| DATE DUE | | | |
|---|---|---|---|
| | | | |
| | | | |
| | | | |
| | | | |
| | | | |
| | | | |
| | | | |
| | | | |
| | | | |
| | | | |
| | | | |

# POWER WITH GRACE

The Life Story
of Mrs. Woodrow Wilson

Mrs. Woodrow Wilson at the time of her marriage
to President Wilson. The official painting, now
in the White House, by Adolf E. Muller-Ury.

# POWER

# WITH GRACE

## The Life Story
## of Mrs. Woodrow Wilson

## Ishbel Ross

G. P. Putnam's Sons, New York

# Contents

Illustrations will be found
following page 128.

# POWER WITH GRACE

The Life Story
of Mrs. Woodrow Wilson

# 1. The Climb to Fame

WHEN Woodrow Wilson, twenty-eighth President of the United States, married Edith Bolling Galt on December 18, 1915, she moved with grace into a historic role. She came into his life at a stage in his career that was crucial both personally and politically. Profoundly depressed over the death of his wife of twenty-nine years, Ellen Axson Wilson, he floundered in indecision as the Allies tried to convince the United States to fight in a war that had been in progress since August, 1914.

Heading reluctantly into the international whirlpool, not as the peacemaker he had hoped to be, but as a participant, he was torn by doubt and criticized at home and abroad for his laggardly attitude. It was not the best of times for Woodrow Wilson, but Edith Galt brought fresh courage and stimulation into his life, and he, in turn, gave her a wealth of love and made her his bride.

By chance she became one of the most powerful women in White House history, in reputation and in legend, if not in fact. Within three years after her marriage she was known as fascinating and influential, seen at the President's side by cheering crowds in Paris, Rome, London, and Brussels. Within five years she was known as the "Presidentress," running the country and isolating the White House from the outside world while her husband lay desperately ill after a crippling stroke.

Edith Wilson died on December 28, 1961, surviving Woodrow by thirty-seven years. At the age of eighty-nine she was still insisting she had never been more than a helpful wife, fulfilling a brief stewardship of six and a half weeks while her husband's life was at stake. Her so-

11

*Power with Grace*

called Regency, she said, had been a matter of medical necessity. But her role was unique. No other President's wife faced comparable responsibility in a period of national crisis.

The most important years of Woodrow Wilson's life followed his marriage to Edith Galt, as did the tragedy that ended his career. World War I blazed, followed by the Peace Conference. Then came Wilson's long and bitter fight to get the United States into the League of Nations, and finally his collapse in 1919 with partial paralysis. Their nine years together encompassed a succession of dramatic events and Edith Wilson was as helpful to her husband in his hours of triumph as in the dark days of his decline.

Their romance was a love story of classic proportions, that grew in depth the more the President needed her and reached its peak as she helped him fight his way back toward health. It was not young love, but a romance of full maturity, since he was fifty-nine and she was forty-four, fifteen and one-half years his junior, at the time of their marriage.

When they met in March, 1915, Wilson's austere presence, scholarship, and swift climb to the Presidency from the Governorship of New Jersey, had made him distinctive among the public men of the era. His record for liberal legislation was impressive, and he had weathered prolonged academic feuding at Princeton University. Edith was aware that he aroused fanatical devotion in those who believed in his philosophy and aims, and unstinted hatred in those who spurned them—a pattern that followed him to the grave.

Edith Galt was not particularly interested in the war issues or in politics when she first met Woodrow Wilson. She had a large circle of Southern friends and relatives, and her days were filled with church and philanthropic activities, family gatherings, running her household, and with travel. Well-off and independent, she lived the life of the cultivated matron. No one thought of her remarrying, attractive though she was. Her life was self-contained and she was at peace with the world in her secluded small house on a quiet Washington street. Although all talk in the capital centered on government, she had never had political ambitions of any kind. Still less had she thought of herself even remotely in connection with the White House, until destiny took hold.

Although gossips suggested Edith Galt set her cap at the President,

12

she was actually reluctant to marry Wilson while he was still in office. But he courted her insistently and with more assurance than he had shown as the bashful young man who waited patiently for Ellen Axson for years. Now he was one of the world's outstanding men, used to having his own way, and he had won the support of his daughters in bringing Edith Galt into their lives. But she was instinctively reticent and she dreaded the limelight, until her years with Woodrow Wilson gave her self-assurance. It was the man who mattered to her, not his office. It took her some time to make up her mind to accept him, but when she made her decision she enjoyed her role to the full.

Woodrow Wilson was considered a handsome man by many. Edith Galt made much of his good looks and told him at times in her laughing way that he was the best-looking man in the world. They made an impressive appearance together at official events, for they were well matched. She was five feet nine, only two inches shorter than the President. He was stiff-backed and of spare build. His lantern jaw suggested determination.

Both Woodrow and Edith Wilson had gray eyes. When not lit with interested concentration, his eyes were distant and unfocused. A mild stroke he had suffered while traveling in Europe in 1906 had left him with a serious defect in his left eye. He had full lips and a dominant nose; his hair was lightly threaded with silver when Edith met him, but during his illness it turned white almost overnight.

Mrs. Galt had a lustrous look of health and vitality. In her forties she still had the beauty of her early years, with luxuriant dark hair and a delicate complexion infused with color. Her eyes were close-set but alive with warmth and interest, and she smiled easily. Although thoughtful and serious, Edith's natural bent was for spirited conversation, and she sparkled in any gathering. Her speech had the soft intonations of the South, with what her friends called the "Shenandoah twist."

Like the President, Edith was born in Virginia and had family ties all through the South, some of which interlocked with his. Her father, William Holcombe Bolling, a lawyer and circuit court judge, as esteemed as he was popular, had settled in Wytheville, Virginia, when his family lost their plantation near Lynchburg after the Civil War. He had served in the Confederate Army, a memory still fresh to him when

Edith was born on October 15, 1872, the seventh of eleven children, nine of whom survived. She was the fourth daughter in a family consisting of Rolfe, Gertrude, Annie Lee, William Archibald, Bertha, Charles, Edith, John Randolph, Wilmer, Julian, and Geraldine. The two who died in infancy were Charles and Geraldine.

Judge Bolling was a scholarly man, with strong convictions, but he was gentle and understanding. Edith idolized him, and she found in Woodrow Wilson some of her father's characteristics. The Bollings were a well-known family dating back to the days of the Revolution. One fact quickly brought to light after Edith's engagement to Wilson was her descent from Pocahontas, the daughter of King Powhatan, who had married John Rolfe in the legendary colonial romance. Edith's broad cheekbones, dark shining hair and close-set eyes were her Indian heritage, an image fostered by the press. So was the steady air of endurance that carried her through the great crises of her life.

Edith had already led a well-rounded life before she met Woodrow Wilson, as the wife of Norman Galt, owner of Washington's leading jewelry and silverware establishment. When she first arrived in the capital from Wytheville in 1890, an eager girl of eighteen, she met Galt, who was nine years her senior and formidable in a worldly way. After a long courtship she married him, and her life broadened considerably.

Edith was an avid traveler, familiar with the best in art, music and the theater on both sides of the Atlantic. But Galt died suddenly in 1908 after twelve years of marriage. Edith Bolling Galt was left well-off, with his business to run, or to liquidate.

In the seven years between Galt's death and her marriage to President Wilson Edith made annual trips to Europe. In spite of these worldly interludes she was always glad to get back to her family and her quieter life in Washington.

Her early schooling, sketchy in scope, was enriched by her quick absorption of impressions as she traveled. All her life she was known to have an extraordinary memory. In her childhood she received countless hours of home tutelage from her scholarly father and from her crippled grandmother, Mrs. Archibald Bolling, who was as exacting as she was informed. When Edith was finally sent to Martha Washington College at Abingdon, Virginia, at the age of fifteen, the results were disastrous. Her chief objective was to study music, but the classrooms were freezing and the nutrition was abysmal. She became painfully

14

thin, and her father brought her home to recuperate from the experience.

During this nightmarish period Edith reached her full growth, and as she flowered again in her home environment she was courted by a man of thirty-eight. Judge Bolling disapproved and sent her to the fashionable Powell school for girls in Richmond, where she had a completely happy year. But the fees were high, and there were still three young brothers to educate. Although Judge Bolling took pride in Edith's intelligence and zeal for study, he thought it more important to get his sons started in life. Girls played the guitar, sewed, kept house, dressed up, and went to dances, but except for the study of French and music their education was not a matter of life or death. So Edith was not enrolled for a second year, and it was then that she visited Washington. Altogether she had received less than three years of classroom study.

But she had listened to the talk of scholars, bankers, and businessmen at the dinner table, while she was married to Norman Galt. When she met Woodrow Wilson her friends included bankers and lawyers. But she was still unknown to the public on the evening of September 6, 1915, when Joseph A. Tumulty, the President's secretary, close friend, and public relations man all in one, handed copies to the press at the White House of a two-line announcement of her engagement. It had been typed by Woodrow Wilson with Edith Galt looking over his shoulder, by the light of the reading lamp he had used while studying law at the University of Virginia.

Overnight Mrs. Galt became a figure of international consequence. Headlines announced her emergence on the Washington scene. Newspapers and magazines explored every aspect of her life. This was her first taste of fame, which she would always experience and rarely enjoy. She moved into the limelight in a matter-of-fact way, and the gloom over the White House lifted. Their marriage ended a courtship that had stirred gossip in Washington, for there had been many clandestine meetings in Rock Creek Park, long country drives, and quiet dinners at Mrs. Galt's house and in the Executive Mansion.

They had always been chaperoned by Margaret Wilson or by Miss Helen Woodrow Bones, the President's cousin and his first wife's secretary, who stayed on as his hostess. Miss Bones and Rear Admiral Cary Travers Grayson, the President's physician and personal friend, had brought them together, hoping to lessen the President's gloom, but no one foresaw the intensity of passion he immediately developed for Edith Galt. It swept him off his feet and startled her, as well as his family and close advisers.

She was well equipped for her social role in the White House, but as war was soon declared she was swept almost at once into nine eventful years. As Woodrow Wilson moved into the forefront in world affairs, a new era dawned in American history. Edith Galt was a potent force in his life from the day she married him until he died, murmuring her name as he lapsed into a coma.

She did not function like the sibyls of the French Revolution, and she laughed when this comparison was drawn in the press. No one needed such treatment less than Woodrow Wilson before his collapse. He was never a man to tolerate interference, but he valued her thoughtful counsel and her presence at his side. She conceded inconsistencies in his actions at times, and was concerned about the strength of some of his prejudices, but she recognized that she was up against an immovable will. He would listen to her when he would to no one else, but in the end he made up his own mind.

This did not deter Edith from telling him what she thought during their conversations. She had strong prejudices and dislikes, and those who considered her an ambitious, scheming woman pointed out that her rise from her girlhood days in Wytheville to the White House had been spectacular. Inevitably she was accused of being a meddler, of injecting her own ambitions into her husband's affairs, and of estranging his closest friends and advisers.

She had a hot temper which flared chiefly when Woodrow Wilson was hurt. Her ambition for him was boundless; she had none for herself. These storms blew over quickly, or she would veil her resentment with wit. Although she maintained a public air of dignified courtesy, she showed a deadly wit behind the scenes. She knew the great men of her day at home and abroad, and she had shrewd opinions of many.

It was well known that she trusted David Lloyd George less than Woodrow Wilson did. Her early enthusiasm for Lord Balfour cooled when she found him veering away from her husband. She looked with disfavor on Robert Lansing, Secretary of State, and Colonel Edward M. House, the President's closest adviser for years, and she made no secret of her dislike for Senator Henry Cabot Lodge after he had fought her husband to a finish on American's entry into the League of

Nations. This opinion she expressed in public and private without hesitation, but while her husband lived and for years afterward she preferred not to talk politics or to comment on public figures.

Mrs. Wilson frankly acknowledged that her husband kept her informed on all issues of consequence from the time he met her, and that she was frequently present at conferences on war issues and on political matters. The diaries and books of his associates show her always in view, a charmer at the dinner table, a good listener at small conferences, a note taker, an intelligent counselor when asked a question, a buffer when he was ill or disinclined to battle opposition. She sat with him in his study as he prepared his speeches, and she rehearsed him in some of them. Right up to the time of Woodrow Wilson's collapse she knew as no one else did what he was thinking and planning.

Constantly at her husband's side, Mrs. Wilson shared secrets of the diplomatic world, since she coded and decoded the most confidential messages in the closing days of the war. In her own words, "I was never a stranger to any subject, and was often able in small ways to be of help." This was a modest appraisal of her work and she scoffed at the suggestion that any of it might be interpreted as a power play. As long as she lived she would tell the world that she was merely fulfilling her wifely duties. And this she did in a most accomplished way, creating an atmosphere of warmth and optimism around him, insisting on the quiet he needed for his work, raising his spirits in moments of depression, and sharing his moods of exaltation.

Woodrow Wilson lived on two levels, according to Edith's analysis of his moods. When he worked he closed his mind to all distractions; he was the scholar, thinker, and statesman, detached from his surroundings. When he relaxed he was completely committed to his diversions. Edith, joining him on both levels, knew how to move without a pause from gaiety and fun to catch his deeper mood with a quiet intelligence of her own. However complex he might seem to others, to her he was a simple man of unswerving purpose. They could laugh together, play together, work together.

William Allen White wrote that in Edith Galt President Wilson found "devotion, high spirits, an infinite capacity for sprightliness, play, joy, and lightness of contact. She gave him those, together with an untiring, beautiful, self-merging common-sense that sustained him for nine years. . . ." White commented on Wilson's liking for the gentle ways of women and their "intuitive cross-cuts to sagacity." Besides beauty he responded to a lively and stimulating wit.

"Father enjoyed the society of women, especially if they were what he called 'charming and conversable,'" said his daughter, Nell McAdoo. Edith Galt was both. Although the President's image in public was dignified and stiff he was a totally different man with his family—talkative, amusing, kind, and loving. The Wilsons liked to jest, to tell stories, to sing, to read to one another. It was an old family custom and Edith had her eyes opened when she first saw Woodrow Wilson clowning, dancing jigs, whistling and singing, making strange faces, and mimicking the smug.

In Mrs. Galt he had found as inveterate a storyteller as he was himself, and one who never tired of his jokes, limericks, and twice-told tales. They had many tastes in common. Both were excellent sailors and enjoyed leisurely cruising. Both were interested in the theater, books, art, historical landmarks, and family gatherings. Both considered good conversation a fine art, and practiced it with their friends. Both were deeply concerned about the young—their education and their well-being. In the second year of her marriage to Norman Galt, Edith had a miscarriage and learned then that she would never be able to have a child. This was shattering news for her, since she had been brought up in the tradition of a large and loving family. She lavished her strong maternal feeling on a succession of young nieces, cousins, and other relatives whom she helped in innumerable ways.

Those who thought Mrs. Wilson frivolous—and many did in the early days—learned in time that much as she enjoyed fun, games, parties, and fashions she had a strong feeling for those who needed help. Her pragmatism was highly developed, her interests had substance, and she brought commonsense to bear on difficult problems. Her laughter and her sense of humor took the edge off her serious purpose.

Although admittedly extravagantly fashion-conscious, she laughed at herself for the feathered, plumed, and quilled hats associated with her public appearance and ridiculed by her critics. She was generally recognized as one of the most chic of Presidents' wives, a style setter known for her furs, hats, and orchids. But Mrs. Elizabeth Jaffray, housekeeper at the Executive Mansion, estimated that Edith spent less on her clothes while in the White House than Mrs. Harding or Mrs. Coolidge.

# The Climb to Fame

Neither she nor Woodrow Wilson took any stock in the social life of the capital. Aside from the essential functions, they made light of the social climbing that went on around them. They strove to keep out of view of the public and get away by themselves, an impossible goal for any President. They were separated only when Wilson was in the Executive Offices, or when officialdom had him in its grip, and even then Mrs. Wilson was sometimes allowed to make an appearance. In Paris they had their first real sense of separation when the President spent endless hours in conference. Even there, though, some of the consultations of the Big Four were held at his residence, where Edith saw the great men coming and going, and sometimes gave them tea.

"I myself never made a single decision regarding the disposition of public affairs," she wrote. And she is supported in this by Dr. Arthur S. Link, director of operations sponsored by the Woodrow Wilson Foundation and Princeton University, and editor of Wilson's papers and collected works. He could find no evidence that she made any attempt to determine or even to influence national policies and decisions. "For her it was enough merely to love Woodrow Wilson and be his wife," Dr. Link concluded.

While he lay desperately ill between the time of his breakdown and his slow improvement, she called herself a mere "courier" channeling official papers in the right direction and following medical orders. During his illness she brought her greatest powers to bear as a protective wife, shielding him from intrusion through a fierce blaze of criticism on Capitol Hill. She helped to keep him alive under the most desperate circumstances. "The strength, the fortitude, the courage, and the constancy of Mrs. Wilson were the greatest I have ever known," Admiral Grayson wrote after working with her day and night during the silent interregnum at the White House.

When the President was threatened with toxemia after his stroke, Edith overruled the doctors whose medical judgment was to operate, and he survived. For four years she devoted all her time and energy to helping him fight his way back to partial recovery, after the initial days of standing guard and defying the men who insisted that the welfare of the country depended on their seeing the President in person. Instinctual patriot though she was, Mrs. Wilson said to one suppliant in a burst of exasperation, "I am not thinking of the country, I am thinking of my husband!" On another occasion she wrote: "Woodrow Wilson was first my beloved husband, whose life I was trying to save, fighting with my back to the wall, after that he was President of the United States."

Since Edith never gave interviews or said anything for quotation while she was in the thick of things, it was not until *My Memoir* was published in 1939, fifteen years after his death, that the public learned how much a part she had been of Woodrow Wilson's political life. Her inner knowledge of the great years came to light as she revealed facts, supported by documentary evidence, that startled both her friends and her critics. This was the Mrs. Wilson the public had never known, with resentment for those who had made her husband suffer. She pictured him as a godlike figure, soaring above his fellow men. The book had charm and considerable bite, and she surprised many with her acid judgments. Her own version of her romance with Woodrow Wilson was told with explicit detail and engaging candor and the public loved it.

After her husband's death she worked for nearly forty years to honor his memory and disperse the shadows that clung to his history. She rounded up papers for his biographer and traveled the world over reminding people of the work Woodrow Wilson had done and the principles for which he stood. She went round the world in 1939, visited Japan twice, and Europe many times. Her presence was welcomed regularly at the League of Nations in Geneva. She attended the Democratic conventions at home and was a patriotic worker all through World War II. She was hostess at her house on S Street to the war leaders and visiting celebrities from Europe, Africa, and Asia.

By degrees she developed a career of her own, with many fresh interests filling her already abundant life. She had always been Woodrow Wilson's alter ego; now she was herself, but whatever she did was always on his behalf. All memorial plans were submitted to her. She helped in the restoration of Wilson's birthplace at Staunton, Virginia, and guided the evolution of the Woodrow Wilson Foundation. She attended meetings without end, bringing a combination of charm and acumen to bear on all business deliberations. It saddened her that among all the national leaders gathered in fierce disunity in San Francisco in April, 1945, to shape the United Nations, only Jan Masaryk, of Czechoslovakia, invoked the name of Woodrow Wilson, who she believed had started it all.

As she aged Edith Wilson remained a notable figure in the capital, attending official functions and taking in the best theatrical and musical events. She still went abroad, dressed in the height of fashion, played bridge constantly, and took up all the new games. Her house on S Street was noted for its hospitality and fine Southern cuisine. It was always filled with visiting relatives—often young people on their way to school and college. She had friendly relations with her successors in the White House and marveled a little at Eleanor Roosevelt. She watched the New Deal with interest and then concern, as things went farther than she felt Woodrow would have approved. She lived long enough to see his prophecies fulfilled as the country was torn apart by World War II. But her point of view mellowed, and the old hurts faded except in the case of Senator Lodge. She aged with spirit and thankfulness for the life she had led. She had traveled from the heights to the depths with Woodrow Wilson, and she guarded his interests and revered his memory to the end.

In her last years Mrs. Wilson was plagued by high blood pressure and a heart condition, but she never complained of her ill-health. Her days were too busy for self-preoccupation. She died in her eighty-ninth year on the 105th anniversary of her husband's birth. She had planned to unveil a plaque that day at the dedication of the Woodrow Wilson Memorial Bridge across the Potomac. The weather was icy, yet no one doubted that she would be there. But quietly, the night before, Washington's Great Lady of the war years and the 1920's had finally given up the battle.

# 2. A Businesswoman

NOTHING was more surprising to Edith Galt when her engagement was announced than the cold shoulder given her by the Cliff Dwellers of Washington because she happened to be "in trade." It had not occurred to her that her leisurely drives to Galt's in her electric brougham to attend conferences, go over records, and direct operations, had made her a person apart. Of strong Virginia heritage, she viewed this with more amusement than concern, but did not forget it. She had never belonged to the official set nor had she cared about politics.

Trade, politics, and fashion were not intertwined as they came to be in the 1970's. The wives of major shopkeepers were not warmly received in the upper social echelons then. Exceptions were the A. T. Stewarts, the Wanamakers, the Marshall Fields, and the Tiffanys.

Edith Galt was aware of the difficulties she faced as she stepped from anonymity to unassailable precedence as the President's wife, but she thought the trade angle ridiculous. Women all over the country were running businesses and her case seemed remarkable only when she moved into Woodrow Wilson's life. Businesswomen had flourished in the White House before her, and they would again. In her time women owned much of the wealth of the country and they were already clamoring for the vote.

The Cliff Dwellers were familiar enough with Galt's, since it had been a city landmark since 1802. It was closely identified with great events at the White House and with marriages, receptions, baptisms, and balls of the fluctuating diplomatic and Congressional set. Mrs. Abraham Lincoln had been one of its customers, and its silverware, jewelry, china, and stationery had been popular through a succession of administrations.

When Edith Bolling married Norman Galt he was the senior partner of the old silversmith firm. He and his brothers bought out their aging father, the founder of the firm, and then Norman bought his brothers out and ran the business himself with considerable success. Edith concerned herself little with the business details. She was busy running her home, and her days were filled with social engagements and philanthropic work. Her friends in the Southern community abounded, and her husband had brought bankers and big businessmen into her life. He was well known to the leading families of Washington who dealt with him in a business way. His courtly manners and impeccable tailoring inspired confidence and were always pleasing to Edith. He was as tall as she was, his smoothly pomaded hair was dark, and he was inclined to be serious. She had been slow to accept him—his courtship had lasted four years. It was never a blazing romance, but she enjoyed her twelve years as Mrs. Norman Galt.

She met him soon after she arrived in Washington in 1890 as a girl of eighteen, eager to sample life in the capital. She stayed at the home of her sister, Mrs. Alexander H. Galt on G Street, between Nineteenth and Twentieth Streets, and came home in a rapturous state one night from Albaugh's Opera House where she had heard Adelina Patti sing. It was her first encounter with the world of high fashion and good opera, and Norman Galt, her brother-in-law's cousin, who had come in for supper, was fascinated by her sparkle and fluency.

She seemed a mere schoolgirl in a green plaid school dress, but she was well developed and beautiful. The family friend who invited her at the last moment had given her no time to change into something glamorous for the great occasion. But she had no thought of herself as she studied the gathering of the most fashionable women in Washington, bejeweled and in evening dress. They had front row seats and the "Jewel Song" sung by Patti seemed to rain diamonds on her head.

For the next four months, while her family gave her every opportunity to enjoy the capital, Norman Galt sent her flowers and sweets and was often her escort. She thought nothing of this; it was the gallantry to which she was accustomed in the South. She thought of him, nine years her senior, as an older man. It was not until he followed her to Wytheville, met her family, and was helpful to her brothers with jobs and schooling that she realized how serious he was. She returned to Washington for another winter and continued to see him, but she had no wish to get married. Her life was full and busy; she was earnest about her music, and she was happy in her home. She had not fallen in love with Norman, but he adored her. After four years of this kind of courtship she decided to marry him. The ceremony took place in St. John's Church, Wytheville, on April 30, 1896.

He was living in his father's large house on H Street and they settled there, then took a modest house of their own which they called The Palace. Two years before Galt's death they rented from his father's estate the house at 1308 Twentieth Street where she would live until her marriage to Woodrow Wilson.

Life took on a warm glow for Edith Galt with means at her command. She ran her house with care and charm, dressed in the latest

23

fashions, and was a familiar figure driving in her electric brougham to pay calls, shop, or go to the theater. She was one of the first women in the country to own one of these fascinating runabouts, and it gave her great satisfaction.

Every Sunday Mrs. Galt was seen at St. Thomas's Church, where her husband was a vestryman, and she attended all church events. With her new prosperity she was able to do many things for her beloved mother—a "saint" who had worked so hard and denied herself so much in bringing up her children.

The Galts went to Europe twice early in the century, and new vistas opened up for Edith. They stayed at luxury hotels, attended the theater and the opera, and were indefatigable sightseers. Edith did not have to remind her husband to take her to Worth's, and she proved to be one more pet American customer for the noted couturier, who called her figure so splendid that he would like to have her as a model. She was a regular customer after that and she wore a Worth gown when she married Woodrow Wilson.

But health troubles beset her early in her married life. Soon after her miscarriage in the second year, her husband's father and his brother-in-law died. Then his oldest brother Charles became a helpless invalid and had to be taken care of by them. The death of her father, Judge Bolling, at this time came as the most crushing blow of all. After his funeral she remained in Wytheville to arrange for the breakup of their home and the relocation of her mother, her sister Bertha, and her two younger brothers.

Mrs. Bolling had decided that she could not stay on alone after all the happy years together with the judge. There were more people and new houses in Wytheville, but the topography was essentially the same. Edith was remembered as a serious girl who walked a lot and worked hard with her music. She was popular at parties but in her early years she was considered something of a tomboy with her large collection of brothers. Now she was a worldly woman with stunning clothes.

She took her mother and Bertha to Washington for the time being, and her husband invited Julian to live with them on Twentieth Street while attending a private school. Mrs. Bolling went back south to winter with Annie Lee Maury in Tennessee, and settled for a time in Bridgeport, Connecticut, with Randolph, Wilmer, and Julian, who

24

were in business there. Eventually Edith brought them all back to Washington, and for the rest of her life she was extraordinarily resourceful and kind, helping them to solve their problems even while she faced crises in the White House.

She and Norman were about to leave for Europe on their third trip abroad when she underwent an emergency appendectomy. She was quite ill and her convalescence was slow. Before she had fully recovered Norman was stricken with an obscure liver ailment and died suddenly in 1908, at the age of forty-five. He left Galt's to her, and she had to decide whether to take in a partner, run it herself, or close it down. It had many old employees, and rather than let them go she turned over full responsibility to Henry Christian Bergheimer, who had worked for her husband and his father for many years. He became her manager and she learned from him, for she had no knowledge of the intricacies of the business. With the aid of Wilmer Bolling, and her lawyer and friend Nathaniel Wilson, they ran Galt's for years. Mrs. Galt made the final decisions, shared in all the conferences, and helped the shop morale when she appeared in her husband's old office, always luxuriously attired and wearing a spectacular hat.

She budgeted her own affairs at this time, returning profits to the business. There had scarcely been time for her husband to pay off all his indebtedness to his father's estate, and to his uncle and brother whom he had bought out. Galt's could get unlimited credit. Edith never failed to point out that the name of the firm on a piece of paper had always been as good as a bond. But she decided not to seek credit. It became a matter of pride to seek no favors, but to keep their friends and their independence.

Things worked well until Bergheimer died. Then Mrs. Galt had trouble finding someone sufficiently knowledgeable in the business to take over. The man she selected as manager was unequal to his task, and the staff was discontented. The business was suffering and Mrs. Galt decided to sell it to the employees for a price none thought exorbitant. At last she was free and solvent. She was very well off when she met Woodrow Wilson.

Mrs. Galt took her sister Bertha abroad in 1910. They toured Holland and Germany and saw the Passion Play at Oberammergau. They were about to go abroad again in the summer of 1911 when she met a seventeen-year-old girl named Alice Gertrude Gordon, who would play a part in changing the course of her life. Gertrude, or Altrude, as she came to be known, was the daughter of James Gordon, a mining engineer from Scotland who had made and lost fortunes in Texas, and had a hand in the completion of the first cross-country railroad and other engineering feats. His wife, a beauty from Virginia, had died not long before Mrs. Galt met Altrude. Several of the Bolling women had known her, and in 1911 Mrs. Galt saw Gordon and his daughter often.

Altrude was the nominal mistress of their large house at 1600 Sixteenth Street, with the help of an aunt, a paid companion, a cook, and an assortment of servants. She was a clever girl, an ambitious student, and always an individualist. She went to the best schools, took courses constantly, and studied languages with the same enthusiasm she devoted to riding. When she made her debut in 1910, she wrote in her diary of her new role as a social butterfly: "I have just worn my first train and worn my hair up on my head—coiled and held down by a bandeau. All of my friends say I have gotten frivolous, but I have just never been really carefree and educated (hurrah) before. . . ."

Just as she was beginning to enjoy her new freedom and was spending her days motoring on the Speedway, riding, playing tennis, dancing, attending football and baseball games with a succession of beaux, life went blank for her. Gordon had cancer and on April 27, 1911, she made an entry: "Father saw the doctors. I am dreadfully blue. . . . Drive with Father. Mrs. Galt at dinner. Father better." Two nights later she made another entry: "Dinner at Mrs. Galt's with Father. No better."

Mrs. Galt was calling regularly to see her father and was having long talks with him about his daughter's future. Torn with grief, Altrude watched her father dying. She read to him through long bouts of persistent pain, and in their conversations he prepared her for his approaching death.

Not long before his illness he had taken Altrude through the areas where he had done his pioneering, and she had come to understand what an adventuresome and courageous man he was. They traveled through gorges, canyons, and frontier land. He had taken great pride in her riding and she was an accomplished equestrienne. The Gordons had many friends of social status, but he was particularly anxious to

# A Businesswoman

have Mrs. Galt give his impetuous daughter worldly guidance. He sent for her just before he died and asked her if she would take on this responsibility. She promised that she would and before leaving that night she had a talk with misty-eyed Altrude and assured her that she would do anything she could for her. She found her shy, appealing, defenseless. Trudy was tall and graceful, with masses of glossy hair, and her dark eyes were large and beautiful.

On June 10, 1911, a bleak little entry in her diary told the final story: "At 2.30 A.M. my darling father went away. He just peacefully stopped breathing. I was in my room."

He was buried with her mother in Rock Creek Park, and on June 24 Altrude wrote that she was sending out 200 sympathy cards and many notes, and was receiving a vast amount of mail, including "many ridiculous letters to tempt me to invest my $2,000,000."

Mrs. Galt was visiting family friends, Mr. and Mrs. Hugh L. Rose, in Geneva, New York, when word reached her belatedly that Gordon had died. She wrote on June 21, 1911: "Dear Stricken Little Heart: I have only learned within the hour of your dear father's falling asleep. You know how genuinely I share your loss and sorrow with you. My *Home* and *Heart* are open to you, and I offer you the enfolding tenderness of the pitying sympathy by one who has known the depths through which you are groping. . . ."

Altrude turned instinctively to Edith Galt. She felt lost without her father, and on July 5, 1911, she wrote in her diary that she had "left home for the first time without my darling father. . . . I am beginning to feel homeless."

Mrs. Galt proposed that they go to Europe to get away from the loneliness of their homes, and Altrude agreed although she added, "I don't really care to go anywhere." Their five months abroad proved to be a restorative experience and the beginning of a lifelong friendship. They sailed for England on the *Lapland* on August 12, 1911. Altrude found Edith Galt a wonderful companion, both at sea and on land. She was good-natured and indefatigable as they went sightseeing, shopped, dined in the great restaurants, went to the theater and opera, and ran into familiar Americans at every turn.

Edith found Altrude "lovely to look at, very intelligent and, like me, lonely." They missed nothing as they toured France, Germany, Swit-

27

zerland, Italy, and Holland. Edith Galt studied the history of each place they visited, and Altrude took it all in, from the 2,000 statues that made "frozen music" of the Duomo at Milan to the bathing costumes at Ostend, which she found quite shocking. Altrude's grief lessened in a world of constant movement and excitement. The two companions had much fun together as they read to each other in every spare moment. There were always escorts from the embassies for Altrude, who felt that her true education had begun.

Mrs. Galt liked to tell later of their financial difficulties in Paris when through an error the money drafts they expected at American Express went astray. They were too proud to ask their friends for a loan, so they cut their meals to two a day and walked everywhere instead of taking cabs, ate chocolate bars to quell their hunger, and moved from the costly Crillon to the Hotel St. James et d'Albany. They had spent so much money on clothes that they were literally broke, but they dined with friends at Larue's, Prunier's, or Le Voisin, ordered clothes from Worth, went to the opera, and took French lessons. Now and again Altrude longed for home, and on November 21, 1911, she made a diary note: "A sort of colorless existence over here, just for self." She was missing her many beaux, her horseback riding, the tang of life around her vigorous father.

They met Isadora Duncan, then at the height of her fame. They had "dreamy weeks" on Lake Como and visited the Château Trevano where the Lombards' own professional orchestra gave concerts in the white marble theater—including the first performance of Gounod's *Faust*.

They were back in the United States on December 12 and all that winter Edith Galt strengthened her friendship with Altrude. She was fulfilling her promise to James Gordon, but she had also become much attached to her ward. Mrs. Rolfe Bolling, Mrs. Wilmer Bolling, and other members of her family had known Altrude's mother as well as her father and they all did their best to draw her out. As the period of mourning passed she swung into her old pattern of parties and outdoor sports, going to Princeton and Yale for the games, and attending the races.

In the summer of 1912 Mrs. Galt went abroad again, this time with Bertha. It was election year but she was scarcely aware of the identities of the candidates. They were in Paris when Woodrow Wilson and Thomas R. Marshall were elected. "I was glad because the Democrats had won," said Edith Wilson years later. "But beyond the fact that they were Democrats, Messrs. Wilson and Marshall were little more than names to me."

On their return home she grew conscious of the new President through the blaze of publicity that surrounded him and his family. And Mrs. Rolfe Bolling (Annie Litchfield) who had campaigned for Woodrow Wilson talked of him so insistently that Edith studied *The New Freedom*, a compilation of his speeches, and asked how such plans could ever be accomplished. Edith decided not to attend the inauguration in March with her sister-in-law but relented sufficiently to go to a performance by Billie Burke at the National Theater because the President and his family would make an appearance there. Edith thought he looked tired and bored and she caught him yawning behind his program, but Annie was ecstatic. When Tumulty arranged a special meeting for Annie with the President in recognition of the campaigning she had done, she urged Mrs. Galt to go with her, but Edith was deaf to this and drove around the circle to pick her up when she came out of the White House. But she went to the Capitol and listened attentively to his speech before the Joint Houses of Congress, an innovation that had not been tried since the time of John Adams. She was impressed.

After she went to the first big reception of the new administration, she was asked how she had felt when her hand first touched Woodrow Wilson's. She said that she felt nothing. It was the "push-along" technique at which he was adept, and which he later taught her to use herself. She recalled having seen him once at the Bellevue-Stratford Hotel in Philadelphia when he was president of Princeton University. He was addressing the alumni, and the hotel manager suggested that Mrs. Galt and her friends might wish to take a look. They did and soon forgot all about it. That was the extent of her contact with Woodrow Wilson as she embarked on another voyage to Europe with Altrude on August 2, 1913. They sailed on the *Minnetonka* and had an even better time than on their first trip.

When they reached London they were soon shopping at Liberty's, visiting the National Gallery, dining at the Café Royal, and Simpson's, lunching at the Carlton, and having tea at Hampstead.

Then it was Paris again—Fontainebleau and the village of Barbizon, lunch at the Ritz, dinner at Prunier's, tea at Pré Catalán, and fittings at Worth's. They toured the château country and visited Lourdes, then went on to the Pyrenees. The contrast when they moved on to Biarritz and joined the world of fashion at the Hôtel du Palais was startling. They explored in San Sebastián and proceeded to Burgos and then to Madrid. There they attended a bullfight, but fled home to bed "too sick to speak of what we had seen." F. F. Dumont, the American consul, shepherded them around, taking them to various parties given for President Poincaré, who was paying a state visit to the King of Spain.

Altrude watched Edith Galt chatting with Poincaré at a garden party at El Retiro, but forgot all else when she was "whirled off to the Royal Theater and put in a box with four French and four Spanish men— beautiful."

Toledo was a "fascinating day in the Middle Ages;" Seville and Granada came next. They went through the Alhambra alone, and zealously read Washington Irving day after day. They stopped briefly at Algeçiras and when they reached Gibraltar they decided to set foot in Africa, taking a Cook's man as their guide. Altrude found walking in the "dirty, picturesque streets of Tangier" a fascinating experience but Mrs. Galt was repelled by the dirt and noise. In the evenings they saw some native dancing that she considered "vulgar and uninteresting." They did the conventional tour of the period, with guides controlling their movements.

They sailed home on the *Saxonia* in October and Edith did not visit Europe again for five years. Her life was about to change dramatically. On the ship she talked to Mrs. Robert Lincoln, a traveling companion, of the past, not the future. As the daughter-in-law of Abraham Lincoln, Mrs. Lincoln had memories of the Civil War, a subject on which both were well informed.

Just after returning home, Edith gave a dinner for her young ward. Then she and some young friends went on to a barracks dance and, in Altrude's own words had a "wonderful time—met Dr. Grayson." This was destiny for Edith Galt as well as for Altrude. Edith and the admiral began a friendship that lasted a lifetime and brought her into Woodrow Wilson's circle. From the start he considered her a remarkably witty and intelligent woman.

Admiral Grayson had been personal physician to President Theodore Roosevelt and President William Howard Taft, and his post as

# A Businesswoman

Naval Aide to President Wilson had developed into close personal friendship. He was popular in the capital and was well known for his discretion, worldly ease, and medical skill. He was a catch for hostesses, always impressive in his naval uniform, a martinet about physical fitness, and a superb dancer. He had dark hair and eyes, a sharp profile, and he was as much at home in the forest as at a White House ball.

Altrude caught his eye at once. She had flowered in a most distinctive way and Edith had developed her interest in clothes. She was taller than he was, but he was so much of a presence that no one ever noticed. Edith Galt saw at once that Cary was the man for Altrude. His name began to appear constantly in her diary in conjunction with Mrs. Galt's. On April 2, 1914, it was "Dr. Grayson at dinner. To Speedway with Mrs. Galt and him." And on April 26, 1914: "Church. Rock Creek. Luncheon with Mrs. Galt and Dr. Grayson. Riding in Park. Mrs. Galt at supper here. Motoring with her and Dr. Grayson. Spent night with her." On May 6 a significant entry showed Miss Gordon attending the circus in President Wilson's party. Dr. Grayson, Miss Bones, and Margaret Wilson were present—"most exciting"—but Edith Galt had not yet come into that picture.

On October 17, 1914, Altrude saw Mrs. Galt at the wedding of Senator Robert Taft and Martha Bower, whom Mrs. Galt knew well and had been seeing in Europe. On December 27, 1914, Altrude made a cryptic little entry: "Snow made us very late getting back to Washington. Dr. G. and Mrs. Galt met me at station. Went to her house!!!"

The teas and drives and dinners and theater parties continued. Altrude now had an electric brougham of her own and was immensely proud of it, but she soon discovered that fast drives were what she truly enjoyed, not leisurely ambles. She often played the hostess now as she felt more self-assurance. Tea dances had come into fashion and Altrude was always eager for those, particularly if Dr. Grayson or George L. Harrison, the two men she would marry in the future, attended. She had gone to a White House reception given by President and Mrs. Wilson in May, 1913, but had not been at the White House since.

The first Mrs. Wilson's seventeen months in the White House had not been happy ones. "I am naturally the most unambitious of women and life in the White House has no attractions for me," she wrote to

31

William Howard Taft when her husband took office. But two of her daughters were married there—Jessie to Francis B. Sayre on November 25, 1913, and Eleanor to William G. McAdoo on May 7, 1914, in a ceremony of much splendor held in the Blue Room.

Mrs. Galt had been aware of Mrs. Wilson's physical decline since the latter first fell ill in June, 1914. It was no secret in Washington that Mrs. Wilson had fainted after shaking hands with a thousand guests at an official reception. She lost weight rapidly and although Dr. Grayson called in a number of specialists nothing could be done to save her. She had Bright's disease, with complications.

Always interested in social causes and work for children, she had campaigned zealously for slum clearance in the capital. Aware that she was dying, the Senate and House rushed through the bill she had backed to clean up the area, so at the end she was aware that her work had counted. She died as war broke out in Europe, but the President was too stunned to take in the importance of this event. For two nights he kept a vigil alone in her room. She was buried with her mother and father in Rome, Georgia, and when he returned to the loneliness of the White House his grief was so overwhelming that he could not speak of her to anyone until Eleanor finally reached him as he paced back and forth in the darkness of the East Room. House and Tumulty, as well as his family, feared a breakdown, and Dr. Grayson, fully persuaded of this possibility, insisted on early morning golf, exercise, and some sort of diversion to break up his brooding. His political worries were acute. On September 21, 1914, Dr. Grayson wrote to Edith, who was holidaying in Maine with Altrude, that the President was having a "very trying and hard time" with so many complications on domestic and international issues.

Dr. Grayson added that Wilson seemed to be feeling the loss of his wife more than ever and had been so unwell that Grayson had ordered him to bed. On visiting the President that morning, he had found him with tears streaming down his cheeks. "It was a heartbreaking scene, a sadder picture no one could imagine—a great man with his heart torn out," Dr. Grayson wrote.

Edith Galt answered at once: "My heart truly goes out to the President and I most truly hope he is better ere this, and that, physically at least, he may soon recover from this awful shadow."

The President had persuaded his daughters to return to Cornish,

32

New Hampshire, after their mother's death, and Dr. Grayson had hoped to join Mrs. Galt and Altrude on their camping trip, but one crisis after another kept him in Washington. He sent them letters and telegrams from time to time, providing glimpses of Woodrow Wilson's moods and activities. Anxious to continue his courtship of Altrude, Dr. Grayson now depended on Edith Galt to back him up. Altrude had promised to think things over in the wilderness.

They were having some adventures of their own away from Washington. They had started out in approved fashion with plenty of gear to make a trip in the Rangelay Lake region, but they stopped at Kineo, hoping to meet Dr. Grayson there. When he failed them because of urgent business at the White House they abandoned most of their clothes and moved on to Jackman, in the northern part of the state. There they ran into heavy floods and had to shed everything but the bare essentials—stout boots, waterproofs, and camp clothes. They shouldered their own packs, but the going was rough as they traveled by day and camped by night. They covered many miles by water and on foot, and their guides showed them how to whip a stream and cook their catch on the spot.

Back in Kineo to recover their trunks, Mrs. Galt got ptomaine poisoning. She struggled back to Washington in a state of collapse after curing herself (she thought) with deadly-looking pellets sold locally as the "Cholera Cure."

Dr. Grayson took over her case at once and called regularly at her house, mostly to talk about Altrude, Mrs. Galt decided. Altrude was being difficult and indecisive. She and Cary met. They quarreled. They made up. They had one misunderstanding after another, but Edith was so persuaded that they were right for each other that she would never give up as intermediary and peacemaker.

In her talks with Dr. Grayson she heard how things were going at the White House, although he was discreet in what he said. Mrs. Sayre and Mrs. McAdoo now had their own homes and family interests. Margaret, whose conversation the President always enjoyed because she was the daughter most like him in her ways, disliked the social life of the capital intensely. She was artistic and was deeply interested in music and good causes, like her mother, so that whenever possible she went to New York to follow her own interests.

Helen Bones, always retiring and fragile, had shut herself in after

Mrs. Wilson's death and had become quite ill. Dr. Grayson asked Mrs. Galt to help get her out into the open, and in this way the drives and walks in Rock Creek Park began that led to the ultimate meetings of the President and Mrs. Galt, and to their marriage.

# *3.* *An Ardent Courtship*

IN her later years Mrs. Wilson liked to tell of her first meeting with President Wilson. On visiting Mrs. Eisenhower in the White House forty years afterward, she showed her the exact spot with a gleeful laugh. It had been a merry encounter, and she remembered her muddy boots and Worth suit as well as the twinkle in the President's eye.

She was not prepared for her sudden meeting with the great man as she stepped out of the elevator on the second floor on a March day in 1915. Helen Bones had told her that he and Dr. Grayson were out playing golf, and the coast would be clear. She and Helen had been walking in Rock Creek Park. They were splashed with mud and were quite untidy, a condition alien to the immaculately groomed Mrs. Galt. On their way to clean up before having tea in the Oval Room they walked to the turn of the hall after coming out of the elevator, and by chance came face to face with the two golfers.

"Turn a corner and meet your fate," Mrs. Wilson would say at this point in her story, recalling an old adage. The spark was lit for one of the great romances in White House history. At a glance she saw that Admiral Grayson, usually as trim in his golf togs as in his dazzling naval uniform, was in some disarray, like the President, who cared little about his clothes at this time. Edith was conscious at once of the laughter that lit up Woodrow Wilson's face as he looked at her and Helen

34

Bones. A quick rush of explanation followed, and it was settled that they would all have tea together in the Oval Room when they had freshened up.

When Mrs. Galt settled with the others around a crackling fire she was natural and spontaneous. The President, always quick to respond to a good conversationalist, was drawn to her at once. Her soft speech, her quick wit, the lively play of expression on her laughing face, were appealing. When he told her some of his stories, she topped them with some of hers, and was her most entertaining self. Helen begged her to stay for dinner, but she thought she had gone far enough.

It was clear that Dr. Grayson and Miss Bones had been trying to get Mrs. Galt into the President's orbit, and now they had succeeded. Things moved fast after that, but he was in love with her for some time before she thought of him as more than a friend. He was determined to marry her despite the opposition of his closest political advisers to making this move so soon after his first wife's death, and with the national election approaching.

Several days after their first encounter Mrs. Galt dined at the White House. The President had taken her for a drive in his Pierce Arrow. He seemed to be troubled and was silent. She made no attempt to interrupt his chain of thought as he sat with the chauffeur in the front seat. She rode in the back with Helen Bones. All through the dinner that followed he had the same preoccupied air, and she realized how great his worries were. But the clouds lifted when they settled by the fire in the Oval Room after dinner and he read to them from the classics. This led him to talk of how exacting his father had been in finding the *mot juste*. Soon Woodrow and Mrs. Galt were deep in a spirited conversation about their family roots and life in the South. This would always be a strong link of communication between them, and it served now to bring them closer together.

Mrs. McAdoo was the next Wilson to arrive at Twentieth Street and take Mrs. Galt driving in a White House car. The feeling prevailed that someone had come into the President's life for whom he cared. Late in April Mrs. Galt received her first letter from him. Many more would follow, for Woodrow Wilson was an accomplished letter writer who believed in keeping his contacts alive through correspondence. His first gift to Edith was a book—Hamerton's *Round My House*—which came with a message: "I covet nothing more than to give you pleasure—you have given me so much."

Two days later Dr. Grayson, Altrude Gordon, and Edith dined at the White House. The President had sent Edith a corsage of what she called "golden roses," and pink ones for Altrude, who hastily changed her dress to ensure a harmonious color combination. It was an evening that Edith always remembered, for she could not fail to see the love in the President's eyes as he studied her. She knew that she looked particularly well in a black charmeuse gown with a jet panel, again a Worth model. Her gold slippers and her roses were the only contrasting touches. In the morning he left with Helen Bones and Dr. Grayson for Williamstown, to attend the baptism of his first grandson, born to Mr. and Mrs. Sayre.

On their return Mrs. Galt was invited to the White House, where the President had assembled a family gathering to meet her. He had taken them into his confidence about his feelings for Mrs. Galt, and she faced the McAdoos; Margaret Wilson, his sister; Mrs. George Howe, her daughter; Mrs. Anna Cothran; and her elfin granddaughter, Josephine; as well as Helen Bones and Dr. Grayson. By prearrangement they all left the President and Mrs. Galt alone after dinner while he proposed in the most formal manner.

According to her own account of this historic event he drew his chair close to hers and then with the "splendid, fearless eyes that were unlike any others I have ever seen," he declared his love for her —"speaking quietly and with such emotion the very world seemed tense and waiting."

It all came as a shock to Mrs. Galt, and she told him hastily that he scarcely knew her. He pointed out that he could not go on seeing her unless they were married, because of the gossip caused by her visits to the White House and their drives. They discussed the situation for an hour and then she told him that if it had to be yes or no at once, the answer was no. It was agreed that they would continue to see each other as before, but with constant chaperonage by members of his family, and also with their approval.

Mrs. Galt was well aware what she would face if she moved into the Wilson orbit. Her friendship with Dr. Grayson, her knowledge of capi-

## An Ardent Courtship

tal affairs, her links with her Southern relatives, her newspaper reading, had kept her well informed. She recognized the prevailing belief that Ellen had been instrumental in Wilson's rise to the Presidency—through the lean years of scholarly pursuits, through a succession of homes and surroundings, through frugal living and ceaseless attention to their three daughters, and through the high and low days of twenty-nine years.

The Wilson girls had adored their mother as they did their father, and all were strong individualists. They had received an unusual upbringing, with scholarship, the arts, and high standards always before them. Men of achievement had passed in and out of their lives, and their mother had encouraged their interest in music and the theater. Books had been daily fare from their earliest years, when they all read the classics together and listened to their father's compelling voice.

All three were spirited, vigorous, and good-looking. Jessie was blond and blue-eyed, lanky, and a little taller than Margaret. She had been engaged to a missionary before marrying Francis Sayre, a professor in the family tradition. Margaret resembled her father in her looks. Like Jessie, she was blond with blue eyes, but she was eager and restless, a high-strung girl always in quest of some elusive goal and lending herself to many strange causes. Eleanor, more generally known as Nell or Nonnie, was the beauty of the family—a brunette with unforgettable blue-gray eyes.

Mrs. Galt knew that there were hurdles where the McAdoos were concerned. Nell was intensely loyal to the handsome Secretary of the Treasury, who had political aspirations of his own. He was the father of three daughters when he married Eleanor and in this respect his was not unlike the second marriage of Woodrow Wilson. Nell played the social game with considerable skill, and she recognized Mrs. Galt's capacity in this field, although Edith had no social pretensions of any kind.

She was none too sure where she stood with the McAdoos when the President and Helen Bones escorted her home after the proposal. She was silent as she thought of the strong force that had come into her life with little warning. The gown she wore that night—a white satin and lace sheath with a square décolletage edged with green velvet, and matching green slippers—was carefully put away.

Only half committed at first, when they understood the depth and urgency of their father's feeling for Mrs. Galt, his married daughters, as well as Margaret, who had been seeing a lot of her, came to his support and she, in turn, showed tact and consideration in dealing with them. Helen Bones was annoyed with her for not having accepted the President at once. They met next day in Rock Creek Park and she reported that he was in a miserable state of mind. They discussed the way in which things had developed from such simple beginnings, but now they had moved beyond Mrs. Galt's control and she was alarmed.

The evening drives along blossom-scented roads during April and May before their engagement were touched with magic, and Edith wrote that "when problems confronted him, which they did in every hour of these tragic years, it seemed to clarify things for him to talk to me as we sped along in the cool April night."

In May she joined his party, sailing to New York on the *Mayflower* for a review of the Atlantic Fleet. Tumulty, Admiral Grayson, Altrude Gordon, Margaret Wilson, and Mrs. Howe with her daughter and granddaughter were aboard. After dinner the President and Mrs. Galt leaned at the rail while he discussed his political worries. He was having trouble with his old friend and backer, William Jennings Bryan, a pacifist at odds with him on his war policies. Bryan was anxious to resign, and the President asked Mrs. Galt if he should let him go. She made a quick retort that she was to regret in her later years; she told him that Bryan should be replaced by someone who could command respect for his office both at home and abroad.

He also discussed with her the wisdom of making Robert Lansing Secretary of State, and Mrs. Galt dismissed him lightly as being a junior in the department, without experience. The President argued that an older man might be too rigid and, since old-time diplomacy was no longer effective in a world changing so rapidly, they should move with the times. Lansing was appointed, but Mrs. Galt never changed her mind about him. She thought him indecisive and not helpful to her husband in spite of his good intentions.

The President was not romantic that night; he was abstracted and troubled over mutiny in his Cabinet. By morning they were laid low by a wild storm in Chesapeake Bay, except Wilson and Mrs. Galt, as both were fine sailors, but even she succumbed in the end. Altrude, a bad sailor, was worst of all. And Admiral Grayson himself, trying to minister to a full house, lay stretched on the deck briefly at the President's feet.

But the sun shone in New York. The water sparkled and crowds were out to catch glimpses of the naval review. The President spoke at a luncheon, reviewed a parade, and attended a dinner. Mrs. Josephus Daniels entertained the women in the Wilson party on the USS *Dolphin.* She invited the wives of the commanding officers and some well-known New York women to meet the fascinating Mrs. Galt. People were already whispering that the President was infatuated. As he stood on the bridge he looked young, alive, and happy, and Mrs. Galt's radiance was noted even by the most critical. The flutter of signal flags, and the national anthem, played over and over, excited Mrs. Galt. She was not accustomed to such pomp and power. They swept downriver, saluting each warship they passed. Between her patriotic fervor and her situation, it was a dramatic day. This was only the first of the spectacles in which she would share, for war was already in the air. Everyone realized it as the fleet was reviewed. Edith was more convinced than ever that if she married Woodrow Wilson she would be entering a world for which she was unprepared.

Helen Bones persuaded her to accept Margaret Wilson's invitation to visit Harlakenden House, the estate of Winston Churchill, the American novelist, at Cornish, New Hampshire, rented for the President as the summer exodus from Washington began. Mrs. Galt was sure he would be so busy with the long drawn-out German negotiations that she need not expect to see much of him at this mountain retreat. In a sense this was a relief, for their meetings were not easy during this period of indecision. She dreaded publicity and feared that she might be thought to be in love with the Presidency rather than with the man. She was not wholly wrong in this assumption. Her appearance in Cornish and the role she played with Margaret at a garden party given for the colony of artists, sculptors, and writers settled there, were cues that Mrs. Galt might soon be in the White House.

It was the first public function given by any member of the President's family since the death of his wife. Ellen and her daughters loved the bohemian life of the colony, and the magnificence of their surroundings. They dressed as they wished; they did what they liked.

Mrs. Wilson, an accomplished artist, wandered off to the fields and woods with her easel, stool, and pallette, to paint by the hour, with none to intrude on her privacy. Margaret busied herself with the local children and with amateur theatrical productions, and Jessie was courted there by Francis Sayre. The President had found little time to enjoy Harlakenden during either summer, but he made the most of his brief visits while Mrs. Galt was there. They walked by the Connecticut River every morning and took long drives, exploring rough roads that kept the Secret Service men on edge. They stopped off for tea at country inns and drove home through splendid sunsets for leisurely dinners and evenings on the terrace.

Mrs. Galt's last doubts about marrying Woodrow Wilson faded in the romantic atmosphere of Cornish. Late in June she let him know that she would marry him, but not until he had left the White House, and she assured him that if he were not reelected she would be ready. She cornered Dr. Grayson to let him know that his wish had come to pass and that she would marry Woodrow Wilson. In the busy household it was difficult to have a private conversation and the news was still to be kept a secret. In the midst of her own happiness she was trying to help Dr. Grayson win Altrude. On June 28, 1915, Mrs. Galt wrote to him after telling him of her engagement: "I really wanted to tell you myself what I have told you tonight—and I think the President has wanted you to know all along, but I know you understand why we did not. I have told no one—not even Mother—and I want to talk to you and tell you all that is in my thoughts. Don't think that because of our own happiness, either of us can forget yours, and when you came upstairs tonight, he said, 'I love Grayson, so I would give everything to see him happy.' I have written this because we have so few chances to talk—and I want you to know I am still your champion."

Determined not to let Altrude slip away from her perfect mate, she arranged a meeting. They rode along the river road near Cornish while she probed gently into their latest quarrel. "She was so full of sorrow that she had hurt you," Edith wrote to Dr. Grayson on July 19, 1915, while she was still at Cornish. "She was terribly distressed that you should have gone without her being able to clear things up. She went into Windsor and I had 20 minutes with her at the Station alone and she is heartsick."

An Ardent Courtship

Mrs. Galt asked Altrude if she might write to him, and was told that she might if she wished.

"Then I said, 'What shall I say?' And her reply was, 'Say anything you like. I give you carte blanche!'

"Then I asked: 'May I tell him you are going to marry him in the Fall?' And she said *'Yes.'*

"I told her . . . that she *must not retreat again,* that it must be *final.*" Mrs. Galt wrote, adding: "Just be happy, for she is worth all you have been through and the future will prove it. Stand firm—but don't be afraid and remember that I am now and always your devoted and loyal Miss Edith: Thank you again for all you did for me. I will never forget it."

When the President returned to Washington Mrs. Galt went to Geneva, New York, to stay until September with family friends, Mr. and Mrs. Hugh L. Rose. Their love was still undeclared and Edith was holding out for time. Back in Washington, with Dr. Grayson by his side, Woodrow wrote to her constantly, discussing his problems, and emphasizing his longing for the "sustaining power of love." He was ready to resume the barrage in person when she returned in September. Her house was fragrant with flowers from the White House, and a note awaited her, reminding her that in Cornish she had promised to dine with him at the White House on her first night home. As she waited for him in the Red Room, Helen Bones warned her that he was under great strain, and Edith could see this at a glance when he strode in from the Blue Room and clasped her hands in both of his. They went driving after dinner, but the President was in no mood for light talk. He dwelt on the imminent danger of war and told her that there now seemed to be no way of staving it off.

On their way back through Rock Creek Park he said to Edith, according to her own account of this drive, that he had no right to ask her to help him in sharing this "load that is almost breaking my back, for I know your nature and you might do it out of sheer pity."

Disregarding the Secret Service man in front with the chauffeur, and Helen Bones beside her in the back seat, she put her arms around his neck and told him, "Well, if you won't ask me, I will volunteer, and be ready to be mustered in as soon as can be."

On the following morning—September 4, 1915—Margaret and

41

Eleanor were told that the engagement was official, and the word spread fast in family circles. The date for a public announcement was discussed, and Mrs. Galt proposed putting it off for a year, until the election was over and things had calmed down. A number of elements entered into this as she felt the pressure of the President's advisers to postpone their marriage. Democratic leaders conferred about the need to warn him that he might lose the election if he persisted in going ahead so soon after the first Mrs. Wilson's **death**. Cabinet members were at odds, with Postmaster General Albert **Burleson** insisting on a showdown, and Secretary of the Navy Josephus Daniels standing by Mrs. Galt. No one had told him yet, but he was sure that Mrs. Galt had won the President's heart, and he approved.

Washington buzzed with tales of the forgotten Ellen Axson Wilson and of a President who could think of nothing but Mrs. Galt. It was a period of sharp political conflict, of feuding among his own closest associates, of divided sympathies and growing anti-German feeling. Fresh flames were lit when a story originated in Los Angeles that Mrs. Mary H. Peck, who had become Mrs. George Hulbert through her second marriage, was ready to make trouble for Woodrow Wilson.

The storm that followed was quickly subdued, but it was one of the most severe in White House history, and almost wrecked the President's new romance. Mrs. Galt was startled to find that her own appearance in his life had brought Mrs. Peck back into view. She was well aware of Mrs. Peck's history; there had been talk about her in Washington since 1907 when Woodrow Wilson met her in Bermuda, where he had gone to rest after long drawn-out dissension over the administration of Princeton. Mrs. Wilson was never a gossip and in spite of her love of a good story she spurned malicious tales about members of her own sex.

In any event, it was all a thing of the past when Edith Galt came into the President's life, and as long as she lived she insisted that he and Mrs. Peck had been friends only and never lovers, and that he had merely tried to help her and her invalid son. Every scrap of evidence that she could find in his papers to bolster this conviction was eagerly seized on and put in perspective by the second Mrs. Wilson.

Mrs. Peck was a worldly woman with means and considerable dash. Her house in Bermuda contained a picturesque assortment of treasures from many lands. She entertained the colonial set and any celebrity who visited the island. There was no inkling when Woodrow Wilson arrived for a rest that he might yet be President of the United States, but as a scholar and writer he fitted well into her social and literary circle, which included Mark Twain, among others.

She came from a well-known family in Grand Rapids and she grew up in Duluth. A cosmopolitan, she was interested in the theater, and was a musician of sorts. Her witty conversation, interesting parties, and fashionable attire stimulated the tired president of Princeton, and in later years when he returned to Bermuda with his wife they were all good friends. He saw her from time to time in New York, where she had a house in the Gramercy Park area, and he asked her to help his wife buy suitable sables for his first inauguration. Mrs. Peck often visited the White House after that, and was on friendly terms with the President's daughters.

Colonel House and McAdoo conferred about the mysterious letter from Los Angeles that had created the fuss. At first the President ignored the matter altogether, then had a meeting with Colonel House, Helen Bones, and Dr. Axson at which he told them that there had never been anything but a platonic friendship between them, and that it would not matter if they published every letter he had written to her, although he conceded that some might not have been prudent. He said that blackmail was incompatible with Mrs. Peck's character, and he explained that he had taken over mortgages on a fruit farm she owned in southern California when her business failed. One-half of the $15,000 entailed had already been paid.

With his custom of writing detailed, witty, and affectionate letters to friends, Mrs. Peck was only one of a number of women who treasured letters from Woodrow Wilson. Various women's names had figured in his career as he traveled, lectured, and wrote; and among the talented and attractive friends whose companionship he had enjoyed were Mrs. Harvey Fielding Reid, wife of a Johns Hopkins professor, and Mrs. Crawford Toy, who was married to a Harvard professor. But Mrs. Peck's was the name that continued to haunt him on more serious grounds; and it now stirred up trouble for Mrs. Galt.

Colonel House said that the anonymous letter from Los Angeles was a total fabrication, but Mrs. Galt insisted that he and McAdoo were

43

jockeying the matter between them to force the President's hand. If so they succeeded, for Mrs. Galt, waiting for Dr. Grayson to take her driving with the President on a warm September night, was faced suddenly with a crisis. When Grayson arrived, plainly upset, he told her that House and McAdoo had just laid all the details about Mrs. Peck before the President and had pointed out its menace for his reelection.

Dr. Grayson assured her that Woodrow's concern was all for her, and not for the political implications. Wilson knew how she hated publicity. At first he had tried to write to her but had thrown down his pen, "white to the lips," and unable to continue. Then he asked Cary to see her in person and explain the situation, telling her that his only alternative was to release her from her promise to marry him. Mrs. Galt took the blow in silence. It was obvious to Grayson that her pride was hurt, but her chief concern was for the President, knowing what it would mean to him. Instead of giving him the reply he expected she said that she would write to Woodrow herself. All night long she sat at her window, sleepless, looking into the future. Toward dawn her "hurt selfish feeling" was gone and she had decided to follow the road "where love leads." With his love as her shield, Mrs. Galt wrote, she would fear neither gossip nor threat. She would stand by him "not for duty, not for honour—but for love—trusting, protecting, comprehending love. . . ."

She sent off her letter at once. It was October 19, a Sunday morning, and for two days she waited for an answer, but none came. On the third day Dr. Grayson arrived and begged her to go with him to the White House. The President was ill, and he could do nothing for him. He neither ate nor slept.

"Did the President ask you to come?" Mrs. Galt demanded.

Dr. Grayson told her that he had not and that when he proposed getting her, he said it would not be fair to Edith, and it was weakness on his part to ask for her presence. It took her only a few minutes to don her hat and drive with him to the White House. Dr. Grayson led her at once to Woodrow's room. He lay in shadow with Brooks, the President's valet, at his side. When he saw her come in, his face lit up and he stretched out his hand. It was icy cold. She took it firmly in hers. His relief at seeing her seemed to be overwhelming. No explanations were necessary, although she asked him if her letter had reached him. They talked at once of an early wedding. Colonel House noted in his

44

diary that "if he does not marry, and marry quickly, I believe he will go into a decline."

The atmosphere around the White House changed overnight as his family, House, Tumulty, and McAdoo all saw that nothing could prevent this marriage. With the election close at hand, fast counter-propaganda was needed to offset the damage done by all the gossip. They closed ranks for the sake of the party and Mrs. Galt was viewed as an asset. But she never forgot where the opposition was strongest. She was touched, however, by the article written at this time by Dr. Axson about the home life of President Wilson. It was syndicated in twenty papers and widely distributed in pamphlet form.

No one knew Woodrow Wilson better than "Stock," who had lived for long periods with him and Ellen, and had been close to him for a quarter of a century. He was a brilliant scholar, a gentle and unassuming man, as withdrawn as Woodrow Wilson was strong and affirmative, but they had similiar tastes and understood each other's wit. Now Dr. Axson wrote that tenderness was his brother-in-law's outstanding characteristic and that he was the most considerate man he had ever known—"so gentle in his home life that he had appeared to some too domesticated." At Princeton he had been accused of such absorption in his family life that he did not know the ways of men. "His intimate friends often expressed to me the wish that the President would marry again, as he was utterly desolate." And Dr. Axson added, "We who love him feel that God Himself must have directed the circumstances which brought Mrs. Galt into the White House circle."

She had been so tactful with Stock that he had succumbed to her charm and he called her a "*vivid* person, most sweet and lovely." Mrs. Galt was too realistic to consider herself heaven-sent, but having taken a stand she decided to hold her ground. Their own lives were what mattered, she argued, and not political expediency. But she could not fail to see that the President's plan for world peace was a strong and lasting issue in his thoughts, and that he needed another term in office to give it meaning.

A few days before their engagement was announced the President sent a friendly and impersonal letter to Mrs. Hulbert in which he told her that he was marrying Mrs. Galt, whom he felt she would love, as everyone else did. There was no reply, and Edith weathered the storm.

# 4. *Mrs. Galt Meets the Public*

AFTER the engagement announcement had been handed out on the evening of October 6, 1915, and before the next day's storm of publicity rained down on Mrs. Galt, she was a sparkling figure at a White House dinner given for all the Bollings within range, and for the Wilsons. Her mother, Mrs. William H. Bolling, more than a little awed but not altogether surprised that her wonderful daughter should have captured the President, sat proudly at his right, and for the time being all the personal complications that had preceded this event were forgotten. Woodrow Wilson was at his best and wittiest. Merriment prevailed.

For the next two days he introduced Mrs. Galt to the public in a succession of appearances in New York and Philadelphia, climaxed in a popular way at a baseball game. As she came into view at Woodrow Wilson's side, crowds cheered them everywhere, and the headlines in both cities told the same story: FIRST LADY HAS OVATION HERE. CHEERING CROWDS AT EVERY APPEARANCE. MRS. GALT MUCH ADMIRED.

Her good looks and vivacity made an instant impression on the public and she in turn found it exciting to be part of a Presidential cavalcade, with traffic being held up to make way for them, and thousands cheering at a World Series game between the Red Sox and the Phillies. She rooted for the Red Sox. The President cheered for the Phillies. In the ninth inning Colonel Starling went along the aisles asking people to keep their seats until the President had left. He and Mrs. Galt were reluctant to move until the game ended, but their train was waiting for them at the depot, and they were cheered all the way.

Their most conspicuous public appearance during the brief period of their engagement was at the Army-Navy game at New York's Polo Grounds late in November. Their wedding day was at hand, and an unusual number of women had turned out to see Mrs. Galt. The field glistened from the rain that had been coming down in sheets all morning, but it stopped as the game began. At halftime the President and his party moved from the Navy to the Army side, and all eyes were on Mrs.

46

# Mrs. Galt Meets the Public

Galt, in black velvet and ermine, walking gracefully at the President's side. The ovation they received persuaded her that "everyone seemed to be our friend." Mrs. McAdoo was in the party, wearing the latest in French couture, and Margaret was serious and thoughtful, watching her father with Mrs. Galt. They all wound up a memorable day with a theater party, seemingly a united family.

Their dinners and theater parties in New York were a source of great satisfaction to Mrs. Galt. Although experienced in these worldly pleasures, it was thrilling to have an audience rise en masse as they entered a flag-draped box at the Empire Theater to see Cyril Maude in *Grumpy*. On this same trip they took in vaudeville at the Palace, entertainment of which Woodrow Wilson never tired. Although this was not her own particular taste, she liked to laugh with the President and to see him relaxing from his cares.

Although she had often visited New York and knew her way around the shops, museums, and theaters, she was now seeing the world from a fresh angle as the fiancée of Woodrow Wilson. Alive with the excitement of her new role, she bought with characteristic care, a past mistress herself in knowledge of fine fabrics and good workmanship. It was an era of furs and huge muffs, of aigrettes and dazzling jewels. It had never been the Wilson custom to indulge in personal luxuries or lavish display of any kind, but sables and orchids were already associated with Mrs. Galt.

On the President's next visit to New York he gave careful attention to the selection of an engagement ring from one of the leading jewelers of the period. When thirteen rings were submitted for his attention, Cordell Hull, then a Congressman from Tennessee and a close friend of the President, urged him to return one, since thirteen was an unlucky number. But Woodrow Wilson laughed, pointing out that it happened to be his lucky number. He was inaugurated in 1913; there were thirteen letters in his name; and the luck did not stop there, for he would land at Brest on December 13, 1919, the hero of the day, committed to making the world safe for democracy.

The leading Democratic women in New York saw little of Mrs. Galt on her shopping trips, for she avoided engagements, eluded the press as much as she could, and held herself in readiness at all times for a sudden call from the President. The portrait by Arnold Genthe given

47

out with her engagement announcement made her recognizable wherever she went. She disliked being photographed, but Altrude Gordon, who was having a sitting with the noted Genthe, persuaded Mrs. Galt to go with her, and to let him photograph her. She preferred his portrait to all others, and it became known around the world, giving an alert, glowing impression of the White House bride.

Both Tumulty and House were intent on helping the romance when the marriage seemed inevitable. The public appearances of the President with Mrs. Galt were carefully arranged. He usually stayed at the Colonel's house while Mrs. Galt and her mother were at the St. Regis. On each visit they followed much the same routine—a long drive followed by lunch at Cleveland H. Dodge's house in Riverdale. In the evenings there were dinner parties, followed by the theater and late suppers. Dodge was a Princeton classmate and an old friend of the President's. He was a financier with banking interests and was treasurer of the American Commission for Near East Relief, with strong Red Cross affiliations.

Wilson and Mrs. Galt had many friends in and around New York, and both were inclined to do the unexpected. They chose their guests and went where they wished, and their candor at some of the dinners preceding their theater parties shocked Colonel House, who felt that they talked too freely of political matters within the hearing of waiters. A soft-spoken man himself, the colonel was committed to a hush-hush attitude on public affairs and was concerned over the President's remarks about some of the American officials in the foreign field, and in particular James W. Gerard, ambassador to Germany.

The war was having repercussions all over America, but the Anglophiles had their greatest strength in New York. The *Lusitania* had just been sunk and daily dispatches from Europe detailed the rising tide of death and destruction. Many Americans were already involved in flying squadrons and ambulance corps. Submarine warfare kept the public in a state of anxiety, and all were looking to Woodrow Wilson to meet the situation with some decisive action. It was a time of doubt and uncertainty in a country committed to peace and isolationism.

The President's visits to New York in the final weeks before the marriage created uneasiness in government circles and were criticized by many. They were semiofficial in character, but the city, with its strong pro-German feeling, was a danger zone for President Wilson. Rumors of plots against his life abounded. He usually had what was described as an "awesome" Secret Service detail, which neither he nor Mrs. Galt appreciated. It was often necessary to form a wedge around his car as people tried to shake hands with him, and women studied his fiancée and her fashionable attire.

Colonel Starling called him a brave man, wholly without fear, going through the war years and the Peace Conference without concern for his person. On his first visit to a theater after the United States entered the war, his guard insisted on his occupying a back seat, instead of his usual place in the conspicuous corner of the box. He did this once, but never again.

Dr. Grayson found him fatalistic in his outlook and his wife shared the President's philosophical calm, but was alert to the dangers he faced, and his refusal to take precautions. Colonel House was concerned at all times for his safety, particularly when he was in New York. In Washington the situation was different, and there was little opportunity for social interchanges as official engagements and pressing issues kept him busy. But he talked every day to Mrs. Galt on a direct telephone line that did not go through the White House switchboard. In this way he not only kept assuring her of his devotion but he also continued the interchange of opinion and comment with her that had already become a habit.

Slim, dark-eyed little Miss Bones was a courier between them, and sometimes she brought Mrs. Galt foreign and domestic information illuminated by the President's penciled notes, to which she would occasionally respond with comments of her own. Already she seemed to be on the periphery of government, the beginning of a "partnership of thought and comradeship unbroken to the last day of his life."

Colonel Starling viewed the lighter side of their courtship as he guarded Mrs. Galt's house when he visited her in the evenings after their engagement had been announced. "He certainly has me on the go these days. . . . He is hooked hard and fast and acts like a boy in his first love-experience," he wrote to his mother on October 29, 1915. It was understood that no pictures were to be taken of the President arriving at Mrs. Galt's house or leaving it. Photographers lurked at some distance in the bushes, but were constantly frustrated. The President and Starling usually walked home together around midnight, unless a White House car waited for them along the street. He was invariably in high spirits as he went sprinting along with his natural lightness of foot, jigging as he waited for traffic to move. The moon and the stars of clear October weather contributed to the feeling of romance in the air.

The President showed the same buoyancy when he walked with Mrs. Galt in Rock Creek Park, laughing, talking, gesticulating, and holding her hand. As they followed woodland paths he leaped over obstacles or jigged around them. "He was having a wonderful time," said Starling, but Edith had a more informed understanding of his heavy cares. Helen Bones was always at hand on these occasions, glad to see the Tiger, as she called him, free from his White House cage. Mrs. Galt's devotion impressed all those who saw them together and when the President brought her to Josephus Daniels' office in the Navy Department, his Cabinet Minister noticed that he called her "sweetheart," while she hung on the President's stories and conversation with enthusiasm. Daniels decided they were utterly wrapped up in each other as he showed them John Paul Jones' sword in a case in his office and told them its history.

It was apparent to the public that the President was emerging from his state of gloom. Every appearance he made with her in public suggested his happier state. This was most evident at the White House where he went around whistling and singing in the old manner and in spite of his political cares. Irwin H. Hoover, chief usher, known to everyone as Ike, noticed that he was more attentive to his clothes and personal appearance. Mrs. Galt was giving him strong support, but he was still elusive to his advisers, and they blamed this on his preoccupation with his fiancée.

Colonel House had been studying Mrs. Galt with deep interest from the moment he realized how vital she was to Woodrow Wilson. He found her "delightful and full of humour, and it makes me happy to think the President will have her to cheer him in his loneliness," he wrote in his diary late in September, at a time when opposition to the marriage was developing.

The situation was of immediate interest to him, and he quickly gauged the depth of the President's love for this sympathetic and worldly woman. He saw that it was not a passing infatuation, but a deep desire for someone to take the place of his lost wife. As time went on House found, however, that beneath her warm and witty exterior she could be like steel where her husband's interests were concerned.

Their first extended talk was at a luncheon at the White House late in September, 1915, at which the President discussed foreign affairs, the delicate negotiations under way with Mexico, and his own prospects for the future. Realizing that he might be defeated in the upcoming election, he became unusually personal, and said that he had decided to make Washington his home when he was out of office, and that he would like to settle in Georgetown.

He was emphatic in saying that he would never play the role of elder statesman, like Theodore Roosevelt, who was then pushing hard to get the United States into the war on the side of the Allies, or William Howard Taft, who was campaigning for peace in his own way.

Mrs. Galt listened thoughtfully to all of this and after lunch she invited the colonel to have tea with her in the Oval Room, and then to meet her for a private talk. She was well aware that he was one of those who had been trying to delay her marriage until after the election, and she was more than half persuaded herself that this might be the wiser course. She asked Colonel House bluntly if he thought the President should run again, and was told that reelection might be something of an anticlimax after the completion of his brilliant legislative record.

Shortly before her wedding the colonel decided to coach Mrs. Galt on what she might be facing. In a private talk he warned her of the efforts that would be made to get her to influence the President for particular ends. He urged her to withhold nothing from her husband, and to let him be her sole confidant. He warned her against talking politics to anyone or trusting even her closest friends with Presidential secrets.

Mrs. Galt listened attentively to what he had to say. Although it was her habit to talk with great ease and facility, she had a strong sense of prudence—one of her virtues, in Woodrow Wilson's estimation. Although not overly self-confident, she felt less unsure of herself than the colonel seemed to think. He had no conception of the encompassing support Woodrow had already thrown around her—and that the President trusted her implicitly.

Just before the wedding Colonel House dined alone with the President to discuss his trip abroad. He was leaving for Europe on a mission. After dinner they called on Mrs. Galt and talked intimately of the wedding plans. They showed House where they would stand and described the details of the ceremony, but he had not been invited to attend.

She managed her own affairs with quiet efficiency as letters and gifts poured in. The announcement of her engagement brought an avalanche of gifts, something the President and she had hoped to avoid. They had planned a small family wedding, with a simple announcement sent to all the appropriate people when it was over. But Ike Hoover was soon listing silver and glassware, rugs and objects of art, pictures and prints, jewelry and ornaments. A white bearskin rug from South America, Chinese porcelain, a brass desk set, tapestries, and a tablecloth of Russian lace were in the collection.

Mrs. Galt prized the portraits of her parents sent as a wedding gift from her native Wytheville, and a silver loving cup from the Virginians in Congress. A gold nugget from California was a native gift that pleased both of them. A ring was fashioned for Mrs. Galt from a small piece of the metal processed for this purpose. Later it yielded a scarf pin, reproducing the official seal of the United States enameled in natural colors, that the President wore as long as he held office. It was noticed on the day he drove to the Capitol with Warren Harding, but was not seen again. A seal ring that he used at Versailles when signing the treaty came from the same gold nugget. It embodied the shorthand characters that he used in his personal memoranda. But a wedding gift that amused Edith was the original drawing by C.K. Berryman of a cartoon he did for the Washington *Evening Star*—a cupid standing beneath a tree on the White House lawn.

# 5. *A Simple Wedding*

FEW of the small group of intimate friends and relatives watching Mrs. Galt's glowing face as she stood beside Woodrow Wilson on her wedding day, were aware of the storm she had survived, or of the crucial decisions the President faced even as he took his nuptial vows.

It was the second wedding for both. Mrs. Galt had been married sixteen years earlier to Norman Galt in Wytheville. Now she was marrying the President of the United States as the ravages of World War I swept Europe. His own first wedding had been held in Savannah, Georgia, when Ellen Louise Axson became his bride on June 24, 1885.

Now, thirty years later, on December 18, 1915, Mrs. Galt stood by his side in a black velvet gown with a dashing black velvet hat tilted at her favorite angle. A feather plume swept her cheek and a diamond brooch given her by the President glittered on her bodice. In spite of her passion for orchids she wore a corsage of lilies of the valley that day.

She had awakened early to a realization that there was much to be done before the evening ceremony. By eight A.M. the President had called her on their private wire. She breakfasted with her mother and sisters, and had scarcely finished when he stopped in to greet them all. He was on his way to sign letters and documents that would clear the way for their wedding trip. Though both could be superstitious, neither seemed to have qualms about seeing each other before the wedding ceremony.

The day was sunny and clear, with a touch of frost in the air. Christmas preparations were under way and evergreens were piling up in the streets. Carriages rolled up to the house on Twentieth Street bearing Mrs. Galt's fashionably attired relatives arriving from out of town. Messengers came and went and in the midst of all the bustle Edith sat and wrote thank-you letters and welcomed the new arrivals.

After lunch she committed herself to the hairdresser before taking her customary drive with the President at four thirty. It was less relaxing than usual because Edith knew he was feeling the strain of the day's events. In spite of all the precautions they had taken to keep things quiet and simple, a President's wedding could not be overlooked.

He was grave and quiet until he went driving with Mrs. Galt in the afternoon. On his return he was buoyant as he checked the details of the ceremony with Ike Hoover. "Nothing must go wrong," he said, and he spoke of the close timing. Although a number of experts were looking out for his interests, he kept it all strictly personal. Most punctual of men, nothing annoyed him more than a delay in keeping appointments. Hoover assured him that he would not fail to summon him when the moment came for him to appear.

He laughed and answered, "Do you think I'll need that, Hoover?"

The President left the White House for 1308 Twentieth Street half an hour ahead of schedule, alone except for his Secret Service escort. In cutaway coat, white waistcoat, and gray-striped trousers he seemed young and agile as he hurried upstairs to Mrs. Galt's library on the second floor, and saw her for the first time in her wedding attire. She seemed a vision to him, her face alight with excitement, but they could not settle down to the usual comfortable chat, with carriages arriving and guests being received downstairs.

Hoover, well used to White House protocol, had taken over all the wedding arrangements and converted the narrow house, four stories high but only two rooms deep, into a miniature flower garden. The choicest flowers, ferns, and plants that the White House greenhouses and the leading florists of Washington could supply were arranged in lavish style. Mrs. Galt approved the arrangements but had left things in the hands of White House strategists and the State Department. The capital's leading caterer supplied the wedding cake.

The President and she agreed that everything should be as simple as possible—no uniforms, no military or naval aides, no official touches of any kind. The announcements sent out after the wedding read "Mr. Woodrow Wilson." The guest list at first was limited to forty but last-minute appeals expanded it to more than fifty, which made for a tight jam in the small, compact house. The drawing room had been cleared of furniture, and the dining room had been arranged for the wedding supper.

When Hoover tapped on the library door to announce that it was eight thirty the President and Mrs. Galt thanked him and walked downstairs through a lane of American beauty roses into a room heavily scented with flowers and softly lit with candles. They took their vows under a canopy of greenery, shell-shaped and lined with heather, symbolic of the President's Celtic heritage. He was pale and solemn as he knelt beside Mrs. Galt at a white satin *prie-dieu* that had been used by other members of the family. A large mirror behind the canopy reflected banks of crimson roses and mantels strung with orchids.

## A Simple Wedding

The service went quickly as Dr. Herbert Scott Smith, of St. Margaret's, pronounced them man and wife. Dr. James H. Taylor, of the Central Presbyterian Church, assisted him. The tone was ecumenical and both families were satisfied. The prayer book used had belonged to Judge Bolling, the bride's father.

A string ensemble concealed in a mist of ferns played softly as the guests crowded around to kiss the bride and congratulate the bridegroom. The tension had been broken and the President stood relaxed and smiling beside his bride. The only Cabinet member present was McAdoo, coming as a son-in-law with Nell. Mr. and Mrs. Sayre and Margaret took Edith into the family with warmth, and the blend of Wilsons and Bollings went smoothly in the modest house on Twentieth Street, while the waiting press hungered to know what was going on inside.

Joseph Tumulty had his mind on the press. Although the wedding went smoothly, Edith made a precipitate move at the last moment that almost wrecked the careful plans. Both families had been dismayed and confused by the clash that developed suddenly over the bishop who was to be the chief celebrant.

The Galts were firm Episcopalians. Norman Galt had been a vestryman at St. Thomas's, which Edith had attended regularly until she moved to the nearer and more fashionable St. Margaret's shortly before her wedding. Two days before the ceremony the bishop, arriving at the Shoreham Hotel, sought an invitation for his wife. Mrs. Galt explained the limitations of her guest list, but when he persisted she lost her temper and wrote him a note that the President advised her not to send. Edith persisted, and the bishop was informed his services would not be needed. She felt he had shown disrespect for the President of the United States. Dr. Scott and Dr. Taylor were glad to fill the breach and there was a quick last-minute shuffling. Only her close relatives knew until afterward that Mrs. Galt's will had prevailed over the President's on this vital day. She had announced that she would postpone the wedding date rather than invite the bishop's wife.

Now it was all over, and the noise and chatter around the supper table enabled the President and Mrs. Wilson to slip upstairs ahead of schedule to change. When the bride reappeared she wore a broadtail coat over a brown velvet suit. A crowd had gathered for the historic event, but the surrounding streets had been roped off. Press cars were

55

waiting to take up the traditional pursuit. Their chase ended in failure, for the getaway plans were so artfully planned by the White House Secret Service that virtually no one knew where they were headed. Even Wilson's aides packed both summer and winter wear.

Shades were drawn and the crests on the automobile doors were covered. A large crowd waited at Union Station, believing that they would be leaving from there, while actually they were speeding to Alexandria with ten press cars in pursuit. Fifteen miles out of Washington they shook them off and drove more slowly. But Edith was oblivious to all this. In *My Memoir,* she recalled, "We had a lovely drive over in the moonlight with the world lying white with snow around us."

The moonlight drive came to an end when they reached a siding close to the Alexandria freight yards. Their private railroad car would connect with the train bound for Hot Springs. Colonel Starling of the Secret Service waited there, and when their Pierce Arrow arrived he blinked his flashlight three times and jumped aboard to guide the chauffeur. Brooks, the President's valet, and Mrs. Wilson's maid had preceded them and worked all day putting things in order. Sandwiches and fruit were in readiness for the abstemious President and his bride. The strain of the day was over. Nothing had gone wrong. Edith laughed a little about the silly things they had done in the trainyards before boarding. She would soon learn how zealous Colonel Starling was, and about the dangers the President faced.

In the siding at Hot Springs next morning Starling quietly entered the private car to see if all was well. What he saw he never forgot. The most dignified of Presidents was dancing a jig and singing a popular song. In the colonel's words, "Emerging into the sitting room I saw a figure in top hat, tailcoat, and gray morning trousers, standing with his back to me, hands in his pockets, happily dancing a jig. As I watched him he clicked his heels in the air, and from whistling the tune he changed to singing the words, 'Oh, you beautiful doll! You great big beautiful doll. . . .'"

Woodrow Wilson would dance a jig when the spirit moved him, or whistle or sing—the solemn statesman at play, often a puzzle to his friends. Starling was quite familiar with the jig—Wilson sometimes did it in the street. It was not a graceful jig but a hop that seemed to express inner tension. By chance, Edith too was an excellent whistler.

# A Simple Wedding

She was wary of jigs but she liked to see Woodrow happy.

Their Pierce Arrow waited at Hot Springs to take them to The Homestead, and it was not long before the public knew where the Wilsons were. The focus shifted at once to their luxurious haven, but the guard set up around them by Starling ensured their privacy. Secret Service men slept outside their suite, and they could sometimes be glimpsed strolling on the grounds, always under guard. One headline read, THE ETERNAL TRIANGLE—WILSON AND HIS BRIDE GUARDED WHILE THEY WALK, EAT AND SLEEP.''

Their rooms overlooked the golf course and a wide vista of snow-capped mountains. Wood fires burned in their living room, which was gay with English chintz. They had a private dining room, two bedrooms and baths, and rooms for their servants. They golfed in the mornings and took drives in the afternoons over terrain familiar to Woodrow Wilson from his childhood. Some of the roads were rough, and the floods they ran into bothered the Secret Service, but it was clear that they lived in a happy haze. Mrs. Wilson thrived in the mountain air.

Dr. Grayson had considerable success rebuilding the President's health after his deep decline when Ellen died. Grayson insisted on early morning golf, regular exercise, a simple diet suited to his gastric idiosyncrasies, eight hours' sleep, and entertainment at the theater or restful voyages on the *Mayflower*.

Woodrow Wilson had never been strong, either in youth or early middle age. At Princeton he frequently underwent treatment for stomach upsets, and he had suffered three nervous collapses during his life. Although he had no organic illness, Dr. Weir Mitchell, a specialist in nervous disorders who had treated him at Princeton, had prophesied that he would not survive his first term. But he grew steadily stronger. "He was the most obedient patient a physician ever had," Dr. Grayson wrote. "He worked as few Presidents have worked and bore burdens such as few men have been called on to shoulder . . . at the conclusion of the Armistice he was stronger than he had ever been in his life, notwithstanding all he had gone through."

Golf ceased to be martyrdom, with Edith by his side. Although he kept at it he was never a great golfer. He took up the game late in life, his natural bent being the sedentary life of the scholar, and a serious defect in his left eye affected his game. He chose his partners with care, lest he be approached about political issues on the links. In Washington he avoided the fashionable Chevy Chase in favor of Kirkside or the Washington Country Club across the Potomac. At times he also used the Town and Country, a Jewish club. He could be scornfully funny about his golf, but Dr. Grayson kept him at it, with the connivance of Mrs. Wilson.

She was not a zealot about the game but she knew how to play, and she found it enchanting to go swinging over The Homestead course with Woodrow. On the fairways he would tell one of his funny stories, often in dialect, illustrating his points with flourishes of his club. Colonel Starling was struck by the fact that neither one seemed to care about the score. He fixed the President's average at 115 and Mrs. Wilson's at 200. At one point Wilson took instruction from Charles Lewis, a native of Devonshire who had settled in Oklahoma and counted among his stable of celebrated students King Edward VIII, King George VI, and Lord Balfour.

Mrs. Wilson was not truly athletic and it always amused her to be able to report that she had beaten Woodrow or Dr. Grayson. This did not often happen, but she had one brilliant coup at Hot Springs when she insisted on using a putter against her caddy's advice while far from the green and by some miracle holed out. The President was not so happy when he saw her flounder once, trying to drive her ball from a mud hole. She made seventeen tries, her neat plaid skirt swirling and dirt flying in all directions. They laughed together over this. He already knew how persistent Edith could be.

She insisted on a niblick for most shots and Colonel Starling admitted in his reminiscences that he could not refrain from cheating for the fascinating First Lady, by retrieving balls she had driven into the woods and dropping them on the edge of the fairways. The Wilsons used black and red balls for identification purposes when playing in snow.

In their hours of talk away from official cares Edith found a new understanding of Woodrow Wilson. "No greater mistake was ever made than to say Woodrow Wilson was all mind and no heart," Josephus Daniels wrote of him. This Edith knew to be true. "He was not," she said, "a man whom the world judged cold, or a human machine, devoid of emotion." In spite of his strength of purpose in public affairs, he was a different man informally, with what seemed to her to be an

58

unquenchable need for love, attention, and relaxation. Wilson wrote of himself, "My constant embarrassment is to restrain emotions that are inside me," and in another revealing comment he said that if the lava did not seem to spill over it was because people could not look into the volcanic basin and "see the cauldron burn."

William C. Bullitt, a journalist with wide ambassadorial experience, was convinced that Woodrow Wilson's Presbyterianism and the influence of his father and mother were the deep determining factors of his life, mellowed to some extent by his two wives. From early childhood he had lived in a world of women. His mother, daughters, cousins, aunts, and other relatives who gathered from time to time in his various homes had warmed his life with affection, while his father had influenced his decisions. He had a deep sense of responsibility for all his young relatives, whom he helped to receive the best available schooling.

This fundamental responsibility was something Edith understood and shared. The President's much-quoted phrase, "I bless God for my noble, strong, and saintly mother, and for my incomparable father," served for her, too. Comparing their early days, they talked at length about Judge Bolling and Edith's extraordinary grandmother, Mrs. Archibald Bolling, who had affected her life profoundly. Thrown from a horse in her early years, Grandmother Bolling was badly crippled and spent her days in a rocking chair, sewing, knitting, reading, and instructing the young. She taught Edith, her favorite, to read, write, and count, and speak a little French. Edith slept in her grandmother's bed or in the trundle underneath and Grandmother Bolling nursed her when she was ill. The old lady was tiny, spirited, and sharp-tongued. Her likes and dislikes were strong (a quality that Edith thought she herself inherited). She wore hoop skirts, tight bodices with bishop sleeves, and it was Edith's task to iron her lace caps to perfection, as well as to care for her large collection of canaries. When Edith left home for any reason Judge Bolling always reminded her to take careful note of what she saw and heard in order to entertain her grandmother on her return with tales of the larger world.

Edith's maternal grandmother Logwood, who also lived with the Bollings at Wytheville, was entirely different—elegant, leisurely, and committed to Southern tradition. She was tall and held herself proudly. In the evening she read and sang to the children. Both grandmothers were of great help to Edith's mother; they lived happily together in the curious pink and gabled dwelling that was actually three houses linked together. Although a balcony ran all the way around, each had its own staircase, its own chimney, and its own character.

The large library upstairs had been the girls' haven for receiving their beaux. Judge Bolling's work as a circuit court judge took him away from home for long periods, but when he returned he was interested in their work and their romances, and he was a genial confidant. He admired their dresses and sympathized with their troubles. The judge read them the classics with a voice that Edith considered second only to Woodrow Wilson's. As a lay preacher he paid close attention to their Bible instruction, which came at home, not in Sunday school. Edith was such an apt pupil that she was ready for confirmation at the age of nine.

Edith's good-looking father, tall, bearded, with fine eyes and a thoughtful smile, had married her mother, Sallie White, while he lived at The Plantation. She was slender and tall, with gentle ways and a great love for William. However busy with her children, she wrote to him every day he was away in beautiful script. Their first two children were born at The Plantation, which they lost after the war. They settled in Wytheville because Grandmother Bolling had inherited a house there. Edith's father took up law and the firm of Terry and Bolling scraped along through the postwar days.

And now Edith was the wife of the President of the United States, and Sallie White, a beauty when William Holcombe Bolling married her, was alive to give her away. It all seemed miraculous to Mrs. Wilson as she gave Woodrow Wilson a picture of her early days.

It was like his own. They exchanged their memories with total understanding. In Jessie Woodrow of Staunton he had a proud, strong mother who quietly dominated the home and insisted on good manners. She was an accomplished musician and did not mingle freely with her neighbors. Woodrow was a flaxen-haired boy who was heavily freckled and wore spectacles. He was nine before he learned his letters and he was the family baby until his brother Joseph was born when he was ten. His two sisters spoiled him. When the war broke out, his father's brothers fought with the Northern forces. His father was an army chaplain, and his uncle James Woodrow was in the Confederate service. Like Edith he grew up on tales of the Civil War although he himself remembered nothing about it. The Bones family was related to the Wilson family through Marion Woodrow, an aunt of Wilson's, who married James W. Bones. The President and his bride commented on the interlocking relationships of their two families. The days were magic for them at Hot Springs, and their privacy was honored by their fellow guests. A Christmas tree was set up and decorated in their honor in the private dining room, and they gave a reception in the public lounge on their last day. Over their personal happiness hung the dark cloud of bad news from Europe. The President had hoped for three weeks of peace, but an urgent message from Secretary of State Lansing made them hurry back to Washington on January 3, 1916.

Edith now faced both families together, since from Hot Springs she moved into the enveloping circle of the Wilsons as well as the Bollings. A family group had gathered at the White House for the Christmas festivities while she was on her wedding trip. It was an unostentatious way for a new White House bride to take occupancy—a midterm arrival without any inaugural flourish. This was providential to both in a period of national crisis.

The family welcomed them warmly but the President was caught up at once in consultations and official responsibilities. The familiar look of anxiety and tension returned. While he attended to his business she attended to hers, without ruffling the steady flow of White House procedure.

As 1916 began, Edith considered herself triply blessed—to be married to the man she loved, to be the wife of the President of the United States, and to live in the stately house she had been passing for years, with admiration but without curiosity about what went on inside.

# 6. *The White House*

MRS. EDITH BOLLING WILSON, already familiar with the President's family life in the White House, took up her official duties with skill and diplomacy. She brought her own personality and experience to bear on it, without disturbing the established pattern. She had no wish to upset the Wilson daughters or to stir criticism in unfriendly circles. Assuming this role in the middle of a term was an uncommon experience but Edith was quite equal to it.

The past animosities and fury that followed her engagement were tempered now that she was in the White House. Many who had snubbed her tried to ingratiate themselves. After the first few functions in January, 1916, there was general agreement that Mrs. Wilson was a hostess to be reckoned with, and even the most critical of her guests conceded her dignity, good looks, and consideration for others.

There was intense interest in the new First Lady and a lively social season was expected. The White House was no longer a place of gloom, but the President had decreed low-key entertaining. After the sinking of the *Lusitania* war was in the air. Preparedness was the word of the day. Since the time had not yet arrived to abandon all social events, they met the scrupulous demands of protocol. Wherever Woodrow Wilson went, his bride was at his side.

Characteristically, her first White House dinner was an intimate family affair to celebrate her mother's birthday. After that she was swept into a round of official events, beginning with a reception on January 9 for the delegates to the Pan-American Conference. This superseded the customary diplomatic reception, since the representatives of the warring nations could not be invited together.

Through a mixup in the invitation lists crowds stormed the White House for the Pan-American event, and before the evening was over Mrs. Wilson had shaken hands with 3,329 guests. She was no novice at entertaining but this was not what she had planned. In later years, after scores of stately receptions in different parts of the world, she recalled the special pride she felt during her first public appearance as the wife of Woodrow Wilson.

After welcoming the Cabinet members in the Oval Room, the President and Mrs. Wilson led the procession down the marble staircase, with naval and military aides forming an escort. The Marine Band played "Hail to the Chief" and a burst of spontaneous applause greeted Mrs. Wilson when she appeared, wearing a white gown with a long train, brocaded in silver. Tulle draped her shoulders, a flowing arrangement that she called her "angel sleeves." She carried orchids that the President had given her.

She bowed repeatedly to the crowd that watched the procession move from the Blue Room to the East Room, where the receiving line suddenly became a scramble. Things seemed chaotic to Mrs. Wilson as she and the President coped with disorderly people, many of whom had obviously come for a close look at the new First Lady. As they pressed in on her she decided that invitations had gone out too freely. A new order followed, giving the White House supervision over future invitation lists. All requests from the House and Senate were to be referred to the President; others were to be handled by Mrs. Wilson's social secretary.

Two days after the Pan-American reception the first state dinner for the Cabinet went smoothly, and on January 14 Vice President Thomas R. Marshall and Mrs. Marshall gave a large dinner for the Wilsons at the Willard Hotel. One reception and dinner followed another all through January, and in between Edith received ambassadors and their wives informally. She decided to see them in sequence rather than in groups. Each one had thirty minutes for tea before an open fire in the Red Room. She was well briefed on their background by her social secretary before receiving them. Recognition was an important element in the Presidential circle, and Woodrow Wilson studied photographs of Congressmen, so that he would know them by sight.

Mrs. Wilson was just beginning to make herself felt at the White House when she left with the President on January 27, for a quick trip west as part of the preparedness campaign. It was no secret in diplomatic circles that the country was totally unprepared for war, but this was not emphasized as he reviewed troops and attended parades.

The new First Lady was on view across the country as the President spoke in New York, Cleveland, Milwaukee, Chicago, Des Moines, Kansas City, Pittsburgh, and St. Louis. She learned what campaigning was like as politicians boarded the train to emphasize regional interests. The President was quietly assessing the sentiment of the country on war. "If America suffers all the world loses its equipoise. . . . I beg of you to stand by your government with your minds as well as your hearts," he told an audience of 18,000 in Kansas City. They cheered when he announced that 500,000 citizens would be trained for their defense, and in St. Louis he spoke of a Navy that would be "incomparably the greatest in the world."

As the much discussed bride of the White House, Mrs. Wilson was warmly welcomed and appraised at every stop. This was their chance to see her firsthand, and she did her best to prove herself a good campaigner—the tactful wife, the thoughtful listener. She saw that the people were deeply interested in what the President had to say, but that Europe was far away and there were pressing problems at home.

Back in Washington early in February, Mrs. Wilson resumed her adjustment to White House life. Each President's wife has approached the Executive Mansion in a different spirit. When the first Mrs. Wilson went upstairs after the inaugural parade and studied the formal garden with its gravelled paths and geometrical flower beds, she said she would change it into a rose garden surrounded by a high hedge.

Edith had no plans except to make things as comfortable as possible for the President. Orderly and practical, she responded well to planned schedules. She rearranged things with an instinct for comfort, while retaining the dignity and austerity of the President's own quarters. But crackling fires, flowers everywhere scenting the air, soft cushions and chintzes, books, magazines, and games all were part of the picture. The White House had long been cold; now it glowed with life. She simplified a number of things for her husband's comfort, insisting on total quiet when he worked. The bedroom arrangements changed at once. The President and Ellen had used the same twin beds as the Tafts, but now the great Lincoln bed used by Theodore Roosevelt was brought back into favor.

When Mrs. Wilson's brother Wilmer Bolling and her maid Susan closed her house on Twentieth Street after she left on her wedding trip, they transferred a few of her own possessions to the White House— her books, her piano, and her bedroom furniture, which all looked inconsequential in their new setting. But public interest quickly focused on her Wilcox & Gibbs sewing machine, an early model still on view in the Woodrow Wilson house in Washington in the 1970's. It served for her home dressmaking, for Red Cross work, for household linen, curtains, and anything that needed stitching. Aside from her own exquisite needlepoint and embroidery, Edith was expert at fashioning clothes.

# The White House

She did it in her prosperous as well as in her impoverished days. She could run up a dress in a day or twist a hat into shape in a matter of hours.

The passion for orchids spread rapidly across the country, and they became the luxury flower of the 1920's. Edith invariably appeared in public with one high on her left shoulder or in a cluster at her waist. Ike Hoover rounded up quantities for her, in or out of season, to please the President, but Woodrow liked to give her roses too—American beauties or the yellow rose that she called his "golden rose." Edith was no less fond of lilies of the valley and violets, and later, as fashions changed she moved to gardenias and never tired of the camellias identified with her youth. But as long as she lived, the purplish orchid was her special flower. She lavished her abundance of orchids on her nieces and friends.

Edith had experts at her command, to help run the White House. Her social secretary, Miss Edith Benham (later Mrs. James M. Helm), was an admiral's daughter who had traveled, worked in embassies, and who knew Washington society well. She understood the etiquette of the day and functioned with the pride, independence, and wit that Mrs. Wilson valued. In Ike Hoover and Mrs. Elizabeth Jaffray she had two White House veterans.

While war clouds blanketed every move President Wilson made in the first year of his marriage, Edith worked mightily to keep him in buoyant spirits. She learned that there were two Woodrow Wilsons—the scholar, statesman, and heavy thinker, and the merry prankster who surprised her with his antics. She had never known anyone to shift interest so quickly and she learned to move smoothly from frivolity to his more natural role as the austere, dignified President.

If Woodrow wanted to dance a jig in the Oval Room after dinner to the music of a Victrola, Edith applauded. She encouraged his interest in tap dancing and always responded to his moods. Unless he was preoccupied with work or quiet thought, she diverted him with merry conversation. He was most disposed to do this clowning and grimacing after a wearisome White House reception. He told Edith wryly that his face needed stretching after all the greetings and smiles. He could move his protuberant ears and outdo the cartoonists' wildest magnification of his looks. Without warning he would elongate or broaden his face ludicrously, amusing his family but sometimes startling his friends.

Edith found this frolicsome side of her awesome and dignified husband endearing. He had played the same games with his daughters and Ike Hoover observed, "they pampered and petted him and looked up to him as their lord and master. He could do no wrong in their eyes." It was easy for Edith to fall into this joyous pattern.

Wilson liked to play jokes on others and to tease, but Edith never tired of his nonsense, limericks, jokes, and rhymes that bubbled up so readily. This was part of every day, like the Bible chapter he read, or grace before meals. McAdoo had a way of forgetting this rite, in spite of Nell's constant warnings. When called on to say grace himself on one occasion, all he could think of was an explosive "Jesus!"

The President had fresh stories for all occasions, and he sometimes surprised his fellow statesmen in Europe and his Cabinet members at home with his apt wit. He liked stories about preachers, but frowned on anything irreligious or profane. Dr. Grayson found that no one knew better how to lighten a serious interview with humorous repartee or anecdote. "He was by nature dignified but assumed no artificial dignity. . . . He was impatient with pompous people and intolerant of those who sought special favors from the Government. . . ."

Wilson's courtesy to the servants was proverbial. He addressed them formally by their full names and never complained about anything. Ike Hoover found him the easiest to get along with of all the Chief Executives in his experience. Edith did not need much coaching, for she was an admirable and experienced housekeeper in her own right. The servants liked her. She expected them to know their business and reprimanded them if they intruded on the President while he was working or resting or if they failed to jump to their feet when he came in.

The White House arrangements were on such a vast scale that she could do no more than indicate to Mrs. Jaffray her wishes, especially where the President was concerned, but one of the novelties of her role was seeing the regal little housekeeper setting off in a carriage every morning to do her own picking and choosing at the city markets. Be-

66

fore long Mrs. Wilson realized how established the White House procedure was, no matter who lived there.

"Mrs. Wilson was what I would call a perfect wife," said Mrs. Jaffray, who had fared well with the Tafts but would cross swords with Calvin Coolidge on grounds of economy. "She was a wonderful companion for President Wilson, sympathetic and understanding and very gentle. For hours on end she would sew or embroider or knit while the President worked in his study. . . . He always wanted her near him."

Mrs. Jaffray's self-assurance and independence stirred comment in diplomatic circles. She dined alone in formal evening clothes every night in her suite on the third floor, and she lined up the staff for inspection before they went on duty. Mrs. Wilson was hesitant about asking for a slight change in the President's breakfast procedure. Because of their early-morning golf she wanted it served upstairs at six o'clock, offering to cook the eggs herself if things were left out for her. But Mrs. Jaffray would not hear of this and no matter how early they started out their breakfast was ready.

While approving the sophisticated fare for official occasions, Mrs. Wilson kept constant watch over the President's meals. He ate sparingly because of severe stomach upsets. His needs varied from time to time. During the Peace Conference he avoided veal and pork. He ate little meat but was particularly fond of chicken salad. Mrs. Wilson always had late snacks for him, since he was apt to ignore his dinner. He liked ham and boiled eggs for breakfast. He was known to take hominy and grits or rice, for Southern-style cooking prevailed under Mrs. Wilson's direction. Edith's taste ran to seafood, and wherever she went around the world she looked for shrimp, oysters, lobster, or local shellfish.

Among the few changes that Mrs. Wilson made at the White House was a rearrangement of the dining room tables for intimate luncheons. Expecting a visit from the Duke of Devonshire, Governor-General of Canada, she wanted an effect that would be dignified but not stiff. The sight of the tables used for state dinners standing empty during luncheons offended Mrs. Wilson. She and Miss Benham decided to do some exploring, and in the old basement kitchen they found a handsome circular table with a rope edge, large enough to seat sixteen guests. Restored and polished it seemed ideal for official luncheons and small parties.

Her own working day began when she settled down to her mail with Miss Benham. She was rapidly coached in the pitfalls of White House procedure. They discussed guest lists, the order of precedence, and courteous letters of refusal. Her own mail was an enlightening course in public opinion, but it soon grew too large for her full-time attention. She was swamped with letters from people needing help, appeals from the suffragists, demands for appointments by relatives of men who had voted for Woodrow Wilson, and with pleas that she urge him to act on the war issue.

Before she settled down with Miss Benham, Edith had already done a morning's work with the President. After the early golf game she studied papers with Woodrow until his private stenographer, Charles Swem, appeared at nine o'clock. The President dictated swiftly and clearly until eleven o'clock, then he went to the Executive Office.

Colonel Starling observed how happy the Wilsons were together. The President would signal to her from downstairs if he wanted her to walk with him. They would go through the garden or meet briefly in the sheltered arcade. Edith clung to his arm as they walked together, talking and laughing. He would kiss her good-bye and then return to kiss her again before disappearing into the Executive Wing.

Whenever possible the Wilsons lunched together at the White House, frequently with guests. Edith kept the conversation on a cheerful nonpolitical basis, and when the President was in a good mood he magnetized them with his stories. When they could, they disappeared for weekend cruises on the *Mayflower.* Captain Robert Berry prepared all for their comfort and privacy. They bundled up in rugs in wicker deckchairs and relaxed. A deep cap shaded the President's eyes as he read, and Edith sported the latest in yachting attire. The Hammond typewriter was at hand, and Swem was usually on board, but Edith was capable of taking notes as her husband thought things out.

Sometimes they cruised far from the marina, visiting small islands. They had a favorite fishing village from which they brought back crabs for Sunday lunch. Like Calvin Coolidge, Woodrow Wilson did not like it known that he spent Sunday on a yacht instead of in church. It was their custom to attend both Presbyterian and Episcopalian churches and they often went to St. John's, the official church for Presidents. Woodrow Wilson would find a Presbyterian church wherever he traveled and would sing the psalms with volume and conviction, for he had been brought up in the tradition of keeping the Sabbath holy, and Edith's family, while less intense, was also deeply involved in church work.

While the social and political life of the White House kept her ceaselessly on the go, Edith never neglected her family. She brought them into the White House circle at every opportunity. She and the President usually dined with the Bollings on Sunday or had them come to the Executive Mansion, but they kept Saturdays for themselves and often took long motor drives if they were not on the *Mayflower*. Mrs. Wilson missed her electric brougham, but Dr. Grayson, a cheerful martinet about health measures, did his best to keep all the women around the President in good trim, and Mrs. Wilson was a willing accomplice. He insisted on regular exercise for the President, and that meant getting Edith into action, too. She had reached an age where exercise was not the breath of life to her, although some women she knew were already systematically standing on their heads. The women's colleges developed a generation that swam, rowed, played tennis, golf, and croquet, and climbed mountains, in addition to the older arts of riding and hunting.

The bloomered girl on the bicycle had become a familiar sight along the highways and, although Mrs. Wilson never admired the eccentric in attire, she knew that her husband had a nostalgic passion for the wheel. When he was out of office, he told her he would like to do some leisurely bicycle touring in Europe. She never tired of listening to him talk about his trips in his college days, stopping at wayside taverns to chat with farmers, townsmen, and itinerants.

Since bicycles were luxuries in southwest Virginia when Edith Bolling was growing up, she never learned to ride one. A Columbia wheel was brought to the White House and she practiced in an area sixty feet long that had been cleared for her in the basement. The President and two Secret Service men went down with her at night, only to see her fall off time after time. The President teased her and she soon gave up, not only because she was black and blue, but because she did not like to do anything less than well. Golf remained her sport. Inevitably she was a spectator at all manner of big sports events in her official days, and she particularly enjoyed horse racing. She followed football closely, with so many college and prep school boys in their two families, and the old Princeton tradition. Baseball was Randolph's game and she backed him in this, although to her it was not the all-absorbing sport that it was to Mrs. Coolidge.

But Woodrow Wilson's love of cycling was mild compared to his interest in automobiles, particularly when he had Edith at his side. In this, as in all else, he developed a fixed pattern. His favorite drives out of Washington were known to the staff as Number One Ride, Southern Maryland Ride, Norfolk Ride, and Potomac Ride. Alexandria never failed to catch his eye as he passed through what he called the "only finished city in the United States."

Life in one sense was frugal in the White House, since the President had decided to save $2,000 a month while in office. Even before the stringency of war time, small economies were practiced. He did not scatter cigars and cigarettes among his visitors; in fact, he did not smoke or drink anything but an occasional glass of wine, a sip of champagne as a courtesy, or whiskey when Dr. Grayson ordered it for his health. But Edith saw to it that there was always champagne for gala events. Both were generous with their relatives, paying railroad fares, tuition fees, and remembering them with gifts.

Edith Wilson knew how to manage frugally, too, although this instinct was not as ingrained in her as in the President. Early in life she had learned the value of money, but she had moved into another world with her marriage to Woodrow Wilson. She was keenly aware of the millionaires of both parties who had come into view during his reelection campaign. He would need their resources now with the task that lay ahead of him as the Allied leaders in Europe kept a watchful eye on the White House, and war seemed inevitable.

Edith Wilson was thought to be extravagant about clothes but she was keenly aware of the necessity to look her best in the eyes of the world. As the wife of Woodrow Wilson she was constantly in the limelight, sharing in some of the great events of the era. Her clothes were much discussed, and she became a fashion leader. Like the parsimonious Calvin Coolidge, Woodrow Wilson wanted to see his wife elegantly attired. When she gave up mourning after Norman Galt's death, the lilacs and grays that she wore as half-mourning were so becoming that she continued to use them, and was most often seen in gray, beige, lavender, many shades of purple, or in black and white.

At all times conscious of fashion, she looked her best in the chiffon velvets, smooth satins, and clinging crepe de chine of the period. In her later years she was handsome in heavy brocades and lamé. She was fond of furs, and the long sealskin coat she wore in the early days of her marriage was recurrently mentioned in news dispatches. As the years went on she acquired a good deal of valuable jewelry, but she did not greatly care for it, except for Woodrow's carefully chosen gifts. At the time of their marriage he gave her a diamond and platinum ring and a large square aquamarine. His idea of the perfect gift for anyone was a book.

Women then were covered from mid-calf to chin. They wore high-necked blouses and big fur collars. Through every stage of fashion Edith Wilson chose a low décolletage in the evening to show off her neck and shoulders. Her hats were the most conspicuous part of her costuming, large, dashing, and tilted at provocative angles. The tiny scraps of flowers and veiling that served as hats during World War II and sat precariously on Mrs. Truman's orderly head were not to her taste.

She would never appear anywhere without being perfectly groomed, unlike her husband, who did not worry much about his attire, but she got him away from loose box coats and ill-fitting trousers, and he was soon wearing the most approved fashions with ease.

It took Edith some time to get used to having a guest list submitted to the White House when the President dined out, a rare occurrence. She soon absorbed the essentials of her role, but in private moments neither she nor her husband felt particularly reverent about the details of protocol. His thoughts were usually in the clouds, and he had been heard to remark that if the earth opened up and swallowed the social crowd they would never be missed.

Wherever the President and Mrs. Wilson went after Germany's flat declaration of unrestricted submarine warfare they saw the tide was rising. The preparedness campaign was catching fire in 1916. Along with the customary annual events, it all seemed like a whirlwind to the

White House bride. Late in May she attended the celebration of the anniversary of the Mecklenberg Declaration of Independence at Charlotte, North Carolina.

In June she went with the President on the *Mayflower* to Annapolis for the graduation of the midshipmen, and a few days later they traveled to West Point. Watching the young cadets, in their trim white uniforms, she speculated on the future of these young men, now so close to war. She knew that behind the scenes preparedness was becoming a reality. Shipyards were in action and arms were being forged.

Edith Wilson's day often started before five o'clock in the morning and Woodrow was apt to work far into the night. In the evenings she sat with him when they did not have engagements, shut off from the world in their crimson-curtained room. He worked at his desk, while she sewed, knitted, or read. Sometimes he would stop to read her something he had written. He was learning how shrewd and perceptive her opinions could be, and how firm her convictions. As the daughter of Judge Bolling, Edith had considerable knowledge of the law. She had learned discretion at an early age and knew when to hold her peace. Keeper of vital secrets as the wife of Woodrow Wilson, she was rarely, if ever, known to embarrass him with an unwise revelation. Her own horizons broadened as she listened to him; he set standards for her that no one else could ever match.

The President's devotion to Edith amazed observers and sometimes irritated Colonel House and Tumulty when they could not reach him with their problems. In March, 1916, when House hurried to Washington to report the British government's attitude on having Woodrow Wilson dictate the peace, House found him in a state of happiness. Clearly the marriage was working well. House's appointment at the White House was delayed a day because the Wilsons were cruising on the *Mayflower.* On a two-hour drive the following afternoon he gave a full account of the results of his mission, with Mrs. Wilson sitting between them, as interested as her husband in what was being said.

Colonel House had conferred with Sir Edward Grey and other members of the British Cabinet in London, and had gone to Berlin and Paris to sound out the political hierarchy on President Wilson becoming the mediator. He emphasized the fact that the aim would be peace by conciliation, and that the American President would be completely neutral. But the Allies, like the Central Powers, wanted to win on their own terms and would accept Woodrow Wilson's mediation only if it were the only alternative to defeat and peace terms dictated by Germany.

Sir Edward, with Colonel House, drew up a memorandum promising an American call for a peace conference at a time appointed by the Allies. The President listened to this attentively but without conviction. Late into the night, after their visitor left, they discussed the implications of this report.

Edith thought that Woodrow needed a vis-à-vis who would stand up to him and not be as acquiescent and "wishy-washy" as Colonel House was. No one knew better than she that her husband's will was immovable on major issues. In many instances she held quietly to her own convictions; but quite often she was swayed by his. He could not shake her in her judgment of men, however, and he realized this.

When she had been in the White House for five months she and the President were quiet observers at the marriage of Admiral Grayson and Altrude Gordon. This gave both of them deep satisfaction, although it had taken time to come to pass. Altrude had finally succumbed to Cary's persuasion and dogged character, but they had put off getting married until Mrs. Wilson was well established in the White House.

Two days before his own marriage the President had invited them for dinner at the White House, knowing what was coming. It was an event of the deepest personal interest to him and to Edith, who were finding much happiness in their own union. The Graysons were married in St. George's Chapel in New York on May 24, 1916. Only close friends of the bride and groom were invited, and nothing was made of the fact that two of the guests were the President and Mrs. Wilson. They arrived from Washington with Helen Bones and Randolph Bolling with just enough time to get to the church after a quick change of clothes at the apartment of Charles R. Crane, diplomat and millionaire manufacturer of plumbing supplies. Mrs. Wilson, in pale gray taffeta with a misty gray picture hat made of tulle, stood close to Altrude, who was calm but fragile-looking in a white chiffon dress. When it was all over the bride clung to the President and he responded affectionately. He congratulated his handsome aide, who by this time was a trusted friend as well as his physician.

The wedding cake was made by Shiro Tauruaski, the Japanese steward on the *Mayflower,* who worked for ten days on the icing and was brokenhearted when the papers credited it to the White House chef. But Mrs. Wilson saw that this wrong was righted. Ike Hoover, devoted to Dr. Grayson, insisted on sending to New York "everything but the kitchen stove," she wrote to Altrude, warning her that the flowers would be irises on the magnifico scale.

On their return to Washington Mrs. Wilson wrote tenderly to Altrude on May 29, 1916, assuring her that she had been a lovely bride and that she had handled everything well on her wedding day. By this time she and Cary were at The Greenbriar at White Sulphur Springs, West Virginia. "Remember always how tenderly interested I am in all that concerns you both—and that you have me always just the same in spite of our two splendid husbands," Edith wrote. "Tell *yours* that mine is as well as can be—but full of work to his eyes—and that we both want you to stay away as long as you can." She assured Altrude that she need have no qualms about "clinging and kissing" Woodrow, for he had told her that he thoroughly approved of such "unmaidenly ways."

With Cary away from Washington Mrs. Wilson got out her own neglected Electric and "went on a real spree" with the President. Writing to Altrude on June 20, 1916, she said, "I have been running the Electric (and it does seem like old times) so we stole off last night and went around the Potomac drive and had a beautiful time, with only faithful Jamieson in his own car trailing behind. . . . We are both perfectly well and, I guess, hard work agrees with us."

Although the public caught many glimpses of the Wilsons in Washington, little was known of their private life during these hectic days. "I am sure there was never anyone in the world who loved personal privacy more than Woodrow Wilson," his wife wrote. Even a chauffeur was an intruder. Although his official trips were usually taken at the mad clip of a guarded Presidential party, his drives with Edith were slow and tranquil. Exhausted at times by all the pressures around him, he would lean against the shoulder of the woman he loved, sometimes half asleep but always soothed by her presence.

Altrude was glad to see that Mrs. Wilson was being so well received by the public, for she had been a close observer of all the antagonism

Edith had had to face when she married the President. She wrote to Edith on March 19, 1916, after catching the reaction of the audience to a newsreel of the Wilson family:

> There was applause when Mr. McAdoo appeared, more for the President, and an outburst of enthusiasm for you! Nothing has ever pleased me more, for it was certainly a true test of public sentiment. . . . You must be so glad, Miss Ede, to know that you are helping such a wonderful man—and so helping his work and the whole country. Those latent powers, abilities and charms of yours have found their opportunity—and are being used to such wonderful advantage and good purpose.

Cary Grayson had opened up the way to Edith's marrying Woodrow Wilson, and she had helped him to win the elusive Miss Gordon. The four-way romance had now reached its climax, and Mrs. Wilson was filled with quiet satisfaction. All four remained close friends for the rest of their lives.

# 7. *An Effective Campaigner*

WHEN the President was nominated for reelection at the Democratic national convention held in St. Louis in June, 1916, Mrs. Wilson was already established as an admirable White House hostess, and she was becoming increasingly popular with the public. But the campaign that lay ahead was challenging, with the war fever rising fast after the sinking of the *Lusitania*.

The President was kept so busy in Washington that it was early September before they were able to move to Shadow Lawn, the well-protected estate near Asbury Park, New Jersey, that had been rented as the summer White House. It was one of the more pretentious summer cottages adding classical variations to Victorian bric-a-brac and smothering swathings. "Awful but comfortable," was Mrs. Wilson's verdict after she had studied its seventeen porches, its Pompeian room, its billiard room with armor, its French salon, its marble statuary, and its decorated bookshelves behind velvet curtains, an eyesore to Woodrow Wilson who in moments of stress liked to rearrange the books in a library, dipping into them as he did so.

The lounge, suggesting an auditorium, had a staircase leading to a platform where a gold piano stood. A massive statue that faced arriving visitors raised a problem for the puritanically inclined. It was draped for propriety, a gesture by prankish Tumulty that led to much publicity. The second-floor sitting room opened on a porch suggesting the deck of a steamer.

Not wishing to use the White House for his political campaigning, the notification ceremony was held at Shadow Lawn on September 2, with 8,000 chairs arranged for guests and a speakers' platform set up at the house. Delegations arrived by train until the grounds were filled with old-time campaigners and the going got rough. Mrs. Wilson had never seen anything like it, but she entered into the spirit of the occasion and smiled dimly when the flowerbeds were flattened and the beer bottles were flung around.

The day had begun with rain and mist, but the sun shone by noon. Senator Ollie M. James of Kentucky made the notification speech, and then the rollicking crowd became hushed and attentive as the President gave what his wife considered one of his finer addresses. After summing up the achievements of his administration on domestic issues he swung into a lofty plea for America to take the lead in world conciliation. It was an intimation of the future, but it kept the war issue in abeyance, as he refused to face the urgent mood of many for action. If reelected, he announced in his unemphatic way, he would be a "servant of the whole people."

That night he left for Kentucky to dedicate the shrine at Lincoln's birthplace.

"Little did I suspect how near to us were those hideous burdens of war which had weighed Lincoln down," Edith recalled of the round of campaigning with her husband that followed. It ranged from simple picnicking to the famous banquets of the Traymore Hotel in Atlantic

City, with fish and game locked in pyramids of ice, colored lights playing on their shining eyes and fluffed-up tails. Frozen eagles were featured for election year, and spun sugar confections whetted the gourmet tastes of the era but were apt to weary abstemious Woodrow Wilson.

The suffragists were at his heels here, too, and although the salt air refreshed him, Edith reported that a "suffragette meeting, a charity concert and people, people, people drained away the benefit of it all." Although they strove to win her attention, the eager and earnest-minded leaders who had gathered for this occasion annoyed Edith with their determination to force the President's support. She smiled and thanked them when they decked her with white orchids, but she wished that they would all go away.

A family tragedy struck the Wilsons suddenly on their return to Shadow Lawn. Mrs. George Howe, the President's sister, felled by a stroke, was critically ill at New Haven. They hurried there, to find that she was beyond help and did not recognize Woodrow. They waited for several days, first at the Mohican Hotel, where he was besieged by politicians, and then on the *Mayflower*, where he could escape them. When they were told that Mrs. Howe might linger indefinitely, they returned to Shadow Lawn. Two days later word came that she was dead.

With the great love for his family and his special devotion to his sister, the President was profoundly upset. She had always been the liveliest member of the family group, joining him for all special occasions, and she had given him warm support when he decided to marry Mrs. Galt. Other relatives had been less enthusiastic.

He and Mrs. Wilson left at once for Columbia, South Carolina, for her funeral. She was buried from the little church in which she had been married, and Edith had a chance to visit the simple, dignified house where Woodrow had spent part of his boyhood. She would see it next as a memorial.

Back at Shadow Lawn, the President played golf with Edith, Dr. Grayson, and visiting friends, took drives, and saw something of the family children when not busy with political discussions and his mail. The McAdoos, who had a cottage nearby at Spring Lake, came over nearly every day. The Sayres and Margaret, who now spent much of her time studying music in New York, traveled back and forth, and Mrs. Bolling and Bertha were never far from Edith's side. The numerous spare rooms of Shadow Lawn were always available for family use, and Mrs. Bolling thought it a treasure house.

Meanwhile the political wheels ground on, with delegations coming on Saturdays and noted visitors arriving constantly. The President used the platform that had been built for the notification ceremony to give brief talks to groups ranging from 500 to 2,000. In some respects they led more of a public life than they were used to at the White House, and Colonel Starling's men had a hard time protecting the wandering family contingent when they got free from the well-protected estate. Wherever Edith Wilson was, there were always relatives to be shepherded about.

She met all the social demands when the men backing her husband's campaign came to call. She had her first brief glimpse of Ignace Paderewski when he arrived to ask the President if he would set aside a day on behalf of the suffering Poles. She would later come to know him well, but her first impression of him was a mournful face, shadowed by a nimbus of hair, looking pleadingly at her husband at Shadow Lawn.

Henry Ford, who was carefully appraising the President, showed schoolboy delight, she thought, in displaying his collection of watches —paper-thin, some edged with diamonds or rubies, and one made entirely of platinum. Jacob Schiff, of banking fame, was received by the President but Edith inadvertently missed his wife. Dr. and Mrs. Simon Baruch were well liked callers. Their son, Bernard, would soon figure prominently in her husband's administration as head of the War Industries Board.

Some of the campaign events seemed to Edith to have their inappropriate moments. She assured Woodrow that he looked "very stunning" wearing cutaway and top hat as he rode up and down the lines, reviewing units of the New Jersey National Guard at Sea Girt. Well aware of campaign needs, he laughed this off as being one way of "emphasizing the civil authority over the military." Before leaving early in October for a round of campaign engagements he spoke to 1,500 members of the Young Men's Democratic Club who had paraded through the gates of Shadow Lawn with bands playing and flags flying.

His advisers at this time proposed that he modify the lofty tone of his speeches and deal with specific regional issues as he traveled west, but this had less appeal for his wife than when he spoke on behalf of mankind. However, she saw its practical value from the reception they received in Omaha. With the top Washington correspondents on board their train and the energetic Tumulty beating the drums in the Corn Belt, Edith lived in a whirl of receptions, applause, flowers, and demonstrations. They were mobbed as they moved from place to place. It seemed an endless round of talking, smiling, and shaking hands, of waving from the back platform of the train at crowds that seemed to spring from nowhere. Edith had gained such stature during her first months in the White House that the earlier criticism had cooled. She added a glowing presence to their appearances on this tour, although she tried to stay in the background.

In Chicago they were joined by Senator Thomas J. Walsh of Montana and Mrs. George Bass, chairman of the Woman's National Democratic Committee, shepherded Mrs. Wilson. The woman's touch was needed, since the Hughes train traveling from coast to coast on behalf of the Republican candidate was constantly on the front pages while Wilson went almost unnoticed. Mingling with the most elegant women members of the party was a strong and assertive contingent of suffrage fighters. All were dedicated to gathering support for Charles Evans Hughes at every stop, but among them were a few women correspondents who were also believers in women's suffrage, and the country was flooded with such inflammatory stories that the feuding and bickering came close to wrecking the expedition. Hughes stood aloof, making dignified appeals to the voters at given points, skirting the war issue with ambiguity but without rejection. He was counting on the women's vote, but the Hughes train excited more ridicule than support.

The only male correspondent on board represented the New York *Times,* which in itself was an insult to the embattled forces. Why a *man?* But he quickly had Park Avenue stirred up with a front page story entitled "Rings In, Rings Out," accusing the more worldly on board of turning their diamond rings around when they moved from the country clubs to the slums. This was scarcely the Wilson way of doing things, but he, too, paid close attention to the women's groups in the West, where the feminists were getting results.

They were back at Shadow Lawn for Mrs. Wilson's birthday and she awakened that morning to find Woodrow standing beside her bed with a platinum brooch. He was already busy with shorthand notes for an address he was due to make. They had a big family party that night, since Bertha, Dr. Grayson, Helen Bones, and both of the McAdoos had October birthdays, like Edith. Two days later they left for more campaigning in Chicago, then Cincinnati again, Indianapolis, and finally Buffalo at the end of October before the grand finale at Madison Square Garden.

This was the traditional gathering place for Democratic rallies and the square was so jammed with people that the mounted police had trouble clearing the way for the President's party. Mrs. Wilson climbed a fire escape at the back of the building in order to get in through a window. Along the campaign route, most of the President's speeches had been delivered without much preparation and often had been purely spontaneous. But little of what he had to say was heard on this occasion as a crowd of 30,000 roared and cheered, and bands played the songs of the South and of the sidewalks of New York. Alfred E. Smith introduced the man who would both support and fight him in the course of his political career. Smith and Wilson seemed to Edith to be a study in contrasts but united in their appeal to the people.

After this evening of excitement the President and Mrs. Wilson were picked up by the *Mayflower* and they calmed down as they steamed with Margaret and Helen Bones toward Atlantic Highlands. They were back at Shadow Lawn by morning and the President spoke once more from there, his final campaign gesture. A group of 250 friends from Princeton arrived with the usual delegation on the Saturday before election day. The most intimate of their old associates stayed on for an evening of talk before they all retired on the blustery night of November 4.

A great storm and violent downpour kept Edith awake all night. Now that the campaign had ended she was depressed about her husband's prospects, even while she reviewed in her mind the brilliant coups of the last four years. In August he had averted a nationwide railroad strike by pushing through the Adamson Act that gave railroad workers the eight-hour day. Wilson's tariff reforms and graduated national income tax would affect the structure of American government for years to come. The Federal Reserve banking system was organized in the face of tough banking opposition, and the Clayton antitrust measure challenged big business at the basic level.

Though she believed in the magnitude of Woodrow's achievements on the domestic front she was not convinced that he could defeat Hughes. Her husband had dynamic appeal for the masses but there was great wealth in the other camp, and she feared he would fall short on electoral votes. For once her keen judgment and her optimism failed her, and she wondered if their marriage would prove to be a factor in the final count. But Woodrow spread cheer when he came into her room on election morning, fully dressed for the day, and laughed at her for talking defeat. One should not court failure, he pointed out. "If it comes, accept it like a soldier; but don't anticipate it, for that destroys your fighting spirit."

After an early breakfast they drove to Princeton. A storm had windlashed the coast and the world looked bright and clean, with blue skies and a blanket of sunshine. Edith's spirits rose as they approached the old engine house where her husband had always cast his vote. The press were waiting and she stayed in the car to avoid them. New Jersey had not yet given its women the vote and it is unlikely that she would have used the franchise in any event. Later, as a resident of the District of Columbia, she could not cast a vote. She never did as long as she lived.

The President was warmly cheered in the college town where his image had been so strong, so revered, so maligned, and so hated. But now the battle was far behind him and, win or lose, he was unassailable. They returned to Shadow Lawn for lunch. Frank Sayre joined them later in the day after casting his vote in Pennsylvania. He and Dr. Grayson were their dinner guests, and afterward they gathered in the upstairs sitting room to await results. The President had decided to get the news by telephone from the Executive Office set up by Tumulty at Asbury Park, instead of using a special wire. He seemed calm and unconcerned but Margaret moved like lightning every time the telephone rang. Her father proposed the game of Twenty Questions to make them all settle down. Edith watched Woodrow to see the effect, but Tumulty later said that on this occasion his imperturbability matched Grover Cleveland's.

They all looked dashed when Margaret received a call from a friend in New York that the red signal had flashed at the New York *Times* building, spelling defeat for Wilson. Dr. Grayson hurried over to the Executive Office but got no consolation there, since a bulletin had just come in from the *World*, carrying news of Hughes' election. Tumulty, ever articulate and often eloquent, was speechless. Dr. Grayson's spirited approach to things faded into gloom. Margaret, wild with disappointment, kept telling her father that it was too early to concede. They all agreed on that, but he anticipated the worst. Finally he had a glass of milk and went off to bed, saying he did not want to stay with them, since they were all so blue. But when Edith followed him he was already in bed, and she realized at once the depth of his disappointment. He told her that she had been right about the outcome. He had not expected defeat, but he was facing it now and looking into the future. "At last we can do some of the things we have always wanted to do," he said, but as he spoke she knew that what he wanted at that moment was victory. And so did she.

He fell into a sleep so profound that she would not let Margaret waken him when she came to her room at four in the morning with encouraging news. She had just heard from Vance C. McCormick, chairman of the Democratic National Campaign Committee, that there was still a vestige of hope. Edith could scarcely keep Margaret from bursting in on her father but she insisted that it was better to let him sleep. She had left for New York to keep a music engagement by the time he wakened, listless and tired. Life had gone dead for him and for Edith. They studied the morning papers with dismay. Headlines proclaimed a Republican victory. The President had said that Hughes' speeches were only "blank cartridges" but evidently they had drawn fire. There were pictures of Hughes and his family, but Edith pointed out hopefully that the returns were not yet all in and the element of doubt remained. The close Hayes-Tilden election of 1876 was recalled, and so the vigil continued at Shadow Lawn. The lights burned all night at Asbury Park and Tumulty neither ate nor slept.

While Hughes went motoring on November 9 the Wilsons played golf at Spring Lake. They were at the eighth tee when Dr. Grayson arrived to tell them that California seemed to be safe, the crucial state at that point.

Although Hughes had made a clean sweep in the East and Middle West, Wilson had caught the Progressives, Independents, and women's groups in the Prairie and Far Western states. The advocates of peace supported the man who typified the slogan "He Kept Us Out of War" and talked peace himself. The President's statement when the *Lusitania* was sunk in May, 1915, was still fresh in people's minds, soothing some and infuriating others. He had said there was such a thing as being "too proud to fight," a phrase mocked around the world.

82

## An Effective Campaigner

Edith tried to explain it by saying that it applied only to Wilson himself and not to the country. He kept silent, she added, rather than stoop to justify himself under attack. Tumulty called it moral grandeur but said that the President did not fully realize his gift for making "striking and quotable phrases." In any event, the impression prevailed that Wilson won because he kept America out of the war.

In the final count Wilson had a majority of 23 electoral votes, and 9,129,606 popular votes compared with 8,558,221 for Hughes. When they left Shadow Lawn for good, the Wilsons still did not know the final figures, but the clouds had lifted and Edith Wilson was in high spirits.

They motored to Sandy Hook and boarded the *Mayflower* there. They paced the deck most of the night, watched the lights of New York through the darkness, and slept fitfully until Brooks brought the President a message at seven thirty A.M. that told him the battle was won. It was November 10. The ordeal had lasted three days.

A special train with their private car (also named the *Mayflower*) attached to it met them at Rhinecliff. Crowds gathered at the boat and train to cheer the President, and Edith stepped aboard hugging a lavish bunch of Hudson Valley violets that had been thrust into her arms. As she settled in the train she finally accepted the fact that there was no doubt of the outcome. Four more years in the White House stretched ahead and her mood changed to one of jubilance. Although she had been assuring Woodrow that defeat would mean peace for them, with more time to spend together, she knew from the expression on his face that victory was everything to him at that moment.

There were fast reactions abroad. Messages poured in from around the world. London welcomed Wilson's reelection, and the German Chancellor announced on December 12 that his government was prepared to negotiate. Japan read peace into Wilson's victory. It was clear to many that peace had been the dominant issue.

As always when he was involved in crucial issues, the personal and family life of Wilson continued with a steady stream of warmth and satisfaction. His sister was gone, but new life had come into his family. His first act after winning the election was to travel to Williamstown, Massachusetts, for the christening of Eleanor Axson Sayre, the second child of Jessie and Francis.

He was anxious to keep the election celebration on a low key, but the people of Troy demonstrated as he passed through. Banners waved and burning brooms lit the night as students serenaded him and Edith at the home of Dr. Harry Garfield, president of Williams College and son of the assassinated President. Later he spoke with quiet earnestness from the porch of the Sayre house to the crowd that gathered there.

The press across the country was commenting on one of the strangest reversals in the history of the Presidency. Mountains of mail awaited Wilson's return to Washington, and people were clamoring for appointments. He was faced immediately with the preparation of his message to Congress, and he was showing signs of strain.

Only two weeks after the election Edith noted that Woodrow was "quite unwell." He was getting professional massage to ease tension, and as he faced the excruciating pressure of the world situation and the official demands of his office, he found solace and refreshment only in their quiet hours together. They listened to opera on their electric piano or Edith played and sang for him. Lansing, House, and Tumulty all annoyed him. He seemed to be at odds with nearly everyone and everything in his life—but not with Edith, who always managed to mollify him. On December 9, 1916, Starling noted that he was a "hard man to handle, especially at this time. He was always hard-headed, but ordinarily he was not contrary or irritable, and above all he was reasonable and thoughtful. When he began to be otherwise I knew the load was telling on his strength."

Wilson insisted on attending the Gridiron Dinner but Dr. Grayson made him cancel his engagement to attend the Army-Navy game. He let him go to New York on December 2, however, for the illumination of the Statue of Liberty. From the *Mayflower* he and Mrs. Wilson watched pioneer flyer Ruth Law pilot an open plane from which she "dropped white fire, making the place look like a giant comet."

The statue was flooded with light as the flaming torch blazed in the night—a symbol, in Woodrow Wilson's words, of "that which is to make the world alight when all men, everywhere, have Liberty." This was followed by a dinner at the Waldorf-Astoria, where he said that peace would come only with liberty, and that there could be no liberty so long as "small groups determined the destinies of peoples."

When the President delivered his annual message to Congress that

84

same week his flow of words did not halt for a moment when a small group of suffrage advocates unfurled their yellow and white banner over the balcony rail. But Edith was outraged. They were cropping up with some regularity now wherever he appeared, and they insisted that their cause was the most urgent of the day.

In the midst of all this she and the President snatched some time to do their Christmas shopping together. On Sunday, the day before Christmas, they went to St. Margaret's Church and after lunch heard children sing carols at the Treasury Department steps. According to custom they trimmed their tree in the Oval Room, and Jessie's baby and little Josephine Cothran were brought in for the festivities.

Woodrow gave Edith a gold mesh bag that Christmas, something she had always wanted. They breakfasted together downstairs on Christmas morning and then went up to the tree, which was ablaze with lights. Mrs. Wilson left this family scene to take communion at St. John's Church and to visit her mother. All day long visitors arrived at the White House and in the evening there was a gathering of both families. Christmas poinsettias abounded and they played charades, using the upstairs hall as a stage and the bedrooms for dressing rooms. The Wilson girls were so expert at this sort of thing that the performance seemed semiprofessional. On the following night the Graysons and the Houses, in from New York, dined at the White House. But a volcano was about to erupt. The days of peace came to an end.

# *8.* *Inauguration on the Brink of War*

EDITH WILSON began the year 1917 with outward calm but deepening concern as she prepared for the inaugural ceremonies and another four years in the White House. Those who thought her frivolous and carefree as she went from one diplomatic reception to another misread the signs. No woman in Washington knew better what the country faced. Edith shared Woodrow Wilson's anxious nights as well as his busy days.

Between December 12, 1916, when the German Chancellor announced that his government was prepared to negotiate, and April 6, 1917, when the United States declared war, the Wilsons lived through one crisis after another. The President was running against the tide of national feeling as warfare in Europe grew more intense and both sides waited anxiously for Woodrow Wilson to act.

When his plan to act as mediator got a chilly reception, Wilson had concentrated on his "Peace Without Victory" plan, embodied in a statement made to the Senate on January 22, 1917. Its principles had been germinating in his mind for a long time, and House and Sir Edward Grey had been talking in terms of a postwar organization of international dimensions. Wilson now envisioned the United States abandoning its isolationism and joining the other nations of the world in an organized plan for peace.

Edith considered this one of his finest state papers; Woodrow had impressed on her his belief that his plan might prove to be the great work of his lifetime. She had watched him sweating it out and had read his notes to him as he typed them in primary form on his Hammond. He asked the belligerents to make peace by negotiation, and the powers of the world to preserve that peace with mutual exchanges such as were later developed at the United Nations. The basic principles outlined in his "Peace Without Victory" speech became part of the Fourteen Points, given to the world early in 1918. But at the moment the door was closed, since his plan served only to anger the combatants and puzzle Americans clamoring for action as the Central Powers followed one hostile move with another. Irreversible forces were at work, and events moved too fast at the very moment when the President believed that he had found the answer to peace without victory.

Delivering his annual message on December 4, 1916, Wilson had ignored the war issue and urged Congress to pass laws to end the railroad strike. But in Britain a coalition government was being formed and peace feelers were coming from Berlin. The President's offer to act as mediator, infuriating to the war-weary leaders of both sides, was followed by Germany's sudden proposal on December 12, 1916, to enter into peace negotiations. The message was so vague that Lansing and House warned Wilson that he might find himself in virtual entente with Germany.

On December 18 he sent a note to the combatants, asking for a joint explanation of their aims. The Germans, suspecting a double cross on their own projected plans, failed to reply. Sir Edward Grey's efforts to pull things together had failed, and the British were bitter. At home, Lodge, Roosevelt, and other powerful figures demanding the country's entry into the war on the side of the Allies were loud in their protests.

In the midst of this impasse the President took time to remember Edith's birthday with a black opal pendant. She was forty-four on December 18 and she looked no more than thirty. As she fulfilled her social engagements she kept close track of every move being made in the projected peace plans and she failed to understand why both sides should not have welcomed mediation by her husband.

Wilson brought Walter Hines Page and James W. Gerard home from London and Berlin in November to confer with him and his two chief advisers, Lansing and House, on his plans for peace by negotiation. Gerard was struck by Mrs. Wilson's obvious familiarity with the situation abroad and impressed by the pointed questions she asked.

Wrestling with world problems of enlarged scope, and with his long adherence to neutrality nearing an end, the President turned more than ever to Edith for discussion and understanding. He lived on two separate planes of thought and action. While he worried about industrial unrest and faced public hostility over the plot to blow up the Welland Canal and other indications of enemy action at home, he was drawn deeper into the international problems that his emissaries could not solve.

Germany's delayed answer came in startling fashion on January 31, nine days after the President laid his case before the Senate. It was a declaration of unrestricted submarine warfare to begin on February 1 in the zone around the British Isles. To add insult to injury it specified the route that a restricted number of American ships might take through this zone. All neutral nations were warned of the situation.

"This means war," the President told Edith when he returned from the Executive Offices with an Associated Press dispatch in his hand

and a grim look on his face. When Tumulty gave him the official German note from the War Department he noticed a "sudden grayness of color, a compression of the lips and the familiar locking of the jaw which always characterized him in moments of supreme resolution."

On February 3 Wilson announced to both Houses the rupture of relations with Germany. Count Johann-Heinrich von Bernstorff, the German ambassador who had so assiduously sought favor at the White House, was handed his passport—the end of one of the most curious diplomatic interludes in American history. His subordinates, Boy-ed and von Papen, were deep in intrigue, but von Bernstorff maintained a correct demeanor, was popular with many, and kept in touch with Colonel House up to the last moment. Edith had followed his curious brand of diplomacy with close attention, since it was one of her husband's annoyances. Von Bernstorff was the most discussed diplomat in Washington at the moment and he had many friends in the British set. He had noticed a chill at the White House for some time, and when the President's engagement was announced he asked Colonel House if he should write to congratulate him.

Von Bernstorff's name came up often when there was gossip about telephone leaks at the White House and elsewhere, as one major development followed another on the international front. The President was much more suspicious of von Bernstorff than Colonel House was, and Edith got inklings daily of his smooth approach to the unwary. He had a long diplomatic history and high rating in the corps stationed in Washington.

While the President coped with his deepening problems Mrs. Wilson was stricken with a grief of her own. On February 25, 1917, Randolph arrived with the news that their sister, Annie Lee Maury, was critically ill and faced an operation. Without further warning she died. She had just left for Roanoke with her daughters, Anne and Lucy, after the Christmas family gathering at the White House, and had been expected back for inauguration with her husband, Matthew H. Maury.

Annie Lee was Mrs. Wilson's favorite sister and was much like her—vivacious and witty. She had dark eyes, features suggestive of her Indian heritage, prematurely silver hair, and a glowing complexion. Annie Lee was so alive and gay that she made her sister seem serious by comparison. The shock was so severe that Edith could scarcely accustom herself to the fact that they had lost her, but she took firm hold as she always did in moments of family crisis. Mrs. Bolling collapsed and could not go to the funeral, so Edith brought her mother to the White House and arranged to have her moved with Bertha and Randolph from the apartment they had occupied for many years to the Powhatan Hotel. Her servant, Mathilde Broxton, who had served her family for a lifetime, had become too old to work any longer.

Edith characteristically subdued her personal grief. She strove to show a cheerful front at the dinners and receptions preceding inauguration day. Because of the war situation the President had considered limiting official functions but then decided that this might spread alarm. So she went through it all, sorrowing over the death of Annie Lee and not knowing from hour to hour what news the President might bring home from the Executive Office. They had decided to keep a steady front, giving no indication to the public of the chaos behind the scenes. A game of golf, a daily drive, a walk in the rain, a visit to the Corcoran Gallery where the President sometimes found refreshment from his cares, and the usual round of official functions reassured observers.

The Cabinet dinners were elaborate, and not the least of them was given by Secretary of the Treasury McAdoo and Mrs. McAdoo. Mrs. Wilson found it a novel situation to be formally received by her own stepdaughter. It was all done in Nell's finest style. But although Edith had come to enjoy the social functions in Washington the threat of war made it all seem senseless. "The round of official entertaining," she said, "began to seem trivial indeed."

March 4 fell on a Sunday in 1917, so the oath of office was taken in informal fashion in the President's special room at the Capitol. It rained on their way there and Woodrow went to work signing bills until Chief Justice Edward D. White came in and chatted with Edith. Finally he rose from the desk where he had been working and was sworn in on the Bible that had been used four years earlier, and also when he became Governor of New Jersey. It was the simplest of ceremonies, quickly over, and Edith preferred it to his formal inauguration on the following day. Starling noticed that at the first swearing in "with shining eyes she watched her husband, proud of him, her head held high, a little smile on her lips."

Again it was dark and gloomy when they set off next day for the Capitol, but the sun came out as the day wore on. They were heavily guarded by regular troops and Secret Service men, an escort that both disliked. Threatening letters had come in saying a bomb would be thrown from a roof overlooking the route of march. The roofs were lined with guards, and the papers proclaimed it a "wall of steel."

Edith Wilson was heavily veiled and her usual smiles were missing as they drove to the Capitol in a carriage drawn by four horses. The air of suspense was strong on this occasion and the crowd listened quietly to Woodrow Wilson's second inaugural address. He said that America wished nothing for itself that it was not ready to demand for all mankind—"fair dealing, justice, the freedom to live and be at ease against organized wrong."

With quiet emphasis that caught the attention of his listeners Wilson said, "We are provincials no longer. . . . There can be no turning back. Our own fortunes as a nation are involved, whether we would have it so or not. And yet we are not the less American on that account. We shall be the more American if we but remain true to the principles in which we have been bred . . . we have known and boasted all along that they were the principles of a liberated mankind."

The President said that the United States had been deeply wronged on the seas and that the injuries had become intolerable. He was still preoccupied with the filibuster raging in the Senate over the armed ship bill when he and Edith took their places on the reviewing stand.

Three days later the President was ordered to bed with a severe cold. He used this period to study the reports of the Attorney General, the Secretary of State, and the Secretary of the Navy on his right to arm merchant ships without the consent of Congress and, if so, how he should proceed. The measure had been defeated by the filibuster, but he was determined to carry it farther. While being sworn in to office in the President's room, the fight had been raging on the other side of a thin partition, with Senator La Follette in a passion of protest. Now Wilson was stubbornly pursuing the issue, convinced that if the Senate did not amend its rules "we are made helpless and contemptible without remedy."

Edith read him the reports as he rested in bed, and she protected him from all intrusion for more than a week, giving him a chance to study

90

this knotty problem and to recover. On March 11 he seemed to be feeling better, so she devoted an evening to one of their diversionary games, with her mother, Bertha, and Randolph, all of whom were depressed over Annie Lee's death. This time it was the Ouija board, a fad at the moment, and frequently brought into use when someone died. Colonel House, summoned from New York for consultation at this time, took note of the games now being played after dinner and made an entry in his diary: "This is an innovation the President has inaugurated since I was last here. He says he finds that it diverts him more than reading." Or after dinner they would go downstairs to the billiard room to pass an hour.

On this particular visit Colonel House told Edith that he thought the President should be more diplomatic and show the bipartisan spirit by consulting such outstanding Republicans as Hughes, Root, and Lodge, whom he thoroughly disliked. Edith agreed, but pointed out that she was even worse than her husband in this respect—neither of them could trust anyone they disliked.

The President continued to temporize in spite of public insistence for action. He still believed that the submarine threat could be met by armed neutrality unless some overt act were committed. This came soon enough when within a few days after inauguration eight American vessels were sunk by U-boats and seventy-two lives were lost.

Woodrow Wilson finally made up his mind and called a special session of Congress for April 2, 1917. At long last he would ask for a declaration of war. Lansing and House joined him in his study, waiting for a clear-cut decision. When it came, there was nothing more to be said. The subject was closed. Colonel House described him as restless and silent, walking up and down, picking up books and rearranging them on their shelves.

With his mind made up, the President shut himself in to write his war message. "We closed the door," Edith recalled, "and gave orders that no one was to disturb him." But she stayed within call and continued to decode fresh messages that came in. He followed his usual procedure of making a shorthand draft, then correcting it with a combination of shorthand and longhand before typing it on his Hammond.

After hours of work Wilson went to bed exhausted, but was restless and could not sleep. Edith heard him go downstairs to the South Portico and the typewriter tapping began. The Secret Service men mounted guard, knowing that the President was not to be disturbed for anything. When all sounds stopped except the faint hum of insects, Edith feared that Woodrow had fallen asleep. She went to the kitchen for a bowl of crackers and milk, which she left on a tray by his side without saying a word. The typing resumed and by morning he was studying what he had written. He started writing the historic message on March 30, and he finished it after attending church on Sunday, April 1.

Frank I. Cobb, of the New York *World,* a friend and counsellor on journalistic matters, was summoned to the White House to discuss the message and the way in which it should be expressed. After von Bernstorff was sent home Colonel House worked with *World* editors to play down the sensational angles and refrain from disagreeable references to German-Americans. Ralph Pulitzer, publisher of the New York *World,* favored this policy.

Cobb did not reach the White House until one A.M. but the President and Edith were waiting for him. Cobb was shocked by Wilson's appearance. He looked as if he had not slept for weeks. It was clear to this experienced editor that Wilson was still plagued by uncertainty, that he had no wish to head great military operations, and that he feared the Constitution might not survive such a war. Cobb reassured him that there was no alternative but the declaration of war.

Colonel House described Woodrow Wilson as "too refined, too civilized, too intellectual, too cultivated not to see the incongruity and absurdity of war." He said that it would take a man of "coarse fiber and one less a philosopher than the President to conduct a brutal, vigorous and successful war." Edith listened to House's argument that everything in this emergency had been coped with time and again in other countries, and that the President might find it less of an ordeal than he expected if he took experience as his guide.

In spite of their late night with Frank Cobb Edith had Woodrow out for golf at Kirkside early in the morning. It was a holy duty to see that he had his daily exercise, no matter what great events were pending. Congress did not meet until noon and the President delivered his message in the evening. A troop of cavalry accompanied the Wilsons through the misty night, and although the crowd was almost as large as it had been for inauguration, there was no disorder. It was a quiet crowd that had long been hungering for action and seemed conscious of the solemnity of the occasion. The torpedoed ships and loss of American lives had been the last straw.

The Capitol dome, illuminated for the first time that night with indirect lighting, seemed to shimmer through the lightly falling rain. When she parted from her husband with reassuring words, Edith and Margaret were escorted to front-row gallery seats. With both Houses called into session, every seat was taken and both floor and galleries were jammed with standees. The members of the Supreme Court, the Cabinet, the diplomatic corps in full array, all filed in, and the Senators, many of them carrying small American flags, took their places before the President walked in. Mrs. Wilson leaned forward expectantly and "my heart seemed to stop its beating," she recalled, as all rose in a body to applaud him. He smiled up at her before beginning to talk in quiet tones without a hint of rhetorical emphasis. In calling for a formal declaration of war he reviewed the offenses of the Central Powers, and calmly announced: "We will not choose the path of submission."

Chief Justice White, a Confederate survivor of the Civil War, jumped up with a boisterous yell and pandemonium followed. The President waited for the applause to subside and then resumed with a quiet call to arms—"to make the world safe for democracy . . . for the rights and liberties of small nations . . . for a concert of free peoples to bring peace and safety to all nations," and "to make the world itself at last free." Again he had coined a phrase that sank deep into the language of the period. World War I became the "War to Make the World Safe for Democracy."

The President asked for a stronger Navy, a new army of 500,000 men, and full cooperation with Germany's foes. "I may live to be a hundred, but it is not likely that I shall ever witness a more thrilling scene or be more stirred myself," said John W. Davis when it was over. "The President made it clear that "we fight for no selfish purpose, but only for our rights and the rights of all the world."

The President was pale and silent as he drove back to the White House. Both he and Edith were overwhelmed now that the ultimate step had been taken, after all the wavering, the sleepless nights, the endless consultations. The march of events had settled the issue, and Woodrow Wilson was an unhappy but a determined man. Tumulty pictured him drooping over his desk and weeping on his return to the White House. The applause had meant only one thing to him. "My message tonight was a message of death to our young men. How strange to applaud that!" he said with bitter realization of his role.

The debate on the declaration of war lasted for three days, but there was never any doubt of the outcome. The final vote came at three A.M. on April 6, with overwhelming majorities in both Houses. The day dawned cold and dismal. Colonel Starling kept a close watch on the President as he took a morning walk. As usual he would not wear his overcoat, and he stepped out briskly, swinging his walking stick. He and Edith went through Lafayette Park and saw a crowd waiting at St. John's for the Lenten service. They walked on, passing 1308 Twentieth Street, and Starling noticed that both hesitated and looked at the house that had romantic associations for them. Then they ran into Oliver Wendell Holmes, who was also out strolling, and they chatted with him. Mrs. Wilson paused to look at some dresses in a shop window before returning to the White House at twelve thirty P.M.

Everyone knew that the war was on, but the word was not yet official. The repressed excitement was evident among the churchgoers. Some peace groups had waited around the Capitol while the President was making his speech. It was a time to guard the proud person of Woodrow Wilson.

He and Edith were lunching with Helen Bones when word came from the Executive Office that Rudolph Forster, the President's executive secretary, had received from the Senate a printed copy of the War Resolution, signed by the Vice President and the Speaker of the House. Forster was told to bring it at once to the White House. The Wilsons hurriedly finished their meal and the President met Forster just as he was entering Ike Hoover's office with the declaration of war.

"Stand by me, Edith," he said as he sat down to sign, with Forster, Hoover, and Starling looking on. Hoover held the blotter and Starling noticed that as he read the document the President's jaw set and his "countenance was grim." Edith had asked him to use a gold pen that he had given her, and this was one of several she kept for life.

After signing with a "firm, unhesitating hand" he got up and escorted his wife and cousin to the elevator. At two o'clock he left for a Cabinet meeting and the wheels of war began to turn. That evening he and Edith spent alone, aware that the world had changed for both of them. All irresolution vanished. His dream of worldwide peace was shattered for the time being, but he was ready for full-scale action. The peacemaker became the Commander in chief.

# 9.   *An Expert on Ships*

WITH war declared Mrs. Wilson compared the comings and goings at the White House to the rise and fall of the tides. After the first week she took to her bed from exhaustion, strong though she was—a performance she never repeated except when seriously ill. She saw at once the toll it would take of her husband and announced, "I needed no one to tell me what my most important war work would be." Her constant care of the President was already an established habit—now more essential than ever.

Before the fighting ended she became a tireless war worker herself. Washingtonians accustomed themselves to the sight of Edith Wilson in a striped uniform with bib apron and Red Cross cap serving coffee and sandwiches to soldiers on their way to war; of Mrs. Wilson christening seized ships and naming new ones coming off the assembly lines; of Mrs. Wilson playing hostess to "Papa" Joffre, Lord Balfour, and other heads of foreign missions; of Mrs. Wilson running her sewing machine for Red Cross supplies; of Mrs. Wilson using buses to conserve gasoline and upholding all austerity measures at the White House. Aside from the reviews, parades, and Liberty Loan drives in which she figured as the President's wife, she did the same everyday things as other American women and she saw a good many relatives off to war. Women all over the land responded to the patriotic challenge, however they felt, as they watched their men go off to war. They practiced economy at home; they knitted and worked and prepared for death and destruction.

Washington was its loveliest, misted with blossoms, as the country mobilized. Universal conscription was quickly enacted and by the end of the summer millions of young recruits were in training camps. The brains and energies of the nation were commandeered, and Washington welcomed an influx of talented, dynamic men in every field. The President appointed the ablest men he could find to head the new agencies, regardless of party. He was under pressure night and day to reconcile the new elements and back up his Cabinet in the tussles that followed.

Edith Wilson saw it all through her husband's eyes. She was doing what she said she would do—devoting herself wholeheartedly to her husband's well-being, and in the midst of her own engagements she would rush at a moment's notice to be at his side. The hours spent with her remained Woodrow Wilson's essential source of relaxation.

From the day war was declared the public was barred from the White House grounds. The doors were triply guarded and there was further protection on the top floor. The traditional state dinners and receptions were dropped, except for visiting dignitaries on missions from foreign countries. Even before war was actually declared Mrs. Wilson had coped with separate diplomatic dinners and receptions for the representatives of the countries at war. There was constant wrangling by staff members of diverse political sympathies, too.

All were warned to be careful about what was said on the telephone, for there were known to be leaks from the White House, and Washington buzzed with gossip about the flow of life around the Wilsons. Early in 1917 Colonel House accused Tumulty of telling his friends that the State Department had tapped the wires of the German Embassy, both in New York and Washington. House insisted that he was opposed to the continuation of this practice.

But the old game of love and espionage worked its spell at home and abroad in Mata Hari tradition, while the Secret Service amassed information on the conversations of high officials with their "affinities." The mistresses of some ambassadors were involved in the wiretapping operations.

# An Expert on Ships

Immediately after the declaration of war, the Allied missions invaded Washington to discuss coordination of their military efforts and to appeal for more support. President Wilson, instinctively averse to joint command and determined to run things in his own way, was cool to this idea. But the commissioners were handsomely entertained at the White House, with Edith Wilson charming each in turn.

Lord Balfour won Mrs. Wilson at once with his easy grace and ranging interests. She liked a man who could listen as well as talk. "A cultured man of the world, easy to know," she commented, crediting him with the manners of a courtier and the scholarship of a don. But at the moment she thought that he looked "war worn and weary" when she took him to the South Portico to show him the gardens and he spoke of the gloom and shadows of wartime London. She noticed that Woodrow and Lord Balfour got on particularly well, discussing architectural design, the swing away from the classics (which both deplored), and the suffragists (on whom they were also in agreement). The President was in good form and told some of his Lincoln stories.

The French mission followed the British, and Marshal Joffre, who had saved Paris and checked the Germans at the Battle of the Marne, came on the scene. Edith warmed to the kindly warrior who was so anxious to have his wife share the Virginia ham served to him at the White House that she sent him another to take back to France. Although a hero to the American public, receiving every honor on his visit and a wealth of gifts, Edith knew that he had been eased into the background, except in the affections of his people. General Ferdinand Foch was now the military name that rang bells in France; he and General Henri Pétain, both younger men, had the top commands.

Edith had a preview at this time of the men with whom her husband would have to deal in Paris. She entertained Woodrow with her impressions of them. While he concentrated on the tough realities presented by each of the missions, she based her conclusions on the human side. The Italian, Belgian, Russian, and Japanese missions followed the British and French. Edith was struck by the public enthusiasm for the Belgians, who had done so much to stem the German tide, and for the representatives of the new Republic of Russia. She had a personal family interest in the Russians because Nona McAdoo had married a young attaché of the Russian Embassy.

97

The ultimate effect of the missions was to convince President Wilson of the desperate and immediate need for American help. He dispatched a squadron of destroyers to strengthen the antisubmarine operations of the British Fleet. Criticism exploded all around him over this move.

Since the President would not leave Washington during the first year of war, the two took drives when they could and escaped for quiet weekends on the *Mayflower* when possible, but the problems were endless. In spite of all the able people Wilson had brought to Washington the ultimate decisions were his. Night and day he was on call, and assailed for decisions made against his peace-loving nature.

It took eighteen months to get the country on a full fighting basis and 1917 was a year of confusion in every area. The massive organizational drive was slowed by lack of factories, ships, basic tools of war and, above all, by strikes. Production of artillery and airplanes posed serious problems. The President's Cabinet and advisers fought their own little wars as outsiders of proven skill and dominance walked into his office and commanded his attention.

The only hope of tranquillity lay in Edith's soothing presence, and on one of his weekends on the *Mayflower* Woodrow wrote to Jessie of his relief to be aboard the yacht where he could get away from the "madness"' and escape from "*people* and their intolerable excitements and demands." This was the inner man, well known to Edith and his daughters, but to the public he seemed a potent and triumphant figure, directing vast operations and conducting his "crusade for democracy."

Edith saw it all through her husband's eyes as she sought to fit the startling headlines in the press to the reality of their daily lives. The steady ritual on which Wilson thrived was broken up. In Dr. Grayson's words, "He was a creature of custom, and he always liked to repeat a pattern, to take the same drive, to do the same things. It was his escape, his form of rest, a return to some measure of tranquillity instead of battling with problems."

Although Edith knew that the hours he spent with her and the members of his own family remained his essential source of relaxation, she was aware of the criticism for the time he spent on golf, the theater, and on the *Mayflower.* She was in league with Dr. Grayson to see that he had enough sleep and exercise to keep fit. Colonel House did not always agree with them about the protective wall raised to guard his health, but he conceded that Woodrow Wilson could do more in eight hours than any man he had ever known, since he never wasted time or energy on talk or useless argument. When an issue was closed he shifted from the official to the personal side of what he called his one-track mind. In Edith's words, "When he left his desk or office he closed that door in his mind; then he would play with the abandon of a boy."

But play became increasingly difficult as the war pressures mounted, and Edith asked Colonel House if he thought her husband's golf might have an adverse effect on public opinion. He told her frankly that many would consider it frivolous in a time of crisis. The criticism of Theodore Roosevelt's "sissy" tennis, and of William Howard Taft's predilection for the golf course when he was swamped with political trouble was still fresh in the public mind.

Actually, the White House day often began at five or six in the morning and extended far into the night. But when prebreakfast golf became impossible because of the pressure of appointments Dr. Grayson proposed horseback riding in the late afternoon as an alternative more compatible with the President's official duties. He enlisted Edith's aid, since they all knew that he would not take outings without her. She had not ridden in years but she was perfectly willing to try, hoping to do better than she had with her bicycle.

Dr. Grayson, as much at home in the saddle as in the sickroom, approved two mounts for the President and Edith. Starling rounded up more for the Secret Service detail, and the First Lady got a hurried summons to be on hand for a five o'clock ride. She had no riding habit, but Altrude, an accomplished equestrienne, produced her best pair of boots, Jessie supplied breeches, and Nell McAdoo, the most fashionable member of the family, came up with a perfectly tailored coat, a little tight for her more generously proportioned stepmother.

The President, casually dressed, mounted Arizona, the light bay with white hooves that had been chosen for him, and off they went, with the Secret Service detail chagrined to have to chase him on horseback. It soon turned into a merry cavalcade with Dr. Grayson, the perfectly accoutered aide, egging them on. Woodrow surprised them all by riding with the "vigor of a cowboy breaking a broncho, but with none of the skill," since he had a "poor seat" on a horse, Starling noticed.

But he enjoyed himself and liked the exercise, so for a time his expeditions were a daily rite.

Edith joined him when she could, "looking beautiful in her smart black tailored riding habit," Starling observed. She rode sidesaddle, and usually they went along the bridle paths of the Ellipse, just south of the White House. Sometimes she cantered nine miles around the Potomac Drive, but riding an unfamiliar horse one day she took a bad spill when her mount stepped into a hole on a shortcut home.

The President and Starling reached her at the same time. She lay stretched on the ground, her face deathly white and her eyes closed. Woodrow bent over her and said in a strained voice, "Edith, my darling, are you hurt?"

Her eyes opened slowly and she smiled with recognition. "No, Woodrow, I think I'm all right. Just shaken up."

They put her carefully back on her horse and rode to the stables, but the President was "anxious and fretful," as he always was when anything happened to her. She rested that night, felt better in the morning, and the rides continued. They still played golf occasionally when the President had the opportunity, but now that the country was at war Starling posted men at a discreet distance and usually hidden in the bushes. To save time Edith got into the habit of bringing a bundle of mail, the morning papers, and her knitting with her and often sat in the car working while Woodrow and Dr. Grayson played a few holes of golf.

"I think about the only piece of wearing apparel I bought that summer [1917] was a riding habit," she said. She and the Cabinet wives had taken a pledge to reduce expenses to the simplest level, to buy few clothes, and not to demand the out-of-season delicacies so popular in official circles. They gave up their regular social meetings, initiated by Edith in the previous year, to have more time for wartime work and relief. Mrs. Daniels surprised them by driving up in a limousine for their last regular meeting. They had all been using carriages, but the group was rounded up to admire the new treasure and Edith pronounced it "stunning." Although she still preferred the horse-driven carriage she enjoyed her own electric brougham.

The United States was not a war-minded nation, but the appointment of the Committee on Public Information, headed by George Creel, was an effective tool in preparing people for action. Propaganda flooded the country. Posters of historic interest abounded. "Work or fight" was the message. All the newest means of communication were used, with radio broadcasts supplementing the flow of copy for the papers and magazines. "Four-minute speakers" appeared in clubs and theaters to project the Wilsonian slogan that this was a "crusade for democracy."

The President and Mrs. Wilson were star performers in the Liberty Loan drives, along with bankers, professors, actors, and men and women of all persuasions, including suffragists. The Wall Street area was jammed when the President stood before the statue of George Washington and made a personal pitch for bonds. There were many occasions in 1917 and 1918 when Edith knew that she was being roped into the propaganda machine, and she was always a little skeptical of George Creel's stunts, but they worked with the public and the pattern was repeated all over the country.

There were times however when the President insisted on dead silence as he moved about. His visit to Yorktown early in August, 1917, went unheralded and unrecorded. The Wilsons slipped quietly out of Washington on the *Mayflower,* as if for their usual weekend trip. By morning they were in the York River, where the ships destined for action were secretly at anchor.

It was not an impressive showing for a country so deeply involved, but Josephus Daniels, full of good cheer and enthusiasm, sailed up in the *Sylph* and the two yachts moved together past thirty-five ships, grimly camouflaged but brightly decked with signal flags. The President had asked that the traditional gun salute be omitted, but the bands played the National Anthem lustily as ensigns were dipped in salute. Sunburned sailors, young, eager, and immaculately turned out in their white uniforms, lined the decks, aware that the President and Mrs. Wilson were with them.

After the review the Wilsons joined the Secretary and Mrs. Daniels on the flagship *Pennsylvania* and Edith found herself the toast of a score of admirals. The President was eager to talk to the sailors and after lunch the decks were cleared and officers and men assembled to hear him. Edith was touched by the youth of the sailors and the eagerness with which they listened to what she considered one of Woodrow's most inspired talks. He appealed directly to the noble and heroic in their natures, emphasizing the role of the lowly as well as the top brass. "It came from the heart and I think it went to theirs," she commented.

Wilson asked the men to use their brains in ferreting out the hornet's nest in submarine warfare, instead of chasing the hornets all over the farm as the British did. He had lost patience with the "prudence" demanded by the English naval experts when American proposals came up for consideration. He told them to drop the word "prudence" from their vocabulary and to practice "audacity to the utmost point of risk and daring." He would depend on them for brains as well as training, courage, and discipline.

This was not what the admirals and senior officers expected from Woodrow Wilson and it startled the sailors with its novelty and drive. The ship rang with their shouts and cheers as the President stood bareheaded, in his white flannels and blue jacket. The man who had been so slow to get them into war now urged them to go at it "with a whoop."

The American troops were supposed to arrive in Europe in contingents of 30,000 men, but because of the shortage of ships and the submarine activities they crossed the Atlantic in trickles. Forty divisions were in France when the Armistice was signed, but because of the prodigious preparations and attendant confusion, it was not until June, 1917, that the first American troops became visible in Europe and it was late in October before they went into action, in a quiet section of Lorraine.

"You have come, thank God," said Papa Joffre when General John J. Pershing reached Paris with the first contingent. The city went wild when they marched through the streets on July 4 and the general laid a wreath of roses at Lafayette's tomb. But with this much achieved, Edith quickly grew aware of the new problems the President faced, with Pershing demanding more men, and his headquarters at Chaumont becoming a battleground of its own, as he held out for independent action and set up a network of technical arrangements for the movement of troops.

Ships soon became a preoccupation of Edith's and took much of her time after Edward N. Hurley, chairman of the Shipping Board, asked her to rename the German ships that had been taken over by the government and to christen all the new ones coming off the runways to get men, munitions, and food across the Atlantic. Steel, wood, and reinforced concrete were used to hasten the flow, but the fabricated steel ships, assembled at wartime shipyards from separate parts supplied by the steel plants were the most trustworthy. Soon fifty of the hastily built yards adjoined one another in a single row at Hog Island in the Delaware River, close to Philadelphia.

Mrs. Wilson found it a simple matter to reshuffle the names of the eighty-eight German ships. Often it meant no more than making the *Amerika* the *America*. Those named after Presidents, such as the *George Washington,* remained untouched. Her work on the ships interested and sometimes amused her husband. He was apt to surprise her with comments and suggestions as they sat together in his study. When she was slow in deciding what to do about the *Vaterland* he laid down his papers and told her matter-of-factly, "Well, that one is easy, for it would *have* to be the *Leviathan.*" They laughed together over the tiniest of the ships and he found the answer quickly. It became the *Minnow.*

Josephus Daniels, Secretary of the Navy, complimented her on the work she had done on the ships and wrote, "When women decide to become cabinet officers the Secretary of the Navy's portfolio should be assigned to you. Indeed, there seems to be fitness in this for in the Navy we always call a ship 'she.'" He told her that she had shown the "fine Virginia touch" in her way of handling things.

As the new ships came from the yards she worked with zeal and efficiency, but she had to show ingenuity to avoid duplication in finding suitable names for so many. Study of several issues of *Lloyd's Register* persuaded Edith that the more obvious names had all been used, so she proposed a sequence of Indian names. This idea was rejected at first on the ground that they would be unfamiliar and difficult to spell. She then considered the names of American rivers, cities, mountains, and lakes, but again ran into duplication. Finally she reverted to the Indian idea— not, she explained, because she was of Indian descent, but to avoid repetition, and early in August 1917, she christened the first ship to leave the newly finished Hog Island shipyard. It was named *Quistconck,* Indian for Hog Island.

The next appointment on Edith's social calendar was the marriage of the President's niece, Alice Wilson. Her home was a modest one in Baltimore but he wanted to give the daughter of his brother Joe a White House wedding. Mrs Wilson made it a happy occasion for everyone, in spite of a thunderstorm that whipped the bride's veil around a tree as she was being photographed on the South Portico.

Early in September, 1917, the President saw a chance to take a few days off for a leisurely cruise. He had noticed that Edith, always so strong and vivacious, seemed to be showing signs of strain. They left the capital quietly by train at midnight and were picked up by Captain Berry off the Twenty-third Street wharf in New York. Both were so exhausted that they rested in their cabins and slept as they cruised up Long Island Sound to New London, where Margaret, Jessie, and Jessie's aunt, Madge Elliott (Mrs. Edward Elliott) joined them for a leisurely dinner. They watched a sunset from the fantail deck and engaged in light family talk.

They sailed through the Cape Cod Canal to Gloucester, where the Houses took them driving along the shore. They visited Mrs. T. Jefferson Coolidge's house to look at the prints and china she had inherited from Thomas Jefferson. The President on this occasion described himself as a "Democrat like Jefferson, with aristocratic tastes." Intellectually he was entirely democratic, he said, which was unfortunate because his mind led him where his taste rebelled. Lunching later at Magnolia, he and House discussed Lincoln while their wives listened, and agreed that Washington would continue to be considered the greater man.

Wilson then surprised them all by telling how nervous he was when he had to make a speech. He thought he had mastered this, but when he had to walk to the speakers' stand he felt that he would drop before reaching it, but immediately afterward he refused to show alarm when they ran into a submarine scare at the south end of the canal.

Captain Berry announced that they would have an escort of three destroyers, because of a German submarine sighted off Nantucket. Berry was obeying Navy orders, but the President told him to make a dash for New London. The convoy accompanied them as Edith watched the *Mayflower* being transformed into a battleproof vessel, with a gun crew to man its antisubmarine guns.

Both she and the President refused to take the submarine threat seriously, and after Margaret had joined them at New London they went up the Connecticut River by motorboat to Lyme and studied Sir Christopher Wren's church there. They visited old Princeton friends along the way, and by the time they boarded the *Mayflower* again all talk of the threatening submarine had subsided.

They refused an escort when they took off for Nantucket to visit Jessie, who summered at Siasconset, driving eight miles in carriages across the heather-scented moors from the port of Nantucket to the picturesque little village. Poised by the Atlantic Ocean, it now was filled with menace for the traveler. The President played with his grandchildren on the beach in front of the Sayre house and built a sand fort to amuse them, but when a heavy fog rolled in they left for Nantucket in two surreys and retraced their way across the moors with the help of the extrasensory perception of the driver, who took soundings from the earth.

They sailed from Nantucket into sunshine and blue waters, with the President sitting on the top deck reading to Edith while she went on with her knitting. But their spontaneous journey had given the State and Navy Departments some anxious moments. Presidents had been known to escape to the wilds before, but a great war was raging and the submarine menace was no empty threat. There would be no more cruises on the *Mayflower* with Captain Berry, who had been their friend as well as a naval aide. He had been trying desperately to get into active service and he was now assigned to command the *Manley*, a destroyer doing hazardous work in the North Sea. There would be other yachts in Mrs. Wilson's life but this was the one she loved.

Within two weeks after their return to Washington she was stricken with a severe case of influenza—the virulent kind that raged in 1917. She was in bed for more than two weeks, and although the President wanted to read to her they all conspired to keep him at a distance, lest he too become a flu victim.

On October 15, her forty-fifth birthday, Edith still felt weak, but her day was brightened when the President gave her a ring with a black opal. In the afternoon she received diplomats and their wives. Among them were Viscount Reading, Lord Chief Justice of England serving as special envoy to deal with financial affairs, and Sir Cecil Spring-Rice, the British ambassador, whose wife was one of her favorites. The new Greek Minister, E. Venizelos, told her that President Wilson had "sanctified" the war. Boris A. Bakhmeteff was a new face on the scene, and Edith was interested in the fact that his talented wife had learned English in three months.

Edith approached the diplomatic set cautiously, scrupulously observing the ground rules laid down by the State Department. Most of the diplomats had been closer to the Republican leaders than to her husband, and she had suffered personally from their slights and gossip. But a new group was emerging in wartime, and her own instinctive gift for entertaining enabled her to maintain the strongly democratic attitude insisted on by Woodrow Wilson where rank and pomp were concerned, but to keep the duchesses happy, too.

All shared a common interest in Red Cross work and other relief activities for the soldiers. Edith worked enthusiastically long before the United States entered the war, and early in 1917 established her own small Red Cross unit at the White House. The sewing machine she had used on Twentieth Street was moved into a small room adjoining Helen Bones' quarters, and here the President, impatient always to have Edith with him, would wander in looking for her. Miss Benham, Helen Bones, Mrs. Bolling, and Bertha took turns, busying themselves with fabrics and patterns, cutting out pajamas for the wounded. Edith joined them when she could spare the time. None was speedier or more expert than she. Her knitting needles clicked endlessly as she sat in the President's study, watching him work. Shortly before Christmas, 1917, she gave her first knitted trench helmet to Woodrow's cousin, Captain Woodrow Woodbridge, when he came to say good-bye on his way to France.

The First Lady did not always look her most fashionable while doing canteen work for the Red Cross, but she impressed the men on their way to war. She laughed a little at herself as she donned the blue and white striped wash uniform with an enveloping bib apron, and the dark blue cap with Red Cross insignia that wilted in the heat. She chose the afternoon shift and left her evenings free for the President.

When troop trains steamed into a quiet siding behind Union Station and khaki-clad youths jumped out for a brief respite, Edith and other Washington matrons worked with youthful beauties passing trays of

An Expert on Ships

sandwiches and buckets of coffee. As they hurried into the canteen for tobacco, candy, and postcards, an occasional youth from the South would recognize her. The President sometimes stopped at the canteen to drive her home and his appearance was the signal for cheers and handshaking. He knew better than they what lay ahead for these young soldiers, and he listened gravely to Edith after a canteen session as she spoke of their spirit and patriotic fervor.

Many farewells were said at this time and her own family circle was involved. Repeatedly the President had to turn down requests of all kinds, but his most embarrassing decision, politically speaking, was to deny Theodore Roosevelt's offer to command a brigade. The warrior of the past had been circulating in Washington commenting on the conduct of the war and vowing that he would find some way to serve. The President received him in the Red Room, and Tumulty reported that "nothing could have been pleasanter or more agreeable than the meeting."

The President talked of the attitude of the General Staff toward volunteer service. There were no exceptions, and he conveyed the idea that he would favor the plan were it within his power. When Roosevelt left, the President said to Tumulty, "There is a sweetness about him that is very compelling. You can't resist the man. I can easily understand why his followers are so fond of him."

Roosevelt's age was cited too, and Edith blandly wrote that the decision to deny his request had been made "after much thought and consultation in which politics had no part." Wilson was also criticized for refusing to send General Leonard Wood to France. He had asked General Pershing for suggestions, and Wood was not on Pershing's list. Wood blamed the general and not the Commander in chief, but Roosevelt's many friends thought otherwise of the former President's rejection.

Late in October, 1917, Colonel House was again sent abroad by President Wilson, to attend interallied councils on the progress and strategy of the war. General Tasker H. Bliss represented the Army, Admiral W. S. Benson the Navy, and Gordon Auchincloss was secretary. Various representatives of the civilian war boards were in the party, such as Bainbridge Colby, Vance C. McCormick, Oscar T. Crosby, and Bernard Baruch.

The President wrote affectionately to House as he left, saying it was an "immense comfort to me to have you at hand here for counsel and for friendship. But it is right that you should go. God bless and keep you both! . . . Mrs. Wilson joins in all affectionate messages."

The mission sailed secretly on armored cruisers, convoyed by a destroyer. They were only halfway across when they learned that the Austrians and Germans had descended on the Italians at Caporetto, undoing the progress of two years and crippling the Allied front. This was followed almost immediately by the overthrow of the Kerensky government by the Bolsheviks and their demand for an armistice. Everything had crumbled at once and the shadow lay heavily on the White House.

The war effort was in total confusion as the French and British governments watched their two leading allies, Italy and Russia, failing them in a time of desperate need. The conferences that had been planned were abandoned. The situation seemed worse than at any time since the war's outbreak in 1914.

Vital though American aid had become, Colonel House cabled President Wilson of the mission's futility. The messages Edith Wilson coded and decoded between her husband and House contained only bad news. Although the code room of the State Department ordinarily handled the President's foreign communications, he and Colonel House had a supercode in matters of top secrecy, known only to the two principals and to Mrs. Wilson, who spent hours over them and became expert at this work.

A particularly disheartening message arrived just as the Wilsons were about to leave for Buffalo where Woodrow would address the American Federation of Labor convention in Broadway Auditorium on November 11. He delivered the prepared speech, an optimistic message proclaiming the certainty of victory, and added, "While we are fighting for freedom we must see, among other things, that labor is free."

It was an arduous experience for Edith. The crowds, the applause, and the underlying anxiety cut through her consciousness. They had done it all in a day, returning to the White House at eleven o'clock at night. Within a matter of hours she was busy decoding further messages from the Colonel, including one that told the President his Buffalo speech had brought some encouragement into the picture.

# An Expert on Ships

Mrs. Wilson worked far into the night with her husband as he prepared his annual message to Congress and she heard him deliver it on December 4. She had insisted that he golf that morning, the first exercise he had had in days. His brother Joe came from Baltimore and they had the usual family gathering to hear Woodrow make one of his major addresses. Speaking quietly, he proposed a declaration of war against Austria-Hungary as well as Germany; he promised that nothing would turn them aside from the immediate task of winning the war, and added, "With victory an accomplished fact peace will be evolved, based upon mercy and justice—to friend and foe."

Colonel House returned before Christmas and Mrs. Wilson heard him give her husband his first report on the situation, with Russia out of the running, Rumania crushed, Italy in a state of chaos, and America seeming to be the last remaining hope. Next day she sat in the study and heard Colonel House, General Bliss, and Newton D. Baker, the Secretary of War, appraise the military situation. Baker later commented on the keenness of her questions and comments and the understanding she had of the foreign situation. Altogether it was a busy day for her, playing a variety of roles. Since it was also her second wedding anniversary in the midst of all his concerns Woodrow paused to give her a bracelet. Jewels, orchids or books—he never forgot birthdays or anniversaries.

Although the mission had failed in its immediate objective, Colonel House had made headway on the social front and told of having been entertained at an intimate luncheon by King George V and Queen Mary, and of finding Margot Asquith "the most irritating personality in all the world" when she and her husband entertained him. At Edith Wharton's he had met Joseph Reinach, the political journalist then campaigning against the spirit of defeatism in France as the war raged.

Colonel House continued to lose standing with Mrs. Wilson on his return from this mission. She felt further doubt about his sincerity after an interview in which she was involved. The President suddenly decided to put the railroads under government control. He consulted Justice Brandeis before he took this drastic step but it came as a shock to the country. Strikes were seriously hampering the war effort and the movement of troops, munitions, and supplies. He drew up a special message for Congress, asking for legislation to cover the compensation to be paid the companies involved, and he appointed McAdoo, his

Secretary of the Treasury, to serve as director-general in charge of railroads.

This message gave him considerable trouble and he asked Colonel House to look over the rough draft and comment on it. The colonel arrived from New York in the late afternoon, found the President busy with the War Cabinet, and paused to chat with Edith over tea. He drew out the draft of her husband's message and went over it, disagreeing point by point. He asked Mrs. Wilson if she would mention the points he questioned and give the President time to think it over.

After dinner all three settled in the study. The President said that Edith had conveyed the message, and he was sorry, because he had weighed every word and worked hard on it. She was taken by surprise when the colonel said that although he had indeed voiced his objections Mrs. Wilson fought so well for her husband's point of view that he reread the paper and now agreed with every word of it. Edith was outraged. "I do not like people to change their minds so quickly," she said.

November and December were anxious months for Edith Wilson as she coped with personal and official problems. She felt that another chapter in her life had been closed when she signed the papers relinquishing her one-fourth interest in the house on Twentieth Street. Her brother Wilmer brought her the papers to sign and she went out at once into a heavy snowstorm to do some Christmas shopping.

On the afternoon before Christmas Dr. Grayson accompanied Edith to distribute gifts to the children who always greeted the President on his way to the golf course. Woodrow was too busy to go with her for this annual rite, but after dinner he joined the family in the Oval Room to trim the tree. The Sayres and Madge Elliott were White House guests and in the morning they all breakfasted in the small dining room before lighting the tree and opening gifts.

In the afternoon Edith, Mrs. Bolling, Margaret, and Frank Sayre accompanied the President to a special matinee for soldiers given at Keith's Theater. As always, this meant crowds and cheers. That night twenty members of both families dined at the White House and two days later Matthew Maury arrived from Roanoke with his daughters. Edith lavished orchids and love on her sister's girls. It was less than a year since the death of Annie Lee, an enduring loss to Edith. The year

110

1917 ended for the Wilsons on a somber note. They knew that desperate issues were at stake, that big decisions had to be made, but both seemed to find warmth and security in the presence of their families.

# *10.* *The Fourteen Points*

ON January 8, 1918, Edith Wilson heard the President present his historic Fourteen Points to Congress in a calm summation of principles that would affect the future course of history. Some had been incorporated in his "Peace Without Victory" speech delivered nine months earlier, but months of warfare had changed the mood of the country. Now even his foes took heed of the detailed demands.

It all sounded familiar to Edith. She had followed it stage by stage: "Open covenants of peace, openly arrived at," and an end to secret diplomacy, freedom of the seas, the reduction of armaments, the evacuation of occupied territory, the impartial adjustment of colonial claims, the independence of Poland, and the formation of an association of nations to guarantee political independence and territorial integrity to great and small nations alike.

Edith Wilson believed that her husband had never received such universal acclaim for a public utterance. The Republican as well as the Democratic papers viewed it as the hope of the future, and Theodore Roosevelt was enthusiastic. But while lofty idealism raised men's hopes for the future, things went badly on the domestic front.

Storms raged. The capital was wrapped in snow, and glazed with ice. The public coped with unfamiliar food and fuel and transportation restrictions. Two prominent Republicans, Herbert Hoover and Harry A. Garfield, son of the assassinated President, had dictatorial power over food and fuel, and McAdoo ruled the railroads.

Congress was sharply critical of the management of the war, and the Cabinet members, with their divergent views, bickered and added to

Wilson's troubles. Between January, 1917, and December, 1918, he and Edith showed outward calm while living through one crisis after another. They were often seen walking in the streets, or in church singing hymns, or at wartime benefits and official events, but in the Executive Office and in the quiet of the White House study the issues to be faced were overwhelming. Edith knew of every step being taken, and sensed the public reaction.

While her husband backed drastic measures and coped warily with the web of political intrigue spun by some of his advisers, Edith was conscious of the massive efforts being made by the public to meet the government demands and hasten the end of the war. The capital assumed a cosmopolitan air as the hotels were overrun with strangers from different parts of the country and visitors from abroad, all committed to some phase of the war effort. New buildings, some as frail as cardboard, went up everywhere. There was exhilaration and patriotic fervor in the air, as well as anxiety.

But the gasless days, the fuelless days, the icy days, and the food restrictions brought misery to the poor and discomfort to the affluent. As attacks in Congress against the President's management of the war grew in ferocity, Edith Wilson invited Colonel House to dinner. Although he had a severe cold, when the Colonel called, Wilson was able to get up and dine in the breakfast room. House asked if the attacks did not worry him, and he answered, "You would think they would know me well enough by now to see that they cannot force me to do what I consider unwise."

Lindley M. Garrison, Secretary of War from 1913 to 1916, had thought Woodrow Wilson too laggardly in preparing for war, and Bryan, who was all for peace, had already gone. The President had a fresh crop of advisers, notably Bernard Baruch, who appeared at the White House with increasing frequency, and usually paused for a chat with Mrs. Wilson. Theodore Roosevelt, staying with the Longworths, was urging universal training and a Munitions Cabinet. As he conferred with experts he spread the impression that he was in Washington to help speed up the war.

"Work or fight," was the message of the most encompassing propaganda campaign in America up to that time. While Creel smothered the nation in wartime propaganda, the Hoover Food Administration pounded home its message of ruin and starvation in Europe.

# The Fourteen Points

The President was more amused than concerned when in the midst of major storms a breeze stirred over sheep let loose on the White House lawn to eat the grass and thus save manpower. The trouble began when the original eight sheep multiplied so fast that the grounds seemed to be filled with frolicking lambs. Children gathered to watch them, just as their great-grandparents had enjoyed Tad Lincoln's leaping goats, and their parents had become attached to Pauline, President Taft's famous cow.

Wilson was accused of allowing the White House grounds to be defiled by the sheep, but Edith would not yield. She defended their presence and confounded her critics when ninety-eight pounds of their wool were sent to the Red Cross and distributed among forty-eight states and the Philippines. The "White House Wool," as it was called, was sold at auction for $100,000.

Wheatless, meatless, and coalless days were scrupulously observed at the Executive Mansion, and when gasless Sundays were proposed by the Fuel Administration, there was always a horse conveyance of some kind. The President was a persistent walker, and during the war years the man supposedly shut up in his ivory tower could be seen striding rapidly from point to point. He seemed to Starling to be particularly reckless on a May day in New York, in 1918, when he announced that he wanted to slip out without a guard. He and Edith were staying at the Waldorf-Astoria, and Starling went along with him as he walked, talked, laughed, and acted "like a kid," dashing out into Madison Avenue without heeding the traffic. After his solo sprint that day they went to Colonel House's for dinner, then to the Globe Theater to see Fred Stone in *Jack O'Lantern*.

On the following day the President led the Red Cross parade on Fifth Avenue to the reviewing stand at Twenty-sixth Street where he was joined by Edith, who received special applause for her Red Cross work. Henry P. Davison, chairman of the American Red Cross Council, joined them both for the parade and the demonstration that night at the Metropolitan Opera House. War-weary though people were, they could still muster spirit for these occasions.

Like Starling, Colonel House always had special fears for the President when he was in New York, and it was a relief when he was safe on the train to Washington after two days of functions and risky forays in the streets. But he and Edith were again in the public eye the next day in Washington when they attended a musical benefit for Italian soldiers at Poli's Theater. Caruso and Madame Alda were the stars of the evening and the great Caruso, sweating profusely as he always did, struck Edith as being nervous when he was brought to their box. She stood quietly in the background, studying him as she heard Woodrow say, "You are a great artist. I have been thrilled."

Edith was thrilled, too. She always was when she entered an opera house. Margaret was still determined to be a professional singer. She worked hard at it, took lessons regularly, and practiced morning, noon and night, flooding the White House with sound. Her father was sympathetic and Edith backed her loyally. Margaret's philanthropic impulses brought an assortment of gifted and bohemian friends into the White House circle.

From the time war was declared Margaret had been groping around, determined to get into action one way or another. In the idiom of the day she called herself a slacker, but Edith pointed proudly to the contributions Margaret made to the Red Cross. She donated substantial earnings from two concert tours she had made. But her goal for some time had been to go to Europe to entertain the soldiers, as she had done in the camps at home. The President told her that hers would be just one more mouth to feed. In the end he let her go, so she was in France when he and Edith arrived for the Peace Conference. But war tension was shattering to Margaret and she headed into nervous collapse.

On May 15, 1918, the President and Edith attended the inauguration of the first airmail route between Washington and New York. The ceremony was held in Potomac Park and the First Lady sent a gold thimble weighing an ounce to an aviation enthusiast in New York. The departing pilot circled the White House and dropped a sheaf of roses for Edith.

On July 4 she shared in a ceremony at Mount Vernon, attended by diplomats from the Allied nations and various notables of foreign birth. The President took as many of the guests on the *Mayflower* as could be packed aboard. His trips to Mount Vernon always had special meaning for him, and with the representatives of so many nations as his guests he spoke about his ideals and the principles for which America stood.

Everything went off with military precision until the moment came for John McCormack, the Irish tenor, to sing the National Anthem. He had been complaining about his piano and there was a long interval before his voice soared majestically over Mount Vernon. At the last minute he said he could not sing without musical accompaniment, and then he asked to have a grand piano placed in front of Washington's tomb. This offended the committee in charge, but the impasse was finally broken by hiding it discreetly in some nearby bushes, near enough to be heard clearly. Much less disconcerted than his hosts, he wound up with a triumphant flourish, and it was not until afterward that Edith learned what caused the long delay. By this time she was a practiced hand at smiling her way through public mishaps.

The Liberty Loan drives were always launched with fanfare, and Woodrow Wilson chose to make one of his most important speeches at the opening of the fourth drive in the Metropolitan Opera House in New York on September 27, 1918. The emphasis now was swinging from war to peace terms and settlement. It was a thrilling night for Mrs. Wilson, even though she was accustomed to the ovations accorded her husband. It was also a night of great anxiety. All the news from Europe was black and before leaving the capital she had decoded cables that were ominous, but the President and she sailed through the ceremonies with smiling composure.

As they entered the opera house, soldiers and marines stood at attention on the platform, the band played, and the audience rose spontaneously to welcome them. The President's speech was described as a "marvelous intellectual performance" although it left bitter echoes in some quarters. Without going to the core of the League of Nations he outlined the kind of organization it should be:

"We must now serve notice on everyone that our aims and purposes are not selfish  . . we must be brutally frank with friends and foes alike," he said, challenging the Central Powers to come out in the open and avow their purposes. He called it a "people's war" with national interests sinking into the background and the common purpose of enlightened mankind taking their place.

He was flushed with excitement and elation when it was over. It was a recapitulation of the Fourteen Points. Back in Washington congratulations poured in. Lansing called it the greatest speech Wilson had ever made. "It gives the country—the world—a very definite goal to attain," he commented. Lord Robert Cecil called it the "finest description of our war aims yet uttered, and will give us all renewed courage to face the horrors of war.''

All through October furies raged at home and abroad. Spanish influenza was sweeping the country. The shipyards were heavily affected and war work was hampered. Abroad, British troops led by General Allenby entered Damascus, and a week later Beirut fell. September and October proved to be the most hectic months of the war for Mrs. Wilson, with the President on call night and day as crucial negotiations went on behind the scenes. But she was faced suddenly with a domestic move of major significance.

Mrs. Wilson did what she could to prevent the President from making one of the most disastrous mistakes of his administration when late in October, 1918, he addressed an appeal to the American people to elect a Democratic Congress in November. He submitted the letter to her for an opinion after he had composed it on his typewriter, not with his usual air of certainty but slowly and hesitantly.

She read it thoughtfully but with growing concern. Her own political prescience was keen and she knew it to be foreign to his thinking; she also foresaw how harmful it might be when his enemies bore down on him. It suggested plainly that he wanted undisputed mastery in the postwar negotiations and it stated bluntly that a "Republican Congress would divide the leadership.'' He added that he had no thought that any political party was paramount in patriotism. All had suffered and sacrificed irrespective of party affiliation, but the leaders of the minority had been "pro-war but anti-Administration'' and unity of command was as necessary "now in civil action as it is upon the field of battle. . . . In ordinary times divided counsels can be endured without permanent hurt to the country. But these are not ordinary times. . . . I submit my difficulties and my hopes to you.''

Edith challenged him at once and told him that this did not sound like Woodrow Wilson. Strong though he was, she feared that he had been pushed into taking this step. He conceded that the letter did not represent his own views, but he had promised to write it and he would keep his promise. "I would not send it,'' she told him. "It's not a dignified thing to do.''

She took a diplomatic approach and pointed out the danger of antagonizing the powerful Republicans who had worked wholeheartedly for his wartime administration, but when his eyes looked foggy and he locked his jaw, she knew that she could not sway him. In his own words he "bent to the storm that followed" but he had no foreboding of its far-reaching effect. All through the war he had risen above partisan issues, and distinguished Republicans had worked for him without thought of party. They were now the most aggrieved, and through a storm of public criticism the powerful voices of Theodore Roosevelt and Henry Cabot Lodge were clearly heard telling the world that Woodrow Wilson had suggested that Republicans were less patriotic than Democrats.

George Creel tried to placate the outraged by quoting Abraham Lincoln on the folly of "swapping horses in midstream" and citing George Washington's plea for "united leadership" after the Revolution. He pointed out that President Wilson knew that Republicans organized in party opposition in Congress would obstruct rather than assist the processes of peacemaking under his leadership.

"That message was one of the greatest mistakes Woodrow ever made," said Edith, and she was less surprised than he when the Democrats were roundly beaten in November, a few days before the armistice was signed. They lost control of the House by a large majority and the Senate by a single seat. At this point Woodrow Wilson was stripped of the mastery that had sustained him through the crushing difficulties of the war years, and which he would need for the peace negotiations. But he showed less dismay than Edith because of his intense preoccupation with the approaching armistice.

When the Democratic candidates were repudiated in various parts of the country, the feeling prevailed that the voters had been heavily influenced by Wilson's role as international peacemaker. His allusions to the "people's war" had offended many of the conservative-minded. One faction feared that he might be too lenient with Germany. Opponents of his economic policies united with the radical groups that had protested going to war in the first place. To many he remained a cold and austere autocrat—a conception that baffled Edith.

As the electoral battle went on at home, the final struggle was under way in Europe, on the Meuse and in the Argonne Forest, part of the general engagement that was squeezing the German line from Verdun to the English Channel. With 2,000,000 American soldiers in France,

1,200,000 in combat, casualties mounted fast and public anxiety grew intense.

Cantigny, the second battle of the Marne, Château-Thierry, Belleau Wood, and Saint-Mihiel all had taken their toll of American lives when the Central Powers collapsed with astonishing speed. When Metz, their strongest position, came within range of siege guns and a second army prepared for a final assault, the end had come. Bulgaria surrendered later in September and Turkish resistance collapsed. Austria, after a long, hard fight, bowed to Italy. With the American and British forces pushing hard in the West, the German realm began to disintegrate, and on October 3 word came through that they were ready to negotiate for peace.

The President and Edith were in New York for an Italian *fête* at the Metropolitan Opera House when Tumulty hurried to their quarters at the Waldorf with the intelligence report he had just received. Colonel House, reading it to the President, said, "This means the end of the war."

Woodrow Wilson accepted the news with complete composure, whatever fires burned inside. As they went in to dinner he handed the colonel a scribbled note saying "Tell Mrs. W.," and signed it W.W. The colonel had anticipated this and Edith gave nothing away but was her usual vivacious self at the dinner party that included the Houses, the Sayres, Miss Bones, Tumulty, and Dr. Grayson.

As they got into their car to go to the Metropolitan the President asked Tumulty if there was anything to add to the intelligence report he had been given. Then he leaned over to Edith and told her quietly that the German note had arrived. They returned to the Waldorf at 12:30 and the President discussed the German offer with House and Tumulty deep into the night. He had gone through the evening with seeming calm, applauding the speeches and the music, whereas Colonel House was so stirred that he was conscious of little that went on.

The capital buzzed with excitement on their return as one development followed another. On October 7 the Swiss minister made the overtures official by delivering a note from the German government proposing an immediate armistice and asking the President to initiate peace proposals based on the Fourteen Points that he had introduced the previous January. Colonel House was summoned to Washington to give advice on the President's reply, and there were conferences with Lansing, Daniels, and Newton Baker.

"Yesterday was one of the stirring days of my life," the colonel noted in his diary regarding a talk he had had with the President after breakfast at the White House. "I never saw him more disturbed. He said he did not know where to make the entrance in order to reach the heart of the thing. He wanted to make his reply final so there would be no exchange of notes."

Edith was busy that day with a luncheon for the British ambassador. She was well aware of the intense pressure on her husband. It was decided that the colonel should leave at once for Paris to represent him at the scene of action.

This meant a fresh shower of messages requiring Mrs. Wilson's attention. Night and morning for months past, she and the President had kept an eye on the central drawer of the great flat-topped desk he used—a gift from Queen Victoria to the United States government. The most urgent material went into this particular drawer—in large linen envelopes clipped with red squares, the warning signal for "immediate and important."

Sometimes a half hour's delay made a difference, and they had often canceled their evening's plans so that Edith might decode messages. She was vigilant and would not go to sleep, however late the hour, until her task was finished. Now the messages were coming faster than ever and everyone was on guard, but she knew that this was the finale as the cave-in of the enemy forces proceeded.

On November 7 the false armistice set the country wild with rejoicing. Everywhere bells rang, whistles screeched, bands played, and people took to the streets. They danced, they sang, they shouted, they hugged and kissed strangers. Many paused to pray, to weep for their dead. The tumult could not be stilled, even after it was announced that the UPI report of the armistice was premature. The President learned the truth almost at once. The Germans had crossed under a flag of truce, on their way to meet Marshal Foch in his saloon car on a railroad siding near Compiègne, but American soldiers were still dying in the Argonne region and all was not yet over.

Wilson, white and tense, stayed calm. He was waiting for further word, and Tumulty was on the alert. But Edith found the excitement irresistible, and when a band played outside the White House and a crowd gathered in the street she urged Woodrow to appear on the portico and give one of his spontaneous talks. He told her that this would be giving credence to a false report.

Nell McAdoo brought fresh excitement into the Executive Mansion when she came for lunch, looking as bedraggled as if she had been adrift at sea. Edith remarked that she "looked like a chip on the waves" as she told of her adventures in getting from the Treasury Department to the White House. She had been jostled, pushed, lifted off her feet, hugged, and even kissed on the way. The bandbox look, so characteristic of Mrs. McAdoo, was gone, but her blue eyes glowed with excitement. At last the end of the war—they had thought the time would never come.

No one could settle down at the White House except the President, who was quiet and thoughtful. Edith could only guess at what he might be thinking, since he was in one of his silent moods. Her own spirits soared and she decided after lunch to take her mother and Bertha for a drive to see the celebrating crowds. She knew that there was no danger now of things going astray, and that the false peace being celebrated in every city, village, and crossroads in the country would soon become fact. She was stirred by what she saw, but she was quickly recognized and they had to turn back when their car was mobbed and cheers went up for her. She was used to applause as she sat by the President's side, but this was a tribute to a First Lady who had played an active role of her own.

On November 9 the Kaiser abdicated and fled to Holland, repudiated by the German people, who had revolted and formed a republic. This cleared the last hurdle in the negotiations, and next day the President and Mrs. Wilson waited for the confirmation they knew must soon arrive. It was a Sunday and since the flu epidemic had finally subsided people were out, many to thank God that the slaughter had come to an end.

The Wilsons went to church in an old victoria that had been taken from the White House stables and refurbished for gasless Sundays. People paused in the quiet streets to watch the War President and his wife. Inside the church they were closely studied but neither face gave anything away. Woodrow looked grave and attentive, as he always did in church, and he sang the psalms in full voice. Edith was her usual composed and noncommittal self, although she smiled warmly at some of her church friends.

Back at the White House they lunched alone. The false armistice had prepared the staff for what was coming, and they could not conceal their excitement. Mrs. Bolling, Bertha, and Randolph joined them for dinner, but the President looked so exhausted that they left early— except for Randolph, who offered to stay and help Edith with a fresh batch of messages that had arrived. The last was handed to the President at one A.M. No one felt like going to bed and at three A.M. the news was in. The armistice had been signed. It was Sunday, November 11, 1918, and within six hours all guns had been stilled.

The President and Mrs. Wilson gazed at each other in silence. They were drained of emotion and wholly immobilized. In later years, when Edith was asked what Woodrow Wilson and she had done in that historic moment she always gave the same answer: "We stood mute— unable to grasp the full significance of the words."

But action was called for at once, as extra editions reached the streets and the country awoke to the fact that this was the true armistice and the war was over. The celebration began again and swept a large part of the world, with Woodrow Wilson as one of the major figures.

Before leaving for the Capitol with Mrs. Wilson he wrote a brief message for the American people: "Everything for which America has fought has been accomplished. It will now be our fortunate duty to assist by example, by sober, friendly counsel, and by material aid in the establishment of just democracy throughout the world."

At twelve forty-five they left for the Capitol, where the President made a formal announcement of the armistice. He gave a brief analysis of the problems that had to be dealt with to a Congress where the Democrats were still in the majority. The election count was in and this would change the balance almost immediately. He received an ovation from the men with whom he had worked and tangled. He told them bluntly that the victors, in their own interest, would do well to lift the vanquished to their feet. He spoke of the spread of Bolshevism from

Russia and the rioting and devastation in Germany. Armed imperialism such as had been practiced by the masters of Germany was at an end, he said, and would never be revived.

The President's voice was low and husky as he finished, "Thus the war comes to an end."

The crowd tore loose as he and Mrs. Wilson drove back to the White House, and when they emerged again in the afternoon to review the United War Workers parade, the celebrants had increased in number and the streets were packed with a shouting, cheering mob. The President at last was showing excitement, and Tumulty had never seen him look so happy as when he walked out to the White House gates to see the celebrants on Pennsylvania Avenue. His expression was not so much one of triumph as of vindication.

After dinner they drove out again, to see the bonfires, the brightly illuminated buildings, the surging crowds, and happy faces, but the pressure grew dangerous as the revelers surrounded them, climbed on the mudguards to touch them, and resisted the efforts of the Secret Service men to hold them back. Finally a group of soldiers in the crowd locked arms to form a ring around the car, and they moved slowly back to the White House.

The President was elated. He was all smiles and greetings and he did not wish the night to end. Edith, carried away herself, felt that it was a moment for gaiety. November 11 happened to be the birthday of the King of Italy, and they knew that a party was in progress at the Italian Embassy. Although it was not customary for the President to visit embassies, he decided on impulse to look in on this party.

In white tie and tails Woodrow Wilson looked his most impressive self that night, and Mrs. Wilson was stately in a new gown, her first extravagance in many months. They were warmly greeted by Ambassador Cellere, his wife, and their guests, who stood at attention while the President toasted the King of Italy. The ball was in full swing, with an abundance of dazzling uniforms and lovely women. The Wilsons stayed for an hour, then drove back to the White House. The revelry was now indoors rather than in the streets, for the night was chilly. Edith felt that many were exhausted from the frenzy of the earlier celebration, but she was still too excited herself to sleep. With a fire crackling in her room, she and Woodrow talked far into the night. He had been feeling on top of the world all evening, but the night's elation was fading. Already he was looking to the future. The war was won; now he had to battle for world peace. He knew from his emissaries that the settlement of terms would not be easy. Before going off to bed he picked up his worn khaki Bible and read his nightly chapter.

Edith could not sleep. Her thoughts kept revolving. She realized life might never be the same for her, but her only concern was for Woodrow. Her love for him had deepened in their three years of married life; her admiration for him knew no bounds. Now his responsibilities would be heavier than ever, and she hoped that she could help him. Edith fully believed that he needed her, and those who knew them best agreed. The war had closed one chapter in their lives; she was ready for what would come next.

# *11.*   *Close to the Seat of Power*

ONE of the few people in official circles who wanted President Wilson to go to Europe for the Peace Conference was Mrs. Wilson, and there was never any doubt that she would go with him. They talked it over and she knew that nothing would make him change his mind once he had made his decision. But Congress was against it. His advisers were against it, and he would be breaking precedent in leaving American shores.

On the day after the armistice was signed Secretary of State Lansing called at the White House to tell the President that in his judgment it would be a serious mistake for him to share personally in the peace negotiations. Wilson thought things over for a week and then said he had decided to go and would make a public announcement to that effect. Neither Lansing nor Colonel House could dissuade him. He was convinced that no other man could back his Fourteen Points. A deciding factor was the news that Clemenceau and Lloyd George would not welcome his personal participation.

Wilson's advisers argued that a Head of State would be at a disadvantage dealing with tough-minded statesmen functioning on the political level. Although Congress reacted coolly to his announcement, many across the country believed that his personal appearance would be a master stroke; they pinned their faith on Woodrow Wilson. He was on the crest of the wave in the moment of victory, and he firmly believed that the American people as a whole would back him in whatever course he chose to follow.

George Creel, always the ardent propagandist, said that on the day of the armistice Woodrow Wilson was the most loved and admired man in the world. "Almost overnight they burned candles before his picture in foreign lands, hailed him as an apostle of light and the invincible champion of human rights. In the United States the sweep of victory cleansed the popular mind of prejudice and irritations, leaving only an intense appreciation of the man's true greatness."

Edith Wilson shared in the discussion between her husband and Colonel House about the men who would go to Paris as commissioners. The President suggested five appointees but the Colonel held out for seven—four Democrats and three Republicans. Edith, surprised that anyone but the President and House would be going, suggested Elihu Root and William Howard Taft, but her advice fell on deaf ears. The colonel favored Taft because he was "good-natured and easily led" and he came from Ohio, whereas Root came from New York which, with Lansing, would mean two delegates from one state, a political blunder. In the end the list also included General Tasker H. Bliss and Henry White, a Republican who had served as ambassador to Italy and France and had been a loyal friend to Woodrow Wilson during the war years.

John W. Davis, the silver-haired judge and lawyer who had been President Wilson's Solicitor-General, and was an old-time friend from West Virginia, brought another impressive-looking commissioner into the fold. He had just been appointed ambassador to the Court of St. James's, to the surprise of many who had envisioned Theodore Roosevelt, Elihu Root, or William Howard Taft in this role. Although brilliant at the bar Davis was not a well-known figure, and when he was asked by Lansing to follow Walter Hines Page in London, he was unsure of himself until his sophisticated and ambitious wife played a hand in his acceptance.

Mrs. Wilson was glad to know that White and Davis would be on the Wilson team. Neither the Senate nor the House was represented officially, and this caused public criticism. The men chosen by the President had been his close associates all along. He made it clear that he did not want any wives or families accompanying the scores of assistants and experts assembled for the Peace Conference. Mrs. Wilson, Mrs. House, and Mrs. Davis with their intelligence and worldly understanding were considered assets, and Edith was immediately a focus of interest.

In the short time at her disposal Edith rapidly assembled the clothes she would need for a variety of occasions. Her sense of style had often been noted and commented on during her years in the White House, and she was intent on making the best impression possible in the capitals of Europe, where she would be exposed to the chic as well as the dowdy. It was characteristic of her that she always knew exactly what she wanted and insisted on getting it. She dealt with Charles Kurzman, who handled Worth gowns in America. He sent dressmakers traveling back and forth between New York and Washington for fittings and consultations with her.

He was still in favor after an earlier fuss about her $1,300 wedding gown. At that time he was on the verge of being blacklisted for Germanic sympathies by the dressmakers' syndicate in France, headed by Paul Poiret, the fashion czar of the moment, who changed the contour and attire of women around the world. America was not yet at war, but anti-German feeling was running high. In the end Kurzman was exonerated, and Edith continued to give him her custom.

She was so well organized that everything was in perfect order when the day of departure arrived. As she moved about she was keenly aware of the exhaustion of the public as they waited for the soldiers to come home. The armistice had left a wake of trauma and bereavement, and the final score was formidable, with 53,390 men killed in battle or dead from wounds. The wounded numbered 234,000, and 4,500 men were missing. The war was won but there were many who felt that America should revert to its well-established policy of isolationism

—all of which ran counter to Woodrow Wilson's expansive vision of a united world. By this time the cost of war was all too apparent. The Fifth Liberty Loan would soon be initiated to help meet the enormous debt, and in the end more than twenty-one billion dollars would be raised through these loans and war stamps, with a third of the total coming from the new income tax and other Wilson measures.

Edith was facing a test of her mettle as the *George Washington* headed out to sea on December 4, 1918. She was conscious of her unique situation, bound for Europe with a President who was breaking all precedent, and whose cherished dreams of world harmony were at stake. Her role, she knew, was to give him the utmost support on the personal level, and this began with a quiet regime at sea before facing the tumult that she knew awaited them in Europe.

They had left Washington secretly in their private railroad car, the *Mayflower*, and embarked at Hoboken. As they slipped their moorings the racket began. Bands played and hastily assembled crowds cheered. The news could now be told. All New York knew what was going on as the foghorns blasted, gun salutes came from the forts, and the screech of whistles ripped the air.

They retired to their quarters amazed at the assortment of aides, commissioners, and experts who would be their traveling companions. William Allen White viewed them as a "desperate crew of college professors in horn rimmed glasses, carrying text books, encyclopedias, maps, charts, graphs, statistics, and all sorts of literary crowbars with which to pry up the boundaries of Europe and move them about in the interests of justice . . . and the Fourteen Points."

The French government paid for its own representatives but the American mission proved to be much larger than the President had anticipated. He had asked for simplicity, economy, and an absence of wives and relatives. His son-in-law, Francis Sayre, had been refused permission to sail with him to France. The President's personal staff was small—Dr. Grayson and Miss Benham, both of whom were close to Edith; two secretaries, Charles Swem and Gilbert Close; and Ike Hoover, who functioned with less success as majordomo abroad than he did at the White House. Susan and Brooks, as personal maid and valet, attended on the Wilsons, and the Secret Service detail, familiar to the American public for their proximity to President and Mrs. Wilson on all great occasions, included Colonel Starling, John G. Sly, and Joseph J. Murphy.

The press coverage was formidable and inescapable. This was a pilgrimage of historic interest and correspondents already famous, or on their way to the top echelons of journalism, such as Walter Lippmann, Arthur Krock, David Lawrence, and William Allen White were on board. Every move the Wilsons made was officially recorded and photographers caught them whenever they were allowed within range. Edward Jackson, a small, dauntless photographer also on his way to fame with his pictures of two world wars, became Edith's particular sleuth. She would not let him photograph her, but they had a good understanding and she helped him catch the President to the best advantage. The flicker of an eyelid and Eddie would spring to attention.

One or two guests lunched or dined with the Wilsons in their quarters nearly every day, and they gave one official dinner before disembarking. But the President made a point of spending time with the crew. It was a daily rite to attend a film but instead of going to the theater used by the members of the Peace Commission they went to the "Old Salt," which belonged to the crew, and the President sang lustily at one of their concerts. He was no stranger to the hymns that streamed into the night as the liner moved slowly through waters still strewn with mines.

John Wanamaker had done his decorating best for this historic trip, a labor of love with him. The President had a large sitting room, dining room, double and single bedrooms, and luxurious bathrooms. He used the same Empire desk on his four voyages, and he had a businesslike office. Mrs. Wilson liked her pink and ivory bedroom, and her sitting room gay with chintz. She had all the feminine trappings that became her.

Many of the passengers grew seasick and Miss Benham was one of the first casualties. Mrs. Wilson was not surprised. She had been through it before many times with Edith Benham, with her sister Bertha, and with Altrude Grayson, but Woodrow was in excellent form, inhaling the salt air deeply, doing his daily exercises, playing a little shuffleboard, and tramping the deck with his wife, who also taught him to play Canfield on this trip. There was no talk of war or world affairs in his hours of relaxation, and no irritations at mealtime.

127

The Hotel Belmont had sent its master chef, a favorite of New York's gourmets, to supervise the Presidential fare, but this seemed pretentious and unnecessary to Woodrow Wilson and the chef did not accompany them on their second trip. Because of his delicate digestion, and also his inherited taste for plain food, served without sauces, his own meals were Spartan and unchanging. Mrs. Wilson was more appreciative of the French cuisine, the varied sauces, the desserts, and the lamb chops "done up in pajamas," as her husband put it.

The "Yankee Knight Errant," in White's words, stood aloof, unbending to outside pressures and deaf to scientific theories as he pursued his own dreams of peace and world cooperation. In retrospect William Bullitt described him as the "Christian Statesman" sent to bring light to the capitalist world by paraphrases of the Sermon on the Mount.

But Wilson listened attentively to fellow commissioners and picked experts who came to his study in the morning for consultation and briefings. Edith attended all the briefings involving the official party. Both were more rested and relaxed as they approached the shores of France.

They stood on the bridge of the *George Washington* and watched nine American battleships sail into view to escort them in double formation into the harbor at Brest. Salutes roared through the clear, cold air and destroyers and French cruisers followed them to their anchorage. With the ship finally at rest General Pershing, General Bliss, Admiral Benson, and French officers representing every branch of service crowded into their quarters. Edith accepted the hand-kissing, the clicking of heels, the bouquets of flowers, with smiling warmth. Going ashore on their tender, *The Gun*, she admired the picturesque terraced city of Brest, and its residents parading in native costume.

As they stepped onto French soil they were greeted by city officials, and they drove to the station under triumphal arches. Margaret, who had been ill in France from her war work and privation, joined them at this point and they all boarded the blue train that the President of France had assigned for their use. The Wilsons had their own car and they waved to the American soldiers, black and white, who had gathered to see them off. All the way to Paris spectators crowded the sta-

Edith Bolling, who all through life disliked having her picture taken, showed sulky resistance at the age of two and had to be tempted with an orange before she would pose in the center chair with her brothers and sisters. *United Press International Photo.*

At eighteen Edith Bolling, after a term at Powell's fashionable boarding school for girls in Richmond, paid her first visit to Washington as the guest of her eldest sister, Mrs. Alexander H. Galt. In 1890 she had her first taste of the social and cultural life of the capital, but had no interest in politics. *United Press International Photo.*

Bertha Bolling in 1915, at the time of the marriage of her younger sister Edith (then the widow of Norman Galt) to President Wilson. *United Press International Photo.*

Mrs. William Holcombe Bolling (1843–1925) in 1915 when her daughter Edith became the wife of President Wilson. *United Press International Photo.*

In the foreground, Edith Bolling (later Mrs. Woodrow Wilson) with her favorite sister, Annie Lee Bolling (later Mrs. Matthew H. Maury). When Annie Lee died suddenly Mrs. Wilson named her eight-year-old niece Lucy her "Adopted" and treated her always as her own daughter. *Courtesy Mrs. John E. Moeling (Lucy Maury).*

This study of Mrs. Woodrow Wilson, done by Arnold Genthe when she was the widowed Mrs. Norman Galt, was the official portrait used with the announcement of her engagement to President Wilson in 1915. It became well known around the world and always remained her own favorite portrait. *Library of Congress Collection.*

President Wilson introduces
fiancée, Mrs. Norman Galt,
the public at a World Ser
game between the Phillies a
the Red Sox in Philadelphia i
mediately after the announ
ment of their engagement. M
William Holcombe Bolling, M
Galt's mother, is at the Pr
dent's right. *Library of Congr
Collection.*

President Wilson had aro
the enthusiasm of the DAR
a speech he made at their
vention in April, 1916, an
and Mrs. Wilson are leaving
hall with smiling faces all are
them. *Library of Congress
lection.*

TO THE FOOD ADMINISTRATOR,
    WASHINGTON, D. C.
    I AM GLAD TO JOIN YOU IN THE SERVICE OF FOOD CONSERVATION FOR OUR
NATION AND I HEREBY ACCEPT MEMBERSHIP IN THE UNITED STATES FOOD AD-
MINISTRATION, PLEDGING MYSELF TO CARRY OUT THE DIRECTIONS AND ADVICE
OF THE FOOD ADMINISTRATOR IN THE CONDUCT OF MY HOUSEHOLD, INSOFAR AS
MY CIRCUMSTANCES PERMIT.
                Name. *Edith Bolling Wilson*
                Address. *The White House.*

Number in Household................    Do you employ a cook?...............

Occupation of Breadwinner...........................

Will you take part in authorized neighborhood movements

for food conservation?.. *Yes* ......................
    There are no fees or dues to be paid.   The Food Administration wishes to have
as members all of those actually handling food in the home.

                            DIRECTIONS
    Mail your pledge card to the Food Administrator, Washington, D. C., and you will receive FREE
your first instructions and a household tag to be hung in your window.
    Upon receipt of ten cents with your pledge card and a return addressed envelope, the official but-
ton of the Administration, and if desired, the shield insignia of the Food Administration will also
be sent you.

Mrs. Wilson responded at
to Herbert Hoover's appe
food conservation as V
War I raged in Europe
signed pledge was promi
displayed at the White
and was meticulously ob:
by the President and Mrs
son. *United Press Interna
Photo.*

King George V, President Wilson, Queen Mary, and Mrs. Wilson at Charing Cross Station on December 26, 1918. The Wilsons were paying a state visit to England before the opening of the Peace Conference. From the station they drove to Buckingham Palace in the royal coaches. *United Press International Photo.*

Queen Elizabeth of Belgium, President Wilson, Mrs. Wilson, and King Albert of Belgium in the palace gardens, Brussels, June, 1919. *Library of Congress Collection.*

The Woodrow Wilson House at 2340 S Street, Washington, a landmark owned by the National Trust for Historic Preservation and visited by thousands each year. This is how it looked when Woodrow Wilson left the White House and became a private citizen. It was Mrs. Wilson's home for forty years and both she and Woodrow Wilson died in it. The exterior is now changed but inside everything is arranged as it was in the days of Woodrow Wilson. *United Press International Photo.*

Rear Admiral Cary Travers Grayson leaving the White House grounds after the President collapsed with a crippling stroke. *United Press International Photo.*

*[Handwritten letter from Mrs. Wilson to Senator Lodge]*

*[Handwritten reply from Senator Lodge]*

Mrs. Wilson's last-minute letter to Senator Henry Cabot Lodge on February 4, 1924, telling him bluntly that she did not wish him to attend her husband's funeral, and a fast reply on the same day from the Senator. *Library of Congress Collection.*

...rs. Wilson and her niece, Mrs. John ...oeling, on the SS *Leviathan,* on their ...y to Poland to attend the dedication of ... Gutzon Borglum statue of Woodrow ...ilson at Poznan in July, 1931. *United ...ess International Photo.*

Mrs. Wilson and Mrs. Cary T. Grayson, both of whom had campaigned enthusiastically for Franklin D. Roosevelt, attend the inaugural reception in 1933 for the incoming President. *United Press International Photo.*

Mrs. Wilson at Princeton University for the June commencement of 1947. She is being specially honored, and her companions are (left to right): Mrs. Truman; Mrs. Thomas J. Preston, Jr., widow of Grover Cleveland; President Harry Truman, and Herbert Hoover. *United Press International Photo.*

Mrs. Harry Truman, Mrs. Franklin D. Roosevelt, and Mrs. Woodrow Wilson join hands at a press party given in 1954 in Washington for Mrs. James M. Helm when her memoirs, *The Captains and the Kings,* was published. *United Press International Photo.*

The public's last view of Mrs. Woodrow Wilson. Frail but spirited, she watched President Kennedy at the White House sign a Congressional order for plans for a memorial to Woodrow Wilson. Two months later she died at the age of eighty-nine, her work finished. *United Press International Photo.*

tions, huddled in the fields, and cried "*Vive l'Amérique. Vive Wilson!*" as the train passed by. It was Friday, December 13, 1918, a day Mrs. Wilson would long remember.

The people of France were exhausted, hungry, war-weary, but Paris went wild as Wilson drove through the streets with President Poincaré after an official welcome at the station. Erect and smiling, holding his hat high in the air, Woodrow Wilson appeared the opposite of the small, rotund figure at his side. Things were different in the second carriage where Madame Poincaré rode with Mrs. Wilson, Madame Jusserand, wife of the French ambassador, and Margaret. Madame Poincaré was stiff and formal; Edith was relaxed, smiling, and radiating warmth.

She was quite familiar with Paris. She had seen it as a carefree traveler with Norman Galt, with Altrude, and with her sister Bertha. She knew the shops, the tea rooms, the galleries, the great vista of the city itself. But now through the familiar lavender mist that tinted its buildings she saw things in a dazzling way while roars of welcome greeted them and flowers rained down on her from the sky. The mounted *Garde Républicaine* took formation with drawn swords before cantering into place to head the cavalcade, the horsehair tails on their Roman helmets flipping down their backs. Their uniforms made a bright splash of color as they swept through cleared streets toward the Arc de Triomphe, where the chains barring the entry were withdrawn for the first time in forty-seven years to let President Wilson drive through.

Mrs. Wilson, already accustomed to the applause of crowds in America, was scarcely prepared for their welcome in Paris. Twisting and turning to catch the scene, she noticed that the rooftops were alive with moving figures, windows overflowed, men and boys perched like sparrows in the horse chestnut trees, and "every inch was covered with cheering, shouting humanity." The most seasoned correspondents decided that they had never known Paris to give anyone so great an ovation and Lansing coolly observed when it was all over, "It was a reception which might have turned the head of a man far less responsive than the President was to public applause, and have given him an exalted opinion of his own power of accomplishment and of his individual responsibility to mankind. It is fair, I think, to assume that this was the effect on the President. It was the natural one."

Hector Bolitho called him the "immovably shining, smiling man" in

129

recalling the Paris welcome, in his profile of Woodrow Wilson in *Twelve Against the Gods*. He had listened to Clemenceau, Lloyd George, generals, returning troops, and battle banners being cheered, but he caught a strange note in Woodrow Wilson's welcome: "something different, inhuman—or superhuman."

The American propaganda preceding his arrival had been widespread and formidable and had contributed to some of the ecstatic comments, but the tired population knew that the war issues had to be settled before life could go on, and that the presence of Woodrow Wilson might make considerable difference.

The Murat Palace on the Rue de Monceau, which was to be their residence, looked like a fortress outside but was a place of enchantment for Edith. A massive wall cut it off from the street. It was heavily guarded, and its two gatehouses were flanked by blue and red sentry boxes. When the outer doors were thrown open for the Wilsons their carriage swept up a semicircular drive to the palace steps. Edith caught only a fleeting glimpse of the grandeur that was to be her lot before she was whisked off to the Elysée for a luncheon given by the Poincarés.

Escorted by a guard of honor and saluted by a ruffle of drums, they were led up a few steps by Henri Martin, chief of protocol, to be welcomed by their hosts on the portico, before proceeding to the grand salon where the cream of French officialdom and society awaited them. Although medals and decorations abounded and uniforms were spectacular, Edith noticed that the Cabinet members wore tightly buttoned frock coats. Her husband had been warned in advance that cutaways, or morning coats, were not worn in Paris and that frock coats were essential for formal wear. Brooks had been well briefed in these matters, so that the President was prepared for all variations.

Edith soon found herself being rushed around at high speed by President Poincaré. She likened herself to a "big liner with a tiny tug pushing her out from her moorings." Woodrow seemed to be doing better with Madame Poincaré when they all settled at a long table decorated with Sèvres figurines, and flowers of every color grouped in arrangements of ships, mounted guns, and the flags of the Allied countries. An airplane made of violets with wings spreading two feet was in front of Edith but through it she could see General Pershing, Joffre, Foch and other heroes of the hour.

After lunch formal calls were exchanged, each move being made with a touch of pageantry and the steady drumbeat of war. In the evening Edith had a chance to study the great ballroom and formal drawing rooms of the Murat Palace, with tall mirrors between long windows hung with flame-colored brocade curtains. The dining room and sweeping stairway were of the same majestic order, and when King Victor Emmanuel of Italy visited them he told Mrs. Wilson he could not live in such a place. It was all too overwhelming.

But the Wilsons spent most of their time on the second floor, with suites of rooms on either side of a broad central hall and a library that became a haven in their more troubled hours as discord developed at the Peace Conference. The President's suite was hung with crimson damask and his Napoleonic writing table was fitted in tooled leather. His bedroom was austere, with Napoleonic bees and gilt eagles for decoration.

Mrs. Wilson had what she called the "bed regal" in her ivory-tinted bedroom. It was huge, with a delicate blue canopy covered with lace. The gold and crystal decanters on her bed table were filled with orange-flower water, and the cabinets in her sitting room held rare objects of art. Everything bore the Murat crest, even the gold toilet seat. But she had little time to loll in all this luxury. She had to change so often and so fast for a succession of functions that she particularly enjoyed her dressing room, fitted with the most commodious wardrobes she would see on her travels.

Miss Benham was the invaluable member of the party from the start. She alone coped familiarly with French and she took charge of the switchboard the first day. She unsnarled various fumbles over protocol and took control until more help arrived and things again ran smoothly. Dr. Grayson stayed close to Wilson at all times and knew what was needed for his and Edith's comfort. But protocol made separate demands on him, too, and he became the most popular and sought after member of the entourage.

On the morning after their arrival they went to the Presbyterian Church in the Rue de Berri in the morning and then drove to the tomb of Lafayette in the old part of Paris. Once again the President broke precedent by sending Dr. Grayson to the florist's to select a suitable wreath and by taking it personally to the cemetery. On the accompany-

131

ing card Woodrow Wilson had written: "In memory of the great La-fayette from a fellow servant of liberty," a message later copied in bronze.

They later received both President Poincaré and Premier Clemen-ceau, and Herbert Hoover called to discuss food needs with the Presi-dent. Callers continued to arrive the following morning, and Ambassa-dor and Mrs. Page lunched with the Wilsons before they all went to the Hôtel de Ville, where the "freedom of Paris" was bestowed on Presi-dent Wilson.

After a few words of thanks from Woodrow, Edith was embarrassed to have the limelight turn in her direction. She was presented with a Lalique box holding a pin made up of six doves of peace in rose quartz. The doves rested between slender fronds outlined with diamond chips. This was the city's gift to the wife of the man who had come to talk peace. At the same time they gave him a gold pen with which "to sign the peace, just, humane and lasting."

Edith's days quickly became a blur of noted faces and famous names as rulers, statesmen, diplomats, and military men called at the Murat Palace to see the President. She and Miss Benham followed every move, but she did not join in their meetings, as she might have done in the White House. She watched General Foch from a distance, but she received Clemenceau personally, finding him refreshingly frank and not at all intimidating in spite of his "fierce old face and long white mustachios." It interested her to see her tall, distinguished-looking husband matching words with Clemenceau, stockily resistant to blan-dishments as the Frenchman prepared to fight the "dreamer" and pro-ject his own belief in military sovereignty. Clemenceau gave Edith some scraps of the truce flag brought by the Germans when they signed the armistice terms. As always, he wore his gray cotton gloves and his skullcap, and his English was impeccable. The language barrier was in-hibiting. She would have enjoyed freer conversation, but interpreters were always at hand. This was never a problem with Clemenceau. "I liked the old man. You could count on his word," the President said. And he found Marshal Foch "simple, direct, and fine."

Edith was touched by the sight of the aging warrior, "Papa" Joffre, loaded with medals and walking heavily, being honored by the French Academy. On the following day she went to the Sorbonne to see Woodrow receive an honorary degree. Always at home in the company of scholars, he was a figure of great interest to the academicians. But a disagreement with Madame Poincaré that afternoon was Edith's first unpleasant experience. She had been invited at the last moment to join Madame Poincaré in her box, but there was confusion in the arrangements. When Edith arrived she found Madame Poincaré already seated and in a towering rage because M. Martin, the chief of protocol, had been with Edith instead of escorting Madame Poincaré to her place. Madame Poincaré turned on her embarrassed guest and "almost forgot to be polite," said Mrs. Wilson, who ignored her and settled down to enjoy herself. "This I did thoroughly," she commented, "for it was a very interesting occasion."

After four days of functions and official welcoming, Woodrow was anxious to get down to work, but a meeting he called at the Crillon, where the commissioners were quartered, convinced him that there would be further delay. The British were marking time with an election close at hand and Lloyd George's political future at stake, so it was agreed that official visits to England and Italy would be timely before the Peace Conference got under way. The visiting groups urged it, and the mood of the American people favored the maximum amount of drive behind their wartime President now that he was in Europe. The welcome in Paris made an impression at home.

Before crossing the Channel they planned to spend Christmas with the troops at General Pershing's Chaumont headquarters. On Christmas Eve they went shopping in Paris. The hurrying crowds recognized them and gave them friendly greetings. They drove to the Rue de la Paix and from there walked to Brentano's and to Perrine's, a couturier on the Avenue de l'Opéra. They stopped at a flower market close to the Madeleine and saw mistletoe being gilded. By midnight they were on the President's train while Jusserand kept them laughing and talking to forget the cold. But they were fully aware of the deprivations that had affected every public service in war-ravaged France.

At seven in the morning they were met by General Pershing and driven in his Cadillac to visit the troops. They stopped at farms along the way to talk with American soldiers in their billets. Edith insisted on climbing a precarious ladder to visit some in a loft. Her smiling face and her quick recognition of the regions from which they came pleased

133

the soldiers, who now had thoughts of getting home. Some huddled in the cellars of fine old farmhouses; others slept on army cots by cattle stalls. The men seemed cheerful wherever she and the President went, and there were cheers for the bundled-up party as the snow came gently down and hid the war-torn landscape.

They had to wade through mud to get to the open field where the President and General Pershing were to review the troops. Mrs. Wilson walked carefully over a plank walk that covered a muddy stretch of ground in order to reach the grandstand. She had seen many military reviews but this was the real thing—the last of the fighting men, marching and countermarching to band music. The cavalry, artillery, infantry, and camouflaged tanks streamed and clattered past with all their battle equipment. When New York's famous 77th Division swung into view, with young men whom the Wilsons knew in its ranks, the commander announced that they were making Mrs. Wilson an honorary member. He gave her the blue and gold insignia—the Goddess of Liberty on a blue field. Although shivering from the cold and damp, Edith was a great success with the troops and they cheered her as she stepped daintily through the mud.

The official party shared in the Christmas dinner provided for the troops—an American feast of turkey, cranberry sauce, and pumpkin pie cut in huge army slices. Their day ended at the château where General Pershing and his staff were quartered. Huddled around a blazing fire, they drank hot tea to thaw out. Edith and the President traveled back to Paris by train that night and were on their way to England and Buckingham Palace on the day after Christmas.

# 12. *Mrs. Wilson Meets Queen Mary*

THE state visit of President and Mrs. Wilson to England at the end of 1918 was heralded as an impressive prelude to the opening of

## Mrs. Wilson Meets Queen Mary

the Peace Conference in Paris. The man who had brought the war to an end and had now come to Europe for the peace settlement was received with full honors in spite of England's ravaged condition

Edith learned what it was like to be a guest at Buckingham Palace. She had been well briefed on the role she should play, but aside from the surrounding magnificence of court life, she was surprised to find that King George V and Queen Mary attended to their comfort personally as if the Wilsons were guests at a country house. The King and the President quickly established a camaraderie and Queen Mary and Edith found a common meeting ground in their love of antiques and needlecraft. All four were anxious to have things go well on this historic occasion.

Woodrow Wilson was the man of the hour and the people turned out to welcome the austere professor with dreams of worldwide peace, and his vivacious wife. Edith had visited London many times, but as First Lady domiciled in Buckingham Palace she felt as though she was on another planet.

Even during wartime the sense of ancestral pageantry was strong, from the moment they landed at Dover. Sir Charles Cust, equerry to King George, had met them at Calais and accompanied them across the English Channel in a hospital ship. Convoyed first by French and then by British destroyers, with airplanes in formation overhead, they were welcomed at Dover by the towering Duke of Connaught, Queen Victoria's son.

The President reviewed the guard of honor at the dock and the Lord Mayor of Dover, small and half-lost in his scarlet robe trimmed with mock ermine, conferred the freedom of war-weary Dover on Woodrow Wilson. Here again schoolchildren strewed rose petals along Edith's path before they were driven to the royal train for the trip to London. The Duke of Connaught warned Edith that the British might be more reserved in their welcome than the French had been. But it was Boxing Day, bright and sunny, and everyone was on holiday.

Henry White, one of the commissioners, had cautioned Mrs. Wilson to be careful with Queen Mary, who was "very stiff, but very nice." As she stepped from the train she instantly grew aware of the Queen, standing straight as a ramrod and overshadowing the King. Princess Mary was with them as they walked over a strip of red carpet to join the welcoming notables.

Together the King and the President reviewed the assembled troops before boarding the royal coaches. Clattering along in the high-slung carriages emblazoned with the royal coat of arms was a new experience for Edith. The King and Woodrow Wilson rode in the first, with a mounted guard accompanying them. The Queen, Princess Mary, and Mrs. Wilson traveled in the second coach as the procession set off for Buckingham Palace, with outriders, bewigged footmen, and scarlet liveries brightening the spectacle. The Queen chatted amiably with Edith as her hand moved automatically in a gesture to the cheering crowd; she said that it was all intended for the President and her. A royal procession always brought out a crowd and the public was used to visiting royalties, but the arrival of President Wilson had special significance for many, and some were curious about his wife.

As she looked around her it seemed to Edith that spectators were everywhere, as in Paris. But people were sad and weary and the cheers were subdued.

They drove straight through the Albert Gate instead of circling it in the customary way, and when they turned into the palace courtyard a gathering of American troops awaited them. The wounded on crutches and in wheelchairs were lined up in front, and a shout went up as the President stepped down from the coach, bared his head, and spoke personally to the men he had sent overseas to fight.

The American press had been transported from Charing Cross station directly to Buckingham Palace to be kept out of the way, but according to Arthur Krock, one of their number, they managed to "crash" the royal party's arrival ceremony. Krock noticed that President Wilson spotted them but "he stood there very composed with the King and Queen and Mrs. Wilson."

Inside the palace Queen Mary formally presented the lords and ladies of the household before personally escorting Mrs. Wilson to the Belgian Suite on the main floor. It was at the back and overlooked the gardens. The rooms were fragrant with flowers and she quickly singled out a basket of crimson roses and white heather from Lord Balfour. Printed programs of the planned events lay for inspection on an escritoire. Their arrival set in motion a dizzying, though picturesque, sequence of events.

Edith enjoyed the visible splendor of their reception, although apologies were made for its wartime simplification. The personalities, the costumes, the settings, and historic treasures were of genuine interest to her, but it seemed like a spectacle viewed at a distance. Edith, who had a strong feeling for history, was amazed to find herself a participant. She had to keep in mind, however, Woodrow's attitude to monarchical trappings and his coming assault at the Peace Conference on imperialistic practice.

Her own gesture in this direction surprised those who knew her dislike for drawing attention to herself. She elected not to curtsy to the Queen, who accepted this breach of social decorum with equanimity. Edith took this stand throughout her visit to London solely to show that the wife of the President of the United States was on a par with the Queen. Her concern was not for her own status but for Woodrow's, since she believed that he should get his due in this gathering of rulers. The British aristocracy viewed it as an ill-timed gesture, but it had no real bearing on the warmth Mrs. Wilson generated during her visit.

As a daughter of Virginia, Edith Bolling had been thoroughly schooled in the tradition of the curtsy, and she was not naïve, either socially or politically. But there was less criticism of the President when, as plain Mr. Wilson, he avoided using "Your Majesty" and addressed the King as "Sir." If this bothered some of the court entourage it certainly did not trouble George V, who was determined to have things go well with Woodrow Wilson. He was mindful of the President's desire for simplicity on the eve of the Peace Conference, although the diplomats of both countries had worked to give this state visit the utmost importance and *éclat,* befitting the wealth and power of the United States.

King George and the President got on well from the start, exchanging jokes and stories. The King made a point of showing him his quarters personally and explaining the complicated workings of the bathing system in a bedroom alcove. Both of the Wilsons shivered with cold in Buckingham Palace. There was no heating in Edith's intimidating bedroom, which had the largest bed in which she had ever slept. She understood the wartime conditions, and found comfort in her dressing room, snug and bright, with crimson curtains and a tiny grate fire.

Before the first dinner they appeared on the balcony, and the President spoke briefly, holding a flag given him by Queen Mary. She and

137

King George waved American flags. Then the royal pair escorted the President and Mrs. Wilson back to their quarters and said they would return to dine with them at nine that night.

At last Mrs. Wilson found time to change from the black tailored suit with sealskin collar and tricot hat that she had worn all day. She hastily donned a black crepe gown with broadtail skirt and a Russian blouse effect. Her wide beaver hat had three gray ostrich tips, and Woodrow studied her appreciatively when he appeared—appropriately turned out himself in morning coat, gray trousers, and silk hat. Colonel William W. Harts, his military aide, and Admiral Grayson escorted him, and Miss Benham walked with Edith.

Queen Alexandra, who had been King Edward VII's consort when Edith first visited England, waited for them at the entrance to her apartments. They had already caught a glimpse of her, waving an American flag and throwing kisses to Woodrow Wilson from an upstairs window of Marlborough House as they passed in the procession. Close up, Edith studied her. Traces of her celebrated beauty were still quite apparent, although the enameled complexion was touched with age and she had shrunk in stature. Her eyes were still alive, but they had lost their soft intensity. Mrs. Wilson knew that although she was completely deaf she was finding it difficult to relinquish the reins completely to Queen Mary. Grandmama was still a presence.

Her daughters—tall, slim Maud, who was the Queen of Norway, and Victoria, the princess royal, were with her. The Wilsons passed through a succession of interviews with the royal relatives, signing their autograph albums and making conversation. That evening the King and Queen, the Duke of York, Princess Mary, and the Duke of Connaught dined with them in their suite. Instead of the stiff affair they expected, the evening went well. The King and the President kept them all entertained with their stories. Once the ice was broken by Woodrow, the King responded with tales about American troops—like the doughboy who refused to believe that he was the King of England because he did not wear a crown during a review, and the youngster who cheerfully said, "Put it there," and offered his hand when the King greeted him.

The Queen wore the simplest of jewels on this occasion, with a peach-colored dress. Edith was in blue and silver, and Princess Mary wore white. It became even more of a family party when they chatted around the fire after dinner. Queen Mary took Edith on a tour of her own quarters, pointing up the historical associations of various objects as they traversed corridors, and saying what she thought of some of the pieces she had inherited from Queen Victoria. Edith was awed by the Queen's air of authority and complete command of her subject, as she took her through nine rooms, each decorated in a different period style, from the French to the Chinese salon, where she longed to linger over the jade, porcelain, lacquer, and embroideries. They finally settled comfortably in the homelike room where Queen Mary spent much of her time. It faced on the garden, had comfortable chairs, a handsome escritoire, and a stunning array of photographs. Edith noticed the books, the flowers, the evidence of the Queen's needlework, and it all seemed more akin to her own way of life, but she felt so cold that she could scarcely keep her teeth from chattering while she talked to the imperturbable Queen. Edith was glad to get back to the Belgian Suite and to find Woodrow relaxing by the fire after his first strenuous day in England. Both were too tired to exchange notes on the day's events.

Next day the President lunched at 10 Downing Street with Lloyd George, who had asked the leaders of all the political parties to attend the formal unveiling of the portrait of George Washington in the dining room. Edith lunched with Lady Reading, one of the few times on their trip that she and Woodrow were separated. Here she met Margot Asquith, one of the most discussed women of the day. Edith was dismayed by her lack of reticence; she found her egotistical; plain but clever. It was useless to spar with her but Edith resented the intensely personal note when Mrs. Asquith asked about her romance with Woodrow Wilson and her relations with her stepdaughters. Mrs. Asquith's own frank comments on her romance with Herbert Asquith were not in the Bolling tradition and Edith escaped by leaving Lady Reading's for 10 Downing Street to have tea with Mrs. Lloyd George. They were joined there by the men who had shared in the unveiling of the George Washington portrait. The election returns were coming in and everyone talked of the conservative swing and victory for Lloyd George.

Returning to Buckingham Palace, Edith had to deal with the unfamiliar question of tiaras—to wear or not to wear them. She was told that she alone must settle this matter, regardless of all the advice coming from the American diplomats and their wives. Most of the ladies of the court circle stored their jewels in vaults during the war years, but were now taking them out again for the arrival of the heads of governments for the Peace Conference.

Edith told Lady Sandhurst, wife of the Lord Chamberlain, that she would not be wearing a tiara because she did not own one. In that case no one would wear a tiara, she was assured. But this was dismaying to the President's wife and she instantly said that she would enjoy seeing them on others. It was a small issue in the midst of major historical events, but the American diplomats were concerned that Edith, in her straightforward and independent way, would make a misstep.

The question of the President's attire at the state banquet had already been threshed out. War President though he was, he was also in Europe as the man of peace, and in America the Chief Executive never wore military uniform on formal occasions. It was immediately decreed that the King and the members of his household would do the same.

Edith wore a simple black velvet gown with a long train. Her own lustrous coloring and sparkling eyes accented her quiet costuming, and she wore no jewelry. She was quickly caught up in the pageantry of the evening when Lord Sandhurst and his aide, Lord Farquhar, escorted Edith and the President upstairs to join the Royal Family for the state banquet. The backward march of the equerries, carrying slender wands that all but touched the floor as they bowed at regular intervals, even as they climbed stairs, seemed to Mrs. Wilson "to represent the difference between a monarchy and a democracy."

They were received by the King and Queen in a white oval drawing room, and Mrs. Wilson and Queen Mary faced each other at close range, with the Queen in full panoply. Both were tall, both were stately, and for the first time Mrs. Wilson was conscious of Queen Mary's character and strength. A victim of press photography herself, Edith thought that the public impression of her was false. Wearing a coronet of diamonds, she carried herself superbly in a white gown crossed dramatically by the wide blue Order of the Garter.

The princess royal wore velvet and rubies, but the beautiful Duchess of Sutherland, the Queen's lady in waiting, drew every eye with her daring gown of silver tissue. Her tiara was one of special charm, worn lightly and with grace. Her ropes of pearls and a diamond necklace showed off her long slender neck. Among all the duchesses she was the most noted for her style and beauty. She was relaxed and graceful, avoiding busty, small-waisted figure of the 1890's that still prevailed at court.

Even the President was looking relaxed in the intimacy of this small gathering. They were ushered into a gallery where the ninety-six dinner guests lined up. Few women had been invited and it took the King only a few minutes to present them to the President, but it took some time for the Queen, in her clear voice, to present the famous men of the hour to Mrs. Wilson as they were officially announced.

They were all names Edith recognized. She had decoded some of their messages and she knew what her husband thought of each one, but she found it strange to be face to face with Admiral Jellicoe, the hero of Jutland; with Admiral Beatty of the Navy and Earl Douglas Haig, Commander in chief of the expeditionary forces in France; with Lord Curzon; and her old friend, Lord Balfour. She found that they all looked much like their pictures except for Winston Churchill, who seemed strangely insignificant in the gathering of warlords. Her husband would never come to like this adventuresome young man, but Edith would live to see another Churchill emerge in World War II.

The military guests were ablaze with medals and decorations, and their smart uniforms were in contrast to the quiet black attire of President Wilson and the King. To Edith, Woodrow seemed the most impressive of all the men present as he escorted the Queen in to dinner. Many admiring glances came her own way as she entered the banquet hall on the arm of King George.

A mist of gold and crimson gave a shimmering effect as they walked in. It was the first state banquet in four years, and the gold plate had been brought from the vaults of Windsor Castle. Everything on the table was gold. The tall candelabra held wax candles, and gold bowls between them overflowed with red anemones and poinsettia—the Christmas flower. The red and gold effect was repeated in the Tudor uniforms of the Beefeaters from the Tower of London, ranged around the room as immobile as statues. Liveried servants abounded, some in blue and silver, suggestive of the period of Queen Anne; others wore crimson with buckled shoes and breeches. All wore heavily powdered white wigs.

Edith was surprised to have the King tell her that he was nervous. The rustle of the small sheets of paper with his notes persuaded her that he really dreaded the ordeal. But he was an entertaining dinner partner, giving her the history of the Beefeaters and jesting a little about the musicians' gallery at the end of the hall. As the evening wore on she could hear "My Old Kentucky Home," "Maryland, My Maryland," "Swanee River," and other American songs being softly played.

Edith could see that the King was shaking as he rose to toast President Wilson, paying tribute to him and to America's role in the war. Then it was Woodrow Wilson's turn to toast the King. He did it in characteristic fashion, without notes. "His graceful speech made me thrill with pride," Edith later wrote, but there was a difference of opinion about the effect it had. Even Edith Benham, his faithful admirer, did not think it one of his better efforts. Lord Curzon, who had taken her in to dinner, said he thought there should have been some allusion to the four years of British suffering. The emphasis had been entirely on America's role. Lord Reading shared this view and the diplomats in general thought that President Wilson had struck the wrong note.

At dinner the King had asked Mrs. Wilson if Queen Mary had told her about her private audience for Susan Booth, her black maid. The Queen had sent for her and they had had a friendly chat on what Susan thought about London and whether she was comfortable in the palace. Susan remembered to curtsy, something that the staff had warned her she must do. From a balcony grill she was allowed to inspect the gold room all ready for the banquet, even before Edith saw it. The Queen gave her a royal crown in green enamel set with pearls.

Overnight Susie became a newspaper pet. The American papers played up the story and the English press made the most of her brief whirl with royalty. Every sidelight on the British tour made good reading in the papers at home, but events came thick and fast. The day after the banquet the President and Edith set out again in the royal coaches, with outriders, but this time without the King and Queen. The court was represented at the Guild Hall where President Wilson received the freedom of the City of London, by Lord Chesterfield, master of the horses.

## Mrs. Wilson Meets Queen Mary

Again the crowds cheered as they passed and this time Edith had a chance to see that there were no young men in the streets except amputees. Christmas had emphasized the bereavement in countless homes. The war was over, the peace terms were about to be settled, but the toll it had taken was evident everywhere—in desolate homes, in strikes, in industrial unrest, in harassed humanity. At the lunch in the city the President had a chance to speak with warmth of Britain's role in the war. He had worked this out in the night, after being told that his toast to the King had missed the point.

Through Mrs. John W. Davis, the ambassador's wife, and Lady Reading, Mrs. Wilson covered a great deal of ground in a brief space of time. She met the more political women at a tea given by Mrs. Lloyd George. Lady Curzon she knew as a fellow American. Mrs. Jan Christiaan Smuts interested her because of her husband's devotion to Woodrow Wilson and the League of Nations.

At midnight that evening they boarded the royal train again to go north to Carlisle. This was a sentimental pilgrimage on which Woodrow Wilson had set his heart, for he was visiting the birthplace of his mother. His devotion to his parents was legendary, and he was deeply moved as he stood at the communion rail of the austere Presbyterian church from which his grandfather, Thomas Woodrow, had preached, and spoke about his mother. It was easy for Mrs. Wilson in these surroundings to picture the little girl who had sat each Sunday in this church until she was taken to the United States at the age of seven. She knew how proud his clever mother would have been could she have heard him say, "Perhaps it is appropriate that in a place of worship I should acknowledge my indebtedness to her and to her remarkable father, because, after all, what the world is now seeking to do is to return to the paths of duty, to turn from the savagery of interests to the dignity of the performance of right. . . . It is from quiet places like this all over the world that the forces are accumulated that presently will overpower any attempt to accomplish evil on a great scale. . . ."

Words cut as deep as swords, said Woodrow Wilson, who seemed to his wife to be overcome with emotion as he went into the vestry to sign the register. Through teeming rain they next visited the modest brick house where the Woodrows had lived, and again Edith could visualize the prim little girl who had grown up to mother her great Woodrow.

Manchester was their next stop, and the President was thrown back

143

into politics after his hours of nostalgia at Carlisle. He chose this center of liberal thought and radical action for his reply to a fiery speech Clemenceau had made urging alliances, just after Woodrow Wilson and Lloyd George had established good relations. Wilson condemned any return to the old system that kept unsettling world peace. The press at once spread Wilson's challenge.

The Wilsons were guests of the Lord Mayor at Manchester's Town Hall. Once again he received the freedom of a city—this time a city brisk with trade, torn by industrial unrest, but showing signs of recovery from the paralyzing effects of the war. Many of the merchants had grown rich fashioning the implements of war.

In their tour of the city Edith, who had developed a special affinity for ships, caught her first glimpse of one of the mysterious ships that had been used to such good effect against submarines. Sailing through the Manchester Canal on a murky day, with a strange assortment of craft in view, her attention was drawn to a clumsy freighter giving no clue to its function. When a whistle sounded its sides collapsed and it turned into a man-of-war before her eyes. Fully manned guns rose into view. But there were few marvels of this kind left for Edith to see. Experts had enlightened her on the scientific aspects of warfare, and particularly on things relating to the sea.

Their party returned to London on the royal train and had a last busy day there before going back to Paris. They dined again at Buckingham Palace, this time with a small guest list of thirty. Next morning the King, having learned that it was Woodrow Wilson's birthday, came to their suite with a set of books on the history of Windsor Castle. Both he and the Queen accompanied them to the station and saw them off with the usual formalities. By this time the Queen and Edith were on excellent terms and all four parted with warmth and goodwill.

The echoes of their state visit to London were reflected in the press comments around the world, showing a wide range of opinion. Some papers made much of the fact that Edith had failed to curtsy to the Queen and that the President had shown little concern for royal titles. Lord Bryce came to the conclusion that Wilson's visit to London had stiffened the already predominant sentiment in favor of the League and had increased the general goodwill between the two nations.

Ambassador Davis revealed that the President considered it only a "qualified success." Wilson said that if the need arose he would return to England to muster popular support for the League of Nations. David Lawrence wrote that the visit was a success in the sense that the British press became more friendly. Colonel House, now a little out in the cold, and ill at the time, reported in his diary that the banquet at Buckingham Palace was the most elaborate affair that any of those attending it had ever witnessed. Edith left feeling greater warmth for Britain than when she arrived.

After London came Rome. Edith knew the city well but she had never envisioned anything like the welcome the President and she received on the banks of the Tiber. Although Paris and London had prepared her for tumultuous crowds, the reception in Rome seemed ummatched in volume and warmth. She wrote to Altrude Grayson that the experiences and emotions of a lifetime had been packed into a few weeks. "Fortunately the three countries—France, England, and Italy—are so different in customs, race, and expression there is no danger of confusing the events which marked our stay in each."

In their rapid tour they had been exposed to monarchical custom, to medieval pageantry and to inherited tradition, as well as to the wounds of war and scenes of devastation. As they moved at a frantic pace from one point to another Edith never doubted the warmth the people of Rome felt for the President, irrespective of the political undercurrents to his name. Fiume was on the horizon, but it was not yet an acute issue. He insisted that it should belong to the new Yugoslav state, and not to Italy. The League requirements would be violated, he argued, if the Mediterranean were to belong to a power of which it was not an integral part.

She could not refrain from describing their welcome in her memoir as a contemporary echo of the ancient custom of turning the city into an amphitheater for returning military conquerors or visiting Heads of State. The President was sensitive at all times to the reactions of crowds, and particularly on this tour, with the Peace Conference about to begin. He knew that much was at stake at the peace table, with Italy one of the chief participants, and he was well aware that he would have trouble over Fiume. The large Italian population in America was intensely interested in the Roman reception, and in Woodrow Wilson's visit to the Vatican.

Although the President and Mrs. Wilson were committed to the diplomatic program laid out for them, both showed a touch of independence as they fulfilled all the requirements with a style peculiarly their own. There were some unexpected tangles in the arrangements for Mrs. Wilson, and she and Miss Benham got lost in the general bedlam. They felt the language barrier acutely from the time that they were met at the border by the American and Italian ambassadors and a representative of King Victor Emmanuel, until they left the country. Strict protocol began on the train—the most magnificent they had traveled in since leaving London—with scarlet-coated servants, china and glass with the royal crest, and the finest embroidered linen.

They were met at the station by the King and Queen and after the official greetings and review of troops they drove to the Quirinal through cheering crowds. Rare old brocades and crested velvets hung from the long open windows and American and Italian flags were flying together everywhere. Troops with picturesque uniforms and what Edith called "two-story caps" lined the streets. Driving with the handsome Montenegrin Queen, they were showered with flowers from roofs, windows, and balconies. Violets and mimosa rained down on the low-slung royal coaches, and dark-eyed girls with baskets flung more onto their laps.

Edith and Miss Benham decided that in some respects the Quirinal was grander than Buckingham Palace, and also much warmer. But communication was difficult in its vast spaces, and the President jested with Edith about the two acolytes in red who guarded her door. His quarters were hung with Flemish tapestries. His salon was Florentine, his smoking room Japanese. During the war the palace had been turned over entirely to hospital use, and only this wing had been refurnished, but it had been done in lavish style. The wounded and the sick were still in occupancy. The King and Queen lived at the Villa Savoia outside the city and came in only for official events. But now Victor Emmanuel stood with President Wilson on the balcony while a great crowd cheered them from below.

One of Edith's first duties after she reached Rome was a tour of the palace hospital. Because of her affiliation with the Red Cross in America she was welcomed in each country they visited by the local head of this organization. In Italy the tall Duchess of Aosta, the King's cousin, filled this role. For her the war was not yet over, since her husband was still in the field with his troops.

## Mrs. Wilson Meets Queen Mary

The King and Queen took Edith on the hospital tour and again she was confronted with the restoration done on shattered soldiers. Some of the men lying on iron cots had been the Queen's own patients, for she had worked in the X-ray department during the war and her arms and fingers gave testimony to the overexposure she had suffered. After their tour the Queen gave America's First Lady the enameled order of the Italian Red Cross.

The warmth of feeling between them increased when the President and Edith drove out to lunch with the King and Queen at the Villa Savoia, where they lived in utmost simplicity. The King, bareheaded, ran down the steps to welcome them, opening the car door himself and greeting them in English. The heir to the throne, a handsome four-year-old in black velvet with a lace collar, shyly handed Mrs. Wilson sprays of apple blossom.

The King's bedroom surprised the Wilsons. It had bare floors, an army cot, two chairs, and some toilet articles. The King laughed when they mentioned the discomfort of his cot, and he told them that it prepared him for the battlefield. On their way back to Rome, warmed by a feeling of kinship for the small and sturdy King who seemed to share the President's views, they called on the Dowager Queen and the powerful Duchess of Aosta. The state dinner given for them in the Quirinal that night, in a long gallery hung with tapestries, remained one of Edith's most firm memories. She and the Queen, both in white, looked impressive together because of their matching height and stately bearing.

Studying the crimson-cushioned chairs that suggested thrones, and the superbly appointed table, Edith reminded the King of his remark in Paris about the Murat Palace: "My God, I couldn't live in a place like this!" He quietly reminded her that he did not live in the Quirinal, and "all this does not belong to me any more than the White House belongs to you!"

In spite of all the visible magnificence Edith was well aware that the ravages of long denial showed through the stateliest events, in run-down palaces, freezing trains, shortages and austerity of every kind. But for the moment it seemed like a world of splendor.

From the Quirinal they drove to the Capitol, where a reception was held and the freedom of the city was conferred on Woodrow Wilson. Again there were speeches, and a bronze replica of the figure surmounting the tomb of Hadrian was given to the President. Mrs. Wilson's gift from the people of Rome was a gold wolf suckling Romulus and Remus.

Edith was familiar with the sights of Rome, but when the Queen led her out on a balcony overlooking the city to see the illuminated Forum, Edith felt the march of history. "Twenty centuries look down on you, Mademoiselle," Prince Colonna said to Miss Benham, who later wrote rhapsodically of a "myriad of sacrificial fires burning to this new god who had come from the West to help these war-tortured countries." The ruins were suffused with rose and green light. Classical scholars were offended, but it was spectacular.

Although invited to accompany the President to the Vatican for his official visit, Edith agreed with their advisers that it would be better for Woodrow to go alone. On their way to have tea that afternoon with Countess Cellere, wife of the Italian ambassador to the United States, Edith and Miss Benham decided to follow quietly and see how the crowd responded to the President. A great shout went up when he appeared on his way to the Vatican. He stood up to wave and greet them, and the police had trouble controlling the eager Romans.

Later that day a situation developed that annoyed the President, according to Edith, and she found him "blazing with anger" on her return to the Quirinal. Although every move in Rome had been carefully planned, an independent arrangement had been made for him to pause and speak to an assemblage at the Piazza Venezia after his visit to the Vatican. George Creel felt that the reception arranged by Orlando and Sonnino, the conservative Foreign Minister, had not taken into account the people themselves. Thousands gathered to hear him, but while he was with the Pope orders were given to disperse this gathering lest things get out of hand. Creel maintained that he was deliberately delayed along the way with official greetings and interviews, so that by six o'clock he swept at high speed through the Piazza. Pandemonium followed. Neither the President nor Edith fully accepted the official explanation that the crowds everywhere had been so pressing that they feared they could not be controlled. According to Edith, the President believed he had been kept from speaking lest some allusion to the Fourteen Points or Fiume stir up trouble.

Edith found the crowds in Rome alarming as well as warmhearted. The President did not like being involved in situations without warning, and the confusion, crowding, and helter-skelter rushing from place to place had his little entourage on edge. The endless marble corridors of Rome exhausted even Edith and she felt relieved when they moved on to Genoa. They arrived in a downpour and she took shelter in their car while the President laid a wreath on the monument of Mazzini, after their welcome by the city's chief magistrate. When they reached Milan immense crowds poured into the Piazza del Duomo for a glimpse of President and Mrs. Wilson.

Here again some of the arrangements went wrong. When the President learned at the last minute that he and Edith were expected to attend a gala performance at La Scala on Sunday night he showed his stubborn side. The finest musical talent of Europe had been rounded up to do him honor, but the scrupulous Presbyterian elder announced that he never went to a theater in his own country on Sunday and could not do so now. The American correspondents waited anxiously for the outcome of this piquant issue, and many of them treated it facetiously.

Every seat was already taken and he was discreetly reminded that he must not disappoint the public—or the artists. A little diplomacy was used, with Edith's help, and he was asked if he could bring himself to attend a "sacred concert" at La Scala on Sunday. He agreed, and saw a magnificent performance of *Aida* after several solos had injected the religious note into the program.

The American press described an unusually genial President throwing kisses to the bejeweled ladies in adjoining boxes. And Edith, a music lover from her earliest days, was enraptured by the performance. Knowing that Altrude would remember the setting from their early travels, she wrote to her on January 11, "We stayed at the Palace overlooking the Cathedral in that great square and that night went to the Scala for a beautiful performance. Every box and every seat crowded to the roof & such a burst of welcome from every throat."

Arthur Krock wrote that President Wilson showed his "charming, gay, delightful nature" in Italy when he was not being the statesman and pedant. On the night of the performance at La Scala Wilson, waving a walking stick, led the band from a balcony overlooking the Piazza del Duomo, where more than 100,000 people had gathered. This was no surprise to Mrs. Wilson; it was just the impulse he would follow when the spirit moved him.

Woodrow Wilson again became the scholar at ancient Turin, making five speeches and receiving a degree from the university. Mrs. Wilson wrote that he "looked young and virile" wearing the blue cap of the students. This particular stop had a special quality of its own when a thousand Piedmontese mayors of every social and political stripe assembled to welcome him. Edith noted bankers and village blacksmiths, merchants and countrymen, in from the hills, fields, and valleys, a true cross-section of the life of northern Italy. It was a change from the pomp of courts and the Wilsons were moved by this reception.

They went straight back to Paris from Turin and were at Modane, a border town in the Alps, when word reached the President on January 6 that Theodore Roosevelt was dead. Mrs. Wilson and Miss Benham watched the slow and careful way in which he composed his message of sympathy to Mrs. Roosevelt, seeking the *mot juste* as he changed from one draft to another. "Another White House widow," reflected Mrs. Wilson, as she knitted and thought of Woodrow's future.

# *13.* The Murat Palace

THROUGHOUT their whirlwind tour Edith had been visible on all occasions as the fashionable and stately wife, spreading a certain aura of warmth by the side of an austere President. Back in Paris, with the Peace Conference due to start, her role changed. The French capital, still sunk under the pall of war, was no place for celebration, in the opinion of Woodrow Wilson. He wanted official entertainment kept to a minimum. Edith wished to be as inconspicuous as possible, but she was soon recognized as an important link with the President by the official groups representing the fourteen governments. It was evident from the start that she was not someone to be ignored.

It was not easy at any time to reach Woodrow Wilson, and even the courtly commissioner, Henry White, was relieved that he had made headway with Edith and was finding her a "valuable channel for communication with the President." He was impressed by her "rightheadedness" on the problems of the moment and her keen perception of complicated issues. As the only member of the American mission who could conduct political arguments in French, White aided Edith socially, too. With some hesitancy she practiced her own French, and she could always rely on White or Jules Jusserand for the official events. Her first was the reception that the President and she gave at the Murat Palace immediately after the Peace Conference began. They invited 300, many of whom were seeing her for the first time. She wore a black tulle dress with golden embroidery and won her way with both sexes.

The Armistice was only two months old and the echoes of war were heard every day. Sad-faced women and wounded men were everywhere. From the beginning Edith made a point of driving or walking with Woodrow to the Quai d'Orsay, and Parisians watched her with interest as she kept up with his fast stride.

Although well aware of the raging furies that soon beat around her husband, Edith refrained from political comment and was always self-contained and noncommittal. Miss Benham noticed that neither husbands nor wives guessed how much her judgment counted with the President, "although all noticed that she was constantly at his side, and that a look exchanged between them could sometimes change the tone of the conference."

The conferees had been at work only a few days when a clash of temperaments developed, the first of five crises which were to stretch over a period of seven months, with the total collapse of the Conference only narrowly averted on three occasions—one being the time that her husband threatened to withdraw the American delegation. It seemed to Edith at times that the sessions would remain forever in a hopeless impasse. The President seemed to her to tower head and shoulders over the men with whom he was dealing. She would change her opinion later, but at the moment Clemenceau was "the avowed cynic, distrustful of humanity's ability to rise to unselfish heights." Lloyd George was the "political weather vane shifting with every wind that blew across the Channel." And Orlando "had his ear ever to the ground" lest Italy fail to get something for which she hungered.

"How I longed to be a man so I could be of more help to him," Mrs.

151

Wilson wrote of her husband. "All I could do was to try to soothe him." And here her special talent lay, for she diverted him after the day's storms with a gaiety of mood that masked her realization of what it all meant to him. However diplomatic she managed to be in public during this period, her comments to Woodrow at night were pungent.

But her days were more filled with drama than with frivolity. And she watched what she considered a historic event being enacted at her own dinner table when the President summoned Dr. Grayson to take a copy of his draft of the Constitution of the League of Nations to General Smuts, who headed the South African commission. It was still so secret that he wanted it personally conveyed to the man who had written what Woodrow Wilson considered one of the best expositions of the aims of the League of Nations and their practical application.

The President read it to the Peace Conference late in January with crashing effect. There was instant controversy over the mandatory system it proposed for the settlement of world colonial policy—a fresh approach designed to end the ancient policy of the spoils to the victor. The future world took shape with Wilson's insistence on the development of each area for the people who inhabited it, rather than for the nation controlling it.

He was savagely attacked at once by the French press for his "impracticable ideals," and the atmosphere in Paris became so tense that, almost before it had begun, the Peace Conference splintered over President Wilson's determination to make the League of Nations an integral part of the Treaty. Many thought that this should be left in abeyance until the Treaty itself was signed.

By the end of January the President was beset on all sides, and Edith deplored the "lukewarm support" he was getting from some members of his own commission. Lansing was one of those who thought that the important thing was to get the Treaty put through, regardless of the League of Nations, in which he believed. The President's eyes were opened to some of the conflict going on behind the scenes when Henry White urged Edith to alert Wilson to the situation. White enlightened her on a unique tour of Paris, which he knew extraordinarily well. America's First Lady, dressed informally, and the diplomat who had served in several European capitals wandered together through the dark alleys of ancient Paris. He brought one historical episode after

152

another to life and she was an avid listener, absorbing the picturesque and the horrifying until they were suddenly very much in the present, discussing the feuding in the American commission.

Mrs. Wilson was already alive to the situation for, although Woodrow lived in the clouds and was much too busy to concern himself with gossip, she heard a great deal of chatter over the teacups and often deduced what it meant. She listened attentively to White.

Lansing, he said, as Secretary of State was resentful that the meetings attended by the President should be held in House's quarters in the Crillon, instead of at the Embassy. White thought that Lansing was right. He also let Edith know that the press, seeking information, were told by Gordon Auchincloss to see his father-in-law, Colonel House. White strongly urged Mrs. Wilson to bring these two points to the President's attention, and she did as they motored after church on the following Sunday. Woodrow was incredulous but he got the point and made changes at once.

The press situation was acute, with the French papers, and to a lesser degree the British, attacking him day after day. The American correspondents were indignant because they were being frozen out. "Open covenants openly arrived at" was the Woodrow Wilson diplomacy. He was determined not to surrender to traditional secret negotiations. Both he and Lloyd George had advocated open sessions of the Peace Conference, but France, Italy, and Japan voted them down. American resistance was so strong that Clemenceau finally agreed to admit the press to the full sessions. Arthur Krock was one of three correspondents who prevailed on the principals involved to settle this issue. But when the Council of Ten shrank to the Council of Four, the doors closed again. This did not prevent leaks by the French press of broadsides damaging to Woodrow Wilson. He was accused of being lacking in decision and of delaying proceedings with his insistence on the Fourteen Points.

Finally he agreed to have Ray Stannard Baker act in an official capacity as intermediary between the commission and the press, visiting him at seven every evening for a roundup of the day's events. It was understood that nothing could be released while under consideration, but resolutions, treaties, and completed acts could be recorded.

Edith made a point of being home to share in the daily reviews her husband had with Baker, so that by the time they reached the dinner table she had a fair idea of the day's events and could comment without plaguing her tired husband with futile questions. But there were news leaks in spite of all the precautions, and in talking to Mrs. Wilson and Miss Benham on January 14 Woodrow said that these were seriously disturbing the status quo. He blamed the French for most of them. But, as William Allen White wrote, Wilson had in his portfolio the "promissory note of the Allies for eight or ten billion dollars" and the wherewithal to feed the starving of Europe, which made him "half green-grocer and half-banker" as he roamed the forums of Europe, disguised as a philosopher and elderly professor with a "gentle inveterate grin" and a "faint odor of the sanctuary in his conventional black coat, with nicely creased trousers . . . with his amiable speeches and his noble aspirations. . . ."

The simplicity of the Wilson entourage was a matter of comment at the Peace Conference and was deplored by Colonel House, who functioned in the grand style and felt that the Chief Executive of the United States, with all the power and wealth behind him, should cast an impressive shadow, aside from the personal dignity that Woodrow Wilson always showed, and the easy grace of his wife. His style was considered provincial by the few remaining inheritors of the Metternich tradition. Aloof and independent, President Wilson was slow to delegate authority to others and so was desperately overworked. He did not use the Secretariat and had his work done by two stenographers with the occasional help of Miss Benham. House and Lansing had ample resources and large staffs at their command, but Woodrow Wilson preferred to play a lone hand, maintaining a screen of privacy when away from the public sessions. In his hours of leisure he saw few but his wife, Dr. Grayson, and Miss Benham.

In February, 1918, the President decided to make a quick trip back to the United States to clear up business in Congress before it adjourned in March and to lay the tentative draft of the Treaty before the Senate Foreign Relations Committee for suggestions and possible amendments. The rising tide of criticism at home made this essential. Woodrow Wilson was as heavily belabored by the American press as he was abroad.

## The Murat Palace

Edith was determined to hear him read the Covenant in the Hall of the Clock and to be with him, win or lose, when the vote was taken. There were few occasions in her married life when she was barred from appearing at his side for a major event, but women were not admitted when he spoke at a plenary session of the Peace Conference and gave his message to the assembled commissioners just before returning to America.

The President laughed when she urged him to get her in. Impossible! Did he think she might tackle Clemenceau? He warned her that the Tiger might show his claws, but she reminded him that Clemenceau never failed to wear gray cotton gloves. Then she schemed with Dr. Grayson, who was getting on well with Clemenceau, and who was often called on for delicate missions.

The upshot was that Mrs. Wilson, through half-parted crimson curtains in a stifling little antechamber, would watch her husband put the sum of his dreams to a vote—and win. She would be the unseen spectator to whom it mattered most, but her husband would know that she was there, and Clemenceau himself would help to smuggle her in.

The Tiger had his moments, and he was already aware that Edith was someone to reckon with. He gave orders for her to be admitted to the antechamber with Dr. Grayson. No one was to be told. They were to be in place before the delegates arrived, and they were not to leave until the Hall of the Clock had emptied. The President was quietly pleased when he learned that Edith would hear him. It was a day of strain for him. He wanted to return to America with a signed document that he could lay before the Foreign Relations Committee of the Senate. It summed up all that he had been working for, and only Edith knew how much thought and effort he had put into it.

The chamber in which he spoke was notable only because of the spectacular clock for which it was named. The antechamber was dismayingly small. It was black as night when she and Dr. Grayson settled on two straight chairs that filled it completely. The heavy curtains were drawn and the air was smothering. She peered through the folds, then boldly drew them halfway back as her husband began to speak. She could see him in the distance under the clock, directly facing her.

Without dramatics, and always the foe of rhetoric, he quietly introduced the Covenant to the assembled commissioners. Some found his

155

delivery a throwaway of the principles he was expounding. "Exact, unimpassioned, clear, explicit, and intelligently dull," said William Allen White.

His wife watched him raptly, convinced that he was reaching his listeners as he plowed through the text, pausing from time to time for impromptu explanation of knotty points. To her the sense of drama was intense; it was the unleashing of the Wilsonian dream, and she later wrote that it was a great moment in history as he stood "slender, calm and powerful in his argument." Beyond his immediate audience Mrs. Wilson envisioned "the people of all oppressed countries—men, women and little children—crowding around and waiting upon his words."

The minutes ticked away on the lordly clock, and she and Dr. Grayson sat immobile. The lights were on by the time the balloting ended and the President had scored a total victory. "It was the end of an epoch," White later commented. "It was his last public appearance as the ruler of the world. Ahead of him lay his trip to America and the disillusioned nation which he found there. Behind him lay all his glory."

But Edith was conscious only of the glory. She watched the commissioners crowding around him to shake his hand. When all had left she and Dr. Grayson escaped from the antechamber. The President was already in his car, waiting for them, and said Edith, "Oh, how glad I was to find him and tell him all the things that filled my heart." Woodrow took off his hat and leaned back against the cushions, saying they had made their first real step forward.

They were leaving next day for Brest and Woodrow suddenly switched from gravity to the spirit of fun.

"As a devoted Presbyterian, Mr. President, I can't believe that you want to sail on Sunday," said Dr. Grayson. "Don't you think that we ought to postpone it one day?"

The President laughed. "Don't you think your reason for that feeling may be not because of my Presbyterian connection but because you want to go to the Grand Prix at Longchamps?"

Soon they were boarding the President's train again after what Edith described as "much kissing of my hand and clicking of heels." Colonel House, whom the President had chosen to direct the American commission during his absence, was at the train. Lansing, who as Secretary of State, was second to the President in official rank, was designated titular and interim head, although full authority to act lay in Colonel House's hands. House had worked strenuously for the League of Nations and had fostered the idea since 1916.

Unconscious of the fight he was approaching with Senator Henry Cabot Lodge, Woodrow saw himself as the champion of the oppressed everywhere. "God knows I wish I could give them all they hope for, but only He Himself could do that," he said to Edith. He considered the United States to be in an unassailable position, since it asked for nothing in the settlement.

Woodrow worked every morning in preparation for the case he would present, and in the afternoon he and Edith visited the sick bay to talk to the wounded soldiers who were being brought home on their ship. It was a foggy, difficult crossing, and there was influenza on board. Foghorns wailed when they were off the banks of Newfoundland and they came close to having a disaster near Cape Ann. Mrs. Eleanor Roosevelt, a fellow passenger whom Edith had been seeing, was reading on deck and she jumped to her feet as bells rang, the engines stopped, and passengers ran around shouting that the ship was almost on the beach.

Their arrival in Boston brought Woodrow Wilson and Calvin Coolidge, two vastly different types, face to face before cheering throngs. Her arms filled with flowers, Edith smiled down warmly at the quiet, good-looking man destined to occupy the White House. Their route to Mechanics Hall was lined with soldiers, sailors, state guardsmen, and police. Again she was conscious of Secret Service agents posted on rooftops, for trouble had been predicted.

Many studied the First Lady with a new degree of interest. The papers had not neglected her dashing ways in Europe, and some had been vitriolic about her. She was not surprised to see some militant suffragists coming into view, waving their placards at Woodrow. The afterglow of victory was beginning to fade, she observed on their return to Washington, as unemployment and the unfamiliar problems that followed large-scale war beset the men on Capitol Hill.

The President's first move on his return was to invite the Foreign Relations Committees of the Senate and the House to dine at the White

House and discuss the draft of the Covenant that had been accepted in Paris. He made it clear that he wanted their suggestions for changes or amendments in writing, and some of his guests agreed that they had never seen Woodrow Wilson more human, witty, and amiable than on this occasion. He worked hard to win their support.

Edith, in black velvet, was present at the dinner, although she did not share in the discussion that followed. But she did a little propagandizing of her own as she sat beside Senator Lodge, chairman of the committee. She found him amusing and charming. She knew how much the gathering meant to Woodrow, and she studied the committee members with close attention. Senator William E. Borah, of Idaho, and Senator Albert B. Fall, of New Mexico, had refused their invitations.

The menu was carefully chosen and the flowers were arranged with grace, but afterward Senator Lodge and Senator Frank Brandagee, of Connecticut, one of Wilson's bitterest foes, mentioned the potency of the drinks and the scarcity of cigars. They all agreed that Edith was an adornment, and Senator Lodge, with his pointed beard and curling gray hair, listened to her attentively. He already knew a great deal about her, but he never believed that she influenced her husband's counsels. They skirted political issues and Edith spoke of their welcome in Boston. When the thirty men with whom she had dined went into conference with the President she retired to her own rooms, but later that night Woodrow told her much of what had happened and assured her that he thought he would have their support on the League. They raised a number of points which did not seem to alter it in substance. He told them that he had to deal with stubborn men but that he would do his best to have them accept the changes, although it would not be precisely the document on which they had voted.

When he asked Senator Lodge if he thought the Senate would approve the Covenant with the suggested revisions, the reply, according to Mrs. Wilson in *My Memoir* was, " 'If the Foreign Relations Committee approves it I feel there is no doubt of ratification.' And her husband replied: 'Very well then, I consider that armed with your approval, I can go back and work feeling you and your associates are behind me.' "

Senator Lodge bowed his head in what the President took to be assent, but looking back twenty years later Mrs. Wilson was convinced that even then he was prepared to fight ratification, and she read a subtle inference into Lodge's reference to the Foreign Relations Committee, for he knew that he could block it there.

Senator Lodge was cold about the evening's work and said that he had left as wise as he had come. The President had answered questions for two hours but had told them nothing. Within two days Lodge attacked the Covenant openly in the Senate and gained formidable support. He recalled George Washington's resistance to foreign entanglements and pictured the League as a threat to the Monroe Doctrine. He urged a cautious course, saying that it all needed consideration, time, and thought, and he dwelt on the danger of getting involved in international Socialism and Anarchism.

The President, anxious to bring it all to a head at Versailles, was staggered by Senator Lodge's unexpected rebuff. Edith stormed over the Senator's stand and felt that he had betrayed her trusting husband, but neither one believed that it represented the true sentiment of the country. William Howard Taft had just finished a lecture tour on peace, and he reported that there was growing sentiment for the League of Nations. The press on the whole was favorable, but just as the President was about to sail back to France he was faced with a document signed by Senator Lodge and thirty-six of his fellow Senators that they would not approve the Covenant in its existing form.

This was crushing news which he felt might impair his strength at the Peace Conference, but on the night he sailed his spirits soared when he and Edith attended an enthusiastic meeting at the Metropolitan Opera House in New York. Taft presided and when introducing the President he took up the objections to the League one by one, tore them apart, and stirred thunderous applause for Woodrow Wilson. It all ended on a patriotic note, flags everywhere, and the band playing "Over There." Edith was stirred as she sat in the opera house she knew so well, with Woodrow telling the audience that he would not come back until it was "over, over there," and when he did come back he would bring a League Covenant that the American people would continue to support.

They were still exhilarated when they boarded the *George Washington* once more. Friends had come to see them off and, in kissing Edith good-bye, Cleveland Dodge whispered to her, "God bless you for taking care of this great man whom the world needs." Altrude Grayson said good-bye once more to Cary and Edith. She was pregnant again but showed no sign of her condition in her fashionable clothes. There had been little time for family gatherings during their brief stay in Washington, but the Graysons had been reunited, and Edith had spent as much time as she could with family and friends. Paris styles were discussed and they all wanted to see what she had bought. She seemed smarter than ever, but the hobble skirt had made no hit with this tall and stately lady. Many of the gifts from Europe had been unpacked and she showed the more personal ones to her friends. The gifts of Kings and Queens were much discussed in Washington at this time and the impression prevailed that the Wilsons had been showered with rare and costly gifts.

Edith was aware on the way back that although her husband was enjoying the sea, as he always did, his mood was gloomy. At last he realized the strength of the opposition he faced at home. He was used to disappointments and was disposed to be philosophical, but he knew that this might tie his hands in bringing the Peace Conference to a successful conclusion.

On the last night the crew sang "God Be With You Till We Meet Again" and he joined them in "Auld Lang Syne." They reached Brest on March 14, too late to make the night trip to Paris. Edith stood on the deck watching the moonlight shimmering through the last of a heavy downpour as she waited for Colonel House to end a talk with her husband. He had come aboard by tender with the usual official party and the President had taken him at once to his stateroom to get the latest news from Paris. He was desperately anxious to be filled in on every detail, and to learn what the reaction had been to the Lodge opposition. According to Edith, they talked for a long time and when he left, she found her husband speechless with anger and disappointment. She rushed to him, for "the change in his appearance shocked me." He told her that House had compromised on every side and had given away everything that he had won before leaving Paris.

Edith raged openly, pouring out angry words while her husband stood tense and grim. It seemed to Woodrow that House had compromised until there was nothing left of the master plan. House told him that the hostility of the American press, attacking the League as part of the Treaty, had forced him to yield on certain points lest the Conference abandon it altogether.

Wilson recovered his self-control faster than Edith did. He told her not to worry for he would fight and recover the lost ground. They talked until early morning knowing that they were returning to Paris with fresh antagonism at home and abroad. When landing time came there was less fuss than on their first arrival, and they found this a relief.

Edith's dramatic account of this meeting was later questioned by observers who insisted that the two men met on shore, that Wilson was already aware of the compromises and that he had met the situation with outward calm.

Back in Paris, Woodrow Wilson faced the second great crisis of the Peace Conference, but he was now full of fight and stronger than ever in his faith in the League. He continued to work with House, but never again with the old unquestioning trust, and Edith felt that her fears about House had been confirmed.

# *14. Pocahontas: An Indian Princess*

THE return of the President to Paris on March 14 was followed by the fiercest ordeal of the Peace Conference for him and the constant threat that it would break up in chaos. Vigilant and ever attentive, Mrs. Wilson did what she could to encourage him as tempers flared, but he was working eighteen hours a day and she saw little of him.

Circumstances had changed during their absence, with Clemenceau withdrawn after an attack by a would-be assassin, and with Lloyd George busy in London with the problems of the newly elected government. Although favoring the League of Nations, the British wanted a firm peace with Germany, and while General Smuts and Lord Robert Cecil continued to uphold the Wilsonian principles, he had lost some of his support at Westminster.

Lord Balfour had sponsored a resolution that a preliminary peace with Germany would soon be made without reference to the League of

Nations, and the opponents of the organization were pronouncing it dead. The resolution dealt with all the settlements involved, with the establishment of boundaries, and it determined responsibility for the war, but there was no mention of the League of Nations. The resolution endangered the most important of the Fourteen Points. The President's anger blazed openly and he acted quickly. Colonel House's explanations were clear to him now. In a stern mood Wilson issued a statement that the decision made at the Plenary Session on January 25 for the inclusion of the League of Nations Covenant in the Treaty was final, and that no change of policy was contemplated. Instantly a wave of criticism rolled over him which made the earlier attacks pale by comparison. He took it in silence, and Edith alone knew at what cost. All through March and April the battle intensified.

On their return from America the Wilsons had taken up residence at 22 Place des États-Unis, an interesting house on a small square where they felt more at home than in the Murat Palace. Their own rooms were on the first floor, with the President's looking out on a walled garden in the back. Edith's faced the street, and she was always conscious of Lloyd George's swarming establishment nearby. The ballroom, which was quickly turned into a workshop, and the main dining room were on the second floor. Miss Benham converted a small bedroom into an office for Edith's affairs.

The President sometimes surprised visitors by disappearing through what seemed to be a solid wall in his study. A secret door painted to suggest well-filled bookcases opened to a passageway that led to Edith's sitting room. The house was full of surprises and curiosa and it had a certain charm for her and Miss Benham. It had been built by a collector of Renaissance furniture and carved old pieces abounded. There were paintings by Van Dyck, Watteau and Romney, a Delacroix, some Goyas, a Rembrandt, and a Hobham. A mezzanine gallery for musicians projected over the President's bathroom, which had a large green tub built partly into the wall. There was much laughter when Mrs. Wilson called him to inspect her huge bathroom, which had a sunken tiled pool, gold faucets in the wash basin, and apple trees seeming to shed their petals from above. The plumbing marvels to come were still in their infancy, but the Renaissance echoes remained.

"I think, like the King of Italy, I could not live in this place," Woodrow jested.

162

## Pocahontas: An Indian Princess

His favorite haunt was the spacious and richly furnished library upstairs, where he and Edith tried to forget the day's wrangling with music, games, reading, and harmonious silence when they had a chance to be alone. But these opportunities dwindled as the pressures increased. The Council of Four usually held two long meetings every day. In addition President Wilson attended the meetings of the League of Nations Commission in the evening and they lasted often until after midnight. He had innumerable other engagements. He held conferences with commissioners and frequently consulted experts, notably Herbert Hoover, Norman Davis, Bernard Baruch, and Vance McCormick. House was being eased out of the picture.

The Council of Four found Edith Wilson poised and hospitable as they came and went at Les États-Unis. The house was so arranged that although she kept out of the way it seemed almost like government at home, involving intimate negotiations without official trappings. When he had time to spare, the President saw representatives of the ethnic groups who came to plead one cause or another. Mrs. Wilson studied them with interest. The Poles were prominent, with Paderewski their advocate at the Peace Conference. She was already familiar with Venizelos and his picturesque guards. The Irish, the Italians, the Jews, the Egyptians, the Belgians, and the Africans all sought access to the President. The Japanese and Chinese spoke excellent English, since most of them had been educated in England or the United States. The Japanese were the most silent of all at the Conference, but they were also the most determined, adhering to their interests and their agreements.

The beautiful wives of the Orientals were all over Paris and Mrs. Wilson admired them in their native costumes when she had them for tea. In the closing days of the Conference when she gave a reception for the full membership of the Peace Conference, she decided that the most extraordinary-looking personage present was Prince Faisal of Arabia, Christlike with his long dark hair, pointed beard, and fine features. Rulers, royalty, diplomats, statesmen, generals, admirals, and plain soldiers; writers, artists, sculptors, musicians, actors, and celebrities from all parts of the world signed their names in what came to be known in the Wilson ménage as The Book.

Late in March optimism throughout Europe reached its lowest ebb. People saw Bolshevism, starvation, and industrial revolution, in

Edith's words, "sweeping like a black cloud over Europe." Fourteen small wars raged in various parts of Russia, Poland, and the Balkans. A Bolshevist revolution shook up Hungary and rebellion broke out in Egypt. Strikes and postwar problems plagued Britain. The French were fighting at the Peace Conference for possession of the Saar Valley, Foch insisted that the Rhine should be the controlled frontier of Germany, and Italy demanded recognition of her claims in the Adriatic and Asia. The reparations demands of the French and the British were delaying a settlement, and President Wilson's persistence about his Fourteen Points seemed to many observers to be the most troublesome element of all.

On March 22 he arrived home looking desperately tired, and told Edith that the French wanted to do what Germany had done in 1870 when it annexed Alsace and Lorraine. He had endured altogether too much of the Big Four and knew what they were going to say before they opened their mouths. Orlando, at odds with his Foreign Minister, Sonnino, was threatening to withdraw from the Peace Conference over Fiume. Although the British and French were neutral on this issue, they were unwilling to risk Italian hostility by taking a strong stand with the President. Edith always believed that Clemenceau and Balfour left her husband holding the bag on the Italian question.

She seemed to be more conscious than he was of the maneuvering going on around him. Her intuition was keen and while he thought in terms of the master issues she studied the men with whom he had to deal. She compared them all unfavorably with her own magnificent Woodrow. Creel always insisted that he was not hoodwinked for a moment by the "impassioned nationalism of Clemenceau, the medievalism of Sonnino, or the grasshopper mind of Lloyd George."

Lloyd George did not generate any responsive warmth in Edith. He was the one she watched most attentively as he came and went "full of Gallic quicksilver, a torrential talker . . . all bright ideas, enthusiasms and panics," in Ray Baker's words. She warmed by degrees to witty, stocky Clemenceau but she recognized his formidable power. Orlando, articulate, idealistic, and smooth in manner, was easy to like, but his manner was all too emotional for coolheaded Edith. Sonnino was as baffling to her as he was to her husband. They found him subtle, brilliant, and suspicious. Venizelos won her by his loyalty to the President. Years later she was surprised to find many of her early impressions of these men confirmed.

All who were close to the President saw how strongly Edith worked during the calamitous months of March and April, 1919, to support and divert her husband. Baker, who was seeing him every day, told of finding him utterly worn out when he visited him in the evening. He seemed to be growing "grayer and grimmer," his face twitched with nervousness, and he was visibly exhausted. It was evident to Baker that Edith was of "incalculable help and comfort to the President in these trying days." He recalled later that in every difficult situation in Europe she had borne herself with "fine dignity and with genuine simplicity and graciousness of manner."

Miss Benham, who saw them at close quarters and dined with them every day, wrote to her fiancé, Admiral Helm, that the more she saw of the Wilsons, the more she was struck by their unrivaled home life. She had never dreamed such sweetness and love could be. "She is the most wonderful wife in the world to a man who needs love and care more than any I have ever seen. Without it I don't believe he could live— certainly his work would be greatly crippled."

The President was particularly baffling at this time to the men around him, for he was in a state of suppressed fury. George Creel observed that he had "as hot a temper as ever burned in a human being" but controlled it well. His Irish and Scottish characteristics were evenly balanced, Creel felt. The Scottish strain disposed him to be slow and cautious, and the Irish strain prevailed after a decision had been made. Wilson's fighting spirit took no account of odds but burned inextinguishably once lit.

Lansing marveled that he never showed anger or impatience, even when seething at the way matters went. He was considerate of others' opinions, but his Council colleague failed to understand why a man of such intellectual brilliance could not form an opinion after hours of discussion. Woodrow Wilson followed his own course, but was ever mindful of the reaction in the United States. He knew that he had to have Congress on his side.

It particularly irked Edith to have her husband scoffed at as a facile academician unable to cope with the statesmen of Europe. Like Creel, she believed that he had unlimited courage when his mind was made up, and was not afraid to assume towering responsibilities. John M. Keynes, the British economist, had said that the "old Presbyterian was bamboozled." William Allen White also persisted in viewing him from this angle. When she came to write her own memoir Edith dealt directly with this old area of pain. "I thank God," she wrote, "that there is some truth in the statement. Never did he turn from the weapons of truth and right, as he saw them. . . ."

Late in March the President and Edith made a hurried trip to the devastated region close to Paris. They had been criticized for not having done this earlier, but there never seemed to be time for it. They set off on a Sunday with a small entourage and went first to Rheims and Soissons. Although Edith had read and heard a great deal about the damage done she was not altogether prepared for what she saw. The snow came drifting through the great holes in the roof of Rheims Cathedral. She studied the faces of the women and children who came out of the ruins to see the President of the United States. They all seemed pinched and sad. The wine cellars in which many lived had kept them alive but had not fed them.

Soissons was completely deserted as they passed through it, but after a detour that brought them back to the same spot they were amazed to find the streets alive with American soldiers. Their officers had ordered them into billets because of the President's visit, but when his car left they came out. Edith was indignant that army regulations had kept them out of sight. Her husband liked to meet the people wherever he went and to greet soldiers in any setting. He spoke to them briefly as they gathered around the cars.

Proceeding to the spot at which Big Bertha had come within firing range of Paris, Edith studied the huge concrete base on which it had rested. A narrow-gauge railroad designed to carry ammunition had once been cleverly camouflaged in a woodland setting, but the surrounding vegetation was dead now from the rush of flame that had darted from the monster gun.

On the way home to Paris that night the President was thoughtful and depressed. In the morning he would be fighting the battle of Fiume again, and Edith found time to write one of her engaging letters to Altrude Grayson. Back in Washington, hating to be away from the center of things, Altrude was one of the better informed Washingtonians on the Paris scene. Cary's letters were like a daily narrative, and with what she heard from the Bollings in the capital and Edith's lively letters, she felt only one step away from the haunts that she and Edith had enjoyed a few years earlier. Now she stunned them all with the birth of a second son. It was only March but during their brief trip home she had fooled them with her elegant costuming and delicate air.

"This has taken my breath away—because I thought May would be the time. You looked so trim & lovely that I could not believe it was true even when I read the cable," Edith wrote.

Cary had come in with a cablegram announcing the news and he was "just like a balloon, with the string out." Paris, he said, had never looked so beautiful to him before. The newborn son was named Cary Travers Grayson after his father. Both Edith and the President cheered Altrude with their comments on her husband. The President wrote to her from Paris on March 26, 1919, immediately after the birth of the new baby, saying that in Paris he had viewed the admiral at closer range and more intimately than ever before, and he admired him more than ever.

With full knowledge that Dr. Grayson took constant care of him, Wilson continued writing in the third person: "The simple fact that the President is the world's leader during these grave and critical times—and this is brought very forcibly before you over here—makes one realize more than the Admiral himself can possibly realize just what responsibilities are resting upon him. In many ways he is just as wonderful as the President—and when I say this I am saying it in all sincerity."

From the time of their arrival in Europe, Edith had made a point of indicating to Cary the places she and Altrude had visited, amusing him with many anecdotes. "How little we thought in those days of my returning with *your* husband to say nothing of all the other wonderful things that have happened," she wrote.

In a letter written on January 11, and addressed to "My Dearest Little Girl," she added her own tribute to Dr. Grayson. "I don't know how it would be without him. He takes all of everyone's troubles and stands between us and complaints of all & various sorts. He is always on hand to help and is a constant joy. I feel we are robbing you—but I know you are willing."

167

And again, as the pressures heightened and there were fresh complications involving the men close to the President, Edith wrote that "he and I hold indignation meetings often over things that are said and done by the very people we would have a right to expect support from and we blow off steam and feel better afterwards."

Dr. Grayson and Colonel House were not always in accord. Both men caught all the American gossip that swirled around the President at this time. Edith reported to Altrude on the people from home whom both knew. Richard Patterson, who had been Altrude's most persistent suitor in Washington before she had chosen Cary Grayson, was now running things at the Crillon since it had been taken over by the American delegation. "If he had only been in charge in our poverty-stricken days when he was in love with you perhaps you would have loved him in very gratitude," Mrs. Wilson wrote, recalling the time that she and Altrude had run out of funds in Paris as they waited for money drafts from home.

Now, after the dreary days of the war, she reported to Trudie that "Paris seems to be coming into its own again." The early flower and fruit trees were in blossom in the Bois and "long rows of *chairs*" were appearing along the streets. The café spirit was alight again and Americans seemed to be everywhere. She told of dinners given at Les États-Unis for the Houses, the Sharps of the American Embassy, and Lord Robert Cecil; of having Elizabeth Asquith to lunch and finding her a "brilliant little creature" and much less abrasive than Margot; of dining with Mrs. Martha Brower, Helen Bones' sister as she headed for Verdun to continue her YMCA work.

With her intense love of family, Edith devoured Altrude's letters, as she did those coming from her mother, Bertha, and Randolph. "There is really nothing of interest to write, for you all hold the center of the stage—I am living the life of a recluse and see no one," Altrude wrote on January 30 before the birth of Cary. But Mrs. Bolling had taken her for a drive on the nurse's day off and she told of little Gordon's enjoyment of his limousine ride. He had already developed a "champagne appetite and greatly prefers a Pierce Arrow to a baby carriage," she wrote, knowing how much Edith enjoyed anecdotes about the children.

Woodrow's nights had now become restless; he was coughing and sleeping intermittently. Plagued by his chronic digestive troubles and a touch of neuritis, the stress in Paris had magnified all his ills. For lack of time he had abandoned the strict health regime that Dr. Grayson had worked out for him, with Edith's help. He had to forgo the exercise that was so essential to his well-being as he worked at all hours of the day and night, and sometimes even on Sunday.

"There was the hurry and flurry of official engagements," Dr. Grayson pointed out. "He met most of the important people in Europe. He addressed crowds such as no man had ever faced before. His emotions were torn by sights of pain and sorrow everywhere, in the devastated regions and in the hospitals. . . . Duty for him was superior to his health."

The collapse that Dr. Grayson had feared and had tried to prevent came on April 3, 1919, when President Wilson had a thrombosis, a prelude to the later stroke that ended his career. It came at a critical moment in the affairs of the Peace Conference and the severity of his collapse was blurred by the official announcement that he had influenza. The world heard only that President Wilson was incapacitated for a few days, but the gossip in Paris spread like wildfire, with his enemies giving scandalous implications to his sudden collapse. Edith and Dr. Grayson mounted guard, and after a few days in bed and stern self-discipline he improved. Although neither one approved, the Council of Four, with Colonel House taking the President's place, continued to meet in the room adjoining his bedroom, so that without leaving his bed he could keep in touch with the proceedings. It was a tense moment at Versailles, with Orlando threatening to withdraw the Italian delegation and the French pushing the Saar issue to the limit.

Baker saw the President on the first day he was up. He was in his study, fully dressed, but he looked thin and pale, with hollow cheeks, which emphasized the "extraordinary size and luminosity of his eyes"—a condition that worried Edith, too, as she watched every move attentively and stayed close to his side. After listening to him, Baker decided that his illness had hardened him in his determination to bring things to a head and to force a showdown. There would be no more dragging of feet, no further indecision on his part. The situation had become worse during his absence and he had decided to return home unless his colleagues capitulated on the central issues. He stag-

169

gered them all when he ordered the *George Washington,* then being repaired in Brooklyn, to sail for Brest immediately. He would withdraw the delegation and return to America.

Clemenceau suggested that this was a bluff, but the effect of the President's announcement was apparent at once. His French critics quieted down; the press attacks were modified, and the leaders showed more disposition to settle the basic issues. President Wilson compromised on the Saar, but his steadfast refusal to let Italy have Fiume, which he insisted belonged by right of nationality to the new Yugoslav state, precipitated a crisis with Orlando.

When Orlando summoned a train and abandoned the Conference, the histrionics were so marked that Mrs. Wilson compared them to a showy scene from an Italian opera. Orlando insisted that President Wilson had gone over the heads of the Italian delegates and had appealed to the people.

In Italy the pictures of Woodrow Wilson that had been worshiped a few weeks earlier, were torn down, and the candles that had burned in front of them were extinguished.

But with the Treaty of Versailles well on its way to completion the Italian government did not applaud Orlando's act. The efforts of Clemenceau and Lloyd George to get President Wilson to relent on Fiume were fruitless and, in hangdog fashion, plump, excitable Signor Orlando finally returned. Lloyd George and Clemenceau were in the study with Wilson and Lloyd George was denouncing him as a quitter when Orlando was ushered in. Woodrow told Edith that night that he felt sorry for Orlando, whom he really liked and who had been helpful to him on many Italian issues outside of Fiume, so he tried to greet him casually.

Orlando knew only a few phrases of English, so was always at a loss with mercurial Lloyd George and sharp-witted Clemenceau. He inquired innocently, "What subject are you met to discuss this morning?" And President Wilson wryly replied, "Well, Mr. Orlando, we are still trying to get Fiume on the map." At this point the Italian walked to the window, pressed his face against the glass, and burst into tears. The President led him to his usual chair and dried his tears as if he were a little boy. He knew the Italian had taken a harsh drubbing where it counted.

170

## Pocahontas: An Indian Princess

A basket of orchids with Orlando's card attached reached Edith, but she was less forgiving than the President, knowing what his defection had meant to her husband. Both Japan and Belgium had considered bolting after Orlando's flamboyant gesture. But it did some good, too, for the Shantung settlement was made by the Council of Three with the Japanese in full agreement. This had been one of the President's bitterest fights. Finally the Japanese delegates made a voluntary agreement to give back the Shantung Peninsula in full sovereignty to China, retaining the economic privileges granted to Germany, and the right to establish a settlement at Tsingtao. It was a compromise, and the Chinese, disappointed, refused to sign the Treaty.

Edith was wrapped up in the difficulties over Fiume and Shantung during what seemed to her to be the terrible month of April, when the Queen of Rumania appeared, demanding attention. Queen Marie had written to Edith on March 11, saying that Loie Fuller, the American dancer, had told her of the "loving kindness you have shown for my far off little country. . . . Were I a thousand Queens instead of one I could not alleviate a tithe of the misery thrust upon us in our crucifixion. Our hope for liberty would have been turned to despair but for a glorious message from your husband to mine. It gave us more than hope, it gave us life and future liberty."

On her arrival at the Ritz Hotel in April, Queen Marie sent a message that she would like to receive the President and Mrs. Wilson as soon as possible. They found her looking beautiful in a filmy gray dress that flattered her hair and eyes. With much feminine *panache* she presented her arguments to the President, who listened attentively while Edith looked on with some degree of skepticism. The Queen emphasized the menace of Russia's proximity to her own little country. She saw danger in the new Russian laws on sex and other familial issues. Her frankness was startling to Edith and after a time the President told her that all her claims on behalf of Rumania had reached him before he left the United States and had been thoroughly considered at the Conference. Her Prime Minister, M. Bratianu, he said, had faithfully presented Rumania's case.

Edith found it all too much of a grandstand play and, studying Woodrow's face, she saw that his jaw was set and that "this beautiful woman had met one man whom she had failed to charm." But they had not

171

finished with the Queen, who was being much discussed by the diplomatic set in Paris. She insisted that they dine with her, until Edith assured her that they neither dined nor lunched out, but she invited the Queen to Les États-Unis for lunch. She was accompanied by her two daughters, one of whom later became Queen of Greece and the other of Yugoslavia. The princesses were shy and quiet but the Infanta Eulalia, seated beside Edith, struck her as being clever and attractive. The Queen had moved the seating arrangements to suit herself.

Things went well, with Dr. Grayson, Colonel Harts, Miss Benham, and two young aides for the princesses easing the strain. The President was in high good humor after lunch and they all discussed political affairs, with the Queen again expounding her views at length.

It was difficult for anyone to upstage Edith, who was just as stately in her bearing as the Queen and able to hold her own in any discussion. She relented slightly when she met Queen Marie later at the Grand Palais, which was being used for workers teaching the mutilated and the blind to find their way back to life. "She hailed me sweetly and graciously and I could not suppress an admission to myself that her beauty made her seem an ideal queen."

Immediately after the President's collapse, and in the midst of all his other worries during April, a crisis developed where Colonel House was concerned, with Edith the pivotal factor in a serious break in their relations. She felt that the colonel had gone too far in the usurpation of her husband's power and had encouraged the impression that he, more than Woodrow Wilson, was the guiding hand for America in the peace negotiations. Much of the gossip in official circles reached Edith's ears, and she did not like any jeering at her husband's expense. Colonel House ran a powerful establishment of his own. He had strong social links with the English and had easy access to the press. He made no secret of the fact that he could influence Henry Wickham Steed, who had just become editor of the *Times* of London. He also wrote editorials for the Paris edition of *The Daily Mail*, and he had a reputation for sensationalism.

Edith blazed with anger when she was shown a *Times* story from Paris, dated April 7, 1919. It was called "*The Mills of Peace.*" Clearly it was a barefaced panegyric for Colonel House and a slap at Woodrow Wilson. "If there is now a chance that the Conference may be hauled back from the brink of failure on to relatively safe ground, it is mainly due to the efforts of Colonel House and to the salutary effect of the feeling that the Allied peoples are becoming seriously alarmed at the secret manipulation of their chief representatives."

The article further suggested that President Wilson should have stayed in America and let Colonel House, with all his savoir-faire and conciliatory temperament, complete negotiations. By chance Colonel House called at Les États-Unis that day and was waylaid by Edith. She towered over him with the clipping in her hand and said, "If you are such a good friend of Mr. Steed, perhaps you can explain this."

Colonel House was dumbfounded. He read it swiftly and said that he had not seen it. Word came that the President was ready to see him, so he hurried away, saying that he would explain later. But he did not return to explain, and the matter died, except in Edith's feeling about him. She believed that he had let her husband down on several counts —in agreeing to the exclusion of the League from the Treaty; in leaving out the "freedom of the seas" clause from the armistice terms favored by the President, and in backing Orlando on the Fiume issue.

The President was much less concerned than his wife about the Steed incident, but he no longer trusted the colonel, and their social relations almost ceased. The Peace Conference brought into high relief the growing tide of discord that had existed ever since Edith Bolling Wilson had entered Woodrow Wilson's life. At this time the colonel accepted responsibility for some of his own tactlessness. He wrote in his diary that he had taken too many relatives and friends with him to Paris and that perhaps some of them had gone too far in emphasizing his role.

Mrs. Emilie "Lulie" House was a woman of charm and social experience, and the Houses entertained lavishly while the Conference lasted. This was contrary to President Wilson's conception of his mission, for he and Edith were committed to a totally impersonal way of life. They neither entertained to any extent nor accepted invitations. Miss Benham, on the other hand, moved about with complete independence, attending dinner parties given by the Houses and one in particular for Paderewski. Mrs. Whitelaw Reid was present, and Miss Benham described her as a "handsome old lady encrusted in diamonds, but genuine—her character as well as the jewels."

Miss Benham was well aware that the Wilsons would never miss her, and she made a diary entry in March, 1919, that before going out to a dinner she stopped in to say goodnight to the President and Mrs. Wilson. As usual they were playing solitaire—"his panacea for rest to his mind."

He laughed and said, "I am afraid you will always think of me as an amiable old gentleman playing solitaire."

The social game was of little concern to Edith during these hectic days, but an incident that amused them was the way in which she used her Indian ancestry to offset the snobbishness of one of France's most revered aristocrats, the Duchesse de Rohan. Although most of the French notables from the Faubourg St. Germain had paid courtesy calls on the President and Mrs. Wilson when they first arrived, the duchess had held off, and when M. C. Vesnitch, the Serbian Minister, asked her if she had met the Wilsons, she said she had not. She was sick of hearing about them and she assumed that Mrs. Wilson, being democratic, must therefore be lacking in social background. She had no wish to meet her.

But the Serbian Minister drew from his pocket a clipping from an American newspaper about Mrs. Wilson and impressed on the duchess the fact that she was descended from Princess Pocahontas, founder of the native aristocracy of America, and a sparkling figure at the British Court of James I. Moreover, her mother, Mrs. Bolling, lived at the Hotel Powhatan, freely translated by fun-loving Edith as the Castle Powhatan. The Pocahontas story amused the President but he warned her against playing any tricks on so noted a French lady until he had completed his mission.

Although her Indian inheritance had not attracted much attention before her marriage, the Bolling family had always been proud of their descent from Pocahontas and John Rolfe, two names representing one of the legendary romances of colonial days. After saving Captain John Smith from execution the Indian maiden had married Rolfe and he had taken her to England. She was presented at the court of James I by Lord and Lady Delaware. As first Secretary of the Colony and a gentleman of fine manners and appearance, Rolfe was welcomed everywhere and the girl he had married in Jamestown in 1614 spread a nove charm of her own in royal circles. She died at Gravesend in 1617.

Pocahontas was the daughter of King Powhatan, and her grand-daughter, Jane Rolfe, married Colonel Ronert Bolling. Edith Bolling was a direct descendant of this union in the seventh degree. The Bollings of both sexes showed this inheritance in a number of ways. The men had aquiline noses, straight brows, dark hair, and a love of the woods. Mrs. Wilson could always spot an Indian in any gathering. She cherished her inheritance and welcomed the letters that they wrote to her at the time of her marriage.

The two women soon met formally at a luncheon for Mrs. Wilson at the American Embassy. The guests were mostly members of the French aristocracy, and she was startled when the princess curtsied to her formally as if she were of royal blood. The princess then said that she wanted to give a dinner for President Wilson and Edith, but was told that they attended official functions only, because of the pressure of work. Edith was finally won by her invitation to visit the house that she had turned into a hospital for the wounded after her only son was killed in the war.

# 15. *Jubilant at Versailles*

Edith Wilson waited with an unaccustomed sense of tension for the drama at Versailles. At eleven A.M. and four P.M. every day her temporary home was visited by men arriving for conferences with the President, as he and his colleagues threshed out the final phases of the Treaty. She was on the sidelines while this was going on, and there was not the usual time for consultation.

With her need always to be busy she turned to a typewriter that she sometimes used, but with less success than the President had with his Hammond. This seemed a good time to improve her technique, and it was calming, too. She used it for a note sent to Altrude on May 5, 1919:

"My dearest Trudie from Miss Ede. Woodrow works practically all of every day, and most every evening. I have given up every sort of entertainment except the highly exciting one of having people to tea."

She then proceeded to describe her adventures on May Day, which had come and gone without the excitement that had been expected. Paris was uncannily quiet when she drove to the Quai d'Orsay with the President, leaving him there for a conference. Only soldiers were in sight, since the city was prepared for something more than the usual May Day unrest. All over Europe rioting and destruction prevailed, and no one expected Paris to be at peace on the workers' day.

Guards manned the bridges over the Seine and piles of sandbags were arranged as barricades. The Métro and street railways had been halted. Parisians had been advised to stay indoors, and American soldiers were ordered off the streets. A demonstration in the Place de la Concorde had been predicted but did not materialize.

Edith was restless and decided that she could not stay indoors with the sunshine and the May blossoms at their best, so after returning from the Quai she picked up Miss Benham and they drove to the deserted Bois. Never stopping to think of any danger, Edith sent the car back and they walked home, swinging along with full enjoyment of the flowers, the birds, and the green freshness of spring.

That night she gave the President her usual lively account of her day's doings, but he was surprised to hear that she and Miss Benham had been so reckless. There had been rioting in different parts of the city and loss of life. He told her at once about the German commissioners, who had just arrived and were under heavy guard at the Hôtel des Réservoirs in Versailles. They resented being held as if they were prisoners and two days later when the Treaty was formally laid before them at the Trianon Palace, they were appalled by the terms. They were allowed fifteen days to study the document after they pleaded for milder terms, particularly where the indemnities were concerned. President Wilson, according to his wife, believed that Britain and France had gone too far in this respect. The delegation asked for more time to consider; then they were called back to Germany and were later replaced by a new set of commissioners.

Edith had an infected foot at the end of May and she was on crutches when she went with the President to Suresnes for his Memorial Day speech. On the drive out he was restless and preoccupied, his usual mood before delivering a speech. This occasion had special meaning for the man who hated war. The endless rows of crosses in the cemetery marked the graves of men who had died at Château-Thierry. For the occasion they were intertwined by garlands of flowers with small American flags fluttering among them. On the hillside behind the crosses a gathering of American soldiers awaited Wilson's arrival, many of them bearing the scars of war.

Seated in the car, Edith could see and hear the President as he stood on a platform in the center of the cemetery and gave one of his most affecting speeches. He was not the man who had seemed so young and virile to her as he received his degree at the Sorbonne some months earlier. The intervening stress, his illness, his trip back to America, had all taken their toll, and she noted how white his hair had become.

With the negotiations nearing an end, a gala performance of *Faust* was staged at the Opera House for President and Mrs. Wilson. Edith, a music lover, looked forward to this. The house was packed and there was an imposing turnout of the famous, the rich, and the fashionable. She was conscious of the blaze of jewels as she and the President entered their box, which was draped with the Stars and Stripes and the Tricolor. Between the acts the audience rose *en masse* and focused their opera glasses directly on the Wilsons. They moved to the foyer, where the scrutiny became even more intense. Edith had never known anything like it, although she was accustomed to being stared at. She was glad to go to the dressing rooms with Henry White, who was full of good stories about the ways of the ballet when he was a young attaché at the American Embassy.

While the haggling was going on with the second German delegation, the President and Edith took a whirlwind trip through Belgium. It was unforgettable for the devastation they saw, the speed with which they traveled, and the warm relationship they established with tall, handsome King Albert, whom they had welcomed in Paris, and tiny, white-robed Queen Elizabeth, who was worshiped by the Belgian people for her war work. As the King and Queen arrived by plane to welcome them at the frontier, the American national anthem was played, Bel-

177

gian and American flags flew together, and there were official saluta-
tions before the entire party started on their automobile tour of the
war-ravaged nation.

President Wilson and King Albert rode in the first car, the Queen and
Edith in the second, with the royal coat of arms on the door. The Secret Service detail rode behind, and a long cavalcade of open touring
cars provided by the United States Army carried the other members of
the party and the press. In the Wilson party were Margaret Wilson,
Edith Benham, Dr. Grayson, Herbert Hoover, Bernard Baruch, Norman Davis, and Vance McCormick.

They drove at breathtaking speed over war-torn roads, with clouds
of dust enveloping the passengers in the open cars. They were cheered
and pelted with flowers as they drove through decimated village
streets. They were greeted by town officials and toasted in the midst of
ruins. Edith longed to give her champagne to the sad-faced women
who stood on the fringes of the gatherings, with tiny American flags in
their hands.

At one of the first stops, Margaret, choking from dust in her open
car, asked if she might ride with Edith and the Queen. She was assigned a low jump seat, from which she fell several times as they drove
at high speed. Two huge bouquets of flowers that arrived with her
threw the Queen into paroxysms of sneezing, for she was allergic to
roses and dust. She kept bowing to the public while totally unable to
talk. Their drive became a nightmare of sneezes, streaming eyes, and
malaise, with Edith trying to help her in every way she could. The
Queen became so ill that it was a relief to stop for lunch, which was
served under a huge white canvas tent close to what had once been a
flourishing village. It was now wasteland with poppies blowing in the
Rupert Brooke tradition. The devastation in Flanders was worse than
anything they had seen.

Edith was touched and amazed at every stop to see the children run
at them with welcoming faces and little American flags. George Creel
had blitzed the region with these. But all too many shrank in the shadows, their faces pinched, their clothes in tatters. These were painful
sights for the President and he became white and silent as the day
advanced. Zeebrugge, where they had a guided tour of the famous
mole, was of intense interest to Edith, with her memories of the sub-

marine warfare in which America had been so deeply involved. They moved on to Ostend, which had none of the old gaiety she had seen on her travels with Altrude. But it was in better order than other places they visited.

After a glimpse of the peaceful waterways of Bruges, they left their cars and took a train to Brussels. The red carpet treatment resumed there but the huge palace was completely disorganized. The Germans had stripped it of everything and there had not been time for restoration. The King and Queen were living in the country and came in only for the President's visit.

After a formal luncheon given by the American minister, Brand Whitlock, and attended by the King and Queen, they proceeded to the Hôtel de Ville where the freedom of the city was conferred on the President. Addressing Parliament afterward he announced that he would recommend to Congress the appointment of Whitlock as the first American ambassador to Belgium, thus emphasizing the importance of this small nation.

Woodrow Wilson drew worldwide attention on this trip when he visited Malines and met Cardinal Mercier, the courageous churchman of the war years. In his crimson robes, with a large gold cross swinging around his neck, he welcomed them on the palace steps and served them tea in a long room with shattered mirrors. They saw the sky through a great hole made in the vaulted roof by a German bomb.

The cardinal accompanied the Presidential party to Louvain, where they were speechless when they saw the remains of the historic library. The shell-spattered stone walls still stood, and flowers had been spread to conceal the wreckage. They sat in high-backed chairs on a little platform at one end of what had once been the great entrance hall. As book lovers they were profoundly moved by the devastation.

The hurried tour of Belgium ended with a state dinner at the palace. President Wilson appeared on the palace balcony with the King. Edith was much admired by the side of their beloved Queen Elizabeth. It was a trip that had long been planned and they missed little of the devastation, but the President had to hurry back to Paris as the negotiations with the German commissioners climaxed. They had agreed to sign, and none too soon, since the French, British, and American troops on the Rhine were under orders to march to Berlin if they did not give in.

179

## Power with Grace

The signing of the Treaty was set for three o'clock on June 28, 1919, and the Wilsons planned to leave at once for home. The day dawned bright and clear, and all over Paris flags flew, soldiers patrolled the streets, and an endless procession of cars headed for Versailles. The President seemed relaxed as he prepared for the final ordeal. Before leaving the house he gave Edith a beaded bag in blue and gray that he had ordered from an old lady in Versailles. It was designed to match Edith's gray gown and hat. His orchids had come earlier in the morning and she tucked them into place but put the single rosebud he offered her as a special token of the day into the bag, and kept it until it crumbled into dust.

"I love to think of my husband as he looked that day," Edith wrote, "for already the sense of freedom from that unremitting labor was relaxing the look of strain, and the happy thought of going home made him radiate content."

Edith, Margaret Wilson, and Edith Benham, along with other members of their party, settled in their cars before the President's automobile, flag flying, rushed past. Then the procession followed. Policemen were spaced along the road to Versailles, but when they reached the Avenue de Paris at Versailles, a double line of French cavalry in horizon blue with banners on their lances mounted guard. A company of the picturesque Garde Républicaine lined the staircase leading up to the Hall of Mirrors. But Edith, greeted on all sides as she arrived, barely noticed her surroundings as she went upstairs with Margaret Wilson and Edith Benham. The demand for seats had been so overwhelming that many were packed into a room adjoining the Hall of Mirrors and consequently saw nothing of the actual ceremony.

Although Edith, Mrs. House, and Mrs. Lansing had front seats in the American section, they saw none too well, since the chairs and benches were arranged on either side of the aisle on a level, and they had to look up to the raised platform where the ceremony took place. Edith sat on a backless bench until someone brought her an armchair. "Beside her stood Admiral Grayson, who gleamed, a full-panoplied Apollo on guard, with his hand on her chair of state," William Allen White observed in his high-powered style.

The President joined the other members of the American commission in the room from which each group entered the Hall of Mirrors. As the doors opened and the chattering ceased, Clemenceau came first.

Then came Woodrow Wilson with his small retinue, looking "alert and alive," Edith decided. He smiled at her in passing. Henry White stopped and faced her, making a little bow.

When all the commissioners had taken their places except the Germans, the audience waited expectantly. A bugle sounded and they were led in. Their appearance caused a stir and although they bore themselves with a certain dignity Edith noticed that their legs shook as they sat down, reminding her of "prisoners before the bar of justice."

While the President and the other Americans signed, Edith and her companions rose to watch. The click of motion picture machines and cameras distracted Edith, and Mrs. House gave a little cry. "Please just let me stand long enough to see my lamb sign!"

The Germans signed amid less excitement.

Wilson later confided to his family that although he had signed "Woodrow" with ease he had difficulty adding "Wilson." It seemed ironic to the American delegation that all this should have happened in the baroque surroundings where the German Empire had been proclaimed in 1871.

The gold pen used was the work of a *poilu* and was a gift from Alsace-Lorraine. There were four documents to be signed: the Peace Treaty, the Convention covering Alsace-Lorraine, the Convention on the occupation of the Rhine territory, and the protocol recognizing the independence of Poland, an issue on which President Wilson had fought hard.

It was all over at three forty and the booming of cannon proclaimed that the Peace Treaty was at last a *fait accompli*. After the Germans left there was considerable scrambling and confusion. Order and dignity had dissolved and the President later told Edith that Clemenceau was so excited he forgot his instructions on where pictures were to be taken and led Orlando, Lloyd George, and himself straight into a surging crowd.

Clemenceau had invited the women for tea in the Senate room on another part of the grounds but Edith, watching the mob scene around her husband, decided to stay where she was. The fountains played, their spray like diamonds in the sunlight; the horns of the Americans' cars made a ceaseless din; bells rang; people bustled around getting autographs and saying good-bye.

The President had to stay for one more formality, so Edith and Miss

Benham returned home to find the staff in high spirits, with everything packed for their departure. But another evening's entertainment lay ahead of them before leaving for Brest. The Poincarés had invited them to the Élysée Palace for a farewell reception and, rushed though they were, there was no escape.

They dined quietly at Les États-Unis and Lloyd George came in to say good-bye. In one of his graceful moments he told the President that he could congratulate himself not only on the Treaty but also on drawing England and America closer together than they had ever been before. All was goodwill when they reached the palace and the Poincarés welcomed them as cordially as if the mutual antagonism that had developed between France and America in the intervening seven months had never existed. The great drawing room of the palace was filled with men and women of all nations, from Americans in khaki to turbaned Sikhs. Decorations and medals abounded. The unadorned President and his fellow commissioners mingled unostentatiously with the picturesque assemblage. Woodrow Wilson seemed to William Allen White to be the man apart, the figure on the mountain who found himself all alone at the end. Anger still burned in some of the men around him. But Edith blended smoothly into the scene.

Not to be outdone by the fashionable Parisian women, she wore a stunning new gown from Worth's, a heavy black charmeuse seductively draped around her figure in the tight lines of the moment, and ending in a fishtail train. From the waist up it was made of sequins, shading from gun metal through various lighter shades of gray and ending in white at her low shoulder-line. Worth had designed a circlet of sequins and rhinestones for her hair, and she wore the diamond pin with doves of peace given her by the City of Paris. A huge fan of shaded gray feathers completed a costume much admired at the time.

The reception was going full tilt when the Wilsons slipped away for their final moments at Les États-Unis, to which they had become attached in spite of the stress and strain. The sense of power in her husband's hands had made a deep impression on Edith, and there had been much enjoyment in the social role. The boulevards were still alive with people after the day's excitement, and a crowd had gathered again at the station, where for the last time they went through the official round of red carpet, waving palms, soldiers to inspect, and sheaves of flowers for the First Lady.

## Jubilant at Versailles

Edith was not without regrets as the lights of Paris faded. She stood with Woodrow at a train window, silent and absorbed. Finally he turned to her and said that all was finished but no one was satisfied —"which makes me hope we have made a just peace; but it is all on the lap of the gods."

David Lawrence, a witness, wrote that Wilson had "conceded, yielded, demurred and deferred on points that might break up the Conference." Stung by the criticism that he had compromised too much, he was adamant in the last days of the Conference, siding with the French in their insistence that the Germans be compelled to sign without modification the terms that had been proposed. This led to differences of opinion in his own mission, with some of his advisers threatening to resign. All were convinced that there had been a great change in Woodrow Wilson since he had had his mysterious illness in April.

Now the French phase was over; the problem of ratification would begin. At Brest their spirits rose when they saw the *George Washington* in the harbor, with the homeward-bound pennant flying. Edith, as always, stood by the President's side as the ship got under way, a salute was fired, and he stood on the bridge with bared head while a band played "The Star-Spangled Banner."

He rested and slept for the first four days but again the sea air toned him up and, as Miss Benham put it, "Mrs. Wilson hauls him out every day to walk, which he despises, but does meekly." On July 4 he addressed the soldiers returning home on their ship, and he responded to an appeal from the French brides on board to have their transportation and other technical difficulties cleared up.

He was caught up again in a whirl of officialdom when a transport met them at sea with mail pouches and papers from the White House. The President was coping with this when they reached Sandy Hook and sighted the usual escort of destroyers. Vice President Marshall, Cabinet members, and Governor Alfred E. Smith came on board to welcome them, and Edith was surrounded by friends.

Elusive as ever with the press, in spite of the story she could tell of her seven months in Paris, she held her peace and was glad to exchange the grandeur of palaces for the "simple dignity of the White House" on her return to Washington.

# 16. *The Long Nightmare*

PRESIDENT WILSON'S trip across the country in September, 1919, to urge ratification of the Treaty of Versailles and to throw light on the damaged image of the League of Nations, drew the crowds, applause, and headlines of a triumphal tour, particularly in the Far West. But he also found deep-rooted opposition and chilling indifference at various points along the way.

To Edith it was "one long nightmare," since only she and Dr. Grayson knew how close the President was to disaster as he sought to convert the unbelieving with logic and his own deep faith. The cost to himself was irreversible and she would always look back on the trip as a sacrificial gesture. His collapse close to Wichita and the cancellation of the rest of the tour presaged his total breakdown in the White House after his return. He traveled 8,000 miles in twenty-two days and delivered thirty-two major and eight minor addresses. Small farm groups clustered at stations heard him, as did great crowds in sweltering auditoriums.

Early in August he had decided to take his case to the country personally. Newton Baker, Josephus Daniels, and others close to him advised him not to try it because of his health. It was clear from his reception in Washington that it would be uphill work. Both Edith and Dr. Grayson sympathized with his desire to make this last stand before the issue went to the vote. He wanted to clear up the points that were not understood by the public, believing that the people would hear and understand, even if Congress failed him. In them he would find his final court of appeal.

"I cannot put my personal safety, my health, in the balance against my duty," he told Dr. Grayson, who had warned him that it might cost him his life. He would go, he said, with the look that Edith knew meant immovable resolution on her husband's part. Her own resistance ended at this point, knowing that the trip meant life or death to him. "I don't care if I die the next minute after the Treaty is ratified," he told Herman H. Kohlstaat, a Chicago editor.

Dr. Grayson insisted on a cancellation in August, when the heat was at its peak. He had played for time to get the President rested and relaxed before setting out. With golf and sleep there was some improvement but time was short. Edith made the best of things when they boarded their train at Union Station on a muggy September night. They had more than a hundred correspondents and photographers on board, ready to let the world know how Woodrow Wilson was faring every step of the way. Tumulty was the link between the *Mayflower,* which was the end car, and the press car, some distance away on an uncommonly long train. Edith found Tumulty's "explosive Irish wit" refreshing for the President. She did quite well at this herself, making a point of being her sprightliest as they relaxed in their private car, entertaining him with her stories and comments on the day's events, and coaxing him to eat the sandwiches provided for him late at night, since he rarely had food before he spoke.

The train ran on a tight schedule, making precise connections with visiting groups and slowing up now and again at whistle stops for talks from the back platform. Their route was arranged to reach the areas where the spirit of isolation was dominant. Many of the President's speeches were impromptu but the major ones were carefully aimed at the interests of the region in which he spoke. Edith adapted herself easily to the role she was called on to play, and shook off any concern about her own well-being with a brisk reminder that it was the President alone who counted. Although she stayed in the background, she was always close at hand when he needed her. As he stood in open cars, automatically raising his hat and smiling a little grimly from side to side, she rested her hand firmly against his back lest he lose his balance as the car moved.

Edith was a figure of considerable interest in her own right, although she had no wish to be singled out for attention. The President had insisted that the gravity of his mission precluded any semblance of holidaymaking. But she was feted and flattered and sometimes studied with cold, appraising eyes by critics of Woodrow Wilson and the League of Nations. In general, she was accepted with interest as a dignified and handsome First Lady who had enhanced the Presidential image abroad, as well as at home.

Edith Wilson's months in Europe, rich in experiences few American women had known, had sharpened her perceptions and heightened her skeptical approach to political affairs. She had shared in the birth of a new philosophy, and this period of triumph and of pain had deepened her understanding of Woodrow's ideals and his role in world politics. Now, as their train sped over the plains and she watched a shifting panorama of lakes, forests, and mountains, she was seeing her own country with fresh vision and a broadened outlook.

It was soon clear to her that the parades, banquets, receptions, speeches, endless handshaking, and friendly interchanges were draining away her husband's strength. His fatigue showed in irritability behind the scenes. As the momentum grew he swung between exhilaration and depression, with Edith following him all the way, rising to the high moments when he received ovations, and cheering him when, dripping wet from his exertions, he returned in a state bordering on collapse to the train or to the hotels where they spent some nights.

Through it all she gave their sparse quarters a homelike air, with flowers and cushions. Between stops Tumulty worked with him in a small compartment, while Edith knitted, read, and studied the flaming autumnal views as they sped through forest land.

Their first stop was at Columbus, Ohio, familiar ground to Woodrow Wilson, and here he gave what his wife called his "first impassioned appeal." But in general there was nothing impassioned about his speeches, and as they traveled westward Tumulty urged him to give them more fire and emotion. With cool logic the President explained and defended the League, and particularly the controversial Provision X, which he called the foundation stone of worldwide liberty. All through the Middle West he reminded his audiences that their isolation had ended, whether or not they accepted this fact. Inevitably they would have to play a vital role in world affairs—constructively through the League of Nations, or irresponsibly if they chose to stand alone. At the Coliseum in St. Louis he drove home the dangers of isolationism in one of his most thoughtful and effective speeches. Minneapolis, Kansas City, Des Moines, and St. Paul all received the message with varying degrees of enthusiasm. In Bismarck, South Dakota, which lacked an auditorium, he spoke in a huge tent pitched in a wheatfield. At most of the major stops he spoke several times, varying his text, putting tremendous effort into reaching the greatest number of people.

As the momentum grew and it became apparent that he was making an impression the Irreconcilables and Bitter Enders mounted their heaviest guns to counteract the message that was sinking in. Senator William E. Borah, Senator James A. Reed, and Senator Hiram Johnson followed him up with vigorous speeches against the League. This was manna for the correspondents, who publicized the battle according to the political leanings of their various papers. Woodrow Wilson kept hammering home the message that he spoke not as a Democrat, not as a Republican, but for all the people. At Omaha he said, "I can predict with absolute certainty that within another generation there will be another World War if the nations of the world do not concert the method by which to prevent it." And at San Diego he sounded another prophetic note when he said, "What the Germans used were toys as compared with what would be used in the next war."

Both he and Edith were pleased to see children crowding around. They called their dignified President "Woody." They were the generation who would have "to fight the final war, and in that final war . . . the very existence of civilization would be in the balance." At Billings, Montana, a small boy who lacked one of the flags being waved by his companions drew a dime from his pocket and handed it to the President as the train was pulling out. In one of his Tacoma speeches he mentioned the boy who had given him all that he had—the widow's mite. Five years after Woodrow Wilson's death his wife found a dime wrapped in paper that he had kept tucked in the inner pocket of a small change purse. She liked to think that this was the "widow's mite" that had been much publicized by reporters hungry for human interest material on this trip.

In the national press it all sounded better than it actually was, for the tension behind the scenes was becoming acute. Although convinced that he had gained ground ("I have caught the imagination of the people," the President told Edith), he began to show signs of serious physical decline as they climbed the Rockies on their way to Seattle. The dust, the altitude, the continual meetings, stirred up the asthmatic condition that had troubled him in Paris. He coughed and wheezed and had restless nights. But the worse he felt the more determined he was to fulfill all his engagements. Edith looked forward to Seattle where she hoped he might get some rest, but it turned into a nightmare of activity as he reviewed the Fleet and gave four major speeches in two days.

They were met by Secretary of the Navy Daniels and Mrs. Daniels, and the cheers came in waves as they drove through crowded streets to the dock. But the day darkened for Edith when she felt they were all imperiled in getting out to the flagship *Oregon* for the review. Admiral Hugh Rodman's barge, which was to have convoyed them, had not arrived, and a young and inexperienced aide commandeered a naval launch. The Presidential party, Mr. and Mrs. Daniels, the press and Secret Service men got aboard—a heavy load for so small a craft. It settled down to the gunwales and the officer in command, well aware of the importance of his passengers and shaken by the emergency, gave fast orders that led to a collision with a Navy whaleboat.

They seemed to be in danger of capsizing, but the President, an able seaman himself, refused to take this incident seriously. Edith was furious—not for herself, but because she felt that it was a perilous experience for the nation's Chief Executive. For once she showed her anger in public. In time she accepted the explanation that Admiral Rodman had not been notified of a change in the President's schedule. It was a bitter memory, however, and in her memoir Edith wrote, "Personally I would not have excused the officers who had endangered lives in this way, though the President did." Admiral Rodman was outraged when her book came out in serial form and denied the whole story as it was told by Edith.

All delays and mistakes were forgotten when the President reached the bridge of the *Oregon* with Daniels. Clouds of smoke billowed over the harbor as guns roared their salute from end to end of the long string of cruisers, destroyers, and other war craft. Watching him on the bridge and wondering how much he could stand, Edith saw that he had recovered his old seafaring look and seemed buoyant and young. As always, the sea stimulated him, and the irritation and fatigue he had shown disappeared. His eyes gleamed and his head no longer ached as he received his last salute from the Navy.

From the roof garden of their hotel that night they had another view of the Navy. They sat in darkness and studied the ships, blazing with lights as far as the eye could see. Each one was a sparkling showcase, silhouetted in nautical detail and gaily festooned. It was a dramatic and haunting scene. "It awed us both," Mrs. Wilson wrote and, remembering the effort that had gone into building up a Navy, she added, "Surely America should have been proud of such a sight." It stirred recollections of the magic day in New York before their marriage when the President reviewed a small and inadequate Navy. Since then the war had been fought, millions of men had died, strange new passions and conflicts had sprung to life, the League issue was in peril, and the man beside her seemed to Edith to be the great hope of the moment. He had spoken that night at the Hippodrome and he was still exhilarated. But one of his blinding headaches came on and he slept little.

When Mr. and Mrs. Daniels called in the morning they found that the exalted dreams of the night before had taken flight and Edith for once had trouble concealing her anxiety. Daniels saw that the President had given his last ounce of strength and was in a perilous state. Within two days he had spoken to wildly enthusiastic crowds at the Stadium and Armory in Tacoma, and at the Hippodrome and Arena in Seattle. But he went on to Portland, Oregon, and made two speeches before heading for Oakland and San Francisco. Here Edith was surrounded by some of the smartest and most sophisticated women in the country, but she had little time to think about herself as things went from bad to worse with her husband. His schedule in southern California dismayed her.

As they traveled on to San Diego and Los Angeles she and Dr. Grayson did their best to protect him from the crowds that gathered at every station, and the welcoming committees. A Sunday of rest was planned for Los Angeles, but the President had set aside time to have Mrs. George Hulbert (the former Mrs. Peck) for lunch. There was much interest in this encounter, with its echoes from the past. Edith said she was glad to have her because of the "work scandalmongers had done to make an intrigue of that friendship." In this way she would "show her disdain for such slander."

Mrs. Peck was living in a tiny rose-embowered cottage on the outskirts of town and was badly off. She arrived by streetcar and was taken to the Wilsons by Dr. Grayson. The encounter was not without its painful moments for both women. They were meeting for the first time, although Mrs. Peck had figured so significantly in the life of Woodrow Wilson.

In their books each wrote of the other with restraint. Edith described Mrs. Hulbert as a "faded, good-looking woman who was absorbed in an only son." Mrs. Hulbert viewed Edith Wilson as "Junoesque but handsome, with a charming smile that revealed her strong white teeth."

The President greeted her as an old friend and listened attentively to a vivacious monologue on her troubles. She told of having been persecuted by his enemies, of dropping out of sight and selling encyclopedias from door to door, of working in films as an extra, of struggling to do everything she could for her delicate son. Edith could see that the President was becoming upset as he listened to her. She tried to check her with a jesting comment that offended Mrs. Hulbert and sparks flew briefly between the two women. But the President calmed things down by discussing his tour.

Edith was desperately anxious for Woodrow to get the nap and drive that he needed, but politicians kept dropping in to see him, and still Mrs. Hulbert stayed on. Dr. Grayson tried to break things up by urging the President to come out and talk to a waiting crowd, and Edith was invited to meet a women's group.

From her own troubles Mrs. Hulbert turned to her son's, which were physical and severe. The President looked rather helplessly at Edith and asked her if there was anything they could do. But Mrs. Hulbert spoke up quickly. "Not for me. I'm all right. Perhaps for my son." The President jotted down the youth's address on a little pad.

Darkness had fallen when Edith ordered Mrs. Hulbert's cloak and took her to the elevator. The President accompanied her as far as the hall and said a friendly good-bye. It had been a difficult afternoon but not an emotional one; his thoughts were all on his tour, and the hotel was ringed with people clamoring for his attention. "Poor woman, she did not understand," Edith said.

"The elevator quickly dropped me out of the life of my friend Woodrow Wilson forever," Mrs. Hulbert later wrote, and a few days after their meeting she learned that the man whose mind she had described as a "rod of steel—polished, flashing, inflexible, true," had collapsed and was being rushed back to Washington. She was not surprised after watching him at the Hotel Alexandria.

Things went from bad to worse as the train turned homeward, zigzagging north and east. They stopped briefly at Reno, where the waiting crowd demanded a glimpse of Mrs. Wilson. "Here is the best part of this traveling show," said the President as she joined him and smiled

190

at the upturned faces. There were shouts of laughter in which she joined when a man in the crowd solemnly announced, "I am very much pleased with your better half."

Edith turned to her husband with a mischievous look but she was in a state of acute anxiety. She was hiding it from everyone but Dr. Grayson, and most of all from her husband, who seemed to be reeling with uncertainty. Too often she found him leaning his head against a chair in front of him, trying to assemble his thoughts and surmount his raging headaches.

Tumulty, watching Edith in these anxious days, wrote that in the "smiling face she turned none could have detected a trace of the anxiety that was haunting her . . . she met the mounting throngs with the same powerful dignity and radiant friendly smile with which she had captivated the people of England, France, Italy and Belgium."

They motored through little desert towns on their way to a rousing welcome in Ogden. In a daze of heat and anxiety Edith caught fleeting glimpses of Indian women and singing children, of weathered faces and small boys clinging to telegraph poles—the old familiar picture. Every move was recorded in the national and local press, and big headlines greeted them at every stop, but the press were suspicious and things were becoming uneasy on the train.

Exhausted though he was, the President gave one of his longest speeches to the large crowd assembled in the Tabernacle at Salt Lake City. The doors were locked at six P.M. with 15,000 people inside and hundreds more clamoring to get in. The police had to clear the way for the President and Mrs. Wilson, who reeled a little as they walked into the suffocating temple. The air reeked and was stifling. The rostrum was high and completely airless. Edith turned pale and Siegrid, her maid, thinking she was going to faint, plied her with smelling salts. Borrowing a handkerchief from a Secret Service man, Edith soaked it in the lavender salts and sent it to her husband as he stood dripping wet before the Mormons. She knew that he had one of his blinding headaches and his asthma was severe that night.

When they reached Cheyenne the President no longer made any pretense of not feeling ill. He moved feebly and his sweat-soaked shirts were being changed constantly, but he held his ground until they reached Denver.

The city blazed with welcoming lights and the streets were jammed.

191

He went to the State Capitol grounds to greet a big gathering of children, and then he spoke at the City Auditorium, shouting to make himself heard. Edith and Dr. Grayson implored him to stay and rest at the hotel for a few days. Again he resisted their advice but promised Edith that they would go on a real holiday when they got back to Washington.

He had made up his mind not to visit the fairgrounds when he got to Pueblo but the crowd was so eager to have him that he rode around, wearily lifting his brown fedora into the air. When he reached the auditorium to make his speech in the afternoon he stumbled as he was going in. Colonel Starling thought he would fall and for once he was not too proud to accept assistance in public. Edith was sick with concern but hung on to her composure, smiling and shaking hands.

The President had warned the press that his speech would be a brief one, but it turned into the most affecting address of the tour—or perhaps the aftermath gave it a special aura. This time he spoke of the war dead in emotional terms and recalled his visit to the cemetery at Suresnes on Decoration Day, 1919. For a moment he stumbled and the press watched closely, thinking that he was about to break down. "The world will not allow Germany—" he was saying when he stopped in his tracks, but he quickly recovered and went on with greater strength than he had shown in any of his more recent talks.

He spoke of the wooden crosses, of his own role in sending these men overseas, of the fact that "France was free and the world was free because America had come." He expressed the wish that the men opposing the League might see that spot and feel their moral obligation not to abandon the dead or the men who came home. He paid tribute to the mothers who had lost their sons in battle: "Why should they weep upon my hand and call down the blessings of God upon me? . . . Because they believe that their boys died for something that vastly transcends any of the immediate and palpable objects of the war."

It was an emotional speech for Woodrow Wilson to make and tears flowed all through the gathering. Edith wept too, knowing the supreme effort he had made to get his message across. He had just had word that Lansing, his Secretary of State, was not supporting the League in Washington, and he burned with anger over this sudden blow. Dr. Grayson, watching him, was racked by suspense and Tumulty was fe-

192

verishly trying to keep the press from alerting the country that the President was ill.

His headache, which had subsided while he talked, returned with added intensity. Nothing seemed to give him relief. As they headed for Wichita, Dr. Grayson suggested that the train be stopped at a deserted stretch of pasture to give him a chance to get out and breathe the clear Colorado air. Tumulty told the press that they were not to leave the train or take any notice. Edith and Dr. Grayson walked by his side, half supporting him, but he revived with the strong air.

Back on the train they dined together and he seemed to be in better spirits. They all went to bed early but Edith was watchful as her maid gave her a massage and brushed her hair. They moved quietly so as not to disturb the President in the adjoining room, but at eleven thirty P.M. he knocked at the connecting door and asked Edith to come in; he told her that he felt very ill. She found him sitting on the edge of his bed, with his head resting on the back of a chair in front of him, the pose she had seen repeatedly. He told her that the pain had become unbearable and she must send for Dr. Grayson. Studying his face in the dim light Edith was shocked by what she saw. "I realized that we were facing something terrible," she recalled.

It was instantly clear to the doctor that the breakdown he had feared had come and that the tour must be canceled. With Edith's help he settled the President on pillows in the small compartment that he and Tumulty had used for an office. He gave him sedation and stood guard. Edith prayed through the night that things would be normal when he wakened in the morning but as dawn came and she studied his face she realized that her constant apprehension, her uneasiness about his fatigue and headaches, and his baffling changes of mood, had not been without good cause. Now she faced reality, and later wrote of this chilling morning that life would never be the same for her again, but that she would "wear a mask" in public and carry on. Things had not yet reached this point, however.

As they neared Wichita, Dr. Grayson, Tumulty, and she were discussing the next step to be taken when the President surprised them by staggering in, freshly shaved and dressed for the day's events. To Edith he looked "piteously ill." Pale and earnest, Dr. Grayson told him that if he wished to live he must have a long rest and he recommended cancellation of the remainder of the trip at Wichita and a quick trip back to Washington.

The President looked stricken and was wholly unresponsive. He would never give up, he said. They must go on. "If we cancel this trip Senator Lodge and his friends will say that I am a quitter, that the trip was a failure. And the Treaty will be lost!"

Tumulty, visibly broken up himself, took the President's hands in his and assured him that no one in the world would consider him a quitter. Both men mentioned the fact that if he spoke at Wichita he might collapse on the platform in view of the public and the press.

The President looked pleadingly at Edith, who had listened and said little. But it was she who swayed him in the end when she told him gently that it might be better for the public not to see him as he was that day. This carried conviction, and he accepted their united judgment. "This is the greatest disappointment of my life," he said.

They were close to Wichita when the decision was reached, and the reception committee already awaited their arrival. He was scheduled to make two speeches that day. From the back platform of the train Tumulty announced that all events would be canceled. The President was suffering from a digestive upset and Dr. Grayson had ordered his immediate return to Washington for a rest.

The press car emptied like magic as correspondents rushed in all directions to flash this piece of news around the world. Tumulty and Dr. Grayson worked feverishly, rounding up telephones and dictating messages through the local telegraph office. Washington was notified at once and Tumulty reached the McAdoos in Los Angeles by telephone. Messages sent to other members of the family were low-keyed and reassuring: RETURNING TO WASHINGTON. NOTHING TO BE ALARMED ABOUT. LOVE FROM ALL OF US.

Margaret, who was in New London, and Jessie, with her husband, Francis Sayre, in Cambridge, knew their father well enough to realize that the situation was serious. They left at once for the capital.

On September 26 their train again rolled eastward. They had been traveling since September 3. The tracks were cleared and no stops were made except to change engines. For two days and two nights Edith stayed close to her husband in their crowded quarters, trying "to go on as if the structure of our life did not lie in ruin around us." She knitted, studied papers, and chatted as if nothing were wrong, but there was little response. Woodrow dozed or was restless, and gave no sign of improvement. She drew the shades as crowds gathered to watch the train flash by. The news spread that the President was being rushed back to Washington. The press car was a hotbed of rumors and speculation, in spite of the cautious bulletins that Dr. Grayson released at every stop. These were handed to station telegraphers and the symptoms of illness recurrently mentioned were headaches, nervous exhaustion, and a digestive upset. One said that the collapse was owing to the President's tremendous efforts on the tour. Another cited overwork dating back to his illness in Paris in April. It had been called influenza at the time, and the epidemic of that year was known to have left a deadly trail behind it.

The picture was clear enough to Edith, as the miserable hours passed and she could no longer help Woodrow, no matter how much she tried. Dr. Grayson was assuring the public that his condition was not alarming, and she agreed that every effort must be made to protect the President at a time when he could not speak for himself.

They reached Union Station on September 28, 1919, a Sunday morning. In forty-eight hours they had covered 1,700 miles. Washington was only one of the world capitals that awaited enlightenment on his condition. Both he and Edith were determined that he would leave the train as he always did, walking unconcernedly to his car. Margaret had come to meet him and the police held back the crowd that had gathered in the rotunda. Alice Longworth stood on the fringes, appraising the size of the crowd. She was Senator Lodge's most vociferous advocate, and by no means the friend of Woodrow Wilson or his wife. As she circulated in the capital she made soundings on the response to the President's tour.

The crowd waiting at the station seemed sparse to Alice and unenthusiastic; the kind of gathering customary for the arrival of a President after some publicized event. She checked the White House, too, where several hundred spectators waited. She crossed her fingers and gave the old "murrain" curse of the Irish as the President's car entered the grounds. It was a reversion to the black magic of her youthful days when she had done the same to William Howard Taft as he battled with her father.

195

Unconscious that mischievous Alice was at hand and had uttered her incantation in the spirit of fun and without full knowledge of the President's condition, Edith was relieved to reach the "blessed shelter" of the White House, away from prying eyes. She felt unstrung herself, a weakness that she never again allowed herself while Woodrow lived. The strain of the trip had been overwhelming. The immediate problem was to work out a schedule that would relieve the President of all burdens and allay his anxiety. He wanted to go to church as usual on the morning of his return, but Dr. Grayson would not allow this and suggested a drive instead. Randolph and Margaret lunched with them and every effort was made to preserve the outward semblance of order. The staff were told merely that there would be some changes in the President's working schedule but they were quickly aware that he was kept from observation. Those who saw him noticed that his eyes were unnaturally bright, his face was haggard, and his smile seemed fixed and unnatural.

For the first few days at home he could find no way to rest and he wandered aimlessly from his study at one end of the hall to Edith's room at the other. She did her best to divert and entertain him. The family dined downstairs together and they played pool, but this soon tired him. His sleep was broken, his efforts to work were futile, and he saw no one but staff members in passing.

The press watched closely. Unable to talk to them on the train, Edith had promised to have some of them for tea on her return to the White House. They had hoped to see the President, but he was too ill to join them. She carried it off in high style, entertaining them with her stories and assuring them that her husband was sorry he could not see them. She sparred with them and gave them no chance to dwell on his health, but he had not been seen in the Executive Wing since getting home.

When Sir William Wiseman, newspaperman and secret agent for the British government, insisted on seeing him to give him an important message, Edith told him blandly that the President was ill but she would ask about an interview. She was glad to come back with word that her husband could not see him; the message had not been important enough to warrant his attention. Edith particularly disliked the ubiquitous Wiseman and was suspicious of him. When stung later by charges that she was running the government she recalled this incident and wrote, "This was the only instance that I recall having acted as an intermediary between my husband and another on an official matter, except when so directed by a physician."

The daily drives were no longer soothing to the President and the hours rolled by with brief bursts of good cheer and hours of gloom and suffering. Life seemed suspended as things did not get better. The medical profession was in consultation, and every effort was made to keep him quiet. Mrs. Jaffray had already decided that he was desperately ill and Ike Hoover was aware of a strange change in him. But Edith retained her reserve even with her family and strove to keep everything normal. She was her usual bright and efficient self, telling nothing and giving no sign of her own inner tension.

# *17.* *Silence in the White House*

WHEN the total collapse of President Wilson at the White House on October 2 followed the incident on the train, Edith almost overnight became a hidden power in the land. It was the last thing she would have wished for herself, and her period of control grew out of necessity and lasted only for the first six weeks. Medical advice and Edith's own intimate knowledge of Woodrow dictated that he had to be protected from the stormy elements engulfing him. But the prolonged secrecy blanketing the White House baffled the nation at large and infuriated Wilson's political enemies.

On the third day of their return the President showed signs of improvement and Edith felt heartened as they took a short drive together. In the evening he watched a film in the East Room, and she went out briefly to keep an appointment. During the day he had asked for Swem, wishing to dictate some letters, but this was forbidden by Dr. Grayson. They retired early and he read Edith a chapter from the cherished khaki-covered Bible.

197

## Power with Grace

He wound his watch and she noticed that he left it on her table as he went to his room. This was a lapse from his usual ritual and she took it in to him. He looked puzzled when he saw it, but she reminded him laughingly that she was always forgetting things. Since returning from their trip Edith had made a practice of visiting his room every hour in the night to make sure that all was well. It took him some time to get to sleep on this occasion, but he seemed to be in a deep sleep when she looked in on him between five and six o'clock. She then dozed off herself until after eight.

Going immediately to the President's room, she was startled to find him sitting on the edge of his bed, looking helpless and groping futilely for his water bottle. His left hand dangled limply and she rushed to give him a drink. When he told her that his hand was numb she rubbed it to restore circulation, but without effect. Then she helped him to get to the bathroom but he walked stiffly and leaned on her heavily. She told him that she would call Dr. Grayson and she went off to her own room to telephone on their private line, not wishing to put the call through the White House switchboard. She reached Dr. Grayson at his house and a car was rushed to get him. But the damage had already occurred. On her return she found that Woodrow had slipped from a sitting position in the bathroom and was lying on the floor. Snatching a blanket from his bed, she covered him and put a pillow under his head. He moved feebly as she bent over him, and asked for water. "I did those things automatically, for I was utterly devoid of feeling," Edith later wrote. "I had a curious sensation of having lived through this very thing before—and to know how to act, and act quickly."

She let Dr. Grayson in when she heard him knock. The President and she always locked the doors leading into the outer hall, leaving only their communicating door open. It took little time to confirm what she had already deduced. "A cerebral thrombosis, a stroke," he told her. "His whole left side is paralyzed."

Stunned though she was, she knew that she could not let herself collapse. "Mrs. Wilson was never braver, more composed," Dr. Grayson later recalled. "She and I got him on the bed, and we knew that the giant had fallen. A clot had formed in an artery in the brain though there was no rupture."

Hoover, waiting in the outer hall, pictured Dr. Grayson coming out

198

looking snocked and exclaiming, "My God! The President is paralyzed." From then on the word "paralyzed" was taboo at the White House. It was understood but it was never spoken. Edith was angry when Hoover told of cuts he thought he had seen around the President's temple and nose, with signs of blood on them. She insisted that the usher had seen him in shadow and had been mistaken about this.

The blackout was total and immediate. Specialists were summoned and furniture was moved around in the President's quarters to create a hospital effect, with the necessary equipment. Nurses were on duty within three hours, including Ruth Powderly, who had been with Ellen Axson Wilson when she died. Specialists moved in and out and tests were made. Dr. Francis X. Dercrum, a well-known nerve specialist from Philadelphia, Admiral E. T. Stitt, of the Naval Medical Corps, and Dr. Sterling Ruffin, Mrs. Wilson's family doctor, concurred in Dr. Grayson's findings. Dr. E. F. Davis, a classmate and friend of the President's, was at hand, and later other consultants were called in. They were experts of proven value and together they helped to project Edith into her custodial role. She amazed them with her strength and independence. The list soon included Dr. Hugh H. Young of Johns Hopkins, Dr. Charles Mayo of the Mayo Clinic, Dr. H. W. Fowler, and Dr. George D. Schweinitz.

Edith saw momentary flashes of Woodrow's wit and understanding. She stayed constantly within range through all the medical activity, seeking to give him reassurance, to hold his hand, to smile and refrain from showing her anxiety. Margaret and Nell were summoned. Dr. Grayson's guarded bulletins divulged nothing. Tumulty was besieged by the press. Political leaders at home and abroad waited for word from the White House. The mystery deepened as the public hungered for some announcement more enlightening than Dr. Grayson's bulletins, which said only that doctors agreed the President needed total rest.

Servants were barred from the family quarters at first, except for Hoover, whose services were sometimes required, and Brooks, the President's personal servant. Downstairs the inevitable gossip raged about the strange new regime on the second floor. Soon, distorted stories reached the servants' quarters of Washington's most prominent families. Without authoritative information, a torrent of rumors swept the capital and the newspapers after the initial shocked concern for Wilson.

While prayers were offered in churches and homes for his recovery, Woodrow Wilson was also being pictured as a man gone mad. The barred windows implied danger of suicide, but actually the bars had been installed years earlier by Theodore Roosevelt to protect the glass from his sons' lusty play.

The story that the President was a drooling infant repeating nursery rhymes followed an incident in the sick room when his love of limericks and quotations led him to whisper to Dr. Grayson, after his wife had been trying to feed him some nourishment with a spoon,

A wonderful bird is the pelican,
His bill will hold more than his bellican.
He can take in his beak enough food for a week,
I wonder how the hell-he-can.

The public quickly assumed that the President was totally paralyzed, and tales spread of venereal disease contracted in Paris. Edith was too busy attending to her husband's needs to be aware of this at first, and when it sank in she concluded that their enemies had fed the flames.

But the clamor mounted and it was most insistent in the halls of Congress. In indirect ways the Cabinet members and various top officials learned the true state of affairs. Both Josephus Daniels and McAdoo, the first to know, felt from the start that the secrecy was a mistake. Daniels' experience as an editor persuaded him that full disclosure would have ensured public sympathy and understanding. He took the stand, however, that the President, as well as Mrs. Wilson, had told him to reveal nothing that might affect the League negotiations then under way. Dr. Grayson had the physician's adherence to the Hippocratic oath to consider, and the time had not yet arrived when a President's symptoms could be discussed and demonstrated in detail on televison.

Edith was startled and furious when Lansing called a meeting of the Cabinet immediately after the President's collapse and considered invoking the Constitution on the disability of the Chief Executive. He discussed the possibility with Dr. Grayson and Tumulty, both of whom were outraged by this swift move on the part of the Secretary of State. When sounded out about their willingness to cooperate, Tumulty said that he would never go back on Woodrow Wilson, and Dr. Grayson made it clear that if the need arose he would testify to the President's capacity to continue in office.

Learning of this sudden complication, Edith held a conference with the doctors who had attended her husband. She wanted their prognosis and pressed them for a frank opinion on the chances of Woodrow's recovery. She said he was thinking clearly in spite of his semiparalyzed state. They all concurred, and Dr. Dercrum reminded her of the recovery of Louis Pasteur, who also suffered a stroke and lived to do his most useful work afterward.

Dercrum told Edith that her husband needed total freedom from worry and disturbance, and that obviously he could not yet cope with government problems. Dr. Grayson knew that no one was better equipped than she to stand as a buffer between him and the outside world, and so she assumed the role that was to sustain the President during his last year in office. It developed almost spontaneously, and as one question after another arose, she simply took hold herself, calling it a stewardship. She was uniquely equipped for the role, since she had been Woodrow's confidante as well as his wife through the war and the Peace Conference. Since he was known for his tendency to dash off notes on his typewriter without having copies made, she was primed on matters not committed to paper that he had discussed with her right up to the time of his collapse. Their days together in Paris had brought her into the periphery of power.

She had not always agreed with him, but she had more than an inkling of how he felt on most issues. The actual extent of her influence at this time has not been proved, and there were no large issues to be settled during the interregnum, but she belittled it herself, defining it in the simplest terms: "I, myself, never made a single decision regarding the disposition of public affairs. The only decision that was mine was what was important and what was not, and the *very* important decision of when to present matters to my husband."

Edith's role was magnified into a strange new image of "Presidentress," "Lady President," "First Woman President," "Iron Queen," "the Regent," and other titles more stinging than flattering. "Petticoat government" was one Senator's way of putting it. Had she not been so deeply concerned, she would have laughed.

Far from being a woman of insatiable ambition who had isolated the

201

President from his closest friends and advisers, she was a deeply worried wife applying her intelligence as medical necessity dictated. It was unthinkable to her that Woodrow should be forced into retirement with the League not ratified and his work unfinished. In her heart she knew that this would kill him.

Talk of this possibility focused attention on Thomas R. Marshall, the Vice President, who could at any moment become the Chief Executive. No one was more reluctant to face this prospect than the Indiana lawyer, best known for his salty naturalism and his success as a grass roots speaker. He had popularized the slogan, "What this country needs is a good five-cent cigar," and he was as independent as his chief, but in all other respects he was the opposite of scholarly Woodrow Wilson. Edith was fond of Mrs. Marshall, but she could not see the Vice President filling her husband's shoes.

He took no hand in the intrigue surrounding the White House during the interregnum and he refused to dwell on the thought that he should prepare himself to meet an emergency. He had been Woodrow Wilson's Vice President since 1913 and was something of an institution, although eccentric in many ways. His refusal to face facts was jolted when an emergency developed at the White House just as Edith was beginning her stewardship. Again she was called on by the doctors to make a decision—and this time it seemed to be a matter of life or death.

Few ever knew that by faith or luck she was instrumental in saving Woodrow's life when he was threatened with toxemia from prostatic obstruction almost immediately after his stroke. All efforts to restore the elimination of fluid by local applications and manipulation had failed. His temperature soared and surgery was suggested as a last resort. Dr. Young and Dr. Fowler, both urological specialists, thought it imperative but Dr. Grayson, with his intimate knowledge of Woodrow Wilson, felt that he might not survive an operation. All were agreed on its hazards, but the situation was desperate.

In an interview with Mrs. Wilson, racked by his own uncertainty and doubting the wisdom of the operation, Dr. Grayson put the decision up to her. He told her of his own fears for Woodrow's life. Although she knew she would be defying the advice of men who headed their profession, she quickly made up her mind against surgery. She waited in her dressing room while the doctors conferred and when Dr. Young appeared she was ready with her answer. "I feel that nature will take care of things, and we will wait," she told him.

Dr. Young was incredulous. He felt that she did not wholly understand the situation and he stood in the dressing room drawing diagrams for elucidation while he urged his case. Dr. Ruffin, whom she greatly trusted as an old family friend, backed the opinion of Dr. Young and Dr. Fowler, the two surgeons who would operate. "But something kept me steady and I would not agree," she recalled in later years.

When a nurse came to say that the President wanted her, she left the doctors and hurried to his bedside, with a warning from Dr. Young that toxemia might snuff out his life within two or three hours. In her own narrative she told graphically of her thoughts as the clock ticked away the minutes while she studied Woodrow's ashen face and watched him tossing restlessly. The three-hour deadline set by Dr. Dercrum had almost expired when Woodrow's expression changed from pain to peace. It seemed a miracle to her that the crisis had passed and that his body had resumed its natural functioning.

He fell into a deep sleep at once and when he wakened the mists had cleared and he could see Edith plainly as she clasped his right hand firmly in hers. He was intensely weak after this exhausting experience, but it was a turning point in his illness and he gradually gained ground. Soon after his breakdown he was lifted out of bed each day for a short period and was seated in a chair close to a window. Within three weeks he was able to sign his name to four bills, with Edith steadying his hand and guiding the pen. This raised a rumpus on the Hill. Was Edith signing the President's name on state documents? Was Tumulty performing this function?

Woodrow Wilson's signature was well known to the legislators as a model of strength and clarity. They had seen it on some of the most important documents in American history, including the Declaration of War. Now it passed through various phases, from being almost illegible at first to showing some of its customary strength as his condition improved. In at least one government department it was taken as a barometer of his progress. But it was studied and mulled over by the doubters—a matter of concern to Edith, with its implication that he lacked understanding of the signed documents.

203

Practical and decisive in her own affairs, she made the best of a badly tangled situation when her stewardship began, believing that there was no alternative as the flame of life burned low. Although she always denied that Dr. Grayson made political decisions during this period, other White House observers were not so sure. His medical judgment interlocked constantly with the demand for interviews. Although his sole concern was for his patient's well-being, he had learned to trust Edith's judgment where her husband was concerned; she would not have it otherwise. He was more than ever persuaded of her sagacity as he watched her in her new role. When he commented on the accuracy of her reports, she reminded him that she had been trained by her father to take careful notes on what she saw and heard for the benefit of her crippled grandmother, Mrs. Archibald Bolling, thus bringing the outside world into their home in Wytheville.

Even Tumulty, who had little reason to love her, ultimately admitted that her "high intelligence and her extraordinary memory" enabled her to report to the President on matters of state, giving a "clear, oral résumé of each case," as she laid documents before him in orderly sequence.

Everything requiring the President's attention was brought first to her—to be read and channeled to the appropriate departments. She made brief summaries of requests that she felt should be dealt with directly by him. Legislative reports were sent on their way without comment. Interviews of any kind had been sternly forbidden as too tiring, but when pressure increased Edith received Cabinet members and delegates from Congress. She listened to what they had to say, then went to her husband with their requests. Sometimes she returned at once with a direct answer; more often she told them that the President would give their problems consideration and would let them know.

She was criticized for failing to give access to Colonel House and Tumulty at this time, but these relationships had broken down before the President became ill. The only link that the efficient and hardworking Tumulty had with her during the first six weeks was through Dr. Grayson, who was anxious to help him but had his hands tied.

Josephus Daniels wrote of her: "Edith Bolling Wilson had no thought and interest in life but to nurse him back to health, guard against overtaxing him in his convalescence. . . . She stood between him and a nation calling for his active leadership when she knew the hope of activity lay in the regimen the doctors had prescribed, and of which she was the executor.''

With the deluge of material reaching her, and the fluctuations in her husband's condition, Edith lived through rocky and confusing moments. Letters that she was later accused of intercepting were found unopened years later in Woodrow Wilson's papers. The battle was painfully won as the President moved from total incapacity to a diminished life that became a stern test of endurance. The white beard that grew in the early weeks until he was well enough to be shaved aged him and was startling to those who saw him during this period. But excellent grooming and solicitous care made him seem at times almost like the old Woodrow Wilson. Edith, Dr. Grayson, Brooks, and the Secret Service men took infinite care to make the best of a situation common enough in man but uniquely conspicuous in the White House. During the four years and four months that he lived after his breakdown his days were sparked by the love of his wife and his boundless faith in the cause of world peace.

The Treaty fight still raged in America when he was awarded the Nobel Prize, sharing it with Léon Bourgeois, who had helped to draft the Covenant of the League of Nations. World leaders gave thought to the helpless figure in the White House whose power theoretically was still overwhelming but whose voice was stilled. The irony of the award struck Edith. Her husband, who had given his life to the cause of peace, was now a physically shattered man.

To the public, somber shadows engulfed the White House. Its locked gates and closed doors were forbidding. The Executive Wing alone showed signs of life. In the mansion itself curtains were drawn and most of the rugs were taken up so they would not impede the President's wheelchair or trip him as he learned to walk again. Hoover converted one of the rolling chairs of the Atlantic City boardwalk to ensure the President the maximum support and comfort. Wilson could not sit upright in the customary kind, but when the footrest of the boardwalk model was raised to be in line with the seat there was no need to bend his knees. This chair was used constantly during his remaining days in office. On short journeys to the theater and for country drives he was rolled to the elevator and Secret Service men carried him the rest of the way to the automobile.

They settled him in his car, firmly braced, and keeping his paralyzed side away from public view. These were not like the earlier drives when he and Edith had ambled through the country, talking, laughing, and shedding the cares of state. She still talked to him entertainingly but evoked little response, and she was vigilant when she saw that something was troubling him.

Mrs. Jaffray wrote that Edith "was certainly the Assistant President of the United States," getting from Tumulty the official papers and documents that had to be signed. "A hundred times I have seen her in the bedroom where the President would be propped up in bed, going over the papers with him."

Mrs. Jaffray glimpsed him often as he dined, and she made a practice of putting a rose in small vases of different colors for each dinner. "Often I would glance in at these two dining alone," she wrote. "It was a sight I shall never forget: the President using only his right hand and going so slowly and quietly through his meal."

Ike Hoover's picture of the President, much as he loved him, was even grimmer, and Edith bitterly resented it. He failed to see any improvement from first to last in the man who had "changed from a giant to a pygmy in every way." But the staff, almost without exception, admired him, Hoover added, and turned away from him in sympathy when they saw him coming.

"I want to try my legs," he had said from the beginning, and Dr. Grayson encouraged him when he felt he was strong enough to make the effort. With a blackthorn stick gripped in his right hand, two attendants held him at either side as he took his first uncertain steps with one leg. It was painful for Edith to watch but she smiled at him encouragingly. She detested the mawkish touch of pity applied to proud, independent Woodrow.

When Ray Stannard Baker, visiting the White House, saw the alert and springy President he had known at the Peace Conference taking slow and painful steps, all he could recognize about him was the perseverance he knew so well, and the keen eyes that saw all or nothing. Together they watched a preview of a film of the President's days in Europe. "By magic," Baker wrote, "we were in another world, a splendid world, full of wonderful and glorious events."

Stooped, silent, and immovable, Wilson gave no sign of recognition as scenes in Rome, Paris, and London flashed across the screen in the vast East Room. Crowds shouted. He walked with Kings and shook hands with doughboys. When it was over, he got up and without a word shuffled back to his wheelchair.

One of the first forms of diversion introduced for him was the showing of motion pictures in the East Room. As he slowly improved this became almost a daily rite. He liked the film stars and he had followed the scientific development of the industry with interest. He responded to the western films popular at the time, and saw the William S. Hart and Tom Mix pictures long before they were released to the public. The Hollywood studios cooperated in this and Edith, Margaret, and Nell McAdoo constantly sought the book or film that might hold his interest without disturbing him.

The boisterous desert entertainment was not Edith's favorite, but she was glad if it meant one moment of enjoyment for Woodrow. He seemed to like the gunfire and the clatter of horses' hooves, but the daredevil stunts sometimes upset him. The sight of tears running down his cheeks brought Edith swiftly to his side—to put her arms around his neck and steady him or to have him wheeled away. On his good days he liked to take little Gordon Grayson by the hand and be wheeled into the East Room.

By the end of December the President had gained in strength and in a limited way was devoting himself to public affairs, with Edith ever at hand to inform and read to him. He was seeing a few people, dictating to Swem for brief intervals, and was working hard at his therapeutic exercises under Dr. Grayson's supervision. When Edith came in view his face always lit up and he put out his right hand to greet her. She found that he became nervous if he had time to think and she could see that the League was on his mind. He was still reluctant to let her out of his sight, and she did not leave him for as much as an hour except in the afternoon when he rested and at mealtime. She saw that the stronger he felt the less necessary she would be to him, but for the time being her encouraging comments on his appearance and what he was doing seemed to count. With considerable ingenuity she kept his mind free of political worries.

Speculation about Edith's actual role was a lively issue with the Cabinet, even with such an old family friend as David F. Houston, Secretary of Agriculture, who did not think it possible that the amiable Mrs.

Wilson could be making decisions for the President. He was one of the first to know the truth about Wilson's condition but, like Daniels, he was sworn to secrecy.

Despite the effective role Edith played during the months abroad, she had never been known in Washington as having strong political interests. She had not belonged to the official set before her White House days and her emergence as the secret voice of Woodrow Wilson required understanding.

Although Tumulty was frozen out, the impression prevailed at first that he and McAdoo were the chief advisers. Senator Lodge discounted Edith's power and viewed it as a regency of Tumulty and Bernard Baruch. It was true that Baruch had taken over many of the functions of Colonel House and that he saw both the President and Edith almost from the beginning.

Her guide in all things was the state of Woodrow's health from day to day. There was no question of any decisions until he began to gain ground, and no one ever really knew but Dr. Grayson, a close observer of the scene and a participant in every move affecting the President, how much Edith decided for her husband. She was strong enough to hold her ground on his behalf, and she kept alive his hope that things would change. She was much too busy to care what people said, although she had at least one angry outburst as she studied a pile of hate mail and press comment on her role. "I don't know how much more criticism I can take," she exploded.

The talk on Capitol Hill did not die down; it grew steadily worse. A conflict of opinion developed. What was the President's wife doing beyond seeing that no one got to her husband? Her own penciled notes appeared on many of the documents presumably coming from Woodrow Wilson. They usually conveyed his wishes in a roundabout fashion, but they made the recipients wonder from whose brain they had sprung. The effects were sometimes so conflicting that they did not suggest the explicit Woodrow Wilson functioning at his best.

Lansing told of sending the simplest of memorandums to the President and receiving "answers communicated through Mrs. Wilson so confusing that no one could interpret them." Yet her own mental processes were known to be extremely orderly, even if her handwriting was not. All this was taken as evidence of the President's mental inca-

208

pacity. Major decisions involving diplomatic appointments and policy matters were stalled, a serious embarrassment to Lansing. The impression prevailed that the government was standing still and that a woman in the White House held the key to it all.

# *18.* *"Don't You Desert Me"*

SIX weeks after the President's breakdown, and a month after his close brush with death, he faced the fact that the Covenant was dead. Edith considered the bitter struggle of 1919–1920, coming when Woodrow was most helpless, as the darkest period in their lives. Beyond all others, she knew the pain, the effort, the discouragement of each passing day from the time of his collapse to March 19, 1920, when the League was voted down for the second time.

To most of his colleagues his stand on the Lodge reservations seemed self-destructive and impossible. Even Edith weakened briefly in her desire to see the Treaty approved. But she shared his conviction that Senator Lodge through personal malice had wrecked the Covenant and in 1939, with World War II near at hand, she wrote that Lodge had "put the world back fifty years, and that at his door lies the wreckage of human hopes and the peril to human lives that afflict mankind today."

Edith braved the storm with calm, shaping each day to the President's needs and helping him to fight his way through a nightmare of physical incapacity to partial restoration of his mental powers. Although the press and the public thought of him as a shattered man no longer capable of holding office, she and Dr. Grayson preserved the outward appearance of order, understanding, and great courage on the part of the President. It was a difficult role to play as the battle over the League reached its climax in November, 1919.

Other matters could wait, but the League vote had to be met head-on, regardless of his condition, and Senator Gilbert Hitchcock, of Nebraska, newspaper publisher and Democratic minority leader directing the League fight in the Senate, bore the brunt of the battle. Twice he saw the President, and once even Edith briefly agreed that half a loaf was better than none, and that he should compromise on the reservations in order to get America into the League on any terms. Bernard Baruch, Daniels, Herbert Hoover, Ray Stannard Baker, and others who had been with him in Paris shared this view and swung her briefly away from Woodrow's rigid opinion.

Mild-mannered and sympathetic, Hitchcock liked Edith Wilson, but he found her intimidating as she stood at the President's door challenging him: "You haven't come to talk compromise, have you?" She was dubious about the wisdom of letting him in, knowing that the subject was dynamite with Woodrow; yet she was more than half-persuaded herself of the need for compromise. When Baker reminded her of how stubborn the President was she told him, "He believes the people are with him."

She conceded that she could not be wholly unsympathetic with the viewpoint of those favoring compromise, since she had come to the conclusion at this point that nothing mattered but getting the Treaty ratified. When she urged Woodrow to agree and get this "awful business settled" he looked at her in amazement.

"Don't *you* desert me," he said, making her feel like one of the betrayers. He argued that he had no moral right to accept any change in the document he had signed unless he consulted every other signatory, even the Germans. Edith leaned over him, holding his hand with her customary gesture of support, and heard him murmur, "Better a thousand times to go down fighting than to dip your colors to dishonorable compromise."

She went out to Senator Hitchcock and told him that for the first time she saw her husband's point clearly, and she would never again ask him to do what he believed to be dishonorable. The Senator felt that they had lost a powerful advocate in Edith Wilson, for they had all tried to persuade her to use her influence with the President. If she could not shake him, no one could, but she already knew how immovable he was and she was reluctant to disturb him with the most painful of all issues.

## "Don't You Desert Me"

When she led Senator Hitchcock into the room he was shocked to find a changed man, looking old and weary. It was Hitchcock's first glimpse of the President since the breakdown. Warned not to upset him, he eased his way into the subject, with Edith mounting guard and flashing him warning signals from time to time. But in the end he had to tell Wilson plainly that the necessary votes could not be mustered, that the issue was in peril, and that the only hope lay in compromise.

The President reacted at once to the sound of the word and huskily muttered, "Let Lodge compromise."

A second try by Hitchcock to persuade him to hold out the olive branch to the Massachusetts Senator met the same response. Clearly Wilson had no intention of yielding ground on the Lodge amendments and reservations. The one involving Article X of the Covenant had been a tender spot from the beginning. It would alter the original provision by denying the obligation of the United States to preserve the territorial integrity or political independence of any other country without an act or joint resolution by Congress.

The President said at once that the Lodge resolution, which included his reservations, was "utterly impossible." On the main issue he added that if his opponents were bent on defeating the Treaty, he wanted the vote of each Republican and Democrat recorded—"because they will have to answer to the country in the future for their acts." As he spoke he acknowledged to Hitchcock that he was a sick man.

By this time Edith and Dr. Grayson could see that the President was growing tired. It was an upsetting interview for him and when it was over he dictated to Edith a letter for Senator Hitchcock to take back to the Foreign Relations Committee. He signed it himself and it was dated November 18, 1919. He took note of the fact that the committee was to meet just before the Senate voted, and he assumed that they would wish to have his opinion. He stated it flatly: "In my opinion the resolution in that form does not provide for ratification, but rather nullification of the Treaty. . . . I sincerely hope that the friends and supporters of the Treaty will vote against the Lodge resolution. I understand that the door will then probably be open for a general resolution of ratification."

Even at this point he could not accept the fact that the men he had once so powerfully swayed would not listen and he fell asleep hopeful after the Senator left. But his appeal did more harm than good. When it

211

reached the Senate, where there were mild Reservationists as well as the known Irreconcilables in both parties, the weeks of maneuvering and the scores of amendments and reservations clouding the issue narrowed down to Lodge versus Wilson, and Wilson lost. An interested spectator in the gallery on November 19, when the vote was taken, was Mrs. Alice Roosevelt Longworth, and she got what she wanted. Ratification with the Lodge reservations was defeated by a vote of 55 to 39, and ratification without the reservations was swamped by 53 to 38.

The news was swiftly conveyed to Edith, for she was the one who would tell him. She could scarcely bear to face it, but he took it quietly. For a few moments he lay in silence and then with a spurt of energy he said, "All the more reason I must get well and try again to bring this country to a sense of its great opportunity and greater responsibility."

It was not the end of the story, but for the time being it was enough. Gloom pervaded the White House outside and in. Edward G. Lowry, who had served abroad as a correspondent and embassy attaché, studied the historic mansion on his return to Washington and observed, "Its great iron gates were closed and chained and locked. Policemen guarded its approaches. . . . It all made for bleakness and bitterness and a general sense of frustration and unhappiness."

The issue was revived in the Senate early in the New Year, and the battle began all over again when the President learned that the Democrats might reach an agreement with Senator Lodge on his own terms. Wilson had nothing to say to individual Senators who wanted to talk compromise with him. For a time it seemed as if Senator Lodge might capitulate and support a reservation on Article X that the Democrats would approve, but he soon pulled out of bipartisan discussions and went his own way. William Jennings Bryan campaigned for ratification with the Lodge reservations. William Howard Taft and Herbert Hoover led the field on a nonpartisan basis.

Each move was closely followed in the White House and letters came showering in for and against the Treaty. Taft was a powerful protagonist but Edith questioned his good faith when she learned that he, too, had reservations. They differed from Senator Lodge's, but she wrote to Senator Carter Glass, of Virginia, that the President felt inac-

212

tion might be better than "mistaken initiative." And Wilson himself wrote to Senator Hitchcock insisting again that Article X was a moral obligation. "Either the United States should enter the League with its head high or else it should retire as gracefully as possible from the concert."

His message to Democrats at the annual Jackson Day dinner on January 8 had some of the old Wilson ring. He declared that the overwhelming majority of the people desired ratification of the Treaty without reservations and if there was any doubt of this he proposed a solemn referendum at the next election. There was no doubt that there was a growing demand among influential leaders of both parties to get America into the League of Nations, which had begun to function. Edith rejoiced when the President was asked to issue the call for the first meeting on January 16, 1920.

But when the final vote was taken on March 19, 1920, he lost again. The count was 49 for and 39 against the Treaty, less than the two-thirds majority needed. Twenty-three Democrats combined with the Irreconcilables to defeat the Treaty, and this time a reversal of 7 Democratic votes would have put it across.

When the battle was over Senator Lodge coldly observed that the issue was as dead as Marley's ghost. "Without Wilson's efforts the Treaty would have been accepted by the Senate," he said, a bitter thought for Edith. This was the end of the Wilsonian dream in his lifetime, but not for her. More alert to every development and keener in his perceptions, the President showed more emotion on this occasion than he had over the earlier defeat.

Tumulty broke the news to him and caught the full tide of his disappointment. "I feel like going to bed and staying there," Wilson said in sheer weariness of spirit. He could not sleep that night, and Dr. Grayson stayed near at hand, checking on him hour by hour. This time he sought comfort in the Bible, and toward dawn he asked the doctor to read to him St. Paul's counsel in Second Corinthians: "We are troubled on every side, yet not distressed; we are perplexed, but not in despair; persecuted, but not forsaken; cast down, but not destroyed."

The President relaxed after this. "If I were not a Christian I think I should go mad," he said. But it had given him fresh hope and he called

213

his first Cabinet meeting for April 14, a month after his defeat. At this time he told Dr. Grayson that he was considering retiring and letting the Vice President take over. But he would make this move only if he were fully convinced that the country "was suffering any ill effects from my sickness."

Edith was used to the strange thoughts that came to him in their long hours together, particularly as his consciousness became more acute, so she was not surprised when he visualized the scene in Congress of being wheeled in and making his retirement announcement in person. But she remembered with special pain the dinner she had attended, the lone woman among thirty men, when the President invited the Senators to the White House to discuss the Treaty with them on his return from Paris. She had been duped by Lodge, she felt—"a snake in the grass: not even that. He was a snake in the open."

Among Wilson's foes and critics, Theodore Roosevelt and Senator Lodge led all others. Edith felt history would prove Woodrow right and Lodge wrong, although at times the whole subject sickened her. It had swept the foundations of life from under Woodrow, and she did not underestimate his suffering from the defeat of his master plan.

George Creel, seeing Wilson a few days later, noticed that his eyes "were filled with anguish such as I trust never to see again," and he quoted him as saying, "If only I were not helpless. . . ." But Edith deplored the circulation of emotional comments like this, for the White House policy while she was in charge was consistently proud and affirmative. The chaos and despair behind the scenes were not allowed to show as she met each day with strength and purpose. The League was the tenderest subject of all.

On February 7, 1920, the President, who had long been impatient over Lansing's failure to back him wholeheartedly on the Covenant and had been open in his support of the Lodge reservations, sent him a chilly note asking for an explanation of the Cabinet meetings he had called without authorization while Wilson lay ill. Lansing replied that since the Cabinet members were not permitted to communicate with the President they had to meet informally to deal with pressing matters.

"I find nothing in your letters which justifies your assumption of

Presidential authority in such a matter," the President responded. "I must say that it would relieve me of embarrassment, Mr. Secretary, if you would give your present office up."

This sudden move by President Wilson surprised the country. But there were no regrets on Edith's part. She made no secret that she disliked Lansing. From the beginning she had doubted his capacity, and during the Peace Conference she had felt that both he and House had been perfidious where her husband was concerned, running things according to their own ambitions but without any unity of aim.

Daniels, a Cabinet member himself, felt that the only meeting called by Lansing that seemed unwarranted was the first, immediately after the President's breakdown, when he took soundings on the Constitutional issue of removing him for disability. This quick and unfounded diagnosis had shocked Edith and she could not forget it.

By chance Colonel House, heading home when he heard of Wilson's breakdown, became seriously ill as he sailed from England. His condition grew worse on the steamer and his life was despaired of on his arrival, so that both men—House and Lansing—who had been so closely linked with the Treaty fight, were gone during the closing days of battle.

Friends who feared for the fate of the Covenant had urged House to use his influence with the President for compromise, but House refrained from taking an active part in the struggle while both were ill. He volunteered to testify before the Senate Foreign Relations Committee, but Senator Lodge had checkmated this so he convalesced in New York and tried to follow the mysterious course of events at the White House. On November 24, 1919, he wrote to the President advising him not to mention the Treaty in his message to Congress and on November 27 he wrote again, "Your willingness to accept reservations rather than have the Treaty killed will be regarded as the act of a great man."

Colonel House's role in Woodrow Wilson's life had been dwindling steadily, and the constant stream of affectionate letters had tapered off. He had not seen the President since they parted in Paris on June 28, but they had communicated regarding the mandates of the various allied countries that were approved by the President. Colonel House had been assigned to this complicated task, but there was a brief flurry when the London papers published reports of discord between him and the President. This was nothing new; they had often been reported at odds, and on August 29, 1919, Wilson cabled him through the American Embassy that the "best way to treat it is with silent contempt." But after the breakdown the colonel was convinced that Edith had succeeded in severing the link.

On October 22, 1919, House wrote to her that her failure to tell the President of his return to America indicated that Wilson was more ill than he had thought or that Wilson laid more stress on his remaining abroad than seemed possible. House explained that his work was finished and that there was annoying comment on his continued presence in Paris. "I was so unhappy and uneasy about the President's condition before I left that I should have come in any event, even if there had been no misunderstanding."

He offered to do anything in his power to help the President or Mrs. Wilson, and she answered politely, "Thank you for your offer to be of service. I know of nothing now, for the best cure seems to be rest and freedom from everything." She explained in a second letter that she had refrained from telling her husband of his return lest he worry because House had not stayed in Paris to finish his work there.

This explanation did not convince Colonel House. As his own health improved he noted in his diary that he would be willing to give his time, and even his life, if need be, to help the President, the country and the world, "but since I am barred, I am more than content to await events. . . . I have a philosophical turn of mind and I never worry where it cannot help. . . ."

In spite of these bland words the hurt was deeply rooted, and after the President's death he wrote with more emotion, "My separation from Woodrow Wilson was and is to me a tragic mystery . . . for its explanation lies buried with him. . . . Never, during the years we worked together, was there an unkind or impatient word, written or spoken, and this, to me, is an abiding consolation."

On other occasions Colonel House had blamed the "'bedroom circle'" that was freely discussed in Washington during the early months of the President's illness. Helpless as he was, the President had decided opinions of his own, and at one point he had actually dismissed Dr. Grayson for defending Tumulty. This was a shock to Edith, who knew how essential the admiral was, but Woodrow soon relented and called him back, breaking down with emotion when he saw Cary come in

and calmly take over as if nothing unusual had happened.
However outraged he was, Tumulty, too, in the end gave Edith credit for her attitude during these exhausting months. "No public man
ever had a more devoted helpmeet, and no wife a husband more de-
pendent upon her sympathetic understanding of his problems. . . .
Mrs. Wilson's strong physical constitution, combined with a strength
of character and purpose, has sustained her under a strain which must
have wrecked most women. When the strong man broke, she nursed
him as tenderly as a mother nurses a child."

Mrs. Wilson knew how useful Tumulty had been to her husband as
an expert secretary, imaginative public relations man, and an effective
link with the press in times of stress. He was entertaining and witty and
the President enjoyed his political reminiscences. A clever young
Catholic lawyer, he had opposed Woodrow Wilson's nomination at
first, but had become his ardent supporter when the Princeton professor turned against Alfred E. Smith. With a wife and six children whom
he adored, he was always rushing home for weekends, but he stayed at
the White House for long periods with President Wilson after Ellen
Axson died. During the blackout Tumulty could help little, although he
continued his work in the Executive Office without access to the President.

Edith alone seemed to give Woodrow constant comfort and reassurance, even in moments of disorientation. Her family and friends
watched with amazement, but she never let anyone know how severe
the strain was as she stood in opposition to public opinion. She aged
visibly during the dark months of 1919 and 1920, and she talked little.

# 19. *Confounding the Critics*

WITH the gossip about the President's condition at full tide and
resentment growing over his isolation, the authorship of the State of
the Union message in December was questioned. This stirred up fresh

waves of speculation about Edith Wilson's role. Who was running the country? Was it actually Edith Bolling Wilson? The capital wives were as interested as the legislators, and tea-table talk would not subside.

It was a mystifying situation with grave issues at stake, including the President's special interest, the League of Nations. Work slowed but did not stop and the men in Congress found the message dull. Those who expected comment on the League were disappointed. International issues in general were ignored, and it followed a pedestrian course on domestic issues, from forest conservation to tax reform and employment for war veterans. The feminists, flushed with victory, saw that it took little stock in them.

No one knew better than Edith the pride her husband took in attending to his own speeches. Tumulty and Swem usually assembled the routine material for a State of the Union message. The President would then discuss it with his Cabinet, but the thought and the phrasing had to be his. On this occasion the Cabinet and Department reports were submitted as usual, but with some uncertainty, and the general text was assembled. The message was given to Edith Wilson to read and she added some penciled changes that she said the President wished.

When it had been delivered the gossip about its origin gave Albert H. Fall, a Republican Senator from New Mexico who had extensive oil interests, fresh ammunition to agitate for the President's removal from office. He insisted that Woodrow Wilson in his helpless state could not have written the text, nor could he have known anything about it. Fall and Senator George Moses, of New Hampshire, who came to be known as "Doc" Moses for his constant and lugubrious assault on the President's sanity, were anathema to Edith. It worried her to hear stories of mental incompetence spread. But the skepticism was not confined to the Republican party; it was equally strong with some of the leading Democrats, from Secretary of State Lansing downward.

Much of the animosity centered on Edith Wilson as she warded off intrusion. She heard with amazement that Senator Fall created a scene before the Foreign Relations Committee, insisting that the elected President was not in office. "Mrs. Wilson is President. We have petticoat government," he shouted, pounding his fist for emphasis. He called her the "Presidentress who had fulfilled the dream of the suffragettes by changing her title from First Lady to Acting First Man."

Edith brushed this off as she did many another calumny; she was not a stranger to the gossip of the capital. Her days were so filled with work that she had no time to feel sorry for herself. Her sole concern was the care of her husband and, far from trying to interfere with governmental procedure, she saw herself as a liaison in a time of crisis. But Senator Fall, a strong supporter of Senator Lodge, persisted and the way opened for him to invade the sickroom, study the "incompetent" President, and face the "Presidentress."

A determined "Petroleum Fall" attempted to see for himself the President's condition, but a more immediate issue was the kidnaping at Pueblo of William Jenkins, a United States consular agent in Mexico. Lansing protested at once and hints of war with Mexico were in the air—no novelty during the Wilson administration. The President had handled things his own way in Mexico, not always to the satisfaction of the American oil interests.

When the Republicans learned that Lansing had acted in this case without consulting the President, Fall artfully introduced a resolution calling for a visit to the White House by two Senators and a direct confrontation with Woodrow Wilson. He and Senator Hitchcock, the Democratic leader, were appointed and the meeting was scheduled for December 4, immediately after the State of the Union message had been read to Congress. Tumulty was warned in a roundabout way that if Fall were not received, there might be impeachment proceedings.

Edith and Dr. Grayson were reluctant to have the enemy, Fall, come near the President, who was already suspicious of his oil operations. But when asked he said he wished to receive them. The press was alerted and reporters gathered on the lawn to hear what Senator Fall might have to say about the President's condition.

Everything was carefully arranged so that the President would appear to the best advantage. He was propped up in bed and heavily blanketed to his chin, except for his right arm, which he was able to use freely. His paralyzed left side was wholly covered and the lighting was so arranged as to keep that side of his face in shadow. His beard had been shaved and the look of age was less apparent. A copy of the Senate report on the Mexican crisis lay on a table beside his bed, where he could reach it at will and flourish it in his tormentor's face, if need be.

The President greeted Fall with a jest and a handclasp that surprised the Senator with its strength. Edith welcomed Fall coolly, holding a pad and pencil in her right hand so that she need not shake hands with him. The President said that he would like Edith to stay in the room with them. The Senator looked dubious and became suspicious when he saw her taking notes.

"You seem very much engaged, Madam," he said.

"I thought it wise to record this interview so that there may be no misunderstandings or misstatements made," she replied.

Neither she nor Dr. Grayson had any idea how the patient would react to loaded interrogation, and she watched the two men attentively as they conversed. Fall's long, drooping mustache and showy attire seemed at odds with his obsequious manner. He did most of the talking while Senator Hitchcock listened. To her great relief she heard Woodrow go haltingly into a responsive discussion with the fiery Senator. He reached for the Senate report, flourished it with his right hand, and gave his views on what should be done. He promised to prepare a memo with additional information, not only on Jenkins' case but on other matters pending in the Senate.

By chance Dr. Grayson, who had been called away, came back with a message from Lansing that Jenkins had just been released. This was sheer coincidence but it seemed to Edith to have been heaven-sent. It deflated Fall, but he continued talking. The President, swiftly changing moods, turned blithe and witty and accused Fall of trying to promote a war with Mexico in order to protect his oil interests there.

Edith, still busy with her pad and pencil and longing for him to go, caught the last words exchanged as Fall bent over the bed and clasped the President's mobile hand in both of his: "Mr. President, I am praying for you," said the Senator.

Woodrow Wilson looked up into his face and with a chuckle said, "Which way, Senator?"

The press pounced on the two Senators as they left the White House. Hitchcock was grinning broadly, but he let Senator Fall do all the talking. Knowing how ruthless he had been in his attacks on Woodrow Wilson, all were surprised by Fall's admission that the President seemed to be in excellent trim, both mentally and physically, and that he was perfectly capable of handling the Mexican situation. He described the scene in the sickroom, mentioning his free use of his right hand in holding papers and the mobility with which he had turned his head to address him. "While his articulation was somewhat thick during the conference I could understand every word he said," the Senator conceded.

Edith alone knew the terrific effort her husband had made. Her own role had been a vital factor in the success of the interview. "Those who saw her that day, as she led the way for the Senators to her husband's bedside, said she looked like a Queen," Josephus Daniels reported. She towered over the unctuous little Senator. It was not her ambition to look or act like a Queen, and she took Daniels' tendency to see her through rose-colored glasses with a grain of salt. She felt sure that she had done the right thing in taking notes, and she carefully saved the manila envelope and wrapping paper that Fall had brought. When her pad ran out she had scribbled the last of her notes on this substitute, not wishing to miss a word.

When the Teapot Dome scandal broke a few years later, Fall, who had become Secretary of the Interior, was sent to the penitentiary for accepting a $100,000 bribe from Edward L. Doheny to turn over leases of the Naval Oil Reserve to the oil interests. When President Wilson, who had always been suspicious of Fall's oil negotiations, lay dying, Dr. Sterling Ruffin was one of the medical men called in by another Senate committee to pass judgment on Fall's sanity when he refused to appear before the investigating body. Dr. Ruffin pronounced him well enough to appear and Edith commented, "I could not but recall that this was the man Mr. Henry Cabot Lodge had delegated to pass on the mentality of Woodrow Wilson."

Stage by stage the President gained ground. From the middle of November he could be seen, a muffled figure on the South Portico, with papers beside him and Edith hovering near. By Christmas he was being lifted from his bed to spend brief periods in an easy chair. By March, when the Treaty was being voted on the second time and the debate was in its final phase, he was seen driving again regularly, and from the middle of April he called his own Cabinet meetings—a true test of his improved condition. The stories of tempers and tantrums, of things being thrown, of bursts of sobbing, of an angry and unreasonable President subsided. The nature of his illness was explanation enough to all close to him, and certainly to his wife.

221

Edith gave a luncheon for the Cabinet wives when the President resumed his meetings. She had Altrude Grayson and members of her own family present, as she did whenever possible. To those who knew her best it was apparent that Edith Wilson had suffered. She looked older and had a more serious air.

She was as attentive to the arrangements for the President's first Cabinet meeting as for his encounter with Senator Fall. It was held in his study instead of in the large Cabinet Room, and he was comfortably placed so that he could see everyone without strain. Hoover introduced each member loudly, as if the President had never met them before, and they all treated him with the utmost consideration, trying not to show him that things had changed. Daniels was touched as he watched Wilson in the role in which he had once been so dominant. When they were all seated the President broke the ice with a jest, a Lincolnian touch which had always been his favorite way of getting a meeting going.

After that he sat quietly and listened as they picked up the initiative and gave him brief summaries of their problems. They were all subjects in which he had been most knowledgeable up to the time of his breakdown—the mining strike, the nationalization of railroads, and the roundup of Anarchists by Attorney General A. Mitchell Palmer, who was a particular favorite of the President.

Dr. Grayson looked in from time to time to see how Wilson was faring, and Edith arrived when the meeting ran overtime. It had been scheduled to last an hour. At a glance from her Wilson said, "Holding this Cabinet meeting is an experiment, you know, and I ought not to stay too long."

After that the meetings were called without a break. Some were bright, animated, and conclusive, with the President expressing his opinions freely, cracking jokes, and telling stories; at other times he seemed morose and lost. Edith dreaded them, but they were a barometer of his progress to the Cabinet. It was reassuring to the public to know that the President seemed to be in command again.

Although her vigilance was unabated, Edith could now attend to the business that had been ignored during the first two months of his illness. He awakened at eight o'clock and they breakfasted together. She read him the day's headlines and went further into the news if he showed interest, taking care to avoid subjects that she knew would disturb him. Then she went downstairs to go through the mail and to see what communications had arrived from Tumulty. She quickly decided which matters needed her husband's personal attention. Her pad and pencil were constantly at hand to jot down any thoughts or suggestions he had to offer. Swem was always available, but they could no longer proceed at the old pace. Edith understood better than anyone else what her husband said, even on his huskiest days, and when he groped for a word she knew what he meant.

Before lunch Wilson would be wheeled to the South Portico, and in the afternoon he slept until four. This was Edith's free time, but she walked always on the south side of the house so as to be within easy call should he need her, which he often did. If he seemed in the mood for work when he awoke, he was propped up in bed and they went over various letters and documents. Otherwise, she would read to him, play Canfield, or talk happily.

She often longed for the efficient Miss Benham as she pored over papers far into the night. Busy all day with the President's affairs, she studied official documents after he was asleep and tried to cope with her own correspondence. She finally resorted to using McGee, one of Swem's assistants, and they worked out a series of form letters to meet all social contingencies, for she had not ceased to be a functioning First Lady on the social side.

Edith Benham, who could have been useful, suffered a nervous breakdown after the Peace Conference and was unable to resume her work. It was not the end of their association but it finished their working relationship, which had been starred with high excitement and dazzling events in Europe.

Although a Republican from a conservative family, Miss Benham's work in the Wilson household had turned her into a Wilsonian Democrat. "I had been completely won to Wilsonian Democracy by the President himself," she wrote. "He made no effort to convince me of the worth of his ideas for America and the world. I simply saw the validity of his arguments." She had found it hard "to watch the thwarting of President Wilson's aims by a small group on Capitol Hill."

She recovered and in April, 1921, she married Admiral Helm, who had waited a long time for her. Edith attended the quiet wedding at

Miss Benham's apartment. Jane Hunt, daughter of the army officer for whom Fort Hunt was named, Edith, and an officer friend of Admiral Helm's, were the only guests.

Margaret Wilson, too, fell victim to a nervous breakdown and recuperated in the South. The hectic days in Paris had caused widespread wreckage.

# 20.   A King and a Prince

ALTHOUGH politicians and all other emissaries were barred from the White House at the beginning of the President's illness, his first encounter with the outside world aside from his medical attendants was with King Albert and Queen Elizabeth of Belgium. On October 30, 1919, three weeks after his collapse, he was propped up in bed, bearded and half-paralyzed, almost unrecognizable, to the towering monarch who eight months earlier had been his host at the Royal Palace in Brussels. They had toured the battlefields together, both tall men, physically and in the eyes of the world.

It was a strange and unlikely encounter, and Edith had to steel herself as she watched them together. She had made this exception because of diplomatic necessity and to let the world know that her husband was capable of fulfilling his responsibilities. To her deep satisfaction things went well. The King spoke excellent English, for he had done newspaper work in Minnesota incognito at the age of eighteen. The President managed to crack a few jokes in characteristic fashion and "The King was as gentle as a woman in his sincere sympathy and solicitude," Edith remembered.

Plans had been made with much care for a ceremonial tour by the Belgian rulers. They were at sea when they learned of the President's illness, and their program in Washington was immediately modified to play down the social aspects of the visit. Vice President and Mrs. Marshall took over the official entertaining.

Edith had planned to return the hospitality and friendship shown them by the Belgian rulers, but with her husband still in a precarious state she managed to do it in the intimate way that she thought would be least upsetting for him. Flowers from the White House and a welcoming note awaited Albert and Elizabeth on their arrival, and she called at once on the Queen to invite her and the King to tea at the White House. They came the following day with Crown Prince Leopold and two aides. After tea was served in the Red Room, a handsome polished wood chest containing eighteen hand-painted plates was brought in by an usher.

After the formalities downstairs Edith led the King to her husband's room. Everything had been arranged for his coming, and the President looked at ease propped up in a handsome dressing gown. It was just like one friend dropping in on another, and after they had chatted for a few minutes the royal gift was presented, with a little speech of appreciation. It seemed to Edith to be a rare and beautiful offering as she watched one plate after another, representing historic places in Belgium, being lifted from its crimson velvet tray. King Albert leaned over to indicate some of the places they had visited together—names historic because of the war, and some that had been leveled in combat. Each plate had the same inscription in French as the case: "Souvenir of the King and Queen of Belgium to His Excellency Monsieur Wilson, President of the United States of America."

The Queen gave Edith a fan of Belgian lace mounted on amber sticks with a circlet of diamonds enclosing two "E's" in sapphires, signifying their initials, Elizabeth and Edith. This "circle of friendship" showed the angels of peace chasing the dragons of war, with the emblems of all the Allied countries in the background. On her courtesy call Edith had given the Queen a handsome fan with shell sticks and her name on it in gold.

Elizabeth proved to be a tireless guest at the White House and Edith, who admired her efficiency and beneficent work during the war, had to move fast to keep up with her. She knew from experience that Elizabeth spoke halting English, so there was not the same degree of understanding between them as their husbands had. But when they concluded their tour in the China Room, they found a mutual interest. Together they studied the china acquired by other Presidents' families, and Edith drew attention to the fact that all of it was imported. She had made a point herself of introducing American china at the White House. Half a century later the Belgian plates were displayed in the Woodrow Wilson house on S Street.

When the time came for the King and Queen to leave, the Queen asked if she might take Prince Leopold upstairs, because he was so anxious to meet the President. This was something Edith had not foreseen, but she agreed and Queen Elizabeth and the young prince were ushered in, to find her husband in his shabby old sweater, using a magnifying glass on one of the hand-painted plates. Uncomfortable in his dressing gown, as soon as the King left he had had it changed for the old sweater that had become almost as famous in Europe as it was at home.

He told the Queen that he would have been more suitably dressed had he known she was coming, but she had nursed so many invalid men that she merely smiled. The prince stood in the background, awed and silent in the presence of Woodrow Wilson. When the time came for them to leave, Edith accompanied them to the entrance, not knowing that the Queen would be trapped by the press, who waited for a word about the President's condition.

Elizabeth paused to tell the reporters that she had found Woodrow very cheerful in his "worn sweater." But because of her faulty English "worn" became "torn" in the press accounts. The story traveled far, as did every glimmer of news coming out of the locked and silent White House. For weeks letters poured in reproaching the First Lady for having let the Queen see the President in a torn sweater. Solicitous women sent wool for repairs, a subject of jest when she told the President about it. She made sure that nothing of the kind occurred when they had another royal visitor two weeks after the King and Queen of Belgium. On November 13, 1919, the golden-haired, blue-eyed Prince of Wales, touring Canada and the United States and making news every day with his golf, parties, and romances, came to the White House. John Davis had urged that he be received, but the appointment fell on one of the President's bad days, when his enunciation was particularly slow and painful.

# A King and a Prince

Edith chatted with him first and served him tea in the Blue Room before taking him up to the President. The Prince was late, waylaid on his way from Mount Vernon by an octogenarian who insisted on telling him of being kissed by his uncle, King Edward VII, when Edward visited Washington as Baron Renfrew just before the Civil War.

The young prince's debonair spirit and graceful manners appealed to Edith, but she realized that this would be a more difficult encounter for her husband than his talk with King Albert. He approached the President's bed. Although widely traveled and accustomed to meeting Heads of State, the Prince could find nothing to say when he saw Woodrow Wilson in so helpless a condition. He was intensely nervous, tweaked his tie, fidgeted, and pleated his trousers. Edith watched the two men with a sense of helplessness. Again Uncle Bertie came to the rescue. The Prince asked if, in 1860, his uncle had actually slept in the magnificent bed on which the President lay. Wilson assured him that whether or not Lincoln had slept in the bed on which he was lying, Uncle Bertie certainly had. Moreover, he had slipped out a window one night to attend a party not on the official program. This struck a familiar note with the Prince and he jumped up at once to identify the window, but neither the President nor Edith knew which it was. Edith could see that her husband was intensely tired. The Prince of Wales passed out of her life except for a farewell courtesy call, but she lived to see him renounce the British Empire for an American divorcée.

The royal visits, coming at a time when everyone else was banned at the White House, stirred up a wave of gossip tied to Edith's past. Why was the Prince of Wales received while Viscount Grey of Fallodon, the British Foreign Secretary who had come on a special mission, was ignored? Old and nearly blind, Grey went to Johns Hopkins to have his eyes treated while he awaited the signal from the President. He had three subjects to take up with Wilson—the League Treaty, which he favored; the respective size of the British and American navies; and the ever-turbulent Irish question. Lloyd George, anxious to iron out any difficulties between the two countries, chose Viscount Grey as the man best fitted to cope with Woodrow Wilson.

Both were scholars with many interests in common, but Grey committed the unpardonable sin of siding with Senator Lodge on the Treaty. During the crucial four months of debate, he talked to Senators of both parties and displayed a message from Lloyd George suggesting that the Lodge reservations would be acceptable to the British government.

Except for Lansing, the Cabinet members were incensed over what they took to be a violation of accepted diplomatic procedure, and there were demands that he return to England and stay out of the internal affairs of the United States. He returned home in January, without seeing the President. Edith was thought to have had the master hand in keeping them apart, although no one really knew who was making the final decisions in the White House at this time. Viscount Grey refused to believe that his friend, Woodrow Wilson, was to blame; there had been too much good feeling between them for that. But he was not so sure of Mrs. Wilson. His statement in the *Times* after his return to London that it was important for the United States to enter the League on whatever terms were necessary, angered Mrs. Wilson further.

In addition to his support of Lodge Washington gossips quickly ascribed the treatment given Viscount Grey to an earlier incident involving attacks made on her by Major Charles Kennedy Crauford-Stuart at the time of her marriage to Woodrow Wilson. He was then secretary to Lord Reading, but had turned up again in Viscount Grey's entourage, although the official representative was Sir William Tyrrell.

The major was a well-known gadabout, a gossip, a familiar spirit among the British in the capital. But he was also talented—an accomplished musician who composed songs and was always welcomed by the cognoscenti. He was clever, erratic, and outspoken in his dislike for Americans. He particularly disliked Edith and chattered irresponsibly about her.

In a pianologue at a party given by Mrs. J. Borden Harriman, one of Washington's most powerful hostesses, and a strong supporter of President Wilson, he made fun of her and suggested that she had become Mrs. Wilson by buying off Mrs. Peck. Later he tried to explain this by saying that he was addressing a sophisticated audience in the spirit of light fun.

Mrs. Harriman was intensely angry, but the story took wings, and other riddles and limericks credited to him got into circulation. There was action at once from the White House and Lansing asked Lord Reading to send him back to England. Crauford-Stuart begged to be allowed to stay, since dismissal on such grounds would end his diplomatic career. He promised to keep out of view socially until his term expired, and he swore there would be no more gibes. Edith, who could neither forget nor forgive his unjust implications, thought that Lansing should have insisted on his departure, but he stayed on until Lord Reading returned to England.

She was astonished that he should now turn up again in Viscount Grey's entourage, with his record well known in the State Department. Baruch and Dr. Grayson were up in arms. The admiral in particular had not forgotten Crauford-Stuart's scurrilous wit at the time of the Wilson marriage. Lansing was told that the White House requested his immediate departure but the errant major was merely shifted from his diplomatic billet to a post as a member of the ambassador's household. This took him out of the firing line. He was no longer an accredited attaché subject to dismissal under State Department rules.

Dr. Grayson and others appealed directly to the aging statesman to send Crauford-Stuart back to England immediately, but without response and Edith felt that Lansing, on his way out, had not helped the situation.

The President appointed Bainbridge Colby, a New York lawyer and an old friend, to succeed Lansing as Secretary of State, and Wilson was soon deeply embroiled in plans for the approaching national election. Democratic leaders rallied around the President as the convention of 1920 drew near. Even those who understood his physical incapacity did not wish to ignore him or hurt his feelings, but he held himself aloof and would not commit himself to any candidate.

Late in May, 1919, Homer S. Cummings, prominent in legal and political circles and an old friend of Woodrow Wilson's, visited the White House to discuss candidates with the President and to show him his keynote speech. Together they talked of McAdoo, A. Palmer Mitchell, and Governor James Cox of Ohio, who was quickly discounted by the President. He talked affectionately of John W. Davis, who had fought so many labor battles as Attorney General from 1913 to 1918 and who was now ambassador at the Court of St. James's.

Wilson took issue with only one point in Cummings' speech—that he had been at the point of death. He did not like that. Edith stood by and shook her head warningly lest this sensitive subject be pursued. It was soon apparent to Cummings and to other Democratic leaders who called on him that Wilson seemed to be harboring the dream of a third term.

Edith, Dr. Grayson, and Tumulty were all aware that this possibility haunted Wilson because he believed that he alone could push through the Treaty. When an interview by Louis Seibold appeared in the New York *World,* with a guarded hint of this possibility—a trial balloon —Tumulty went into action at once and asked the President to announce publicly that he had no intention of running for office. The President refused. Why, he argued, should he decline something that had not been offered to him? Tumulty wrote to Edith asking her mediation, but there was silence. McAdoo, with bright prospects as a candidate, decided to withdraw, and Dr. Grayson talked frankly to Carter Glass, chairman of the platform committee at San Francisco, urging him to do everything possible to head off the nomination of the President. He said it would kill him. Knowing how deeply her husband felt, Edith stayed silent while various friends preserved the myth that kept him expectant. She was assured that although his wishes for the platform would prevail, and his name would be honored in all respects at the convention, there would be no push for his nomination. But Colby, who visited the Wilsons before leaving for San Francisco, hoped to have him enter the race. Carter Glass, Newton Baker, Josephus Daniels, and others agreed with Homer Cummings that this would be a tragic mistake.

McAdoo would most likely have won the nomination had the President endorsed him, but Wilson remained silent, resisting the appeals that came pouring into the White House from the West Coast. All requests for endorsement were ignored. It was a period of great stress for Edith. Friends and foes realized that this was an unusual convention, with the President helpless at the White House. His strong image joined them as the delegates entering the auditorium saw a large American flag slowly unroll to reveal a startlingly lifelike portrait of the President. San Francisco was ablaze with personal tributes of one kind or another to their lost leader, but the political machine ground on.

Whatever Woodrow Wilson's hopes may have been—if any—he waited in vain at the White House for nomination. He and Edith followed the voting, ballot by ballot. Cox, whose chances he had discounted, was the winner, with Franklin D. Roosevelt for his running mate. Roosevelt later said that he had felt like backing Woodrow Wilson for another term. In the end it would not have made any difference, since Warren Harding and Calvin Coolidge were the Republican nominees, and soon Harding was in power.

Wrapped in a shawl, the President looked old and haggard when he was wheeled out on the South Portico to receive Cox and Roosevelt on their return from California. Mrs. Wilson noticed how bright and spruce young Roosevelt looked as he bent over her husband with deference.

"Thank you for coming. I am very glad you came," Wilson said with his old courtesy but in a feeble voice.

Shocked by his pallor and his look of helplessness, Cox told him at once how much he had always admired the stand he had taken for the League. The President responded, with a quick burst of energy, "Cox, that fight can still be won."

Before leaving the White House the nominee signed a statement in the Executive Wing committing himself to making the League the paramount issue of the campaign. He had always believed in it, and had been one of its supporters.

The President was cool to the Cabinet members on their return from San Francisco. All were anxious to explain the role they had played in the general confusion. He listened attentively, but only Daniels and Colby seemed to reach him. He was incredulous when Daniels told him that the Democrats would be beaten.

"Do you think it is possible that the American people would elect Harding?" he asked.

"It is not only possible, but they are going to do it," Daniels replied.

"You haven't enough faith in the people," said the President.

Regardless of his low opinion of the Republican nominee, his sense of fairness asserted itself at once when Tumulty came hurrying in to tell him that the Democrats had a fine campaign issue in the story which had just come to light that Harding had African ancestry. Without a moment's hesitation Woodrow Wilson squelched Tumulty's enthusiasm. "Even if that is so, it will never be used with my consent. . . . I insist you kill any such proposal," he said.

Edith was proud of her husband's stand. Immediately before the

231

election he made his closest approach to a speech since Pueblo. He talked formally at a Cabinet meeting on November 2 of the need "to redeem the great moral obligation of the United States," and he predicted that Harding could not win. But Harding did, with a tremendous sweep.

The President told Edith that he wanted to stay up beyond his nine o'clock bedtime to follow the returns, but by nine even he had to concede Harding's victory. He was intensely depressed when he awakened the next day, feeling that in electing Harding the people had turned against him. He felt lost and abandoned. Edith met the situation with tenderness, and Nell, whose husband had lost in the stakes, too, wrote to her "darling, darling Father" that the Democratic defeat was not a repudiation of the League. Jessie found consolation on election night by reading the life story of Joan of Arc, and finding parallels where courage and conviction were concerned. At the end, as in the beginning, Woodrow Wilson could depend on the women in his family to give him unlimited loyalty.

Edith had to work harder than ever now to lift his spirits. He had spasmodic fits of anger that were difficult to cope with, and even an occasional "damn" for the perfidy of politicians. Daniels noted that this was uncommonly strong language for the Presbyterian elder to use. In all the years he had known him there had been no more than five or six "damns" within his own hearing. Now the President assured him that he was just being emphatic and not profane when he was heard uttering a rousing "damn" at a luncheon.

Although his vocabulary had always been rich in varied expressions of love for Edith and the other women in his family, he had no specific expletives for his enemies. Nevertheless, Edith knew that he was not different from other men when his anger was fully aroused. She, too, could be earthy and was not above calling Senator Lodge a "stinker." Her husband's tirades leaned more on intellectual analysis, but he could be stinging in his comments to Edith and his intimates.

His eyes were now fully open to his own situation and the realization was embittering. So much had been spared him that he had not realized the loss of public confidence in his powers. His notes to Cabinet members and department heads had an acerbic touch different from the temperate tone of the past. Edith's own work as intermediary had

232

slackened, with the departments functioning under the old rules. The delayed appointment of diplomats was corrected in May, 1920, and the President received the Bulgarian and Belgian ambassadors, and the minister from Uruguay.

His last months in the White House were a triumph in human endurance as he and Edith together, aided by a skilled professional staff and Dr. Grayson, met with an unbroken front each situation that arose. Up to the last hour the President persisted with his exercises, abided by his established routine, listened to his wife's constant words of cheer and hope, and thought his own thoughts. As his condition improved he also grew more realistic about his incapacity, but he would not give up, nor would Edith let him.

# *21.* *The House on S Street*

ON the day of Warren Harding's inauguration the public realized for the first time the condition of Woodrow Wilson as they saw him ride to the Capitol beside the handsome President-elect of the United States. The visual evidence was more convincing than the gossip that had swept the capital. It was clear to all who saw him that he was a shattered man. Twice in the past he had presented a handsome image on inauguration day; the picture had changed.

He had made up his mind to honor his successor and finish his own term in the traditional manner. He was up early and Edith found him in formal attire with Brooks waiting beside him holding his high hat, gloves, and walking stick. The time had come for him to appear. She walked with him to the elevator and together they entered the Blue Room and greeted the Cabinet members, Senators, and other officials assembled with their wives.

When the President-elect and Mrs. Harding arrived, there were cordial words all around. Dr. Grayson and Secret Service men skillfully helped the President into the car that then moved smoothly away. Woodrow Wilson was leaving the White House forever—the War President who in his wife's words "had given his all in strength and health to make peace."

The day was bright, with a clear blue sky and a whipping wind that stirred the flags and blew off hats. It was a quiet procession with few bands and little excitement. The parade-weary public along the route gave scattered bursts of applause. Many were surprised when they caught a quick flash of the shrunken figure of Woodrow Wilson in the shadow of Warren Harding's hearty presence. Wilson raised his right hand feebly, but his hat was not lifted high in the old triumphant gesture. Harding seemed to fill the car as he stood up and waved his arms in all directions. He was built in the heroic mold, with sharply chiseled features and a shock of silver hair. To some he suggested a strong new spirit in the White House after the Spartan era of war and the President's illness.

Spectators were also having a last look at Edith Bolling Wilson in the role of First Lady. Between December 18, 1915, her wedding day, and the Harding inaugural she had become a figure of international interest and also of power and mystery. She listened to Mrs. Harding's insistent talk as they drove together, but her thoughts were with Woodrow and how he would stand the day's excitement.

She was unhappily aware of both Hardings when they reached the Capitol. Because of the President's inability to climb the steps he had once taken in stride, arrangements had been made for him to be driven to the lower entrance out of sight of the crowd; from there he would be taken upstairs by elevator.

The chairman of the inaugural committee had told the Wilsons that undoubtedly Harding would accompany the President and go up with him in the elevator, instead of the traditional climb up the stairs together. But he jumped out at the foot of the Capitol steps, waving his hat to the cheering crowd, and the car with Woodrow Wilson moved on to the rear entrance.

Edith resented this deeply and instinctively she wanted to follow Woodrow, but she was swept into a round of formalities with Mrs. Harding before she could catch up with him in the President's room. When he had finished walking stiffly from the elevator, newspaperman

234

# The House on S Street

David Lawrence noted that the "man who had driven through the streets of Rome, Paris and London, hailed as the great peacemaker of this generation, sank limply into a chair." When General Pershing stepped forward Wilson said, "Excuse me, General, for not rising."

Edith moved close to him as Cabinet members, judges, diplomats, and old friends from Congress who had sometimes helped him and often fought him, filed past with friendly greetings. He jested with Harding and wished him well. There were bills to be signed, the last act of an outgoing President, and here their paths divided. When he was asked if he wished to go out to the stand for the ceremonies in front of the Capitol he said that he lacked the strength.

He stiffened visibly when Henry Cabot Lodge appeared for the closing act of the President's term. His gray eyes focused sharply on Lodge as the Senator told him that the two Houses had completed their work and were prepared to receive any further communications from him. Edith, standing by, heard the President say in his iciest tone but with perfect calm, "I have no further communication. I would be glad if you would inform both Houses and thank them for their courtesy— good morning, sir."

David Lawrence, an observer, called it the final scene of "perhaps the greatest of battles in American history over the ratification of a treaty." Warren Harding came back as Wilson was being helped into his coat and wished him good health. Edith gave him credit for showing kindness and courtesy in this final exchange. She did not fail to wish the Hardings and the Coolidges "all the luck in the world." She knew what they faced and she had already warmed to Mrs. Coolidge, if not to Mrs. Harding.

A tide of applause for Warren Harding was rising in the Capitol grounds as Woodrow and Edith were driven to 2340 S Street, the house in which Edith would spend the rest of her life. Woodrow, relieved that it was all over, was tired but in a jesting mood. Edith burned with indignation, feeling that he had been shabbily treated. He refused to take her seriously. "Where I was bitter, he was tolerant, where I resented, he was amused," she later recalled.

A crowd waited at S Street and quietly applauded as they entered their new home. Twice Woodrow came to the window and acknowledged their presence with a wave of his right hand. Inside, his familiar setting at the White House had been faithfully reproduced. Two days earlier Edith had seen the house in a state of total confusion, with littered floors and no furnishings. Now everything was in perfect order. The rugs were down, curtains hung, pictures and mirrors in place, and the rooms fragrant with welcoming flowers. Woodrow's favorite chair by the fire, his reading lamp, his books, all saved him the trauma of a major change of scene when he was least able to cope with the unfamiliar.

Edith had planned it all, with the help of her brother Wilmer and Ike Hoover. The President's quarters at the White House had been left undisturbed until he left for the Capitol; then the transfer was rapidly made. Brooks and Susan arranged all the Wilsons' personal belongings and sadly bade them good-bye.

They lunched in the dining room overlooking the garden and, although tired, Woodrow was in high spirits, reminding Dr. Grayson that he was now plain Mr. Wilson when Grayson called him "Mr. President."

"You will always be the President to me," said the devoted doctor who had watched him through the hours of triumph and of pain.

When he reached his bedroom for his afternoon rest, Woodrow paused at the door. Everything was just as it had been at the White House. Edith had ordered a copy of the eight-by-six-foot Lincoln bed to which he had become attached, and the familiar silken Stars and Stripes hung above it. She had also placed a grandfather clock with Westminster chimes on the staircase, for she knew he would miss the White House clocks.

Their new house was four stories tall, with high ceilings and spacious rooms. The entrance hall had ivory-tinted woodwork with a black and white marble floor. It had rooms at either side and the one at the left became Randolph's office. A short flight of stairs led to the main hall, where Woodrow soon was taking daily walks after dictating letters to Randolph. Their handsome drawing room and library were on the second floor, as well as the dining room and a solarium overlooking the garden. Five bedrooms and five bathrooms were on the third floor and Edith, always clothes-conscious, had arranged for an unusual amount of closet space. The servants' quarters and the laundry were on the fourth floor.

Behind the main hall were a billiard room, servants' dining room, and a large kitchen. A brick garage was built for the Pierce Arrow, its roof making a terrace level with the dining room on the second floor. This was another area where Woodrow could walk when he felt able. With an elevator, stacks reaching to the ceiling to hold his 8,000 books, and everything designed for his comfort, from footrests and castored chairs that could be rolled about with ease, to carefully placed reading lights, Woodrow and Edith soon adapted themselves to the new way of life. It came easily to Edith, who enjoyed arranging her house, which she called "unpretentious, comfortable, dignified, fitted to the needs of a gentleman."

At first they had thought of building a house of their own and Woodrow's interest in architecture had led them to study plans. But they gave up this idea and she spent weeks in search of a place that she thought would be right for them. The house on S Street was her third choice, and she never regretted it. The price was $150,000, which was beyond their means, but ten of the President's friends, including Bernard Baruch, had arranged the mortgage for them. When Woodrow realized that this was the house she wanted but that she hesitated to take it, he surprised her by greeting her when she came in from a Philharmonic concert with a deed to the property. The house was four years old and had been built for Henry Parker Fairbanks. To ensure complete privacy for the Wilsons, Baruch took over the adjoining lot and left it in its wild woodland state. For weeks before they left the White House Edith would run over after Woodrow fell asleep to help Wilmer in his preparations.

Here the Wilsons had some of their best days. They had found a haven, away from the public eye, and they could watch with equanimity the shift in party spirit. Their day was over and Woodrow Wilson did not try to fill the role of elder statesman. He made no attempt to interfere in any party issue, nor did he pass judgment on the flamboyance of the Harding administration. Edith was more openly critical of their expensive style, their huge parties, and racy ways.

After the long years of darkness and silence the Hardings had thrown the White House open to the public, with big receptions, banquets, and unlimited hospitality. Always beautifully dressed and carefully coiffed, Mrs. Harding stood beside her buoyant husband while Democrats and Republicans closed ranks to some extent in the inevitable social drift to the White House.

Woodrow Wilson was never altogether the Forgotten Man; his name was too firmly implanted in the nation's history for that, but his wife at times suffered over what she took to be neglect. The party leaders still honored his name. He was always cordial and listened to them attentively but refused to take sides on any issue. On days when his vitality was high he indulged in his old teasing, telling stories and cracking jokes, but underlying all his conversation they caught his unquenchable hope for the future of the League.

When word reached S Street in August, 1921, that Franklin D. Roosevelt had met with his crippling disaster at Portobello, the immediate reaction of Woodrow Wilson was one of sympathy. Up to then he had been somewhat cool and condescending to the handsome young man, but now he wrote, "I am indeed delighted to hear you are getting well so fast and so confidently, and I shall try to be generous enough not to envy you." This was followed by occasional jests about a race between the two great leaders—one with his career over, the other with the whole world ahead of him—as to which would be able first to play golf. Edith saw little of Mrs. Roosevelt at this time, but she understood what Eleanor was facing. And the two men could never again think of each other with indifference. In the days of his great power, Roosevelt was a Wilson worshiper.

Disabled though he was, the former President showed improvement after settling on S Street. The sense of strain diminished and his muscular tone improved. It was a simple life for one who had known such power, but it was in keeping with his desire to stay out of the limelight. Everything was done to protect him from disturbance, but he was wrought up over the confusion surrounding his role at the burial of the Unknown Soldier at Arlington on November 11, 1921.

When an invitation came from the War Department for his presence, Edith sent Randolph to explain personally to the Assistant Secretary of War that her husband wished to pay his respects by appearing in the procession, although he could not take part in the actual ceremony because of his disability. He wished to drive in an open carriage and to follow the cortege to its destination.

But the official orders for the day were precise and no concessions could be made for Woodrow Wilson. He and other government dignitaries were to retire from the procession at West Executive Avenue. As it happened, when he and Mrs. Wilson arrived in their carriage to fall in line ahead of the Supreme Court Justices, as directed, there was much confusion and no opening for them in the long line of cars. Scott sat on the box with their driver and, rather than be crowded out, they wedged their way awkwardly into the line. As they were recognized the crowd broke through a barrier and rushed the Wilson carriage. Veterans in service uniforms, remembering their Commander in chief, formed a solid guard around the carriage as it moved slowly to the point of retirement on West Executive Avenue. Mrs. Coolidge thought that Woodrow looked better than he had on the day of the Harding inauguration, but he was a bitterly disappointed man as he was driven back to S Street.

It was a day of deep emotional feeling to the thousands gathered at Arlington. As they watched the famous war figures pin foreign decorations to the casket cover they sorrowed for their dead, and tears flowed as the final trumpet sounded and ten minutes of silence was observed, initiating a national custom. It took some time to calm the War President and make him feel that he had played his part that day. But he was not forgotten by the soldiers or by the statesmen with whom he had worked in Europe. The great names of the war loomed large on the American horizon in the winter of 1921–1922, as delegates arrived for the Conference on the Limitation of Armaments. The White House was a hive of social activity and the embassies kept up a brisk round of parties. There were many distinguished callers at S Street. Some saw Woodrow Wilson, others just left cards.

It was a shock to some of the men who had worked and battled with him to see him, as keen and scholarly as ever, dignified and courteous, but tiring quickly and stricken physically. He was carefully prepared for these interviews to give the appearance of independent functioning. Edith kept her distance, but at the slightest sign of excitement she moved closer to give him reassurance or smiled encouragingly across the room.

His old friend Clemenceau kissed him on both cheeks and poured out a torrent of words, but there were tears in his eyes as he joined Edith downstairs and said, "Madam, I am deeply touched." When Lloyd George came for tea with his wife, and his daughter Megan, Edith found the Welshman more charming than in Europe. There was much to forgive him, but he and Woodrow had always liked each other personally, and they had a merry afternoon. They had no sooner greeted each other than Woodrow sprang some of his limericks. Soon they were all in gales of laughter.

"While they did not agree very often on public questions, their personal relations had been invariably delightful," Edith said.

She was fascinated by Megan, already on her way to a political career of her own. She had always found Mrs. Lloyd George a colorless wife for so versatile a man, but they got on well together, for Edith was expert at handling the conventional wives of the brilliant men who crossed her path. They must all have noticed a difference in her, too, for during this period she lost her characteristic gloss. Woodrow's illness and her concentration on his care had been exhausting and aging. She smiled and laughed less often now, and her expression was touched with sadness as she watched him with the great figures he had known in the past.

Woodrow sometimes worried about her and urged her to go out more for recreation, but he always needed and wanted her. One guest she did not enjoy was Margot Asquith, who arrived in Washington in February, 1922, and insisted on seeing Woodrow Wilson. Edith tried to divert her, remembering their hectic contacts in Europe. She decided to leave her card at the British Embassy and let it go at that, but before she had time to do so Mrs. Asquith called her directly from the White House, asking when she could come to S Street.

She was invited for tea that afternoon and on her arrival she startled Randolph by throwing her arms around him, peering into his face, and demanding why she had not been invited, but had been forced to invite herself. How could anyone think that she would visit Washington and not see the "great War President"?

When Edith took her up to the library she threw herself at Woodrow's feet and poured out torrents of words, with accompanying gestures. Edith saw at once that she was amusing Woodrow, who liked to listen to the conversation of witty women. On the way out she gave them a demonstration of a new type of dress—one zip from top to bottom and off it came. Edith took stock of the flash of French lingerie in this quick move. Margot reminded her of a hummingbird but Woodrow was less censorious. When they discussed her he said, "Well, of course, I think her a woman of taste, for she told me I was the best speaker she had ever heard."

240

Then Tumulty made a move that cut his strings forever with Edith and shut him off from Woodrow Wilson. Edith's relations with him had always been tenuous, but she could not forgive his message at the Jefferson Day banquet of the National Democratic Club, held in New York in April, 1922, which seemed to commit Wilson to the candidacy of James Cox for President. The invalid raged when he glanced at a morning paper and saw a headline proclaiming this fact.

Tumulty had asked him for a message he could read at the dinner, but the former President wrote that he did not feel the occasion an appropriate one for breaking his silence. Cox, a strong supporter of the League of Nations, had lost in 1920; he was up again for 1924. Tumulty pushed the matter and asked Edith to let him see the "Governor." She stipulated that he must not discuss the election, but she was not present at the interview and so never knew what was said.

The message Tumulty read at the dinner suggested at once that Wilson was backing Cox. A great burst of applause greeted the magic name of the former President just before Cox delivered his keynote speech. The next day, a New York *Times* headline read: COX BOOM LAUNCHED ON WILSON KEYNOTE OF JUSTICE FOR ALL. Denials quickly followed from S Street and a note to the *Times* from the President appeared on April 14, 1922, saying: "I did not send any message whatever to that dinner nor authorize anyone to convey a message."

Wilmer Bolling acted as intermediary for his sister, who called the message a total fabrication. Edith was chiefly concerned over the severe reaction it had had on her husband. Tumulty's half-retraction did not go far enough to suit her, but Wilson, knowing Tumulty best of all and having valued his loyalty, in his own words "let the unpleasant affair fade out."

In gloom the bewildered Tumulty refrained from bothering his idol further, but he wrote in an ambiguous vein to Edith, "I want you to feel, you who have been so wonderful and generous to me in all things, that I shall always be around the corner when you or yours need me. I expect no reply to this letter. I shall understand."

He got no reply, then or ever, nor did he ever talk again to Woodrow Wilson. The stories that circulated after the President's death about the treatment accorded Tumulty gave Edith much concern. She was dismayed to read in the papers that she had refused to let him see her husband before he died and that he had gone through some anguished hours trying to get to the President. He had been seen weeping outside the house, incredulous that Woodrow Wilson should be dying and that he was denied admission. He was told that the doctors would let no one into the sick room and even Dr. Grayson, who was friendly to Tumulty, could not help him. Visitors were coming and going, but Edith was not seeing any of them, nor did she even know that Tumulty was among them, she said.

McAdoo was concerned when he learned that Tumulty had not been invited to the private service at the house, and after speaking to Edith about it a hasty telephone call was made to invite Tumulty and his wife. When much was made of the fact that Tumulty had ridden in the last car of the procession, even behind the servants, Edith explained that this was because of his last-minute inclusion.

The Tumulty situation was never wholly cleared up. Had Edith deliberately snubbed the man who advised the President not to marry her? Had she disliked his influence and some of the prejudices he had brought to bear on the Wilson administration? It had merely been one final straw in the wind. But Tumulty was never in any doubt about the motive, and for the rest of his troubled life he held this, along with much else, against Woodrow Wilson's widow. He died in 1954 after practicing law for a number of years, and then being institutionalized for a mental breakdown. No word of any kind reached his family from Edith Wilson when he died.

# 22. *"The Best of Wives"*

LIFE at the White House came under fierce scrutiny while Woodrow Wilson adjusted to a new form of existence on S Street. He refrained from criticizing Warren Harding as gossip raged about high living and a little house on K Street. Out of his own bitter experience

# "The Best of Wives"

Wilson squelched some of his successor's critics by reminding them that they should not attack the man in the White House without full knowledge of the facts.

Harding had disappointed him, however, by shifting his stand on the League of Nations. During the campaign his position had been equivocal, but his inauguration speech indicated that he was definitely opposed to entering the League. He was not a total isolationist, however, and he advocated American participation in the Permanent Court of International Justice at the Hague.

When the news of President Harding's death in San Francisco on August 2, 1923, reached the house on S Street, Edith could scarcely believe that the handsome fifty-eight-year-old man who had raced up the Capitol steps was dead. The Harding funeral was an ordeal that had to be met by Woodrow Wilson. He sat with Admiral Grayson and Edith in the Pierce Arrow parked west of the North Portico while the services were being held inside the White House. Edith could only guess at his thoughts as the passing troops saluted him, and members of the White House staff came out to greet him. He wore formal morning attire with a black cravat; Admiral Grayson had a black band on his white naval uniform. Edith wore mourning. It was a sweltering day and the surroundings were bright with blossoms and shrubs. The Hardings had done much to beautify the White House grounds.

Suddenly, a cavalry colonel rode up to their car and asked Woodrow where Senator Lodge could be found. Edith did not need to look at Woodrow to catch the cold impact of his voice. "I am not Senator Lodge's keeper." As the embarrassed officer rode away, Wilson said that he must have been something of a madman; then he reflected that he was young and probably uninformed.

Woodrow, deeply depressed that night, told Edith that when he died he wished for a private funeral. From time to time he made remarks indicating that he knew his life was ebbing away. His cherished hope that he could devote himself to writing and get back to his long-delayed *The Philosophy of Politics* was fading. Since leaving the White House many offers had come his way and Ida Tarbell was one of those who urged him to give some of his wisdom to the world. He intended to write his autobiography but never got beyond the dedication. Edith knew from the start that it would never be written, but she treasured the tribute to

her which he tapped out on his typewriter as one of his last acts before
leaving the White House:

To E.B.W.

*I dedicate this book because it is a book in which I have tried
to interpret the life of a nation, and she has shown me the full
meaning of life. Her heart is not only true but wise; her thoughts
are not only free but touched with vision; she teaches and
guides by being what she is; her unconscious interpretation of
faith and duty makes all the way clear; her power to compre-
hend makes work and thought alike easier and more near to
what it seeks.*

*(Signed) Woodrow Wilson*

Now he found it difficult to cope with an article that he had agreed to
do, *The Road Away from Revolution.* It was published in August, 1923,
in *The Atlantic Monthly,* but only after a painful period of rewriting
and expansion. It was a warning to Americans against the materialism
of the period. He urged a social and economic order based on "sympathy and helpfulness and a willingness to forgo self-interest in order to
promote the welfare, happiness, and contentment of others and of the
community as a whole."

Great effort had gone into this piece of work. The old power of communication was missing, and he would waken Edith many times in the
night to jot down thoughts as they came to him. When it was finished
George Creel, to whom it was submitted, dismissed it as unworthy of
Woodrow's talents. He thought that it should not be sent out, since it
lacked substance and needed expansion. There was no hint of the Wilsonian style, he said. Edith knew this to be true, and it was her task to
break the news to him on their next drive. He was deeply upset and
raged about anyone daring to question his work.

When they got back to S Street Dr. Axson heard her sobbing in the
hall. He had seen her through many crises but had never known her to
show weakness or break down. In his gentle way he asked to see the
article. As an English professor he was prepared to do some revision if
necessary. The changes he made were minor, but Edith would not pass
them until her husband had approved them himself. The article ap-

peared and made little impression except that it bore the famous name of Woodrow Wilson, once so fluent, now silent and disabled.

Woodrow longed to be useful again and Edith was startled when he announced that he would practice law with his good friend, Bainbridge Colby. He had studied law in his early days and the legal requirements were easily met for the illustrious Woodrow Wilson. Their firm was known as Wilson and Colby, with offices in New York and Washington. Colby looked after the New York end, traveling back and forth, and Wilson functioned in the capital.

It was a heroic gesture all around and quickly came to nothing. Dr. Grayson would not permit his patient to go to the office, so prospective clients came to S Street. One big offer after another was turned down, for the former President would not consider the use of his name for cases that might lead to embarrassment. Edith urged him to dissolve the partnership, which he did. She saw that Colby was being held back from building up the lucrative practice that soon became his. All three remained the best of friends.

Although impractical from the start, the venture had been good for Wilson's morale. With the one legal fee he had accepted he bought an electric brougham for Edith's birthday in October, a matter of great satisfaction to her. She had always liked the independence of having her own "electric" even when she had the use of the official White House cars. Now she could resume her old practice and even take her husband for an occasional spin. But the traffic rules were changing and the roads were alive with speeding cars. Although for a time they took leisurely runs through the park, by the river, or even over to Alexandria, there was always the danger of the current giving out, leaving them stranded in an inaccessible spot.

Everything was done to suggest a normal manner of life at S Street. This was simpler than it had been at the White House. Randolph, who had spent the last four months in residence with them while convalescing from an operation, took Tumulty's place as a paid secretary when they moved into their own house. His office to the left of the entrance became known as the Dugout. He was a combination of secretary, amanuensis, censor, court chamberlain, and keeper of the gate. He controlled the flow of visitors, handled the mail, and conspired with his sister to protect the former President from any kind of fatigue or disturbance.

Edith kept a tight hand on Randolph's letters, since he could be tactless and even vituperative. He, too, had strong likes and dislikes but she was careful never to wound him. She treated him with tenderness and understanding. She would quietly set aside any letters to be signed by her husband that lacked the objective touch. Woodrow's own letters had always been noted for cool balance and courtesy, however strongly he might feel on an issue. Edith was a tactful letter-writer herself in most instances; she was apt to be more emphatic in her conversation than in her correspondence.

Even though he was no longer President, Woodrow Wilson still received an enormous amount of mail from all parts of the world. The Dugout was Edith's office, too, and while Randolph worked with his letters and clippings she sat close to the fire at the old rolltop desk that she had brought from the White House. She was again the businesswoman, always well-groomed, making quick decisions, except for matters that had to be brought to Woodrow's attention. He, too, would appear occasionally in the Dugout but he preferred to dictate to Randolph upstairs.

Small in stature and visibly crippled, Edith's brother lived in a world of his own. He had coped with pain from early childhood because of lateral curvature of the spine. She did everything she could to enlarge his interests and enrich his life. Classical music was his chief interest, but he was catholic in his tastes and followed baseball and the big sports events of the 1920's with fervor. On a huge table in the middle of the Dugout, he worked day after day on immense scrapbooks of Wilsoniana, a compilation that in time became one of the most remarkable collections of its kind in the country. He finished one a year.

Only a fraction of the material that came in ever reached the retired President. Everything was channeled carefully through Edith and Dr. Grayson, who studied each variation in Woodrow's strength and understanding. One minute he talked vaguely of running for the Presidency in 1924; at another his thoughts dwelled far in the past. Edith usually knew at a glance which course he was taking, and there were days when he seemed as of old. Delegations of various kinds were received and small gatherings in the street cheered him from time to time.

## "The Best of Wives"

The press showed particular interest when Samuel Gompers arrived on a January day in 1922 with a small delegation to honor the President who had been a valiant friend of labor. Gompers had come from the National Theater where one of the meetings to initiate the Woodrow Wilson Foundation had just been held. Edith stood on the steps behind her husband, listening to Gompers' words of praise, but worrying at the same time about the icy wind buffeting her frail husband.

Woodrow had moody and angry days, as well as quiet, depressed ones, and Edith's own spirits went soaring when she saw the shadows of confusion lift. Although in her heart she knew that all the effort was hopeless, she kept an even front to Woodrow and to all her friends and relatives. Her own zest for life and her love of music, bridge, and the theater kept her going, but her entire day was regulated by her husband's routine. She limited her business errands and brief social calls to the hours when he slept or worked over his mail with Randolph. Dr. Grayson marveled at the number of things she could accomplish in the time at her disposal. "She had executive genius and took upon herself the responsibilities and burdens of many," he commented. Even when her husband lay desperately ill, she remembered the needs of her mother, Bertha, her brothers, and young relatives, arranging things for their comfort and pleasure.

The President, as Edith still sometimes thought of him, was wakened at eight o'clock. They breakfasted together in his room or in the solarium, where he also lunched unless guests were coming. Edith went over the papers with him before going down to the Dugout to see what mail had come in and to attend to her domestic affairs. While he lunched, she read or chatted with him. It had always been understood in the Wilson family that his mealtimes should be kept free from stress and political concerns. While he rested after lunch she ate downstairs with Randolph, with other members of her family, or with friends. He kept appointments when equal to it, until it was time for the daily drive. Randolph brought visitors to the library where they sat and talked to him by the fire, for he was always cold.

Their drives were agreeable but no longer the happy diversion they had been before his collapse. He tired in his confined position but Edith diverted him as much as she could. It always pleased him to have people recognize him as they passed. On their return she usually had a social hour for tea and sometimes friends would drop in and talk to Woodrow. At seven, after he had changed back into his dressing gown and slippers, he had dinner. Except to go out driving, he rarely wore anything else, and he dined at a small table by the library fire, for he only entered the dining room in formal attire. Edith read to him in the heavily curtained room, with the fire crackling and a low reading-lamp lighting the pages, and she helped him in the slow process of coping with his food. It was a world apart, and when he had finished she would join Randolph and occasional guests for dinner while her husband was prepared for bed. She would soon leave the table to read to him until he fell asleep. His bedtime technically was nine o'clock. He had a male nurse-masseur, John A. Ruppel, who was on duty from seven in the evening until morning, and in addition he did many handy jobs for the house.

Edith found two devoted retainers in Isaac and Mary Scott, a black couple who leavened the last years of Woodrow's life and stayed on when he died. Isaac went everywhere with him, sitting beside the driver when they set off for the country, accompanying him on their trips to the theater. "I count them high on my list of this world's blessings," said Edith of this pair who grew old in her service. "This gentle and understanding little servant became more and more essential to Mr. Wilson's comfort." Mary was equally loyal and efficient as Edith's personal maid.

Miss Ruth Powderly, the mature and dignified nurse who had been with Woodrow Wilson through every crisis, beginning with the death of his first wife, was waiting for them at S Street on the day they moved in. She was in government service, assigned to the Navy Department, and the retiring President felt that it would not be fair to have her follow him. But when needed she was quickly on duty at Woodrow Wilson's bedside, and Edith relied on her for emergencies. She was with him when he died.

Much as he needed Edith, Woodrow worried at times about the burdens his wife carried. She never showed a sign of fatigue in his presence, but her family cares, aside from being with him, were considerable. Even with her splendid constitution the strain on Edith was beginning to show, and Dr. Grayson feared she might have a breakdown if she did not take a rest. She had not been away from Washington since the autumn of 1919, except for three brief trips: two to New York—one to visit the Baruchs and the other to spend a few days with Mr. and Mrs. Norman Davis—and a third foray to Charles L. Hamlin's country place at Mattapoisett, Massachusetts. This was where she decided to go again in the fall of 1923. Dr. Grayson promised to stay at the S Street house and to take the best care possible of his patient while she was gone. But when she got to Massachusetts she waited eagerly for news of her husband and pounced on the mail when she came in from her long walks with Anna Hamlin and her black spaniel Moses.

Dr. Grayson was giving Wilson electrical treatments and taking him for daily drives. He stayed with the former President while he took his meals, just as Edith did. Bernard Baruch and Louis Brandeis called to see him. When Edith telephoned from the Hamlin house her husband could not understand a word she said, nor did he even recognize her voice. It was time to return. She felt rested and refreshed when she arrived home early in September, but her first glimpse of Woodrow dismayed her. He had not changed, but she was finally seeing him as he was. His decline was steady through late summer.

It was always a matter of concern to Woodrow when Dr. Grayson left town for one reason or another. Only Edith understood his needs better than Cary, and they enjoyed each other's jokes as well. Although constantly on call and a regular visitor at S Street, he bred horses in Virginia, and he and Altrude followed the races. Edith called the ponies their "little four-footed daughters and sons." She kept in close touch and always rooted for them.

Dimly, Woodrow Wilson heard the echoes of a changing world, but disturbing news was kept from him. The League was still in his thoughts, and in his talks Edith saw that the old hurt remained. The isolationist spirit prevailed in various parts of the country, but international problems had become the talk of Washington as President Coolidge coped with the World Court developments.

Woodrow Wilson's last great effort was a radio talk he gave on the eve of Armistice Day, 1923. Belle Baruch and Evangeline Johnson, two friends of Edith's, had persuaded him to make this gesture on behalf of the League. Both were campaigning hard in Paris, Washington, and New York for America's participation, and they talked convincingly to Edith about the weight her husband's voice would carry at this particular time. Both were rich, worldly, and politically informed, and she called them "birds of brilliant plumage."

Belle was Bernard Baruch's daughter and she had inherited his dynamism. Evangeline was a striking blonde, six feet tall, who later became Mrs. Leopold Stokowski and in 1974 was still one of the Beautiful People, a decorative figure at the fashionable resorts, enjoying life and backing a number of constructive causes, as the Countess Zalstem-Zalessky. She belonged to the Johnson and Johnson pharmaceutical family of New Jersey and was no novice in the political field.

Wilson did not like the newborn form of entertainment that now reached millions of people; he thought the voices noisy and discordant. But he worked hard preparing a suitable ten-minute talk and although he had spent the day in bed with a severe headache, by eight thirty in the evening he was standing before the microphone in his library wearing a dressing gown. He always said that he could not speak unless he were on his feet, but now his wheelchair was ever close to his side. All the transmission equipment was outside. Nell stayed in the next room so as not to distract him. Edith stood behind the microphone with a copy of the speech in her hand, ready to prompt him.

Woodrow Wilson could no longer memorize a speech, something he had always done with great facility, nor could he extemporize. another of his special gifts. With his failing sight he had trouble with the typed pages. He started uncertainly, then halted for a moment and looked toward Edith, who prompted him softly until he recovered and went on without a further break. Strange though his voice sounded to many familiar with his crystal-clear delivery, all were impressed by the fact that it was the War President speaking again, and that the League was still uppermost in his thoughts.

Weak and discouraged as he ended, he went straight to bed and slept restlessly, convinced that his talk had not been a success. But the papers ran enthusiastic comments about it and made the point that he had spoken to the largest audience ever reached "at a given time by the human voice." The effort had stimulated him and he spoke again next day—November 11—to a crowd assembled at the house on S Street for an Armistice Day demonstration. The press likened it to a "religious

250

pilgrimage" as Wilson worshipers jammed the surrounding streets, out of range of his voice, but paying him tribute.

Carter Glass gave the formal Armistice Day address and then the former President spoke, with Edith standing protectively behind him, ready to give support if he failed. His words came slowly at first and he seemed to be on the verge of breaking down as he spoke of General Pershing and the soldiers he had commanded. "Pardon my emotion," he said, and then resumed his talk with greater strength. After proclaiming his enduring faith in the principles for which he had stood, he concluded, "that we shall prevail is as sure as that God reigns."

It was his last speech. Edith, who deplored any show of sentiment in public, had difficulty controlling her own emotions. Glass, who was devoted to both Wilsons, called her "simply great"—with human qualities that kept her close to earth but also "bordering on the divine."

During Woodrow's last days they went to Keith's Vaudeville House nearly every Saturday night. They came in through a side alley cleared in advance by the police, and had their own aisle seats, near the back and close to the side entrance. The actors prized Wilson's presence even more than they had when he was in the White House. They brought him flowers and sometimes played directly to him, as Olsen and Johnson did on Woodrow Wilson's last appearance in a theater.

It was Christmas Eve, 1923, and Margaret Wilson had come from New York with Helen Bones to be with him. The hilarious farces of these two comedians had always amused the President, but on this occasion a serious note underlay their performance. The set was a Christmas scene with a portrait of Woodrow Wilson over the fireplace, and the cast lined up before it. As Nan Halpern wished the audience a merry Christmas, addressing herself directly to Woodrow Wilson with tears in her eyes, the showgirls trooped down the aisles with their arms full of flowers to pile on his wheelchair. The audience rose en masse to sing "Auld Lang Syne" with the cast, all faces turned to the dying man. When Chick Johnson boomed "Merry Christmas, Mr. President!" a faint whisper sent back the echo.

As they left the theater Edith was well aware that it might be their last Christmas together, but she responded gaily to the crowd that awaited them in the alley—cast members still coated with greasepaint and mascara, and well-wishers pushing in from the surrounding streets. The air was scented with evergreen as on the day of their marriage. It was indeed Woodrow Wilson's last visit to a theater, but he continued to watch the films supplied to him at S Street, as in the White House. Douglas Fairbanks had given them a projector, and he added a personal touch that charmed Edith when he directed a family film of the McAdoo children. Will Rogers, already the friend of Calvin Coolidge, sometimes called at the house on S Street—not to bother the man he had long admired, but to leave a message, "I am not asking to see him. Just tell him that I love him."

Woodrow Wilson's name still had a certain magic in distant places, but he refused all medals and decorations, although he had been offered enough to cover him from head to foot. For years he moved in a world of military decorations and diplomatic display, but his plain, black-coated figure was distinctive in any gathering. He broke his rule about decorations only once, when he accepted the Order of the White Eagle from Poland in 1922 rather than offend the Polish Minister who bestowed it. He wore it only once—to please Edith at a dinner she gave for her mother on Mrs. Bolling's eightieth birthday in January, 1923. It turned into a costume party with the President wearing the jeweled star of the Order on a wide blue band. Edith was a harem lady, Wilmer a sheikh, and Randolph an Indian chief. The Wilson passion for charades and games persisted through Woodrow's long illness. This party tired him but he liked to see his family being merry around him, and he knew that his time was getting short.

On December 28 he received a birthday gift that delighted his wife. He was taken out to view the custom-made Rolls-Royce that his old friends had given him. It was black, with a thin orange stripe—the Princeton colors—and it had been designed to meet his special needs. The doors had been carefully planned and measured and it had every comfort inside. The President had always been interested in cars and this was the last one he would use, wearing the old gray sweater that had gone everywhere with him. Edith had long ceased to do anything but humor this whim. He had taken it to Buckingham Palace, to the Quirinal, to the Royal Palace in Brussels. Down the years the finest sweaters in the world had come his way but he clung to this one, as he did to the walking stick he had chosen from a picturesque collection to serve as his "third leg" after he had his stroke. His Hammond typewriter was another family legend, but in actual fact, long before his collapse he used the most up-to-date of models.

Woodrow Wilson was a man of habit, Dr. Grayson said, and in nine years of marriage Edith had come to know what he wanted almost before he spoke—a great advantage as his powers of communication wavered. Soon after their night at Keith's she noticed an indefinable change in him.

# 23. *Woodrow Wilson Finds Peace*

TO the end of his life Woodrow Wilson fought his disability, and Edith was the first to know when the battle was over. He attended to a small amount of mail, took his ten-minute walk in the hall and his daily drive until the last week. His final public act was shaking hands feebly with 125 members of the Democratic National Committee who filed past his chair by the library fire on January 16, eighteen days before he died. They had come from far and near, and Cordell Hull introduced each one by name. It was a slow procession as they leaned over and touched the weak hand that the President extended.

After the last one went down the stairs and out into a blinding downpour, Edith was back at his side with encouraging words. Lucy Maury, her niece, had just arrived for a visit and he jested with her in the old way. Edith thought that her presence at this time might help to cheer him, and she gave two small luncheons, bringing young laughter into the house.

Woodrow had a feeling of loneliness that he had never known. Everyone seemed to be going away, except Edith, who never left the house at this time, when she saw how he felt. The Sayres had gone with their three children to the Orient, where Francis was to serve for a

253

year as adviser on international law at the Court of Siam. Margaret
came from New York for weekends, but each time she left he felt he
was being deserted. He had always liked to have his daughters around
him and family was the breath of life to him.

His signature had become a mere scribble, and a magnifying glass
was of little help. He could no longer read and he sat by the fire looking
at picture magazines. When Mrs. Jaffray called to have tea with Edith
shortly before he died, he bowed with the old courtesy and said, "I
know you will pardon me, Mrs. Jaffray, for not rising." And on Ike
Hoover's last visit he said, "I am tired of swimming upstream."

Occasional echoes of life at the White House reached him but they
seemed dim and far away. Edith knew of the changes at the Executive
Mansion. Mrs. Coolidge had made the transition from Vice President's
wife to First Lady, and she was already popular. The quiet family life
of the Coolidges seemed restful after the Harding regime, but it was
oddly at variance with the current mood of spendthrift gaiety, revolutionary fashion, and lawless Jazz Age spirit. Materialism had haunted
Woodrow Wilson and inspired his last words in public. Theatrical and
literary talent was blossoming, but the ills of Prohibition were shaking
the foundations of legal control. Fortunes grew and business flourished. But President Coolidge raised a storm when he vetoed the Veterans' Bonus Bill, a measure that would have stirred up Woodrow Wilson had he been critical of his successors. It was the kind of news that
was not discussed at S Street.

Carter Glass, Senator Hitchcock, Vance McCormick, George Foster
Peabody, Raymond Fosdick, and others made brief calls but they did
not trouble Woodrow with political comment. Arthur Krock, aware of
his failing condition, was surprised to find him thinking so vigorously
even while he noticed the "cast of death on his face." The former
President sat with a long shawl thrown over his shoulders but his voice
seemed strong to Krock, and his manner was full of interest. As he was
on his way downstairs, Krock was surprised to hear Wilson calling after him a final message in what seemed like his old vibrant voice, the
last word from a man he had come to know well.

It was clear to Krock that as Woodrow Wilson's life ebbed he clung
to it tenaciously, but the end seemed near. There had been some improvement in his state when he settled in S Street, away from the strain

of the White House. Edith was in sole command, with Dr. Grayson always at hand to advise her and check each variation in his physical condition. But the arteriosclerosis which had brought on his original stroke made fresh inroads and there were new complications. After each setback he renewed the battle and at times seemed even stronger than before until the autumn of 1923 when minute retinal hemorrhages served as warning signals. He no longer recognized people when he went driving and he had difficulty reading.

In January, Dr. Grayson accepted an invitation to go duck shooting at Bernard Baruch's plantation. He called at S Street to look at his patient and bid him good-bye. On their way downstairs Edith asked if he did not think Woodrow was weaker. They had been through so many crises together that he thought she was unduly alarmed but he offered at once to change his plans and stay. He told her that he would not have accepted the invitation had he felt there was a change for the worse, and he promised to return at a moment's notice if needed.

Edith hurried upstairs to tell her husband what Dr. Grayson had said. She found him sitting with his head bowed, and when she asked him how he was he said that he always felt bad now, and he hated to have the doctor leave. When she told him what Grayson had suggested she offered to go downstairs and stop him, but Woodrow said that this would be selfish. Grayson was tired, too, and needed a rest. After a long pause he added, "It won't be very much longer, and I had hoped he would not desert me; but that I should not say, even to you."

Knowing that this was ominous, she did what she could to lift his spirits, but he had a restless night and in the morning he ignored the papers waiting for his attention and did not summon Randolph for dictation. On the night of the twenty-ninth he was very much worse, and Edith summoned Randolph in the middle of the night to send for Dr. Grayson. There was no doubt about the diagnosis this time. His stomach had ceased functioning and his kidneys were involved. It was not a second stroke, as many assumed, but it was the end. He managed a feeble smile when he saw Dr. Grayson at his bedside and whispered, "I'm a broken piece of machinery. . . ." Earlier he had talked things out with Cary, wishing to know the truth, and had accepted the verdict philosophically; in fact, he had seemed relieved. Now, almost his last articulate words were, "I am ready."

Dr. Grayson stayed at the house continuously. Ruth Powderly was summoned and with two other nurses and the faithful Scott on duty, the dying President again became the object of worldwide solicitude. When Dr. Fowler and Dr. Ruffin, old friends who had attended him when he nearly died in the White House, came in he found strength to crack his last joke with Dr. Grayson: "Too many cooks spoil the broth." It was not the first time that he had said this at the sight of doctors gathering around his bed.

There was little that Edith could do now except carry trays and stay close to the bed where Woodrow could see her in his conscious moments and hold her hand. She was calm because she knew she could not collapse lest he need her. He lingered on, his heart growing weaker, but he was conscious until twelve hours before his death, showing occasional flickers of life even when she and Margaret felt that he had slipped away. In one of those moments he was heard to murmur "Edith." In another he spoke of the League.

Margaret had been summoned from New York by telephone. The McAdoos were hastening east from California. The Sayres could not be reached immediately in Siam. Meanwhile, when news was flashed to the world on Friday, February 1, 1924, that Woodrow Wilson was dying the house on S Street was besieged. But Edith did not move from her post in the silent room. Dr. Grayson appeared from time to time and talked to reporters, acknowledging that the situation was serious. One bulletin followed another for the next two days and finally, white and shaken, Grayson gave a revealing picture. "Mr. Wilson realizes his fight is over. He is making a game effort. It almost breaks one down. He is very brave. He is just slowly ebbing away. He is not talking to anyone but he is still conscious."

People knelt in the icy street praying for her husband's survival as Edith kept her last long vigil. The leading papers had pages of copy set ready to use the moment the flash came in. The embassies registered the interest of world leaders in the passing of Woodrow Wilson. This was not just the death of a President, but of a man who had envisioned a new future for mankind. The war years, Versailles, his fight for the Treaty, his appeal to the people, and his strong domestic reforms had made him an outstanding historical figure.

The police put up lines to hold back the crowds that came from all directions. Waves of sympathy rolled belatedly through the capital for the President who had been ill for so long, and had suffered so much. On February 1 President Coolidge wrote to Edith, "The news of Mr. Wilson's acute illness, and this morning's bulletin indicating its very grave character, have been a great shock to the nation. The whole people will await with deep concern the hoped-for assurance of a turn for the better. . . . If it is possible to do so, I hope you will let your husband know of my great interest in his behalf. . . ."

It was too late for the dying man to learn of this message, but the parade of notables leaving cards continued. Mr. and Mrs. William Howard Taft, Mrs. Florence Kling Harding, Herbert Hoover, and Mr. and Mrs. Charles Evans Hughes were among the first to arrive. Ambassadors, judges, and colleagues on the Hill came in close succession to the house on S Street. Bernard Baruch and Carter Glass were admitted and they sat in the library with Joseph Wilson, the President's brother.

After Saturday night's bulletin that there was no radical change, Edith sent Scott out as darkness fell to say that she wished those who waited would go home. All through the night she and Margaret watched the worn face of their idol. Both addressed him by name in the flickering moments when he seemed to be conscious.

On Sunday morning, as Washingtonians were starting the day, well aware that it might be the last in the life of the War President, Dr. Grayson, haggard and strained, announced that Mr. Wilson was unconscious and that his pulse was very weak. Two hours later he appeared again to say that the end might be expected at any time. "He is holding life by a thread so slight that it may break at any moment."

But after seventy-two hours of steady decline Grayson could still feel Wilson's pulse beat, although the dying man could no longer hear the soft whispers of Edith and Margaret calling him by name. The press prepared themselves with handkerchiefs to signal their telegraphic colleagues down the hill when the final word came, alerting the world to the death of Woodrow Wilson. At eleven fifty-five A.M. he died quietly, with Edith and Margaret at one side of his bed and Cary Grayson at the other, holding his pulse. No words were spoken; he looked as if he had just gone to sleep. It was Sunday morning, February 3, 1924, and he had just turned sixty-eight.

President and Mrs. Coolidge were attending morning service in the

First Congregational Church when shouts from the street informed them of the news. Extras were already in circulation. The service was halted while the minister asked the congregation to pray. The Coolidges were driven at once to S Street, and the cameramen and Secret Service closed in around them.

Mrs. Grayson, Helen Bones, and Dr. Axson went straight to Edith—the first friends to reach her. Helen had brought Edith and Woodrow together, and Altrude's romance was inextricably interwoven with theirs. Both felt that the stress of the years had been wiped away and that he looked young again, in spite of his white hair. Edith spoke of the majesty of death before turning away, but Altrude wept.

Dr. Grayson later said that Edith was in a state of shock after her husband's death. Her fatigue was overwhelming but she insisted on everything being done as Woodrow would have wished. He had asked for simplicity, and when President Coolidge offered her the aid of government departments in making the funeral arrangements, she said that she would wait for the arrival of the McAdoos before deciding.

The news reached Princeton as chapel services ended and at once bells tolled and flags were lowered to half-mast, as they were all over the country. Business in the Senate, concentrating at the moment on the Teapot Dome investigation, was suspended for three days. More than 8,000 messages of condolence poured in from around the world, and carloads of flowers arrived at S Street.

Woodrow had told his wife that he did not wish to be buried at Arlington, and after President Harding's funeral he said that he would prefer a private service for himself. Staunton, his birthplace, was considered but he had no relatives buried there. His devotion to his parents and to Mrs. Howe made Columbia, South Carolina, seem a likely place but he had told Edith after attending his sister's funeral that all the space there had been used.

There were storms of tears when Nell McAdoo swept into the house and Edith discussed the funeral plans with her and her husband. Margaret moved around in a dream after her father's death and would not express an opinion about anything; she seemed to be totally detached from reality. In the end they all agreed that burial should be in the crypt of the Cathedral of St. Peter and St. Paul, the unfinished national cathedral rising majestically on Mount Saint Alban. Edith talked to Bishop James Freeman before making this choice.

## Woodrow Wilson Finds Peace

Arrangements went forward for a quiet service at S Street and burial at the cathedral, with Edith close to the breaking point. McAdoo was at a crisis in his own career. His name was in the news at the moment as having received legal fees over a period of years from Edward L. Doheny. He had hoped to win the Democratic nomination for President at the 1924 convention, and again his prospects seemed doomed.

When Edith learned from the papers that Senator Lodge had been named by the Senate as one of the official representatives at Woodrow Wilson's funeral, she burned with anger. She wrote to him with great urgency and at the last minute, since the news was late in reaching her, "As the funeral is private and not official and realizing that your presence would be embarrassing to you and unwelcome to me I write to request that you do *not* attend."

Nothing like this had ever happened to Senator Lodge and he sent her a handwritten reply that arrived just before the funeral. "When the Senate Committee was appointed I had no idea that the Committee was expected to attend the private services at the home and I had supposed that the services at the church were to be public. You may rest assured that nothing could be more distasteful to me than to do anything which by any possibility could be embarrassing to you."

In spite of a sudden storm of tears and anger that had broken Edith's control, she was composed for the private service at the house. Lodge sent word at the last minute that a sore throat would keep him from attending the cathedral service.

The President and Mrs. Coolidge went upstairs to the drawing room as soon as they arrived. The casket lay in shadow, with a cluster of black orchids from Edith on top of it. When the drawing room doors were opened the guests who had assembled in the library and on the stairs followed the President and Mrs. Coolidge. A copy of Bouguereau's Madonna done by Ellen Axson hung on the wall, a reminder of Woodrow Wilson's earlier life.

A few of the relatives sobbed but otherwise there was total silence, except when the clock on the staircase landing chimed. The Reverend James Taylor, of Central Presbyterian Church, who had officiated at their marriage, repeated the Twenty-third Psalm, Woodrow's favorite. The Reverend Sylvester Beach of Princeton University, another old friend, prayed for a world at peace and for the family. Bishop Freeman, holding the khaki-covered Bible that had been read daily by the

259

President, pronounced the benediction. The three churchmen passed down the aisle and stationed themselves outside the door in the falling snow while eight servicemen, representing the Army, the Navy, and the Marine Corps, carried the casket to the hearse.

Edith came out on Randolph's arm, her tear-stained features concealed by a heavy mourning veil. McAdoo followed, with Nell on one arm and Margaret on the other, both heavily veiled. President and Mrs. Coolidge came next, followed by the pallbearers—Josephus Daniels, Newton D. Baker, Carter Glass, Jesse Jones, Cleveland Dodge, David F. Houston, Thomas W. Gregory, William Redfield, Edward Meredith, Bernard Baruch, John Barton Payne, General Tasker Bliss, Dr. E. P. Davis, and Dr. Hiram Woods. They were a blend of the original Wilson Cabinet members and a few intimate friends. William Howard Taft, who was to have been one of the pallbearers, suffered a severe heart attack on the morning of the funeral. Dr. Grayson hurried in to see him, but found that he was much too ill to leave his bed.

It was three o'clock in the afternoon and the country was already mourning when a long line of cars left S Street for the slow, winding trip to the cathedral. Cabinet members, Senators, and the household staff were driven slowly through the slush and drizzle of a bleak February day. Although guns had been firing salutes at Army posts and Navy yards, there was no military display at Woodrow Wilson's funeral. A line of servicemen saluted as the hearse passed, but the clatter of cavalry and the rumble of gun caissons were missing. The cheers, bands, and shouting crowds were far behind the War President now.

The rain changed to sleet. Thousands had gathered around the cathedral and the bells pealed "Nearer My God to Thee" as the funeral party arrived. Umbrellas dripped as people huddled together and stamped their feet to keep warm.

The eight servicemen who had guarded the casket carried it into Bethlehem Chapel and placed it in the center aisle. Above the entrance the inscription THE WAY TO PEACE was carved in stone. The fragrance from the overwhelming display of flowers and wreaths dazed Mrs. Wilson as she took her seat. Tall wax candles and tinted light suffused the chapel from the Story of the Nativity in the Gothic windows.

Guests for whom there had not been room at the service on S Street now joined those who had come from the house, making more than 300 altogether, including the diplomats. Past and present were clearly defined. The members of President Coolidge's Cabinet sat in one section reserved for them, and President Wilson's in another.

The service was transmitted to every part of the country by radio. At Madison Square Garden, where a memorial service was in progress, silence reigned during the transmission. Chopin's *Funeral March* was played by Warren F. Johnson, a former member of the White House staff. And a favorite hymn of Wilson's was sung by the choir:

> Day is dying in the West,
> Heaven is touching earth with rest.
> Wait and worship while the night
> Gets her evening lamps alight.

A prayer for the family followed the Lord's Prayer and the Apostles' Creed, then the choir filed out. President and Mrs. Coolidge left as the Recessional was softly played on the organ. The wives of four Presidents attended the service—Mrs. Wilson, Mrs. Coolidge, Mrs. Taft, and Mrs. Harding. Two of them were widowed now and Edith stood swaying at the foot of the black steel casket with the small group that stayed after the chapel emptied. Only Nell, McAdoo, Margaret, Dr. Grayson, and Edith remained for the final rites, along with eight servicemen standing at attention. They would move the casket into place to be lowered into the vault when a slab in the aisle was lifted. Its plate read simply: WOODROW WILSON: BORN DECEMBER 28, 1856, DIED FEBRUARY 3, 1924.

Mrs. Wilson fought for composure as Bishop Freeman recited Tennyson's *Crossing the Bar*. Her eyes were too blinded by tears for her to see the casket start its slow descent as Bishop Freeman intoned the final words of committal: "Earth to earth, ashes to ashes, dust to dust." Outside the chapel taps was sounded by the same bugler who had performed at the burial of the Unknown Soldier at Arlington.

The world was cold and wet as McAdoo hurried Edith away from the chapel. Nell and Margaret followed. Many still knelt in the slush and prayed. It was strange to go back to the house on S Street and not find Woodrow waiting for her, but she could now weep away from watchful eyes.

261

After the others had all left, Cary Grayson stayed to see the casket reach its final destination, a long slow process. He had much to remember and he was as broken up as the family; only Edith knew better than he how much Woodrow had surmounted. In his entire life Grayson had never seen such single-minded devotion to duty against all odds, such patience and forbearance with adversity, and such resignation to the inevitable as Woodrow Wilson showed. His final tribute to Wilson was simple: "He was as much a casualty of the war as any soldier who fell in the field. His death was a result of his consecration to the service of his country and humanity."

# 24.  *A Life of Her Own*

AFTER Woodrow Wilson's death, Edith Wilson continued for nearly forty years to enjoy a vital and constructive life. She developed fresh interests and made a career for herself that grew more expansive with each passing decade until she reached her eighties. With an experienced eye she watched the changing ways of the world, and she mellowed. In some respects she seemed progressive; in others she retained the old-fashioned touch. But little was heard of her in the first year of her widowhood.

Silent and half-dazed, she coped with the business of each day, and made quiet trips to the cathedral, to walk in the grounds and to meditate on the man who still seemed a living presence. For once in her life there was no teatime talk around Edith; she was facing a great reality. It took time, but she personally answered many of the letters coming in from all parts of the world; she also had to deal with the financial problems of her husband's estate.

Then, by degrees she moved in widening circles, becoming well known around the world as a courier reminding people of her husband's work for international peace and equity. Her dominant interest all through the 1920's, the 1930's, and indeed as long as she lived, was to glorify Woodrow Wilson's image, approve all the memorials, and care for his letters and papers. His name could not be used without her approval, and she was never in doubt about what she wanted.

Her appearances at the General Assembly in Geneva and at the political conventions were always greeted with storms of applause. Everywhere she went she was received by the nation's leaders, but whenever possible she pursued her own quiet course. It was not personal applause she wanted but the honor due her husband and his aims. Although she could not be persuaded to make a speech and still refused to talk to the press in any part of the world, she conferred with men of influence and lent her presence and support to all approved events, large and small, that concerned Woodrow Wilson.

By the end of the first year of her widowhood she could laugh again, and by degrees her old cheerful spirit returned. She did not speak of the past or indulge in regrets or complaints, for she had come to terms with herself after what Dr. Grayson described as a numbed state induced by shock and exhaustion. Through it all, her devotion to her family and friends was still paramount, and her philanthropic and church work continued, but her interests widened as she voyaged around the world, went seven times to Europe, and twice to Japan.

She kept up her contacts with many of the famous men her husband had known, and when they came to America they visited her on S Street. Bit by bit she relaxed from the rigid patterns and stern discipline of the invalid years and became the spirited Edith of old. She was again a person in her own right, and she was listened to with respect. She could be blithe or serious as the spirit moved her. It took her some time to accustom herself to rising late rather than early and to choosing her own bedtime hour.

Washington now had Republican rule, with controversy over the League of Nations still a live issue. If she felt the chill of neglect, she did not show it. In spite of the overtures made by her successors in the White House, she did not enter it until seven years after the day she had left. After that she became a regular guest and missed few of the official events. Altrude and Cary Grayson, her family, close advisers, and regular bridge partners sometimes got inklings of her private thoughts on the changing political scene, but she refrained from critical comments in public, and knew how to veil an occasional dig with laughter. Sometimes she talked in riddles, for her mind moved swiftly and she was expert at the light approach to deep realities. Although politically naïve when she married Woodrow Wilson, she was now deeply informed and four months after his death she wrote to Bernard Baruch, urging him to keep up the fight for the League and to stiffen those who lacked the courage to come out for it "flat-footed" at the Democratic Convention. She knew it would be one of the underlying issues, and she reminded him that the Allied Conference called by Ramsay MacDonald and M. Herriot would give the Republicans "just what they want—an opportunity to get into what they will claim is their own plan. It makes me sick; no wonder the doctor said I was suffering from shock!"

The Democratic party was split on every major issue of the day—the League of Nations, Prohibition, the Ku Klux Klan, the cost of living, the restriction of immigration, the Veterans' Bonus Bill, and other issues that plagued Calvin Coolidge. Edith longed to be at the convention, and it was a blow to her when Dr. Grayson would not let her attend. She clung to her radio day after day following the political uproar in Madison Square Garden that continued through the end of June and early July. She wrote to Cleveland Dodge that everything seemed to be chaotic.

"Only a progressive could win," McAdoo announced as he arrived in New York confident that this time he would make it. Al Smith radiated confidence and William Jennings Bryan still retained a glimmer of hope that the convention might turn to him on his fourth try. Newton Baker made a brilliant plea for unqualified entry into the League of Nations, which resulted in a unanimous vote for his plank on the subject. John W. Davis, the winner in the end, stayed in the background almost unattended. He kept silent through torrents of talk and had nothing to say to the press. To Bryan he was J. P. Morgan's lawyer and the tool of Wall Street. To Edith he was a sympathetic figure who believed deeply in the League.

McAdoo, whose fortunes Edith watched with the closest interest, refused to release his delegates until the last minute in the longest convention up to that time, and the stormiest since the Civil War. Davis was nominated on July 9 and Edith was satisfied that a friend of the

League had made it, but the Democrats lost to the Republicans and Calvin Coolidge won the national election.

News of the death of Coolidge's young son Calvin subdued the oratory at the July convention, and murmurs of sympathy swept through the gathering. When the news was announced, Franklin D. Roosevelt read a resolution of sympathy for President and Mrs. Coolidge. Tragedy again in the White House, Edith reflected; it seemed inevitable. After Calvin played tennis, a blister on his foot had become infected and he died within a few days.

As Mrs. Wilson followed the convention sessions she coped with financial matters involving her husband's estate. He had made her his executrix and, although an astute businesswoman herself, like other widows she was faced suddenly with an uncertain future. But she had strong and successful businessmen around her to advise her. Although Woodrow and she had lived thriftily in many respects, they had long been close to some of the ablest lawyers in the country and to what the President's critics called the princes of Wall Street.

Almost at once Jesse Jones, Cleveland Dodge, Bernard Baruch, Vance McCormick and others established a special trust fund to cover the first year of Mrs. Wilson's widowhood. They all assured her that should she have any difficulty about maintaining the house on S Street, or feel the pinch in any way, they would come to her aid. She had been advised not to petition Congress at this time for the customary pension given to all Presidential widows since the time of Mrs. Lincoln. She rarely talked about money after this but she made considerable amounts herself on her husband's books and her own writings. He had amassed $250,000, mostly in Federal land bonds. She lived well but not extravagantly, and she managed her business affairs with considerable skill during the prosperous 1920's, when fortunes were made overnight.

In August, 1924, with the convention over, she had her first breathing spell since her husband's death when she went to Maine with Randolph for a total rest. She wrote to Altrude on the thirty-first, "We have both had the best rest—there is nothing like the air here in Maine. It reminds me so of our visit to Kineo where every day is more radiant than the other—and the stars are bigger & brighter than anywhere I have ever been."

Edith was already at work rounding up letters sent out by Woodrow

Wilson. She kept Randolph busy writing to known recipients, and the first cache came from Dr. Simon Baruch. She had many decisions to make and she listened to the men who advised her, with Norman Davis and Bernard Baruch closest to her at this time. Her friends in general were worldly men with business and legal experience. As they worked with her they came to respect her judgment and instincts and conceded that she was often right when she overrode their decisions. And override them she often did.

Henry Cabot Lodge died nine months after her husband—a bitter and disappointed man plagued by diabetes and oncoming blindness. Again Wilson's name flashed into the headlines; both men were dead but the echoes of their feud remained. The tide had turned against Lodge's isolationism and there was growing interest in the work being done at Geneva and The Hague. Edith had a chance to see some of it herself when she sailed for Europe on the *Majestic* on May 17, 1925. Lucy Moeling and Renée Baruch were with her, and they motored to Paris through Normandy. The pink hawthorn trees were in bloom, reminding her of her trips earlier with Altrude and Bertha.

André Maurois, the French author, visited her at the Hôtel Chambord to discuss a sketch he was doing on Woodrow Wilson. She was not altogether convinced that *Ariel,* his recently published book on Shelley, made him the right man for this task. He told her frankly that she need not expect his sketch to be all praise; his approach would be realistic. He wanted to know if it were true that the President had come to Europe without knowing anything about the men he would have to deal with, and that their methods had taken him by surprise.

Edith told him equably that since her husband had been a student of history all his life, it was a poor compliment to suggest that he was ignorant of the difficulties he would face. When pressed about his attitude to Clemenceau and Lloyd George on the League, she said that Woodrow had respected the French leader's willingness to try in spite of his skepticism about it, while Lloyd George simply did not believe in it at all.

Edith could see that Maurois hád no faith in the League but after a visit to Geneva he returned converted. "It works! It lives! It *is!!!* I could not believe it until I saw." Maurois was only one of many people Edith met on this trip who were impressed with the work already under way.

266

## A Life of Her Own

Late in July she traveled to Venice, and wrote to Bernard Baruch that she felt like a different person from the one who had sailed to Europe six weeks earlier. It was the most perfect rest she had ever had, and his daughters had been so devoted that she was getting spoiled and would find it hard to look out for herself in "prosaic Washington" when she got back. Belle and Renée were determined to protect her from exploitation or intrusion.

She reached Geneva in September after a quick trip in August to the haunted castle that Baruch had taken in Scotland. In her later years Edith liked to tell of the nightly groans and rattles that had impelled her to barricade her door with a huge wardrobe. But the chief objective of the summer abroad was her visit to Geneva. She wrote to Baruch from the Villa Bartolini in Geneva, that the work of the Secretariat was a revelation to her. She was amazed at how much had been done in a short period of time—"it seemed to make all the years of pain and heartache for my great husband worth it." She kept wishing that he could have been there to see what she was seeing, but she was convinced that he knew. With unquenchable optimism she chose to believe that the ideal for which he had given his life had become reality. There was never any doubt in Edith's mind, and she often expressed the thought that he had literally died for the League. Edith always felt at home in Switzerland. She and Altrude had taken in all its beauties and its hazards as they drove to the Eiger glacier, had a long, rough trip through the St. Gotthard tunnel, watched moonlight on the Jungfrau, and enjoyed the peaceful beauty of Lucerne and Geneva, now the cradle of the League. Wherever she went in Europe she came across some reminder of her travels before she was Mrs. Woodrow Wilson and before Altrude was Mrs. Cary Grayson.

She wrote to Dr. Grayson of the number of men with whom she had been associated now working at the Secretariat and she was impressed that they all seemed deeply conscious of every country's dependence on the League—a growing tide of confidence. The French were even more articulate than the British in their hopes for its future, although Austen Chamberlain had said at an American Club luncheon that if the world did not have the League of Nations it would have to have something like it. Characteristically, Edith played down her own role at Geneva. She wrote to Dr. Grayson that the head of every country represented wished to give dinners for her, but she declined all invitations and asked the various officials to call on her instead, since she was not taking part in social events. This was ideal for her purposes, as it gave her a chance to talk quietly to the men who were moving the pawns. Particularly skilled at this technique, she learned "many important and interesting things."

On September 22, 1925, again from the Villa Bartolini she wrote to Grayson that every American of note traveling in Europe that summer seemed to have turned up in Geneva. "It is all splendid propaganda and I am delighted." Senators Clapper, Walsh, and Owen all were there. So were Dr. and Mrs. Raymond Fosdick, already deeply committed to the League, and she was particularly glad to see her trusted friend, Dr. Sterling Ruffin.

Early in October she was back in Paris, staying at the Hotel Chambord and shopping with her young companions, Belle Baruch and Evangeline Johnson. They were the most knowledgeable of guides, interested in the arts, politics, and all that was smart and contemporary. They seemed to know everyone of note in Geneva, in Venice, in Paris. As they shopped Edith remembered Dr. Grayson's birthday and wrote to him on October 4, "Just a line, dear Dr. Grayson, to bring you a birthday greeting. I wonder if Trudie will remember it this year—as I am not there to remind her, but I am sure she will, and that you will probably have a grand celebration in your new and lovely home. Always yours, Edith Bolling Wilson."

Trudie was busy at the moment preparing to move into a large new house that the Graysons had taken for their growing family. On her return from Europe, Dr. Grayson could see that Edith had had just what she needed after the years of strain. Rest came first, then stimulation and variety—Venice, the Scottish moors, Geneva, Paris, and points in between. Thoroughly relaxed, she had recovered some of her instinctive flair for enjoying life and was ready to face the deluge of work that awaited her at S Street. In November she was calling Baruch her "publicity adviser" when he warned her against approving or condemning any of the suggestions for Woodrow Wilson memorials. In December she was thanking him and the girls for the Christmas gift they had given her. "I never had dreamed of possessing a real silver fox and it comes as the most wonderful surprise and gratification," she commented.

It was her first Christmas without Woodrow, but she gathered her family and friends around her in the old warm way. There were gifts for everybody, many of them gathered on her trip abroad, and life went on at S Street—its great man gone, his widow a vital presence. She knew that she would return to Geneva—again and again. Disillusionment would come later.

# 25. *Weighing the Evidence*

EDITH Wilson wasted no time in getting to work on her husband's papers and letters, and on settling on a biographer to write his life history. She had worked so closely with him that she had the power to draw in letters and notes from all manner of sources. When she appealed to friends—and also to enemies—she got what she wanted without question, except for some complications with Colonel House, which were eventually straightened out.

Unlike other Presidents, Woodrow Wilson had typed many of his own notes and had not always had copies made. His shorthand notations were sometimes completely his own. She also had many notes of her own, scrawled in her loose rounded script on little pads, as in the case of Albert Fall. This was testimony of a very personal nature. The official papers, covering the war period and the peace negotiations that followed, were of tremendous importance historically, but had many gaps. Woodrow's personal papers were most revealing, and they were full of surprises for Mrs. Wilson.

Well as she had known him, and much as he had talked to her of his past, there were wide areas that her experience had not touched. Her political horizons broadened and her scholarship sharpened as she worked over the papers, so that in her later years she was uniquely well informed, if unfailingly partisan, in all matters relating to Woodrow Wilson. She had expert help from the scholarly men who had been around him, and the voice of worldly experience from such friends as

269

Bernard Baruch and Norman Davis, but she held the helm all the way through, making every decision as she thought her husband would have wished.

She insisted from the start on reading all material before it was sent to the publishers and agreed that no matter how long it took, an adequate and authoritative biography would be the great objective. A number of candidates were under consideration when she found in her husband's papers a note he had written just before he became ill, naming Ray Stannard Baker as his choice for biographer. There was no further indecision after that, and early in 1925 Baker proposed a simple announcement of the project, using the message as a "voice from the clouds."

This was the beginning of a literary partnership that went on for years and represented monumental effort by Baker and a constant drive by Edith Wilson to draw in fresh material, to check debatable points, and clear up any shadows that might dim the shining presence of her idol. On vital personal matters she wrote to Baker herself and from time to time he visited her in Washington for personal discussion, but Randolph was the intermediary who had encyclopedic resources at his command, who checked and counterchecked, who knew where to turn in Washington for missing links.

Edith's correspondence with Baker was revealing. She was firm and insistent on all the points she wanted made, their exchanges were always courteous, and she developed a professionalism of her own. Wherever she went, at home or abroad, she sought for material, and her own conversations with men of affairs brought out fresh points for verification. When she went abroad in the summer of 1925, Baker urged her to get in touch with men who had worked with her husband. "Also some day when you are sitting reflectively on the top of Mt. Blanc, you may think of some suggestions which will help to make our biography the really fine and great work we want it to be," he wrote to her.

It was important to catch people of the older generation who were still alive. He told her that she could control letters no matter where they were, and she then asked him to find out what method the Roosevelt family had used to prevent the use of Theodore's letters. Baker traveled about, interviewing people like Colonel House and following every lead that she suggested. He was not strong and the stress affected him from time to time, so there were delays and by 1933 he felt he had to give up, but he was persuaded to continue. Mrs. Wilson was demanding and eager to have the task finished, but the meticulous checking took time. Baker was a man of independence, with a long history of newspaper and magazine experience. As "David Grayson" he had written, in another vein, philosophical books on contentment, friendship, understanding, and solitude. He lectured and had written *Woodrow Wilson and World Settlement: A History of the Peace Conference,* and with William E. Dodd he had edited *The Public Papers of Woodrow Wilson,* published between 1925 and 1927, so when he embarked on the eight-volume compilation of Wilson's life and letters he was on familiar ground. He worked at Amherst, with Katharine E. Brand, his skilled assistant, at his side to arrange, index, and deal with the papers as they flowed in. Various scholars were engaged in the mammoth task.

Early in March, 1925, what Baker called the "Ark of the Covenant" traveled from the house on S Street to Amherst with 102 packages of Wilson files. The huge van weighed more than ten tons and caused a sensation in the quiet steets of the college town. Edith wrote that she would sleep better when she heard it had arrived. She had personally supervised the assemblage of the papers, and she asked that a four-drawer file marked "No. 2" get Baker's very personal supervision because it contained "so many of Mr. Wilson's notes—both long and short-hand—and typed, and consists of much very secret information." She explained why her own penciled notes were so illegible and badly written. She had made many of them while standing by the President's bed. At this time she told Baker that she would withhold Woodrow's personal letters to her for a number of years. Papers belonging to Mrs. Helm and Dr. Grayson were also withheld for the time being, since both thought that they might wish to use them themselves. Mrs. McAdoo, Mrs. Sayre, and Margaret had promised to cooperate in every way they could.

Overwhelmed by the riches that came his way from many sources, Baker wrote to Edith on January 15, 1926, after receiving some of the more personal material, "I wonder if any biographer ever before came into the possession of such unexpected riches . . . . It furnished just the intimate personal understanding which I most needed. In a very real sense it will *make* our book . . . ."

The work on Woodrow Wilson's early days proceeded smoothly,

while fresh material on the war period was still being amassed. Their collaboration was on a personal basis, and Baker kept it all very much to himself. It was not until the Wilson papers reached the Library of Congress in 1939 that they were subjected to wider scrutiny. By Edith's wish they had been little seen or read except by Baker himself. For thirty years she worked to make the record complete and to protect it.

As material reached Edith, she read it carefully and made many notes, giving her own interpretation of matters relating directly to her husband. Unfailingly she projected her own point of view where she felt that he had been misunderstood. While she went on with her usual social and philanthropic work, traveled, played bridge with growing devotion, took her daily drives, and ran her home, she would drop anything to confer about the papers. Baker tired but Edith Wilson never did. As the work moved on, Edith kept a tight rein on Baker's treatment of personal matters. When the manuscript of the first volume reached her, she was all enthusiasm and complimented him on the way in which he had handled Mrs. Peck and her letters. This was a danger point but she assured him that he had done it in a "most dignified and frank way." Josephus Daniels had told her, she wrote, that he had read every one of the letters and found them—"as of course we already knew—only those of one warm friend to another." She and Baker had discussed the Peck story at length, and she had favored frank treatment of it rather than suppression. It had all preceded her entry into the President's life, and she felt that it needed special care.

But she thought Baker's handling of Woodrow's reaction to his first wife's death was melodramatic. She pointed out that this was "not the man she knew." Baker was upset and claimed that the picture created had come from the President's letters between September, 1914, and March, 1915. The passion and depth of feeling Woodrow Wilson was apt to show in his private letters was clear to both of them.

Baker tried to mollify her by saying that the letters showed clearly how her own marriage to the President had been a determining factor in his life. He cited the "humor, vitality, lightness of touch" that had restored Woodrow Wilson's love of fun and had enabled him to concentrate on his tasks as never before.

They did not argue, but at times the situation became tense as Baker coped with too much work and felt driven by publishers' demands. Edith was always sympathetic about his health and would wait long periods for him to recover. But in the early 1930's Baker grew seriously ill and was ordered to spend more time outdoors. He offered to step aside for a younger and abler man, since he was finding his task overwhelming. But he continued his close communication with Edith Wilson, and completed his task in the spring of 1939. Miss Brand, who had been working with him all along, prepared the papers for transfer to the Library of Congress. Baker assured Edith that she was "one of the most competent and conscientious workers" he had ever known. Norman Davis and Robert Morgenthau had considered buying Edith's house and making it the headquarters of the Woodrow Wilson Foundation, while she continued to live in it. She immediately rejected this proposal, telling them that this would be intolerable to her, since it "would rob a home of its most treasured element—of privacy." The thought of sightseers in her beloved house dismayed her. Baruch then proposed building a ranch-style house on the lot next door. The papers finally went to the Library of Congress. Later, Princeton became a central focus for Wilson material, with Dr. Arthur S. Link, assisted by Dr. David W. Hirst, in charge of operations sponsored by the Woodrow Wilson Foundation and Princeton University. Here the papers came under fresh scrutiny and appraisal. They included copies of the manuscript material in the Library of Congress and a wealth of fresh material drawn from other sources.

Edith remained good friends with Mr. and Mrs. Baker, and when Mr. Baker won the Pulitzer prize in 1940 she sent him a note congratulating him. That year the papers he had held for so long were opened to the public at the Library of Congress, under special conditions laid down by Mrs. Wilson. They proved to be full of surprises for scholars, as Dr. George L. Sioussat, chief of the Manuscript Division, and Miss Brand, their special custodian, coped with the deluge of requests that followed. Edith played an important part, too, in the flow of acquisitions from the men who had been in her husband's Cabinet, and other associates. It was a rich harvest of Wilsoniana.

Baker died of a heart attack in the summer of 1946. His dealings with Edith had been unique in the history of Presidents' wives, and his judgment was one of admiration and respect. She had been exacting, a per-

273

fectionist, a goad when he was slow, but good manners and courtesy had always prevailed. Her lack of objectivity at times had dismayed him; her devotion to her husband's interests had been nothing short of awesome.

In addition to her concern over the President's papers Edith paid close attention to all portraits, busts, and memorials after his death. He had not been averse to posing for artists or being photographed. The painting that aroused the most interest and discussion was done by John Singer Sargent.

Early in the war Sargent had donated a $90,000 blank canvas at a sale to help the Red Cross, stipulating that he would paint a portrait of the purchaser or of anyone designated by him. The subject eventually chosen was Woodrow Wilson. Sargent had already passed his prime when he came to the United States in 1917 to fulfill the commission. Edith was eager to see him, but she found him an exacting guest and when she learned that his League sympathies were with Lodge rather than her husband the door closed tight between them. But she helped arrange for the sitting in the Rose Room. They toured the White House to find the chair that he felt would be right, and a small platform was built to ensure the needed perspective. She and the President entertained him well, taking him to see the Army's camouflaging headquarters and to various events that they thought might interest him. But the chill remained, even though Woodrow was his most interesting self during the sittings. Edith was surprised when Sargent told her that he was extremely nervous about doing her husband. He seemed to be looking for some constant in Woodrow's sometimes impassive, sometimes expressive face.

Colonel House said that they all liked the portrait "fairly well." Edith talked of having a copy done, but House thought that Sargent might be obdurate about this. Her conclusion was that she disliked the Sargent painting intensely. The smooth glorified style was not what she sought in a portrait of her strong-faced husband. It seemed to lack character and it made him look older than he was. The President was diplomatic, but wrote to his old friend, Robert S. Bridges, the British Poet Laureate, on February 4, 1918, "Of course, I do not know what judgment to form of it myself but the family likes it and that is a pretty good test."

# Weighing the Evidence

Bridges had been to see it three times and "liked it hugely." But he took note of the criticism it had aroused, and wrote, "I can see you getting ready to tell a story, with the quirk to the right side of your mouth. None of the art critics seem to like it—*but for me it's you*—and the real human you that they could not see if they tried. I'd stand on that. What they want is a stern-looking Covenanter with a jaw like a pike . . . . Damn 'em. . . ." Although never considered Sargent at his best, it became a popular tourist attraction at the National Gallery in Dublin.

In 1926 there was consternation about a Wilson bust to be given to the League of Nations in Geneva. Franklin D. Roosevelt, Herbert Bayard Swope, Mrs. Charles Tiffany, Edward Bok, and William Allen White were in the group advocating it, and Sophie Irene Loeb, an experienced campaigner and a close friend of Margaret Wilson, then on the New York *Evening World*, was promoting it. The two chose Bryant Baker as the artist. Bryant told Edith he had fashioned the bust from Sir William Orpen's painting owned by Bernard Baruch.

Edith went to his studio in New York and was horrified by the large plaster model shown her, and unimpressed by a smaller one. The large one was gigantic—a "staring, soulless effort; and the other a "mild *sweet* little thing, with no mentality or strength." Even Margaret agreed that it lacked her father's spiritual quality, but she believed the completed bust would be the best yet done of him.

Edith was so worried this would be the permanent memorial to Woodrow Wilson at Geneva that she wrote to Sir Eric Drummond, telling him that she did not like it and she hoped they would make acceptance conditional on her approval. Edith suggested asking Mrs. Leopold Stokowski (Evangeline Johnson) to find the right sculptor, but this idea died.

The clay death mask, set in bronze by Dr. W. Fortunato, caused Edith some uneasiness, but the Gutzon Borglum statue given to Poland was the greatest disaster. In 1929, this well-known sculptor asked her, at Daisy Harriman's instigation, for garments to aid him in his work. "I shall need a coat and a gown—the gown not to be worn—but falling from him—as he abandons it for more public service," Borglum wrote. She gladly helped him with this, but was stricken when she saw the fallen gown later at Poznan.

Edith approved the bust by Jo Davidson that Mrs. Ira Nelson Morris

275

gave to Princeton in 1945. This was eventually installed in the President's birthplace at Staunton. Ike Hoover reported that when the Wilsons left the White House thirty-two busts of the President, in both plaster and metal, were smashed with a sledgehammer. At least ten large oil paintings were taken from their frames, which were then auctioned.

Many of Woodrow's portraits had been done before Edith came into his life, and he was particularly attached to a crayon sketch done by Fred Yates when he was president of Princeton. One of her own favorite paintings of him was by F. Graham Cootes and was designed for the White House. Edith was at the Ritz Hotel in London when she first saw it, and she telegraphed at once to Baruch who was at Fettersee Castle in Scotland. She liked it immensely, she said, but suggested that the artist "take off just a tiny bit of hair on the right side where it is so long—and also make the background above the place on the top more complete for in some lights it still shows."

Eugene Savage, a member of the Commission of Fine Arts, recommended it as being better than the one already in the White House. But he, too, suggested some changes, such as darkening the trouser on the right leg and enlarging the arm on the left side. In 1957 it was conveyed to the White House and became the official portrait of Woodrow Wilson.

Though Edith was deeply concerned about her husband's portraits and paintings, she was resistant to doing anything about her own. Although many thought her vain, she showed no sign of this when she became First Lady. She could have had any artist she wished paint her. It was routine procedure for Presidents' wives, but when Colonel House called on Edith Galt at the St. Regis Hotel in New York in November, 1916, to persuade her to have a painting done as a wedding gift to the President, she was reluctant, and said she would think it over.

In the end she was painted by Adolfo Müller-Ury, a Swiss artist who was in vogue at the time. He had painted Mrs. Jefferson Davis and other well-known Southerners. Edith wore an orchid brocade dress that Worth had made for her trousseau and a dark velvet evening cloak gave depth to the background. This painting hung in her husband's bedroom, both at the White House and on S Street. Eventually it became her official portrait in the Executive Mansion. It was one wedding

276

gift that Woodrow prized. She was well pleased with the portrait done of her by Arnold Genthe when she visited his studio with Altrude Grayson. Although taken on the spur of the moment it turned out uncommonly well and became the official picture that went around the world when her engagement was announced.

Also, Edith never hesitated to make sketches for architects and sculptors to demonstrate her wishes, for she had absorbed her husband's interest in architectural and decorative design. In July, 1924, immediately after his death, she corresponded with Ralph Adams Cram, the noted architect of St. Thomas's Church in New York and the Military Academy Building at West Point, about the canopy over the sarcophagus at the cathedral. Although she liked the design of the sarcophagus itself, she felt that his blueprints of the canopy suggested something too elaborate. Cram wanted to make it his own contribution to the memory of Woodrow Wilson, and he assured her that it was in the best medieval tradition. When she showed him a sketch of her own he was not impressed. She was distressed by a press report that Woodrow Wilson would rest beneath a sword. Word went out at once from S Street that the simple design was not a sword but a Crusader's cross.

# 26. *A World Traveler*

ON a January day in 1926 the Senate voted 76 to 17 in favor of entering the World Court. For seven hours Mrs. Wilson listened to the debate and when it was over she emerged with a look of intense satisfaction on her face. To the country at large it was the end of a seven-year battle against isolation; to her it was the voice of her husband being heard at last. When reservations voted by the Senate were rejected by the World Court, though, hope faded again, and Edith was intensely conscious of the parallel with the past.

President Coolidge continued his efforts on behalf of international goodwill by preparing a conference of the leading naval powers at Geneva. The United States was now involved in the world picture for better or for worse. Edith watched every move and never failed to attend the debates, often with Mrs. Brandeis. The diehards held their ground and certain parts of the country were still isolationist in feeling. But there was a growing tide of alarm as dictatorships followed the chaos left by World War I. Mussolini had ushered in 1926 by proclaiming himself the modern Caesar. In Poland, Jósef Pilsudski led a military revolution in Warsaw and established his dictatorship. Syria had an uprising and there was trouble in the oil-rich Mosul area, claimed by Turkey after the war. The Riffs were fighting their way to defeat in Morocco. Both Asia and Africa were battlegrounds as the year progressed. Much of what Woodrow Wilson had foreseen had come to pass. Hitler was silent after his early bid for power in the Beer Hall Putsch, but *Mein Kampf* had been published, drafting the shape of things to come.

In America the pace was fast and furious as prosperity gilded the land after years of austerity. Taxes were low and tariffs high. The major industries were enjoying their greatest boom since the war, and there was little unemployment. Madison Avenue was conditioning the nation's tastes and loosening the family pursestrings. Lawlessness had reached the point where judges and police officials protected bootleggers and the courts were swamped with untried cases. The gang-war funerals were macabre spectacles. Jazz bands spun whining music across the land as flappers, college youths, and their elders, too, danced the Charleston and the Black Bottom.

Edith observed it all, with a lively interest in the changing fashions but a tight grip on established custom. She was slow to lend her name to anything not directly linked to Woodrow Wilson, although she was deluged with requests to serve on committees, speak before clubs, write for magazines, add her name to all manner of projects. She stayed aloof, living her private life. There were only so many hours in the day and she was constantly busy with Wilson correspondence and the ordered round of family affairs. But she was always ready to appear at patriotic functions, to uphold the veterans' interests, to remember the things that Woodrow would have approved. In 1926 she made one exception to her rule about serving on committees when Mabel T. Boardman, a veteran of the American Red Cross, persuaded her to become honorary vice-chairman of the organization. "Although it has been my custom to decline honorary membership on committees, I feel in this great mission for humanity I will be proud to have my name associated," she wrote to Miss Boardman.

After her husband's death she no longer rode or played golf, although she had done both to please him and give him companionship. She became more than ever a racing enthusiast, partly because of the Graysons, and she followed the polo matches and racing events of the era. She still enjoyed a chance to go yachting with Baruch, Jesse Jones, and other rich men in her circle of friends. She had done all those things as the President's wife, but as his widow she could enjoy them in a more relaxed way without Secret Service men and the public attention that she disliked.

She sailed on the *Leviathan* with her brother Wilmer on August 3, 1926, and she wrote to "Dearest Trudy and Doc" from the ship, wishing them well at Saratoga and describing the splendid quarters to which they had been moved from their own modest bookings. Norman Davis' daugher, Martha, was on board with a friend and they proved to be good companions although the assemblage of passengers in general reminded Edith of a "Zoo full of strange animals." Flaming youth and big-money tycoons were in the ascendant.

Paris meant a whirl of activity, with shopping to be done, friends to see, familiar paths to be trod. Belle had sent advance notice of new plays, recitals, Russian ballet, and Mary Garden's appearances in opera scheduled for the Paris season. Things were forever like this with Belle.

Always in the vanguard where the arts were concerned, Belle catered to Edith's love of music and the theater. She was as familiar with the Left Bank and the expatriate Americans of the 1920's as she was with Patou and the Ritz. Her work for the League of Nations and her father's close links with the New York *World* and its brilliant correspondent, Herbert Bayard Swope, kept her in touch with the newspaper correspondents. Two of them, Lincoln Eyre and Pierre van Paassen, were close friends, but Miss Baruch knew better than to involve Edith with the press under any circumstances.

They went back to the haunted castle in Scotland for the beginning of the shoot on August 12. Occasionally Baruch shifted his hunting base to Czechoslovakia, but he rented a succession of shooting boxes in Scotland. After their bracing encounter with the moors, Belle, Wilmer, and Edith motored through Czechoslovakia to Prague. They were entertained by President Masaryk in the palace, and had five cavernous rooms that Edith said resembled a public highway. Guards patrolled the corridors all night long, and there was no privacy, even in the primitive bathtub.

Edith was deeply interested in the land that her husband had helped reshape after the war. When she and Belle stopped at a little village close to Prague, they studied the children and took pictures. In September they were back in Geneva for the League sessions, and again she was warmly welcomed and brought up to date.

She sent Carter Glass the *Journal of the Seventh Assembly* of the League of Nations, drawing his attention to speeches by Aristide Briand and Gustav Stresemann, two statesmen who had been close to her husband's interests. Alert for any point reminiscent of Woodrow, she studied all the League documents that came her way. As always, she was glad to get home, much as she enjoyed the luxury and diversions of her travels. She was happiest with her family, with her regular bridge companions, with her own car to run her around in Washington. She liked shopping on the Rue de Rivoli, having tea at Colombin's, visiting the galleries and couturiers, dining at LaRue's, but she was always linked to the steady pattern of life at home. Although lavish in some respects, she was curiously parsimonious in others, and could surprise her friends with unaccountable economies. The stringency of her early life had made her careful even in the days of her affluence, when she traveled and moved with the seasons like other fashionable women of the era.

The year 1927 was full of surprises and political activity. Baruch was determined to bring Al Smith and Edith Wilson together. Another political convention was at hand and Smith could well be one of the standard-bearers. They met at his home in New York. Edith had last seen Smith on her return from the Peace Conference in 1919. She was well primed on his earlier dealings with her husband; they had not always been good friends. But on this occasion they met with mutual goodwill and were soon engaged in a spirited conversation. Al Smith showed her the deference that Woodrow Wilson's widow usually received in Democratic circles, but did not altogether win her. His pungent speech and point of view on certain issues did not go down well. She conceded his strength and naturalism, but disliked politicians as much as her husband did.

In spite of the waves of opposition that beat against Smith, he was nominated at the Democratic Convention in Houston in 1928 and Edith was there to see it happen. She carefully avoided backing any candidate, nor were the strong men around her likely to be swayed in any way by her opinion. They simply wanted to honor her and to keep the name of Woodrow Wilson well to the fore. Calvin Coolidge's summer announcement that he did not choose to run again stunned the country and brought fresh hope into the Democratic camp.

Texans observed the stately Edith Wilson with curiosity and admiration. Governor Albert Cabell Ritchie of Maryland and Bernard Baruch had asked her to travel on their private railroad car, but instead she went with Hugh Wallace, former ambassador to France, and his wife. Jesse Jones, millionaire publisher of the Houston *Chronicle,* entertained her lavishly in Houston, but she was not particularly pleased when he got her up on the platform and announced that Mrs. Woodrow Wilson would make a speech. The applause was thunderous and it gave her time to summon up courage to speak briefly in a low-pitched voice. She had not had any warning and she never spoke in public, but she remembered who she was and did her best.

World communication was moving in a new direction that year, since Charles A. Lindbergh had electrified the world with his transatlantic flight. Edith immediately saw this as one way of binding countries together. She was surprised when the golden-haired young aviator and his bride, Anne Morrow, later emerged as confirmed isolationists. But for the moment America turned from tales of corruption and violence to heroism and high adventure.

The winter of 1927 was a busy one for Edith, but in the summer of 1928 she was back in Maine and writing to Altrude from Lincolnville: "Here we are again in this heavenly Maine air and breathing deeply to get it all in our lungs in place of that awful steam we had in Washing-

281

ton." She told of traveling thirty miles down the bay to fish in an area familiar to the Graysons from camping trips.

Belle cabled Edith to join her for a few weeks in Europe, so she sailed on August 28. This time Edith found her staying at the Ritz but enjoying it less than the old Chambord where she and Evangeline Johnson and Edith had enjoyed merry times together. The American correspondents had marked the Ritz bar for their own, and there were always familiar faces from home to be seen, but Edith stuck zealously to the tearooms. Agan there was Geneva to visit, the Scottish shoot, the couturiers, and the races. She followed with intense interest the election results as Al Smith went down to defeat and Herbert Hoover rode into power. The Republicans were back in office, and that was not good news for Edith Wilson, although she could not think of her husband's Food Administrator as being other than a friend.

On March 4, 1928, he was sworn into office in a blinding rainstorm. The crash of 1929 was close at hand, but few saw it coming. Edith escaped its beginnings, for 1929 was the year in which she decided to go around the world. But first she saw her cherished niece, Lucy Maury, married and it was just as if a daughter of her own were kneeling at the altar. The President had felt this way about her, too, ever since she had first started visiting the White House as a schoolgirl. Edith always addressed her in her letters as "dopted" or "adopted."

After the death of her mother, Annie Lee Maury, she became well known first at the White House and then on S Street as a Presidential protégée. She came out during the lively 1920's and Edith made life a constant delight for her with a variety of beaux, beautiful clothes, and a balanced round of diversions. Like Edith, Lucy liked domestic life and fine needlework as well as more worldly pleasures. Her wedding was planned to the last detail by her aunt, who presented her with the magnificent lace veil that she had been given by the French Government. It cascaded over Lucy's ivory satin dress and ended in a train.

Lucy's White House status was headlined when she married John Edward Moeling, of Chicago, on February 23, 1929, in the Chapel of the Annunciation in Cathedral Close, with Bishop Freeman officiating, and with the former First Lady looking on. Lucy's father, Matthew H. Maury, gave her away. Her only attendant was her sister, Mrs. John A. Goodloe. Anne Lee Goodloe, the four-year-old niece of the bride, was flower girl. Lucy's wedding bouquet was of white roses. After the ceremony Edith gave a reception for the bridal party at S Street, and threw a rare tantrum when the cake arrived. The confectioner made the mistake of decorating it lavishly with crystallized red roses. One by one she snatched them off and threw them on the floor before the startled messenger. Lucy watched this proceeding without alarm, for she knew that her Aunt Edith demanded perfection and compliance when she gave orders.

As Mrs. Moeling, Lucy's life centered in Chicago and she brought up her children there. But she continued her close association with Edith and was often a guest at S Street. As long as Edith lived Lucy kept in touch with her by letter, telephone, and frequent visits.

Before the year had ended her aunt's letters were coming from the Far East. Edith had embarked on her most ambitious travels—a trip around the world. Again it was a family affair, with Dr. Rudolph Teusler, his wife, and two teen-age daughters for traveling companions. He was the cousin and playmate of her Wytheville days whose mother, Mary Jefferson Bolling, had married a German who had fought with the Confederate Army and lost a leg in combat. They had moved to Germany after the war and now their son was known throughout the Orient for the work he was doing in Japan.

He headed St. Luke's International Hospital in Tokyo, a model institution with the latest in equipment and techniques.He had founded it on a much simpler scale, but the old building was destroyed in the earthquake of 1923. Immediately afterward he raised funds in the United States and Europe to continue his work and finance the new building.

Dr. Teusler was due to make an appearance at Geneva and Edith did not like to miss her annual visit there, so they traveled eastward, showing the Teusler girls the beauties of France and Switzerland before sailing from Marseilles on a Japanese ship. They crossed to Egypt and soon Edith was writing enthusiastically about the Pyramids, the Nile, the recently unearthed riches of King Tutankhamen's tomb, and the worldly pleasures of Shepherd's hotel.

Although they were traveling quietly, Edith's presence could not be overlooked, and the diplomats and officials did their best by her at every stop. She was censorious of the colonialism still apparent at Singapore, Ceylon, and other points as she studied the people as well as the sights. It pleased her to see how well her husband's name was remembered in distant parts of the world.

Dr. Teusler was so much at home in the Orient that he made the language barriers easy for her to penetrate. She shopped enthusiastically in Hong Kong and Shanghai and dined at princely tables. Peking, which they reached by train, would remain in her memory as the most fascinating city she had ever seen. As usual, she was well informed. She had done specific reading for the trip. A number of her Washington friends were taking world cruises at this time; it had become the fashion before the fall of the market. But she had little time for reflection as they moved from point to point. Twenty banquets and entertainments were given in her honor by the diplomats and by wealthy Chinese and she sickened a little on the exotic foods offered her—sometimes as many as twenty courses—but small and delicious. She was conscious of two worlds—the squalor and dust of the streets and the magnificence of the palaces.

They went by train to Manchuria, stopping off at Mukden before crossing the Sea of Japan on their way to Tokyo. The Teusler house with its walled garden stood on the site of the old American Legation. Much as she disliked hospitals she was stirred by the sight of the nursing staff lined up as in the old days of the war.

The Japanese had stormy memories of Woodrow Wilson and the Peace Treaty, and not all of it was forgotten. His widow remembered well their nights of strain over the Japanese impasse, and the Presidents's strong stand on the restriction of immigration was well known. But the Japanese government paid her all honor and the Emperor's brother, Prince Chichibu, gave her a dinner in the Western manner.

Edith's visit to Japan received worldwide publicity, which she did not welcome. Photographers followed her everywhere, and she laughed at herself for being caught in one of her famous hats and a long dress fishing from the traditional arched bridge of Japan with the celebrated Mikimoto, whose pearl fisheries were well known to Americans. She felt large and clumsy beside the tiny Japanese in his derby hat and kimono, just as she did with the small graceful women of the country. She was convoyed to the oyster beds in an ancient boat resembling a Roman galleon, and she learned how the oysters were worried into creating pearls, the process that had made Mikimoto rich.

# A World Traveler

As she toured the world, Randolph did his best to keep her informed of events at home. She never liked to be out of touch with her family and she watched eagerly for news and letters at the embassies. She sent Randolph a detailed travelogue of her doings from day to day, however tired she felt.

She was home in time for Christmas, 1929, and that year the children received a rare assortment of Oriental toys and games. In 1932 she made another quick trip to Japan for the wedding of Virginia Teusler to Eric Crowe, an attaché at the British Embassy in Tokyo. Virginia was one of Dr. Teusler's two daughters who had gone around the world with her. In between her two trips to the Orient she took Mrs. Moeling to Poland with her on an unofficial mission. Ignace Paderewski had arranged for the unveiling in Poznan, on July 4, 1931, of the statue of Woodrow Wilson done by Gutzon Borglum, and Mrs. Wilson was to be the guest of honor on Poland's day of independence.

Edith sailed again, on the *Leviathan* on June 17, 1931, and Lucy Moeling discovered the pleasures of traveling with her Aunt Edith, who apologized for taking her away so soon from her young husband, "Red." The captain gave a dinner in their honor and one starry night followed another.

Mrs. Wilson read Polish history on the way over, briefing herself for Independence Day ceremonies ahead. Lucy knitted, listened to Edith read, and joined in the shipboard diversions. Bernard Baruch's car met them when they landed and they were taken direct to Paris.

Although she had gone over the ground innumerable times, Edith gave Lucy a thorough tour. She took her to Les États-Unis, to Napoleon's tomb, to the Louvre, and up to Sacré Coeur in the moonlight. Lucy lived in a dream world. "It was the most divine night, a little new moon. Will never forget it," she wrote to "My Precious Red."

It was *La Grande Semaine* in Paris. Edith was given a box for the Grand Prix. Americans gathered around them and Lucy was stunned by the fashions. They were guests at a lunch for twenty-two at the Polish Embassy, where they met the Jusserands again. The Polish ambassador saw them off to Warsaw and Poznan. They traveled through Belgium, stopping briefly at Liège. Since they had bunks one above the other in their compartment, on the first night of their journey Edith climbed nimbly to the top bunk to play cards with her niece until dawn.

At the Polish border they were met by a representative of President

Moscicki, who boarded their train and accompanied them to Warsaw. After that it became complete officialdom, as Edith Wilson was cheered in the streets of Warsaw and her husband's name was shouted on all sides. Poland was *en fête* for its day of freedom and for the men who had made it possible.

Ironically, Paderewski, who arranged it all, was in Switzerland caring for his desperately ill wife, and he was not present for the unveiling. Edith saw both the old and the new, from medieval palaces and great works of art to the gambols of thousands of children who were led each day to the park for play.

The palace itself was an overwhelming experience. Here Edith saw evidence of Russian vandalism, as well as the faded traces of past magnificence. She and Lucy studied the famous Canaletto paintings of Warsaw, some of which had been returned under the terms of the Peace Treaty. Many were still missing. The remarkable clock of Father Time with the world on his shoulders, too heavy for the Russians to transport, was still keeping perfect time.

Then they boarded a train for the unveiling ceremony at Poznan. "Our arrival at Poznan was the most dramatic thing I have ever been privileged to see," Lucy wrote to her husband. A mounted escort with pennants flying escorted them to Wilson Park. Edith sat on a raised dais with the President, two ambassadors and the Minister of Foreign Affairs. The sun blazed down on them as the President unveiled the statue. Even with many eyes focused on her Edith could not conceal her dismay, and Lucy wrote to her husband, "I almost shrieked when I saw it—it's so terrible aside from not having the slightest resemblance. . . . The statue is unbalanced. The queerest impression."

But the crowd cheered and the ceremony went on, with five speeches and a procession of the representatives of many organizations bearing wreaths until the statue was half concealed with flowers. It was a Fourth of July outpouring by a freed people to the memory of Woodrow Wilson, and it touched Edith. But when Mrs. Borglum asked her how she liked the statue, Edith found she could not praise it.

Edith and her party were to be picked up by a train going on to Berlin. There was thought to be an element of risk in her visit, because of the angry feeling that still burned over Woodrow Wilson. Their plans were kept quiet and they moved about like casual visitors.

They were utterly exhausted when they reached Geneva. Their party had broken up by this time and the elder Baruchs had gone back to Paris. The Assembly was not in session, so after lunching in a house in the country that had been turned into a barn—a growing trend—they called on Paderewski. "I fell in love with him," Lucy wrote. "He has the most charming personality. But it was such a sad household. His wife is very ill—so ill that he could not go to the unveiling."

He and Edith were old friends by this time. She remembered the day she had first seen him at Shadow Lawn. She saw now that his mood was gloomy, although Poland was rejoicing over its freedom. Belle took them driving, but her car stalled on the hill leading to his house. She asked the great pianist to push the car for her, but he looked at her helplessly and could do nothing because of his "precious fingers." Edith went to work herself.

Baruch wanted them to tour the chateau country but they were now ready for the trip home. From first to last it had been the "broadening" experience that Mrs. Wilson had promised Lucy. Banquets, receptions, and troop reviews were an old story to the First Lady, but in Poland she was keenly aware of the enduring love for Woodrow.

# 27. *Intolerable Books*

EDITH WILSON knew that a flood of books and magazine articles would follow her husband's death, but she was stunned by the unvarnished hostility shown by the men who had worked most closely with him. It took years for a flow of biographies and war records from other nations to round out the picture of Woodrow Wilson on the international scene, but the American books came at once, with crushing impact, and she found those by House and Lansing particularly intolerable. They made her all the more anxious to get his own records before the public.

Bainbridge Colby wrote to her on May 10, 1926, that it was a passing phase and she must not let it annoy her, since the "great personality they presume to discuss is beyond their intellectual vision or comprehension." Baruch advised her that the "grim silence of facts" was better than an endless number of denials and "the quieter we kept the better." Edith would come to grips with House and Lansing when she wrote her own memoir, but she remained silent while work on the papers continued. Ray Stannard Baker urged caution, saying that the guerrilla warfare proposed by some of the President's friends would only serve to draw attention to the offending books and fatten their sales. It was agreed between them that attacks should be ignored, but Edith quickly spotted what she believed to be errors of fact, giving Baker a chance to check and correct them while he edited the papers.

Lansing's book, *The Big Four and Others of the Peace Conference,* came out in 1921 while the President was still alive but very ill. Edith and Lansing were already at loggerheads and she resented the picture he drew of her husband at Versailles as a man without a program, intent on keeping everything in his own hands, commanding everyone's approval of the Covenant, and functioning in omnipotent isolation. The former Secretary of State pictured him as reaching the zenith of his power at the first plenary session of the Conference and then losing ground until the commissioners no longer took him seriously. In Lansing's opinion Clemenceau's "shrewd and practical methods of negotiation succeeded better than the President's idealism."

Her reaction to William Allen White's book was immediate and severe. Although he was lavish in his praise of her at various points, that was not what she wanted; she could see only misinterpretations affecting her husband, and constant ridicule. His references to Mrs. Peck were particularly distressing to her and the book stung her, but it proved popular with its racy prose and original point of view. His material on Tumulty struck her as being outrageous. She deplored his account of suffrage picketing at the White House, comparing it with David Lawrence's, which she thought more closely approached the truth.

Josephus Daniels' *The Life of Woodrow Wilson, 1856–1924* was published the year the President died, but he had triple qualifications as a Cabinet member, a trained journalist, and a close friend of the President and Mrs. Wilson. He had been working on it for some years and it was wholly friendly.

Dr. Grayson's memoir came out in 1960, shortly before Mrs. Wilson's death and long after his own. It was a sympathetic and intimate study of Woodrow Wilson, with a glowing tribute to Edith. It emphasized the courage with which Wilson had fought and partially conquered his disability, and it illumined his wit and kindness to others.

One of the great sorrows of Edith Wilson's life was the sudden death of Dr. Grayson in 1938, at the age of fifty-eight while he was still in public service as chairman of the National Red Cross. She had known him before she had known Woodrow Wilson, and his wife had been her closest friend and traveling companion. He had shared in her hours of triumph and of sorrow, and he had guarded her health as he had her husband's. Above all, he had been a family friend, whose wit and knowledge had helped them all.

Another of her husband's good friends and supporters, Newton D. Baker, died a few days before Dr. Grayson. Ray Stannard Baker wrote to her, "The generation of the war is slipping off. Newton Baker the other day, and now Grayson. Both good men—*really* good men."

Edith helped Senator Carter Glass prepare his book, reading it chapter by chapter and supplying him with facts. She complimented him on his "splendid loyalty" and his "unselfish friendship" for her husband. But she was far from pleased when she learned that Mrs. Helm had signed a contract in 1930 to publish her own letters to her husband, written during the Peace Conference. With her diary entries they made a particularly bright and witty narrative on the Wilsons abroad, with authentic historical additions to the known facts of that period.

They were written with inner knowledge and a perceptive touch, making clear Edith Wilson's witty and irreverent moments when not in the public eye. Mrs. Helm had been meticulous in meeting all the requirements of protocol in getting Edith to all the appointed places on time, but both were strongly conscious of the ridiculous.

These two good friends who had been through so much together had a caustic exchange of letters when Edith learned what Mrs. Helm had done. She reminded her former secretary that she would have expected her to shrink from making public any correspondence handled by her in her confidential position and as a member of the household.

Mrs. Helm promptly replied that she had always told her she intended one day to publish the letters to her husband when she got them arranged in satisfactory form. She recalled that her manuscript had been taken from the vault when Edith suggested that she read it herself to the President. But she had stopped after a few pages, because she saw that he was becoming upset by the echoes of the days in Paris. Mrs. Helm also reminded Edith that she had given her the material to read at that time, and no objection to the possibility of publication had been made. Now that the contract was signed, Mrs. Helm asked if Edith would like to go over it again, but would understand if she declined rather than be associated with the book. It was written with a "heart full of love for you and the President," Mrs. Helm assured her, and she was sorry that Edith had written to her as she had.

Edith calmed down and sent her a handwritten letter saying not to worry about her feelings, since she had grown callous through much exposure. "All that matters is that we have been too close in all these years to let anything disturb our friendship."

Their paths crossed often in the years that followed, since Mrs. Helm returned as social secretary to the White House when her husband died, and she rounded out twenty-five years of service there. There was an old camaraderie and understanding between them that nothing could destroy. They had experienced extraordinary events together. Both had a feeling for social form, but in an independent and spirited way. Both were wits when the spirit moved them.

As books and memoirs proliferated, it was inevitable that she would write her own, and *My Memoir* appeared in 1939, fifteen years after her husband's death. For years she was urged to tell her own story. But it took Colonel House's book to get her started. She was so angered when she read it and found so much to contradict that she began scribbling notes as she traveled about. She wrote with passion, for there were moments in which she alone had shared. She knew the answers. When Bernard Baruch read her early notes he was enthusiastic and immediately saw the serial and magazine possibilities. Since she was working with Baker on the Wilson series at this time she hoped that he would also handle her own manuscript. He responded enthusiastically at first, but after studying it carefully he had reservations. He warned her that she might run into trouble with some of her frank comments on Margot Asquith, Queen Marie of Rumania, Queen Elizabeth of Belgium, Mrs. Harding, Madame Poincare, and others.

After years of discretion and scrupulous care about not being quoted, Edith's book was nothing if not candid. Baker felt that her dislike of House, Tumulty, and others came through too strongly. She recalled slights her husband had suffered that had passed unnoticed at the time but that rankled in her memory, and seemed out of proportion now. Yet there was no denying that her story was full of life and deeply felt. He told her that it had the elements of a great and moving narrative, having not only personal interest, but much fresh material of historical value. He was struck by her remarkable memory and her gift for bringing facts into focus. After studying the manuscript carefully he saw that it would need careful checking and editing, and he had neither the time nor the inclination to handle it himself, although he would supervise what was done. But Edith was determined to follow her own course in all respects and when her attitude to House was questioned she pointed out that she would show "exactly what she found." She had felt a warm liking for him at first, she said, but her "prolonged and dispassionate" examination of the documentary material had disillusioned her as to his ability and character.

When writing the book she was perfectly willing to concede its literary deficiencies, but Baruch kept encouraging her. She worked quietly until suddenly the pace heightened as the date of publication approached. Facts could be checked, but she was immovable in the field of personal conviction and opinion.

When the question of serialization arose, Bernard Baruch brought in Marquis James, a writer with excellent magazine connections and a solid reputation as a correspondent. He and his wife, Bessie R. James, who helped her husband with research, became close friends of Edith's and were frequently her guests at S Street. They played backgammon together and went in for all the parlor games of the 1930's, as well as a little of the black magic that amused Edith. She became interested in their clever daughter, Cynthia, who was studying music but flitted joyfully from one goal to another.

James was a Cherokee Indian, which was a bond with Edith Wilson. He found her remarkably easy to work with—a natural storyteller. Although Edith, in her introduction, gave both the Jameses credit for their help to her book, it was altogether hers, with a little trimming of what James called her "colloquial and idiomatic" English. He assured her that he liked the earthy quality of her writing. It had pith and sinew.

She was no amateur in this field; she had worked with the most exacting of scholars. And Randolph, "as dependable as a good old clock," did essential checking.

The book was serialized in *The Saturday Evening Post* and brought quick and widespread reactions. It enlightened many and infuriated some. The day of White House revelations had not yet arrived, and the voice of Mrs. Woodrow Wilson, widow of one of the most controversial of Presidents, was now heard echoing around the world.

Although she was well used to newspaper features on her husband, it was exciting for Edith Wilson to see her own story, lavishly illustrated, appearing in the widely read *Post*. She was scarcely prepared for the avalanche of letters that followed, some so abusive that they could not be shown to her, others adulatory. Her sense of humor prevailed even when the cuts ran deep; she had been through it before, but she rejoiced when her readers said that she had humanized Woodrow Wilson and given them fresh bits of history.

The serialization had just begun when the book itself came out carefully shepherded by Edith. She insisted that her name, Edith Bolling Wilson, stand alone on the jacket of the regular edition, without bringing in the name of Woodrow Wilson, since she said she did not wish to capitalize on his fame. Every detail of the presentation had to be approved by her, and tactful editors and publishers were anxious to please her.

Her husband's closest friends were reserved in their judgment, but admired her courage, unless they came under fire themselves. It had widespread newspaper coverage, both in the news columns and the book reviews. "It deserves wide reading," Gerald Johnson wrote in the New York *Herald Tribune.* "Cold, hard fact," said the Chicago *Tribune.* "There is nothing half-way . . . about the lady's punches . . . . A clear compactness of events and the causes behind them."

Henry Steele Commager, reviewing the work for the New York *Times,* wrote that it "does service to Woodrow Wilson because it humanizes him without detracting from his dignity and celebrates him without recourse to eulogy." Lewis Gannett, in the New York *Herald Tribune,* described Mrs. Wilson's book as "human, and official, and will outlast a carload of documents." Howard Mumford Jones labeled it a "significant public document utterly without literary value" in the

# Intolerable Books

Boston *Transcript*. William Allen White, writing for *The Saturday Review*, called it a "work full of historical background," with Mrs. Wilson telling her story "unselfconsciously out of her heart."

Stephen Vincent Benet wrote sympathetically for the New York *Herald Tribune* that he feared the public might view it as a Cinderella story. To him it was a "valuable historic document . . . the work of a devoted wife, a fierce partisan and an extremely feminine woman. It combines great candour with a very genuine dignity . . . the result is as fascinating a human document as a woman in high position ever set down. . . . She does not apologize, she does not regret—she says what she did and leaves it to the verdict of history."

But the Wilson name was in eclipse in Washington, and Edith had many critics. She entered the 1940's a better-known woman, but she did not change her policy of avoiding the press, and she was deaf to the offers that now reached her to write, speak, and give interviews. She had her say and let it go at that until Alden Hatch, who had worked on Wilson papers and was familiar with the family background, wrote *Edith Bolling Wilson: First Lady Extraordinary,* which was published in 1961. It reminded the public that Mrs. Woodrow Wilson was still alive, but she died a few months later.

From the beginning she had strong views on books about her husband written by women, and she disliked a serious and highly praised study of him by Edith Gittings Reid, called *Woodrow Wilson: the Caricature, the Myth and the Man.* It chilled her when it came out in 1934, for although it brushed away many of the myths about him it almost completely ignored her existence and the role she had played in his life. Edith told Baker that she had been "studiedly ignored" and she felt hurt.

She lived so long that she had a chance to read the books of various members of the White House staff, in addition to Mrs. Helm's, and one that upset her considerably was Ike Hoover's *Forty-Two Years in the White House.* It, too, was serialized in *The Saturday Evening Post* and was widely read. Much as she had liked Hoover, and generous as he was in his comments on her, she thought that he gave an enfeebling picture of her husband and a distorted view of events at the White House on the night the President had his major stroke. The picture Hoover drew of Wilson's last years seemed to Edith to be misleading.

Mrs. Elizabeth Jaffray also had her say, in *Secrets of the White House.* She was altogether flattering to President and Mrs. Wilson, hostile to Mrs. Harding, and cool to President Coolidge and his popular wife, Grace. Colonel Edmund W. Starling's book, *Starling of the White House: As Told to Thomas Sugrue,* was filled with piquant and intimate observations on the Wilsons immediately before and after their marriage. He had always admired Edith and this came through strongly in his book.

She found deep satisfaction in John F. Kennedy's *Profiles in Courage* and Hector Bolitho's *Twelve Against the Gods.* Bolitho pictured Wilson as daring everything alone and handling colossal power as "if it were a sword in his hand, sheathing it when he wished, baring it at his own moment. . . . Wilson is in person the doctrine of democracy . . . the peer in romance of anything that has come about in humanity before."

This pleased Edith. Bolitho had visited her on a trip to the United States, and he wrote from Brighton in May, 1947, telling her how much he had enjoyed seeing her at the house on S Street—the tranquil room, the canasta they played, and the hungry birds perched on her windowsill that they fed. He added that the books coming out on Wilson seemed cold.

The steady flow of important biographies and war records mounted with the years, both at home and abroad. Edith kept abreast of them all. Baruch saw to it that any books concerning her husband and League affairs reached her. She moved in a circle of clever and well-informed women, some of whom had strong political interests through their husbands, so she caught contemporary thought from many angles.

*The Priceless Gift,* edited by Eleanor Wilson McAdoo, was published immediately after Edith's death. This was a combination of the letters of Woodrow Wilson and his first wife, Ellen Axson Wilson. Many of them were ardent love letters, a genre in which Woodrow Wilson was proficient. They were held up out of consideration for the second Mrs. Wilson, but she was aware of them through her work on her husband's papers.

She did not live to read *Thomas Woodrow Wilson: A Psychological Study,* by Sigmund Freud and William T. Bullitt, published in 1967.

Both men agreed that it should not come out while she was alive, and Freud had died by that time, too. One of the conclusions he drew was that Wilson's sudden infatuation for Edith Bolling Galt was proof, rather than disproof, of the depth of his love for Ellen Axson Wilson. From profound depression he had moved rapidly to heights of exaltation and "was recklessly in love with the recklessness of the man of sixty who has felt old because a passionate love has passed from his life and suddenly he experiences the miracle of the rebirth of passion and feels young, exalted, full of power, God-like."

This psychological study of Wilson had its origin in a book Bullitt had done on the Treaty of Versailles, with sketches of Clemenceau, Orlando, Lloyd George, and Wilson—all of whom he knew personally. Freud had always been interested in Wilson, so they decided to collaborate on a full-scale treatment, with Bullitt doing the research and Freud drawing the conclusions. On this shaky basis the work proceeded desultorily for ten years, with Bullitt amassing 1,500 pages of typewritten notes, which he took to Vienna to show to Freud. Then Freud wrote certain portions and Bullitt others, creating an amalgam for which both were responsible, after they had amended or rewritten each other's copy.

Woodrow Wilson's worship of his father and the need he felt throughout his life for a "father image" was the underlying theme. His love life with Ellen Axson and Edith Bolling Wilson was analyzed and interpreted in the Freudian manner. Bullitt, who had once been close to Wilson, had become one of his severest critics.

When Dr. Stockton Axson, the first Mrs. Wilson's brother, had a nervous breakdown in the early 1920's, Edith treated him with extraordinary understanding. He wrote to her on December 13, 1924, "I loved you from the beginning of the association of our lives through Brother Woodrow. . . for his sake, for your own sake, for the marvellous way you took us all into your affections and consideration. . . . You have let me feel I am like one of your brothers."

Axson's illness coincided with the publication of William Allen White's book. He blamed himself for having talked too freely about family matters to the editor from Kansas, and he thought that Edith would never forgive him, but she did. She told him to stop worrying about it, since the book would float like an empty box on water and then break up and sink and be forgotten.

Edith invited Axson to all family gatherings, and while her husband was still alive she asked him to stay with them at S Street, which to her was a "haven of peace and privacy and so sweet and homelike." She wrote of their tiny garden filled with fat robins, and described the Kentucky cardinals darting like flames of fire from tree to tree. The bees were swarming when she wrote, and she offered to tuck him in a corner where he could live a "dusty old buccaneer's existence" and see others only when he felt like it.

Dr. Axson found Edith's practical way of handling each problem as it came up, leaving no time for brooding, a much-needed support. Her cheerful and positive approach to life had meant everything to Woodrow Wilson, and had helped to sustain him through his toughest ordeals. Time and again she had rescued members of her family from depressions and had kept a busy flow of life around them. She had learned early in her widowhood not to yearn for the irrecoverable past, but to spread her wings.

In the early 1940's, one of the busiest periods of her life, she was giving some thought to an official film on the life of the President. After his death there were various plans and some abortive attempts to do this in a satisfactory way, but it was not until the 1940's that the plan took shape, with the production of a picture by Twentieth Century-Fox, directed by Darryl Zanuck. It was difficult to find a script that suited her, but Lamar Trotti finally succeeded, and Baker spent months in Hollywood as a consultant. He kept up a steady flow of correspondence with Edith, reporting each move. In a sense she was the director in absentia, an exacting one.

Who would play Woodrow Wilson? She hoped for Alfred Lunt, but he and Lynn Fontanne were engaged in London at the time. Finally Alexander Knox was chosen. Although almost unknown in the cinema world, he was a talented actor with a particularly fine voice, and this was what Edith most desired, since she considered her husband's diction the best in the world. Baker assured her that he seemed to bear some physical resemblance to the President, and he was the son of a Presbyterian minister, a strong point in his favor.

## Intolerable Books

Since it could not be Lynn Fontanne, Edith gave little thought to the actress who would play herself. But Zanuck went slow on that. Twenty-five possibilities were tested before Geraldine Fitzgerald was chosen. Baker approved her looks, her charm, and her intelligence, but he noticed that although she had a cultivated voice she did not know the "Shenandoah language," and failed to catch the nuances of Edith's soft speech. Nor did Miss Fitzgerald bear any resemblance to her.

There was never any question of Miss Fitzgerald trying to look or talk like Edith Wilson. Her own view of the matter was quite simply expressed. "Edith Wilson was one of the beauties of her day. . . . My only concession to authenticity took into account Mrs. Wilson's light-hearted, laughing nature. I kept every scene buoyant, even the very serious ones." She purposely avoided using the makeup of middle age, for she wanted to show her looking as she would have seemed to Woodrow Wilson—young and attractive.

Edith wrote to Baker that Miss Fitzgerald sounded like a girl of independence and character. She was amused by the discussion in the press about her hats. How would Miss Fitzgerald cope with all those plumes and birds? "I can only recall *one* hat that does not have *Birds* but *Wings*. It was one of my favorites in violet," she wrote helpfully.

Altrude visited the set in Hollywood to see what was going on and to report back to Edith. She caught only one episode, done over many times, and she wrote that they seemed to be doing a good job. Knox was a "dignified figure, with a nice cultivated voice" but she did not think that he resembled Woodrow. Altrude felt differently about things after she saw the finished picture.

Altrude became Mrs. George L. Harrison a few years after Cary's death, marrying one of her former suitors. She disliked the Wilson film, feeling that Cary had been misrepresented. Among the points she raised was the informal fashion in which he addressed Edith Wilson, since both she and Cary had always been scrupulous in this respect, not going beyond the intimacy of "Miss Edith," or "Aunt Ede" at times. Also, he never smoked and was not the nervous figure they saw on the screen.

Edith was apprehensive about attending the New York premiere of the film in August, 1944, an uncommon state of mind for her, but she dreaded personal publicity and she feared that it might give a false impression of her husband, despite Baker's assurance. Nor did she like having her first view of it in a public place. She stayed at the Plaza Hotel and after a formal dinner drove to the Roxy Theatre with Belle Baruch and Josephus Daniels. The police had to hold the crowd back as they arrived. They went in quietly just as the lights were going down. She sat transfixed watching it and afterward only said, "I think it is dignified and not cheap."

She sent red roses and a note to Miss Fitzgerald, saying she was sorry their meeting at the opening had been so brief because she "was eager to learn of my alter ego." But she thanked the actress for the "quiet dignity in which she had clothed the part." And Miss Fitzgerald replied, "I feel very humble and very proud to have had the honor of interpreting so lovely a lady."

Daniels, in a letter to Edith, found the picture disappointing, thinking that it "missed the glory of your great husband." He felt that the Hollywood atmosphere had worked against his own enjoyment of the film. "I think on the whole a showing of the film will teach no voters of today that they are looking back to glory," he concluded.

The picture was well received and there was great interest in it in Washington. Edith's nieces, decked with orchids given them by their aunt, who had been deluged with flowers for the opening, had a glamorous evening that ended with supper at the Chevy Chase Club.

Edith would not accept the $50,000 that Twentieth Century offered her, saying that she had no wish "to commercialize Mr. Wilson." When asked to name a favorite cause she immediately suggested the Woodrow Wilson birthplace at Staunton, and everyone was satisfied with that. She kept quiet about the film's view of herself, satisfied that the picture carried Woodrow's story to millions of people and helped support the birthplace.

No President's wife was more strongly committed to the theater, music, and the allied arts than Mrs. Woodrow Wilson. Wherever she went she found the best and enjoyed it. Music remained her most enduring interest, and she settled into a seat in the opera house or concert hall in her seventies with the same zest she had felt at Albaugh's Opera House the night she met Norman Galt, the night her life in Washington had its true beginning.

# 28. *Her Second World War*

EDITH WILSON lived the years of World War I over again in the first half of the 1940's, with the declaration of war after Pearl Harbor, followed by four years that changed the course of the world, climaxed by the death of Franklin D. Roosevelt.

Absorbed and tense, Edith sat beside Eleanor Roosevelt as the President who had most resembled and admired her husband delivered his address to the joint houses of Congress on December 8, 1941, asking for a declaration of war against the Japanese Empire. Both women were conscious of the parallel. With Edith Wilson it was *déjà vu*. And within twenty-four hours Mrs. Roosevelt had commented in her column, *My Day*, "At noon today at the Capitol, I had a curious sense of repetition for I remembered very vividly the description of the same gallery, when Mrs. Woodrow Wilson listened to President Wilson address Congress. *Today* she sat beside me, as the President spoke the words which branded a nation as having departed from the code of civilized people."

Jonathan Daniels, Josephus Daniels' son, wrote that President Roosevelt was showing his "genius for gesture" when he arranged to have Mrs. Wilson present on this historic occasion. He watched her applauding the President with white-gloved hands, and described her as a "well-preserved, still elegantly dressed widow of sixty-nine," more of a period piece than a "symbol for the continuity of times and causes."

The war news next day was so overwhelming that little attention was paid to the joint presence of these two notable women—one with her history behind her; the other with hers in the making. Edith Wilson was fresh from an ovation of her own a few months earlier at the Democratic Convention of 1940 in Chicago. It was an unforgettable experience—not that she liked the limelight herself, but hour after hour she was able to follow the close political maneuvering in Jesse Jones' camp as President Roosevelt held out for Henry A. Wallace as Vice President. When Edith was introduced she came close to being mobbed by the crowd. "It was really dangerous and I had to leave under Police Escort," she wrote to Randolph.

Although she attended one political convention after another she would always remember this as the most exciting. Henry Wallace had become a big political issue. But Edith was much less concerned with politics than with war work as the nation mobilized and she was welcomed as an experienced worker. She had zealously backed Roosevelt at the convention of 1932 in Chicago, and stayed up all night to see this admirer of Woodrow's first roll into power. Now she had seen him nominated for the third time.

Soon she was again a familiar figure around Washington, a former First Lady climbing on buses, carrying her own bundles, cutting down on the lavish Southern cuisine of S Street, keeping the old Wilcox sewing machine busy, and spending long hours with the Senate wives on Red Cross work. She wrote to Lucy Moeling on December 7, 1942, "The weeks fly. I *play* on Mondays, work Tuesday, Wednesday & Thursday at the Red Cross—and try to do home work on Friday, then mow grass & get together usually on Saturday for lunch and gin (rummy)."

She was drawn into many official functions and activities connected with the war. For some time she had been watching with close attention the spread of the New Deal, and now the canvas widened with the outbreak of hostilities. She wrote to old friends that they would no longer recognize Washington—"everything packed with people, new buildings, new methods, new Deals." The pace was fast. The scientific and aeronautical advances of the 1920's and 1930's had made all the difference as war raged in the desert, on Pacific islands, on the beaches of Normandy, in the mountains and along the coastline of Italy.

Day after day Edith studied the newspapers and saw what had come to pass. Her husband had predicted it. Some of his old friends were still in the hierarchy as the Brain Trust grew in power around Roosevelt. Cordell Hull, Jesse Jones, and Bernard Baruch all were her good friends. She saw the parallels with the past but did not dwell on them. It was characteristic of her to refrain from talking politics as she made her rounds, but her correspondence with a few men gave evidence of her ceaseless interest in the major movements of her party, linked to the flow of world events.

In one way she kept aloof from it all, living in the shadow of Woodrow Wilson, promoting the causes he had believed in, and honoring

300

his memory; in another way she was inevitably linked to the social and civic necessities of the period, in the strictest sense of flag and country. She was never forgotten on the official wartime lists; her husband's name lived on, and the Democrats were in power again, with many comparing Franklin D. Roosevelt to Woodrow Wilson.

Christening a ship came naturally to her. Once more at Wilmington, Delaware, as she sent the *Woodrow Wilson* "down the ways" in a flurry of champagne on a February day in 1943, she was cheered and loaded down with flowers.

As the gas shortage grew, she immediately gave up her car and her chauffeur, Shaw. "I naturally will miss both but feel it is the right thing to do," she wrote to Lucy on September 26, 1942. Her friend Mrs. D. C. Sands, an officer of the Ration Board, had given up hers but she used a truck for essential work and sometimes gave Edith a lift.

As she worked with organized purpose and efficiency, Edith managed some lighter moments, too, and reported to Lucy on a benefit luncheon and Hattie Carnegie showing of fashions that she had attended in September, 1942—"and I never saw uglier things." She particularly disliked the hats, but wrote that she was staying away from the shops, and was not buying clothes.

She still went to the theater and concerts when she could. Max Gordon and other producers sent her tickets for their openings—a well-established practice since the days of Woodrow Wilson. Their love for the theater was well known to the profession. With the rush of daily duties her correspondence, usually meticulously kept up, lagged at this time and her apology for failing to answer letters was, "I suppose . . . it is this awful war which disorganizes everything."

But she managed to cope with the benefits and her church work and to hold her own at bridge. She found it stimulating to be in contact with Cabinet wives again and she made a point of going to the Capitol to hear significant debates. She could always depend on Mrs. Borah and Mrs. Brandeis to share her interest in these events, and she was much involved with Mrs. Cordell Hull in the restoration of Woodrow Wilson's birthplace at Staunton. When Hull resigned in 1944 as Secretary of State, she wrote to him that "without your wonderful wife my dream of making the birthplace as a Memorial would never have come true." He was donating the Humanitarian award he had received that

301

year to help support the birthplace, and she wrote that this forged another link "in the long chain that binds the names of Hull and Wilson, both in Washington and Staunton."

Strong though she was, the pace kept up by Edith Wilson in the war days was beginning to tell. She was at Bellefield, the Baruch plantation in South Carolina, when she had what she called a "nasty spell" in September, 1944. Her blood pressure soared to 210 and she was ordered to bed. She was told to act less strenuously. Back on S Street, committed to lying prone for several hours a day, she soon found a way to keep on working. "While I was in bed," she wrote to Lucy, "I cut the ruffles for the curtains & whipped them together . . . my Wilcox works like a breeze." Between her Red Cross work and her own sewing the old machine was in operation as in the days of World War I, with her sister Gertrude at hand to help her.

But with reluctance she gave up her Red Cross work with the Senate wives in November, 1944, explaining that for health reasons she would now have to rest in bed in the mornings. She would miss them and the "delightful little rides to the work room," she wrote. They missed her considerably, since she was a fast worker and a most entertaining conversationalist.

Her family life was changing, too. A new young generation was growing up in various parts of the country—with nephews and cousins going to war, or engaging in war activities, and nieces marrying men in service. Sooner or later, with their brides, friends, and new interests, they turned up at S Street, to visit Aunt Edith and partake of her hospitality. She had become a legend to them.

Jessie Sayre had died unexpectedly from an operation in 1933, but Edith kept in touch with the new generation of Sayres. McAdoo, who had divorced Nell and married a girl young enough to be his daughter, died of a heart attack in 1941 at a hotel in San Francisco. He was seventy-seven, and a disappointed man, having lost his long fight for the Presidency. He left a number of descendants who crossed Edith Wilson's path from time to time.

Again the family tree was shaken in 1944. She wrote to Lucy on February 24, "Of course you saw in the papers of Margaret Wilson's death in India—she was buried there." This item, obscured by the war news of 1944, evoked memories across the country, since Margaret had once been so prominent at her father's side. The soldiers of an earlier generation remembered her as an entertainer at the war camps. It had been difficult to follow her winding course after her father's death. Margaret had always been the unpredictable member of the family, who followed strange gods and took up new causes.

She had suffered a nervous breakdown during the war years and afterward held a succession of jobs—in public relations, advertising, stocks and bonds, and pursuing various arts. But she was restless and always in quest of something she could not find. She had traveled the world over and been touched by the mysticism of the Orient and the spell of the gurus who were active in America in the 1940's. For four years before her death she lived as a member of a religious colony at Pondicherry, in the south of India. In flowing white robes, and looking strangely like her father, she told a visiting correspondent that she had found peace at last and had no wish to return to America. She was fifty-seven when she died.

There was intense activity in Washington in the spring of 1945, and growing hope that the end of the war was in sight. Mrs. Wilson was struck by the great social push going on at the same time, a frenzied crescendo geared to helping the war effort. There were benefits all over town, and much activity at the Sulgrave Club in which Edith shared. Perle Mesta was playing a vigorous role and late in March she gave a dinner for a hundred guests at the club, and another hundred came in later for supper and music. But all social life was stilled and the country was plunged into mourning with the death of President Roosevelt.

The war had yet to be won. Harry Truman was an unknown figure following the strong image of Roosevelt, but the whole world became aware of him when the atomic bomb was dropped at Hiroshima on August 6, 1945. Edith wrote to Lucy Moeling that she had spent a week so crowded with world-stirring events she could scarcely realize the war was over.

She first heard the news at the United Nations Club, where she was attending a dinner for sixteen given by Mrs. F. M. Dillard. They had been invited a week earlier and no one had any idea that it would turn into a victory party. But they listened to the news from Japan coming in on a radio in the private room where they were dining. Twice in her life she had lived through the hours of jubilation that marked the end of a world war, but this time things were more subdued. It was not the wild celebration she remembered from the days of the armistice. The atomic bomb had a sobering effect.

The new President invited Edith to the victory service at the White House and sent a car for her—"which I thought very thoughtful on his part," she wrote to Lucy. She studied with interest the modest-looking man who had had only a short term as Vice President and was thought to know nothing of world affairs. Woodrow's specialty had been history, but what none suspected in 1945 was that Truman had been a zealous reader in this field from his earliest years.

One of the significant events of the decade for Edith Wilson was the international conference held at San Francisco in the spring of 1945 to draw up a charter for the long anticipated United Nations. It broke up in total disunity as the delegates from different countries fought for precedence. Josephus Daniels told her that the spirit of Woodrow Wilson hovered over the gathering, but his work received scant recognition in the midst of all the oratory, and Jan Masaryk of Czechoslovakia alone brought up his name. She was personally honored at the conference and after it was over President Truman urged the speedy ratification of the charter. He had better luck than Woodrow Wilson, for it was approved by the Senate on July 28, 1945.

Edith may have felt some skepticism as the conference ended. She was furious when Nell McAdoo gave a statement to the press early in May from her home in San Francisco that her father died believing the United States was right in refusing to join the League of Nations. When she saw an abbreviated version of what Nell had to say in a Washington paper she sent out a denial at once.

At the time of the President's death Margaret had been similarly quoted. She insisted that her father had said it on his deathbed and that she had heard him. Angry then, Edith was even more so now, and she summoned up for the press her own recollection of what he had said as his life flickered:

> Woodrow Wilson would never have made such a statement for it would have reversed everything in his nature and contradicted his life's struggle for the betterment of all people and all nations of the world. What he did say to me and to many of

his friends who have often spoken of it since then —perhaps it was better that the American people did not join the League of Nations just to follow him, but that they join from their own convictions that they could not stay out, and that conviction would come through the tragic loss of young lives, for in another generation the World War would be followed by another one even more terrible.

This prophecy had been startlingly realized, and the organization that evolved from the San Francisco conference, whether known as the United Nations or not, in her opinion would be based on the principles for which Woodrow Wilson gave his life.

All through the 1940's, in addition to her war work, Edith threw her influence behind the Woodrow Wilson Foundation and the restoration of the President's birthplace. She knew what she wanted and stood firm until she had achieved her ends. Inevitably there were political flurries at the Foundation among the powerful Wilson admirers who had built it up, and by the end of the 1940's a drive for young blood involved much maneuvering and tact on her part. She traveled repeatedly to New York for luncheons, dinners, and meetings of the organization. She always kept in mind the man and the aims that she felt he would have approved. The Foundation's awards were controversial from time to time, and she did not believe in decking with laurels persons who had hurt Woodrow Wilson or his policies.

But she was a proud participant when Lord Robert Cecil, who had kept the faith with her husband on the League of Nations, received the first award at a dinner held in New York in April, 1923. Woodrow was still alive—in her own words a "wounded eagle chained to a rock."

By the 1970's thousands stopped each year at the spacious old manse in Staunton to see everything from Woodrow Wilson's cradle to the documentary film of his life. The restoration was a united effort by members of his family and some of his old friends to assemble memorabilia, but it bore the final stamp of Edith Bolling Wilson. She knew what each object had meant to Woodrow; her own gifts were highly personal. Through her affluent friends she generated interest and financial support on behalf of the birthplace, but she never appealed for funds and carefully avoided the commercial touch in its development.

It held many echoes of Wilson's parents and of the first Mrs. Wilson.

A simple summer dress Ellen Axson had made herself at the time of her marriage lay stretched on his parents' bed. Her pallette, streaked with dried paint, was as evocative as her woodland paintings that hung on the walls and the portrait done of her at the White House a few months before her death.

The guitar that had belonged to Woodrow's mother, his father's rocking chair, the violin he had played as a boy—Edith saw one treasure being added to another from different donors, and often made the decisions on where they should go, from the family crib to the antique doll's trunk in which Grandmother Bolling had kept her love letters from her doctor husband during the Civil War. The grandfather clock that had given Woodrow his lifelong passion for timepieces, an original corner cupboard, the old family Bible on a pedestal, and the bowl and ewer in which he had washed were historic grist for the birthplace.

One of Edith's most significant gifts was the student lamp her husband had used at the University of Virginia and had taken to the White House. It had shone on many historic documents, and it recalled companionable evenings as he worked by its light, and the unforgettable announcement of their engagement. She and Randolph gave the bookcase Woodrow had bought with his first earnings and treasured in the White House even after his well-stacked bookshelves reached the ceiling.

Reminders of his official life included the famous Wilson eagle, the flag he carried on his way to sign the Peace Treaty, four gold guineas from the Federal Reserve Bank, a painting of him signing the Federal Reserve Bill, which he considered one of his most important achievements, and other official memorabilia.

The house developed by stages into a national shrine, and great care was taken by the ladies of Virginia to preserve the historic pattern. Edith and Mrs. Herbert McKelden Smith, of Staunton, worked harmoniously for years on the acquisitions and arrangement, with Mrs. Cordell Hull overseeing. "You have a wonderful sense of the fitness of things," Edith told Mrs. Smith. "I rest assured in the knowledge that each thing done is the right and dignified one." She found after a visit that the only thing needing adjustment was the fringe on Woodrow's parents' big bed, and Lucy Moeling gave a Martha Washington bedspread that she had made, to correct this flaw.

There was great public interest in the acquisition of the Pierce Arrow, which had become something of a stagecoach and curiosity. President Wilson bought it in 1919 for $3,000. Even in a world of speeding luxury cars, he clung to the old Pierce Arrow. Weighing an unbelievable three tons, with a 48 horsepower motor and dual ignition, it lumbered along at twenty-five miles an hour, because Woodrow Wilson would not let his chauffeur, George Howard, go any faster. All Washington knew the car at sight, with its sidelights, tinted glass, and massive presence.

The President drove to the Capitol in it before he became ill, and after his stroke he and Edith took leisurely rides through Rock Creek Park, to Chevy Chase Lake, or out to Griffith Field to watch baseball. He liked the space, the glass partition that shut him off from the front, and the two buzzers he used to catch his chauffeur's attention. Restored and painted up, it finally came to rest at the birthplace, finished off with a small Princeton Tiger hood ornament found in the President's belongings after his death.

The years flowed gently over Edith Wilson. Although her tastes grew more luxurious there was no real change in her thinking. She always returned from her travels ready to settle down to her accustomed ways. But one thing she did learn was the great change that World War II had made in women's lives. She had watched it happen after Woodrow Wilson's war. It was overwhelmingly evident again after Franklin Roosevelt's war.

# *29.* The Wilsons and Suffrage

WHEN the nineteenth amendment granting suffrage to the women of America was proclaimed on August 26, 1920, Woodrow Wilson was still in the early stages of his illness, with Mrs. Wilson constantly at his side to protect him from the intrusions of the outside world. But Mrs. Carrie Chapman Catt, chairman of the National American Woman Suffrage Association, gave him credit for ensuring before his collapse the last vote needed to pass the measure. It came from Tennessee, where he had many friends.

Historically he would be identified with the ultimate success of the fight that had plagued him through his two administrations, and on which he had zigzagged from time to time. In the war years it became acute as the more radical legions of the National Woman's Party, headed by Alice Paul, picketed the White House and Capitol for a year and a half, and sprang up with banners and shouts of protest wherever President and Mrs. Wilson appeared. Miss Paul, an ethereal-looking Quaker with hazel eyes and a melodic voice, combined fragility with the iron will of Mrs. Emmeline Pankhurst, the English suffragette whose tactics she had learned at first hand in London. Like Alice Longworth (Mrs. Nicholas Longworth), she was still alive in 1974 and conscious of the march of the liberationists. Theodore Roosevelt's daughter had not been on Miss Paul's side, but had lived the part, and Mrs. Wilson had watched her use all her political drive against her husband on the League of Nations issue.

For years there was uncertainty as to President Wilson's belief in woman suffrage, but there was never any doubt about his wife's dislike for aggressive, noisy tactics by members of her own sex, a feeling strengthened by every fresh outbreak in public. She had grown up in the Southern tradition and believed that home and family were the true goals of the well-adjusted woman. It was ironic that she should have functioned as a successful businesswoman when her first husband died, and that by chance when Woodrow Wilson collapsed she should become internationally known as the Presidentress, running the country by regency.

This was less than the truth, but it caught the public imagination. The statesmen who had met her in Europe and her husband's colleagues who had watched her at their conferences with the President in the White House, recalled how potent she had seemed and how often he had turned to her for an opinion. "When women decide to become Cabinet officers the Secretary of the Navy's portfolio should be assigned to you," Josephus Daniels wrote to Mrs. Wilson in 1917, as she renamed seized German ships and christened new ones coming off the assembly line for service in the Atlantic.

Mrs. Wilson insisted in *My Memoir* that she had merely played what she called the wifely role, but evidence abounds of the candor with which she expressed her own opinions. The fact that she was married to the President of the United States made all the difference. Women agitators ranked high among her dislikes, and in the campaign of 1916 she listened coldly at a suffrage meeting in Atlantic City to "the only speech of my Precious One that I ever failed to enjoy, but I hated the subject so it was acute agony." The President had been highly complimentary to the suffrage workers on this occasion and to women in general; it was a campaign issue and the election was at hand.

When November 7 dawned the Wilsons were up early and after breakfast they drove from Shadow Lawn, the summer White House, to Princeton where the President cast his vote in the old engine house, a familiar rite of many years standing for him. "That was as near as I ever came to voting at the polls for the Presidential candidate," Mrs. Wilson commented. New Jersey had not yet granted suffrage to women and after her husband's death she lost the right to vote, since she was a resident of the District of Columbia.

The day was bright and sunny and the President was in a genial mood as the press crowded around him, but Mrs. Wilson kept out of their way. Optimistic by nature, she was more doubtful that morning of her husband's chance of winning than he was. When it was all over and he had finally been declared the victor over Charles Evans Hughes, the New York *Times* of November 10 ran a headline: WOMEN VOTERS FAIL TO FOLLOW LEADERS. The states where suffrage was strong had gone for Wilson, although Hughes had endorsed their movement in a much more spectacular way.

The President came face to face with the issue in an unexpected way when he asked Congress for a declaration of war in April, 1917. Jeanette Rankin, the Representative from Montana who had campaigned on horseback for the eight-hour day and equal pay for women, said nay. She later denied that she had wept, the popular legend at the time, but she acknowledged that she had hurt the suffrage cause by taking the stand she had at that particular time. Her colleagues forgave her, agreeing that she had followed the dictates of her conscience. The issue was peace, not suffrage, although both were intertwined.

By the 1970's Miss Rankin had become one of the nationally recognized heroines of the movement, like Mrs. Margaret Sanger, who had shared headlines with her as the nation went to war. When she was sent to the workhouse early in 1917 for opening a birth control clinic in Brooklyn, America's leading protagonist in this field brought birth control and abortion forcibly before the public. This was all tied up with woman's rights, which were entering a new phase as the United States went to war.

The repercussions were minor to the busy man in the White House commanding the vast operations of 1917, but Mrs. Wilson watched them with an observant eye. War and peace and the Malthusian philosophy were in historic collision.

Woodrow Wilson had all the gallantry of the Virginian of his generation where women were concerned, and he had grown up surrounded by women—some docile, others strong-willed, but all inclined to spoil and humor him. His mother had been a quiet force in his life, saying little but teaching him to aim always for excellence. His first wife had been deeply devoted to him for twenty-nine years, pursuing her interest in the arts and showing her idealism in working for children and the poor. Their daughters leaned strongly to the feminist cause as the suffrage movement grew strong in America. Both Nell and Jessie had influence with their father in this respect, and it was one of many interests pursued by Margaret.

On the day the President's engagement became public, by chance or design an announcement that he would vote for woman suffrage in New Jersey was featured across the country. The New York *Times* of October 7, 1915, linked both events in a startling headline:

PRESIDENT TO WED MRS. GALT,
INTIMATE FRIEND OF HIS DAUGHTERS;
ALSO COMES OUT FOR WOMAN SUFFRAGE

There was only one woman in the President's periphery that day, and he seemed to be bewitched by her, but the public immediately at-

310

tributed his change of front on the suffrage question to the influence of his future bride. Hardheaded politicians agreed that it had more to do with the forthcoming election. It was not convincing to the agitators, who insisted that he was so absorbed in one woman—Edith Galt—that he was "ignoring the rights of *all* women."

William Howard Taft noticed the juxtaposition of the two news stories with interest since he, too, was on the firing line about suffrage. Mrs. Elihu Root had warned him that the mere sight of the suffrage workers intent on presenting him with a petition would make him run or look the other way. Taft was doubtful about this since although his wife was not a convert, their daughter, Mrs. Helen Manning, dean of Bryn Mawr, who was good-looking and also well balanced in her views, did not hesitate to take to the platform on behalf of woman suffrage.

Three years would pass after the President's pronouncement, and pickets would storm the White House and be sent to the workhouse, before either man capitulated completely. Taft was won by the evidence he gathered on his lecture tours during the war years that women stood for peace and had the best right in the world to attain equality. Wilson's "conversion," as he called it, came with the realization that the women's movement was a growing force in the settlement of international affairs and a "moral" issue in which America should show leadership. The women of other countries were forming strong alliances and were moving ahead of their bright and articulate sisters in the United States. Added to this was the convincing evidence of the work they had done in the war.

Once persuaded, President Wilson stood firm on suffrage up to the time of his collapse. His political enemies listened coldly when he declared that the war could not have been won without the extraordinary work done by women, aside from the irrefutable fact that they were the mothers of the men who went to battle. Mrs. Wilson reserved judgment at this time, but Woodrow had spoken.

Although she was faced with the suffrage issue in a personal way immediately after her engagement, it was not altogether new to her. On trips to Europe before World War I broke out, she had learned a great deal about the violent tactics of Mrs. Emmeline Pankhurst and her daughter Sylvia. The papers were filled with their exploits, and friends she met in London and Paris talked of the wild new breed intent on kicking policemen, burning letterboxes, getting tied to lampposts, and flinging themselves at the royal coach.

On an August day in 1913 Mrs. Galt and Altrude Gordon visited Madame Tussaud's and lunched at Rumpelmeyers, but were amazed to find that the Houses of Parliament and Westminster Abbey were guarded against suffragettes. Altrude's diary entry testified to this curious turn of events in law-abiding England.

The ladies from Virginia were none too approving, but neither did they like coming under suspicion of being agitators themselves. They thought it an outrage when their luggage was torn apart at customs in the quest for weapons or incendiary trinkets. Visiting Americans were not all Daisy Millers. Some of them had dashing ways and could express themselves glibly. The name Lucy Stone was not unknown in England.

Mrs. Galt was more amused than angry when she ran into trouble at the Tower of London. She was told she could not go in without having her purse searched, and this offended her. Since she had made the tour on earlier visits she told Altrude and a young cousin she had with her to go ahead while she sat outside and wrote letters.

As soon as she settled on a bench one of the lordly scarlet-coated Beefeaters approached her and a crowd gathered to see the fun. She asked him what he was up to, and he told her, "I am here to watch you. We don't trust women these days." He was quickly joined by two other guards, one with a gun in his hand. Her fountain pen was examined and was found to be harmless. Her hatpins came under observation, since the suffragettes were known to jab their enemies, the constabulary.

Mrs. Galt found it all irresistible and brought her merry wit to bear on them, so that by the time Altrude and her cousin Pat had returned, the guards themselves were grinning as they shouldered arms and escorted her off the premises. With the soft chuckle well known to her friends she thanked them for having taken such good care of her, and later she and Altrude were hilarious over the incident.

Remembering this experience, both took note when the movement, which had been germinating slowly in America since 1848, moved into high gear in 1913 with a great parade of women in Washington.

# The Wilsons and Suffrage

The excitement spread, and Altrude, staying with Mrs. Galt at the time, made a modest entry in her diary on February 28, 1913: "Mrs. Galt and I saw suffragette hikers arrived from New York, heard speeches." Altrude's interest was piqued; she loved excitement and novelty, but not the bizarre.

Mrs. Galt was unprepared for the explosive course the suffrage workers followed during her husband's administration. She had her first taste of it during his campaign for reelection when small groups interrupted meetings, paraded in the streets, beleaguered him at Atlantic City, and challenged him to back their cause. They waved banners with abusive messages and shouted and tangled with the police. Colonel Starling was always on guard to ward them off, and he commented, "Sometimes they were a joke; sometimes they were a nuisance; always they were determined and a little frightening to us men."

On inauguration day a small army of pickets circled the White House to band music, waving a gold banner at the head of the line with the message: MR. PRESIDENT, HOW LONG MUST WOMEN WAIT FOR LIBERTY? Later, "He Kept Us Out of Suffrage" matched the popular slogan, "He Kept Us Out of War."

Every move Woodrow Wilson made came under their scrutiny, and Mrs. Wilson watched to see how he was affected when a small group unfurled a banner over the gallery railing while he was delivering his State of the Union message in 1916. He continued without a pause, and with more composure than she felt as she watched them being quietly removed from the gallery. But she showed her displeasure when the Russian commissioners, paying their courtesy call at the White House after America entered the war, had to pass through a double line of suffrage pickets. The huge banner they waved accused the President of deceiving the people of Russia. How could he deny women the vote if he believed in democracy? they asked.

"I was indignant, but apparently no less so than a crowd of onlookers who tore the picketers' banner down," Mrs. Wilson commented. But there was worse to come, and she did not take it lightly when they burned her husband in effigy and sent one of his speeches up in flames.

When Alice Paul broke away from Mrs. Catt's organization, which functioned on an international scale, the new order began, and a tough drive got under way to push through the federal amendment. The suf-

313

fragettes in England who had been playing such a violent role when Mrs. Galt and Miss Gordon were in London in 1913 dropped all agitation for the time being when war was declared in 1914, putting country first and transferring their energies to war work. But when the United States declared war Mrs. Catt continued her efforts on a world scale, and Miss Paul intensified her campaign at the White House and Capitol.

On January 1, 1917, the National Woman's Party began picketing the Executive Mansion and the Capitol, and this continued for a year and a half, to the dismay of Mrs. Wilson. Hundreds of women took turns at this vigil, and when she looked from her windows, or came and went on her busy round of war duties, they were invariably there—always in motion, always making a noise. Some were raffish and bohemian; others were quiet scholarly types who had come to the conclusion that nothing in the world was going to work for them but clamor. A few noted beauties leavened the view for their scathing press critics in the Executive Wing, who deplored the pickets' lack of sex appeal.

President Wilson had moments when he felt sorry for them as they clung to the gates in bedraggled disarray. He was dining with Mrs. Wilson on a particularly icy day, with their banners being ripped by the wind, when Ike Hoover was told to go out and invite them in to warm up with tea or hot chocolate. Ike reported back that the proud ladies had indignantly refused the hospitality of the White House.

"Not they!" said John W. Davis, the Solicitor General. "The crown of martyrdom shall not be snatched from their brows." He added that frozen toes or pneumonia might do them good. Davis, who was close to the White House and aspired to the Presidency, found women with political inclinations nothing short of insufferable. "As long as I believe that suffrage will add nothing to the happiness of women, and contribute no resultant benefit to the state, I am and shall continue to be against it," he said.

Dudley Field Malone, a handsome and able lawyer whom the President had appointed collector of the Port of New York, was pressing hard for his support at this time. His wife, Doris Stevens, was one of the most beautiful and eloquent of the pack but he had already discovered from discussions at the White House dinner table that Mrs. Wilson was immune to persuasion by Doris; in fact, the more the subject was discussed, the more resistant she became. They had been the best of friends and now Malone seemed like a traitor to Mrs. Wilson as he pleaded the cause of "those detestable suffragettes."

On July 26, 1917, he called on the President and tried to force the issue. He told Wilson, with whom he had long been on friendly terms, that national woman suffrage could be put through almost immediately if he were to give it strong support. He pointed out how successful he had been with difficult and unpopular domestic measures. But the President told him flatly that the time was not right to fight this battle, because of the greater demands of the war.

But war or no war, the pickets could not be quelled. Alice Paul had a master touch for keeping things in motion. A day was set aside for the labor forces; another for office and factory workers. There were special days for individual states and she took a suffrage train across the country. Susan Anthony's birthday was celebrated in a downpour, and a pageant was staged on the Capitol steps. Her votaries were sometimes gorgeous in purple, gold, and white surplices; and sometimes grotesque when they tried to hide their banners under drab old skirts and shawls. It became a game to pull them out and flash them when the President and Mrs. Wilson came into view. The inscriptions grew rougher in tone, and were sometimes sacrilegious—a particular affront to Woodrow Wilson.

Although the pickets became increasingly difficult to handle, the White House guards had orders to let them alone. When annoyed passersby tried to haul down their banners or got into arguments with the women who brandished them, there were street fights and bedlam in the vicinity of the Executive Mansion. Finally Alice Paul and a few of the leaders were dragged off to the workhouse. They went on a hunger strike, in the Pankhurst manner, and had to be forcibly fed. This was too much for Alice, physically fragile, but with a spirit so strong that she was removed to the psychiatric division—in short, the madhouse, as things were then—and was treated as one of the insane.

The drawing rooms of Washington and New York buzzed with tales of the horrors that Alice Paul and her friends were enduring. She would never come out alive, the story ran, but she fooled them all by becoming a nonagenarian. A fiery letter of protest to the President about the treatment of the prisoners caused him to ask Tumulty, who was no friend of the pickets, to get a report on conditions at the workhouse. He wanted the officials in charge to know "how very important I deem it to be that there is certainly no sufficient foundation for such statements," he wrote.

Malone, doubly committed as a lawyer and also because of his wife's role in Alice Paul's party, defended them in court. "I was blazing with anger at Malone's conduct, and my husband was deeply hurt," Mrs. Wilson commented. But when the President thought it over his sensibilities were touched. Tumulty argued strongly against the pardon, but after a round of golf with Mrs. Wilson and Dr. Grayson, the President made up his own mind and signed the document giving the prisoners their freedom.

This did not stop them, but the war made a difference—to Woodrow Wilson, to the legislators, to women everywhere. A woman suffrage amendment to the Constitution had been presented to every Congress since 1878, but it was not until 1917 that its passage seemed even possible. Although Alice Paul's flamboyant tactics were an irritant to many, she had kept the subject before the public and vitalized the campaign. But Mrs. Catt, like the President, felt that as long as the National Woman's Party played its obstreperous games at the Capitol and White House, there would be little softening of Congressional opposition. She wrote sternly to Miss Paul on May 14, 1917, asking her to withdraw the pickets, making the point that the militant element was actually delaying the amendment and stirring up public antagonism.

The President and Mrs. Wilson preferred the more peaceful and orderly tactics of Mrs. Catt, who stood for peace as well as woman suffrage, but who also accepted the fact that the war had to be fought and won. She was a parliamentarian in action and above all she wanted President Wilson to get on the bandwagon and round up Congressional support. She wrote to him as well as to Alice Paul and he gave her the same answer that he had given to Malone: the time was not right with the "thought of the Congress" centered on the conduct of the war—an overwhelming task in itself, and becoming more demanding every day.

He admitted to Mrs. Catt that friends whose judgment he valued dissented from this conclusion, but his own contacts with members of Congress had convinced him that he was not misjudging their feeling. Meanwhile he spoke encouragingly to state delegates who came to

# The Wilsons and Suffrage

Washington to argue their case and were sometimes received by the President. Not the least of these were the women from New York State, a vital center of action.

Woman suffrage had become a fashionable cause. In the West Mrs. Leland Stanford and Mrs. William Randolph Hearst had given powerful financial support to the movement early in the century. Mrs. Potter Palmer had set the stage for them at the Columbian Exposition in Chicago, although not yet committed to their ways. The women's colleges had been rich recruiting grounds. The growing interest in sports, the drift to the arts, the suffrage agitation in England all had had their effect. Smart young matrons and aging dowagers with large fortunes at their command were now swinging into line.

Alice Paul was still on her hunger strike in jail when President Wilson received an imposing group representing New York State, where Mrs. J. Borden Harriman, Mrs. Henry Morgenthau, Miss Anne Morgan, Mrs. Frank A. Vanderlip, Mrs. James Lees Laidlaw, Mrs. Helen Rogers Reid, and many others worked effectively for emancipation. Mrs. Norman de R. Whitehouse headed the delegation that combined their call on the President with a picket parade around the White House. But patriotism and her devotion to Woodrow Wilson got the better of Mrs. Harriman when she saw one of the marchers holding aloft a banner inscribed KAISER WILSON. She wrenched it out of the woman's hands. Before she died in 1967 at the age of ninety-seven, Daisy Harriman said, "I am not a militant. I always regretted the picketing." But she had engaged in it with considerable verve at the time. She had supported Woodrow Wilson for the Presidency and he had named her the only woman member of the Federal Industrial Relations Commission. She and Mrs. Wilson remained friends after the President's death, and there was a good deal of visiting back and forth, although Edith was always a little wary of the powerful Mrs. Harriman.

As one by one the states fell into line, 1918 loomed as the crucial year and Tumulty urged President Wilson to send for certain Senators he felt might vote for woman suffrage if he were with them. A vote was about to be taken. The Chief Executive reminded Tumulty that he would weaken his influence in a score of directions were he to depart from the rule he had set himself against sending for Senators. But he proceeded to write persuasive letters to key figures. with little response. Senator Ollie James of Kentucky was his chief ally. On June 20, 1918, he addressed a strong appeal to Senator John E. Shields: "I feel that much of the morale of this country and of the world, and not a little of the faith which the rest of the world will repose in our sincere adherence to democratic principles, will depend upon the action which the Senate takes in this now critically important matter."

Were the times normal he would not feel that he could make a direct appeal of this sort, he wrote, but the fortunes of nations were now so linked together, the effect of American action on the "thought of the world" was so important, that he urged his aid in clearing away the "difficulties which will undoubtedly beset us if the amendment is not adopted." In his letters and conversation he now stressed the moral effect of the stand taken on suffrage, but he flatly refused Mrs. Catt's suggestion that he make an announcement calling the suffrage amendment a war measure. He did not believe that this would accomplish the object in view, and he felt sure that it would further antagonize the Senators. The other war measures were trouble enough at the moment. But he promised Mrs. Catt and her followers continued support and said, "I am, as I think you know, heartily in sympathy with you. I have endeavored to assist you in every way in my power, and I shall continue to do so. . . ."

His words on this occasion were burned later in the day by some of Alice Paul's recruits. They had been heard too many times and no longer had meaning for them. Mrs. Wilson listened attentively when McAdoo called at the White House on September 29 and urged his father-in-law to address the Senate the following day on woman suffrage. His visit was made on a Sunday, and the entire family knew that Woodrow Wilson preferred not to talk politics or business on the Sabbath. But he took in all that McAdoo had to say and then made the point that there was no precedent for such an action. He felt that the Senators would resent direct pressure from the Chief Executive. When McAdoo left he went to St. John's Church with Mrs. Wilson, and conviction must have settled on him there. Later that day she telephoned to McAdoo that Woodrow was working on his speech. He typed part of it on two pieces of paper which he pasted together.

His entire appeal lasted only fifteen minutes, and McAdoo thought it powerful, with a cutting edge. The President asked the Senators to support the suffrage amendment because women's help was vital to the postwar settlement: "We shall need them in our vision of affairs as we have never needed them before, the sympathy and insight and clear moral instinct of the women of the world."

His argument seemed unanswerable. It was a statement of fact that the services of women during the war had been of "the most signal usefulness and distinction." He pointed out that the war could not have been fought without them, or its sacrifices endured. "It is high time that some part of our debt of gratitude to them should be acknowledged and paid, and the only acknowledgment they ask is their admission to the suffrage," said the President.

"Can we justly refuse them?" he asked. But the Senate did. Although his plea, delivered on September 30, 1918, was considered courageous it was deeply resented by all the Senators opposed to the amendment and even by some of those he had persuaded to vote in favor of it. Senatorial tradition did not allow the Chief Executive to plead for any measure under consideration for action. Although the Senators remained obdurate, the Congressmen were more responsive. Many of their wives were personally involved in the movement or sympathized with it. The tea tables and cocktail parties were enlivened by suffrage talk as women stood firm on one side or the other, and the lines were already sharply drawn when the President went before the Senate in person to speak forth boldly for woman suffrage. In spite of his appeal the amendment was defeated 53 to 31.

When Mrs. Catt and a committee of suffrage leaders called on him four days after the defeat to thank him for what he had done, he told them that he did not deserve their gratitude, and added quite revealingly, "When my conversion to this idea came, it came with an overwhelming command that made it necessary that I should omit nothing and use the position I occupied to enforce it. . . . History will deal very candidly with the circumstances in which the head of a Government asked the kind of support that I asked the other day, and did not get it. . . ."

He studied the women before him and remarked in a half-humorous tone but with underlying bitterness, "I have to restrain myself sometimes from intellectual contempt. That is a sin, I am afraid, and being a good Presbyterian, I am trying to refrain from it."

The struggle continued in 1919 and again the militants closed in on Woodrow Wilson. They now had a perpetual delegation of twelve women posted around the White House. When he returned from the Peace Conference they staged a demonstration in Boston, and when he spoke at the Metropolitan Opera House in New York Alice Paul was again in action. In this instance the pickets were clubbed by the police and she and Doris Stevens were jailed for disorderly conduct. But it was not unfashionable to be in this sort of trouble, for the rich and the worldly were now in the ranks of the suffrage advocates.

The war had made all the difference. On both sides of the Atlantic women had found their own liberation in the work they did, the old taboos they defied, the precedents they shattered. Mrs. Wilson had seen its workings in Europe and now she studied the American scene with fresh understanding. It was an unhappy summer for Woodrow as the Senate debated the Peace Treaty and he came steadily under fire. The House passed the Volstead Act, but more significantly, the Suffrage amendment finally passed Congress and went to the states for ratification. It was only a matter of time after that.

On June 11, 1919, Mrs. Catt, Dr. Anna Howard Shaw, and Miss Helen H. Gardener, all of the National American Woman Suffrage Association, wrote to Woodrow Wilson that they hoped the time would never come when the women of America would fail "to hold in grateful memory your splendid efforts in our behalf."

He was winning the fight at Versailles at this time and they congratulated him that his struggle for the self-determination of groups of men had not blinded him to the fact that the time had come in world development when such struggles were in vain if they did not include the mothers of men—"America half-democratic would not mean America the beacon light of liberty, justice, and equality."

On the cross-country tour that ended her husband's political career Mrs. Wilson was conscious at many points of the groups of women still moving into view with the old insignia, but no longer as angry militants. With the states lining up one by one for ratification, the fight was practically won, although the measure did not become law until August 26, 1920.

On April 6, 1920, five months after the President's return to the White House, a broken man, Mrs. Catt's committee sent him a compilation of letters in book form from the presidents of suffrage organizations in the various states, expressing their appreciation of the courageous way in which he had gone before the Senate on their behalf.

An enveloping curtain of silence by this time sealed off the normal flow of life at the White House, and the echoes of suffrage came through only dimly. It had never been Mrs. Wilson's favorite cause, yet now she herself had involuntarily assumed a role that summed it all up, and was without precedent in the history of American Presidents.

On March 8, 1920, after the President's breakdown, Robert J. Bender, a well-known journalist, raised the question in *Collier's* magazine that was being discussed all over the country: Who was the real President of the United States at this time? He listed four names currently mentioned—Tumulty, Grayson, Bernard Baruch and A. Mitchell Palmer. Then he wrote, "The truth seems to be that Woodrow Wilson remained very much President; but if anyone had even a remote right to claim his title temporarily, it was not one of the four names but Edith Bolling Wilson, First Lady of the Land, who has time and again come close to carrying the burden of the First Man."

Linking her directly with the newly achieved emancipation of the American woman, Bender added, "Never an ardent suffragist herself, Mrs. Wilson is likely when the full story of the first months is known to have proved herself the finest argument for suffrage that any woman by her work has yet offered to the cause."

Mrs. Wilson was not impressed. She did not like being called First Lady of the Land. "I am not political," she would insist to the end of her days, and her family zealously backed her in this assessment of herself. But while her husband was alive she would go to the Senate at any time with Mrs. Brandeis or Mrs. Borah to follow a debate that had any bearing on his interests. And after his death she continued this custom for major debates, particularly in the days of World War II. She disliked politicians but she was never indifferent to the march of events, and was always up to the minute on current affairs.

Some of her bridge-playing friends regarded her attitude on suffrage with some dismay, for there were activists among them, and their daughters were branching out into the world of achievement. Many of the women she met in her long and widely traveled life failed to understand why she held herself aloof on this question. She had achieved so much herself and had functioned so responsibly in human relations that women like Mrs. Harriman found it hard to understand her. But she did not forget easily, and much of her feeling went back to the trouble the picketers had given her husband.

In the end Mrs. Wilson was ready to applaud the good work she saw being done. Whatever her early outlook on votes for women, she had a clearheaded appreciation of women who did useful work and who helped themselves. She had done it herself in her early years and she was always sympathetic to Margaret Wilson in her ambition for a career in music, and in her many efforts to find a place for herself in the business world.

The family flair for the academic life continued and it pleased her to see young relatives rolling up degrees and landing posts in the professional and business world—the girls as well as the boys. But above all else she liked to hear of happy marriages, and when the daughter of Mrs. John Moeling, the niece who had always seemed like her own child, combined marriage and motherhood with a successful career, she could not do other than applaud. Young Lucy Moeling had joined the growing ranks of those who did it all. She had always been a brilliant student and Mrs. Wilson had followed her scholastic triumphs with pride, as well as watching her take the jumps at the Horse Show in Madison Square Garden. While attending law school she had fallen in love with a fellow student, Leslie Ralph Bishop. They were married at once and together they practiced law successfully in Chicago, in addition to bringing up a family.

All the younger generation were aware that Aunt Edith had done great things, but to her it had always seemed that she had merely been fulfilling the natural function of a wife. She was touched when Josephus Daniels, who had been so close to her husband over the years, wrote to her from Raleigh, North Carolina, on February 3, 1946, about his memorial to his wife. The form of the inscription was unique: ADDIE WORTH BAGLEY    INTERMARRIED WITH JOSEPHUS DANIELS. He explained that "most men place on the monument in the cemetery 'wife of' and then his own name as if the wife had no identity of her own and is to be remembered only because she married him."

Mrs. Daniels, a clever and independent woman of great experience, had been an advocate of woman suffrage and had talked on the subject

322

at Geneva. Daniels' jesting remark that Mrs. Wilson qualified for the post of Secretary of the Navy seemed to have some point, for she lived to see two women hold Cabinet office—Frances Perkins, Secretary of Labor in the Roosevelt administration, and Mrs. Oveta Culp Hobby, who ran the newly created department of Health, Education, and Welfare for President Eisenhower.

Mrs. Wilson's own role would always remain something of a mystery, for it had no parallel in American history. Her devotion to Woodrow Wilson's interests, both before and after his death, was classic in its intensity. She met emergencies with an unfaltering spirit and played a bold hand in the eyes of the world.

# *30.* *Presidents' Wives Together*

EDITH WILSON'S own highly developed social sense played a part in her relations with the seven Presidents' wives who followed her in the White House. The partisan element did not enter strongly into her relations with her successors, if she happened to like them. She was on good terms with Mrs. Coolidge, Mrs. Hoover, Mrs. Eisenhower and Mrs. Truman. She was cool to Mrs. Harding. She loved Mrs. Kennedy, and she admired but did not always understand Eleanor Roosevelt.

In the 1920's and again in the 1950's she was not at the inner core of events—nor did she wish to be, but her age and her history gave her a bipartisan status. The Presidents and their wives all treated her with special deference as a White House widow still active socially, the survivor of great events, and a personality in her own right. She was a star guest at all events involving international affairs. Clever men liked to be paired with her, for she was a good storyteller who could still spark a White House evening.

She was often in view during the Roosevelt administration, but she had reservations about many aspects of the New Deal. Although her husband had been regarded as a liberal, she thought that the spreading social changes of this era were getting out of hand. But it all brought back to her the excitement of the busy days of World War I, and some of the most noted visitors to America during the Roosevelt period remembered her as their White House hostess in the days of World War I.

When Herbert Hoover became President, Edith was again in touch with an old wartime friend. He had figured powerfully in world affairs during her husband's administration, and he and his wife were well known to her. Later the Hoovers lived next door to her on S Street. She and Mrs. Hoover did not have a close friendship, but they understood each other well, since both were widely traveled and shared a common experience in World War I. The blasts of hate that enveloped Herbert Hoover when things went wrong were all too reminiscent to Edith of her husband's experience.

She had many friendly exchanges with Mrs. Coolidge, who remembered Wilson's much publicized comments on her silent husband. Edith was touched by the concern that both showed over Woodrow's illness, and when he died Mrs. Coolidge wrote on February 3, 1924, "Dear, dear Mrs. Wilson. I cannot refrain from sending you this personal word of sympathy for I want you to know that I am thinking of you in your great sorrow. May God bless you and in His great mercy give you the comfort which He alone can give. Very sincerely your friend, Grace Coolidge."

And when President Coolidge died suddenly of a heart attack Edith wrote to Mrs. Coolidge on January 3, 1933, "My dear Mrs. Coolidge: My heart goes out in deep and understanding sympathy to you and your son in this great sorrow, and I wish I could really be of service. Faithfully yours, Edith Bolling Wilson."

All through the Roosevelt administrations Mrs. Roosevelt made a point of honoring Edith in every possible way, although their views differed on many questions. She had her at concerts, musicales, and all special events as well as at state functions.

Although Franklin D. Roosevelt was hated by some of Edith's rich banker friends, she got on well with him. She took him much less seriously than many of her friends did, and his worship of her husband was a strong point in his favor. He stood for many of the same things and quoted Wilson repeatedly in his addresses.

When Woodrow Wilson's birthplace at Staunton was dedicated in May, 1941, his widow sat thoughtfully by Roosevelt's side and heard him say that her husband had beheld the "vision splendid." To her disappointment he did not mention the League of Nations, but he said that Woodrow Wilson "had taught that democracy could not survive in isolation."

A large crowd, including many who had come in from the Virginia hills, surrounded the old manse where Wilson was born. There were flags, bands, and young cadets in bright uniforms, as well as ancients with tales of the Reverend Joseph Ruggles Wilson, the President's father.

By the time of the dedication the public had a new view of Edith Bolling Wilson, for *My Memoir* had been serialized and published in 1939. Its revelations and recriminations were still being discussed by men in public office, aware that deeply embedded behind her calm and smiling face lay the hurts her husband had suffered. She had not spared the men she considered his enemies.

Mrs. Roosevelt followed the serialization closely and on Janaury 25, 1939, told of going to bed early the night before to read the last installment. The ellipsis of the serialization seemed to bother Mrs. Roosevelt, and in March, 1939, Edith sent her a copy of the book, so that she would have the picture in full. There was silence after that. No sooner had it come out than letters of praise and condemnation poured in to the editors of papers across the country. Comparisons drawn between Mrs. Roosevelt and Mrs. Wilson were embarrassing to both, as their influence over their husbands was weighed.

Edith was troubled by some of the criticism but at the same time she was deluged with praise as letters came in from all parts of the world. It might not have gone down well with the critics but it had touched a great many hearts. She was used to brickbats and the book brought so much pleasure and enlightenment to people in distant places that she decided to laugh instead of worrying about the repercussions. Mrs. Roosevelt, too, was constantly under fire, and they had some fellow feeling in all such matters.

They continued their friendly communication and Edith was in a relaxed mood on Easter morning, 1945, when she wrote to Lucy Moeling, "I got a beautiful Easter lily from the President and Mrs. Roosevelt." Her lilies of the valley bloomed in abundance. A few days later she was sitting beside Mrs. Roosevelt at a charity entertainment when a sudden call came from the White House and the President's wife left hurriedly.

Within an hour everyone knew what had happened. The President had suffered a massive cerebral hemorrhage at Warm Springs. Mrs. Wilson relived the anxious hours. After attending the funeral she wrote again to Lucy on April 17: "Of course everyone here is so shocked by the death of the President that nothing else is talked of." She gave her own view of the ceremonies in the East Room, and drew a little cluster of dots to indicate the seating arrangements. Mrs. Hull and she, who were together, found it all "very impressive."

Mrs. Wilson studied Mrs. Truman and Margaret with sympathy. "Poor things," she wrote. "I feel sorry for them."

From the beginning of the new administration the Trumans went out of their way to honor Mrs. Wilson. She and Mrs. Truman already had an excellent understanding of each other. They were practical women with strong Southern feeling about the way homes should be run and the privacy of family life. Whatever Edith thought about the atomic bomb (her face usually went blank when she was asked about that), she and Mrs. Truman enjoyed each other's company. Edith was conscious of Margaret Truman's deep devotion to her father and she admired her determination to have a career as a singer. Music had always been one of Edith's own special interests, and she had done what she could for Margaret Wilson in this respect.

As time passed her feelings about President Truman veered from esteem to growing disenchantment. She did not think that he carried on the Wilson tradition as Roosevelt had done, and on January 9, 1953, she wrote to Lucy Moeling that she was going to the White House to bid Mrs. Truman farewell. "I do think *she* has been wonderful," she wrote, a phrase that spoke for itself.

The shift from the long era of Democratic rule to the placid days of President Eisenhower meant a total change in the social picture. But Edith and Mrs. Eisenhower exchanged friendly notes and great bunches of flowers from the White House gardens were delivered regularly at S Street. Edith in turn remembered the anniversaries and special occasions in the Eisenhower family, and sent bouquets to Mamie.

On her many visits to the White House after she left it, Edith Wilson was always observant of the changes her successors had made. She knew every nook and cranny, and nostalgia sometimes overtook her. It delighted her to take young nieces and cousins to see the Executive Mansion. One shy young niece incurred her Aunt Edith's wrath when Mrs. Eisenhower invited them upstairs to see the family quarters. They all crowded into the elevator, and she was so tightly squeezed in front that she had to step out ahead of the First Lady.

When they got back to S Street Mrs. Wilson impressed on her that one *never* walked in front of the President's wife. But no one had noticed because she had shown them the exact spot outside the elevator where she first met Woodrow Wilson, in her muddy boots and Worth costume.

On January 28, 1954, she wrote to Lucy that she had attended a dinner given at the White House for Vice President Richard Nixon. "I sat next to him—poor thing, he dropped the Chili sauce all down his shirt front & on his white waistcoat. Mrs. Eisenhower and I took a napkin and ice water and got it nearly off."

All of America was discussing Communism and Joseph McCarthy that spring and she wrote to Lucy on May 2, 1954: "Don't you think that McCarthy investigation is awful?" She had vivid memories of the A. Mitchell Palmer roundup of radicals during her husband's administration, of bomb scares, deportation proceedings, and strong anti-Bolshevik propaganda.

Edith sat up all night to catch the election returns of 1960 and felt jubilant when John F. Kennedy was elected. She wrote at once, "I think Mrs. Kennedy will be a great asset to her husband—as she is cultivated and charming." She was glad to have the Democrats back in power and she already knew the Kennedys. She was well aware of John Kennedy's war history and she could never forget that he had chosen Woodrow Wilson for one of his subjects in *Profiles in Courage*. They had a brief but star-dusted friendship. Edith was soon to die but he gave her pleasure in her last months. Always conscious of style, good looks, and manners, she took an interest in this bright young couple and felt motherly toward Jack.

He in turn made special arrangements for her role in the inaugural ceremonies. Not that she needed much help, for she tackled the unforgettable blizzard that preceded the event with her own brand of independence. A special escort arranged for her by President Kennedy took her to the Capitol on inauguration day, and she was seated almost directly behind him during the swearing-in. Because of her deafness she heard little or nothing of his speech, but her keen gray eyes were alert to every move, so she saw poet Robert Frost helpless at the podium and a cheering crowd welcoming the return of the Democratic party. Truman kissed her at the ceremonies and she was pleased.

Her car was close to the head of the inaugural parade and she insisted on having the top down. Expert at bundling up and staying warm, from her years of parade experience with Woodrow, she turned a smiling face to a young generation that scarcely knew who Mrs. Woodrow Wilson was.

Soon after this eventful day she fell and injured her shoulder, but when she had recovered sufficiently she arranged a luncheon party at her home for Mrs. Kennedy. Ever since inauguration day, she wrote, she had wanted to thank her and President Kennedy for their "charming attentions" to her that day. She enclosed a list of the guests she intended to ask, if Mrs. Kennedy approved. "All Democrats and three of them my nieces," she wrote. "Please tell your indefatigable husband how proud of him we are."

Mrs. Kennedy was late in arriving but she made up for this by lingering on far into the afternoon. The sea crab soup and asparagus on the thoughtfully chosen menu seemed to appeal to her. The young nieces—Jane Bolling, Barbara Fuller, and Mrs. Harry Fowler—gave sparkle to the occasion and later liked to recall that glamorous meal on S Street with two First Ladies—one young, the other now growing old but still bright-witted and active.

If there was a chill anywhere in Edith's relations with her successors it was with Mrs. Harding, although she mellowed a little toward her after Harding's sudden death, when misfortune, ill-health, and some knowledge of what she had weathered touched Edith's sympathies. The letter Mrs. Harding sent her after Woodrow's death made an impression, too.

When they first met, Mrs. Wilson was suffering acutely from the depressing finish to their White House days, and the events at the Capitol on the day of inauguration which had left her in an angry mood.

There was no real rapport from the start between these two dissimilar women. Mrs. Wilson disliked Mrs. Harding's assertive manner and her insistent way of talking as if she were afraid of not being heard. She did not admire her sense of style or her vivid makeup, and she seemed shrill and affected to soft-voiced Mrs. Wilson. But this was Mrs. Harding's habitual manner and when she arrived in Washington she was still unsure of herself and a little staggered by the precipitate way in which her husband had reached the Presidency.

When Mrs. Wilson invited her to tea in December, so that she could tour the White House and discuss the household arrangements with Mrs. Jaffray, there was trouble at once. Mrs. Harding was the guest of Mrs. Evalyn Walsh McLean and wrote to ask if she might bring her hostess. Mrs. Wilson had no wish to have the owner of the Hope diamond in her house. The McLeans had long been enemies of the Wilsons, and the Washington *Post,* which McLean owned, had opposed Woodrow Wilson consistently. It was an old story, with many bitter memories for Mrs. Wilson. She sent Mrs. Harding a second note, saying plainly that she would prefer her to come alone, since she would be busy with Mrs. Jaffray on housekeeping details.

This rankled and Mrs. Harding was on edge when Mrs. Jaffray was called in to be introduced. The White House had twenty-seven servants at the time, and Mrs. Harding was not at all sure that she wanted to keep the omnipotent Elizabeth Jaffray. She ordered the twin beds used by the Tafts and the first Mrs. Wilson brought back to the master bedroom in place of the legendary Lincoln bed.

Mrs. Wilson studied her successor as she laid down the law to the housekeeper, a mesh veil drawn tightly over her sharp features and her glasses worn over the veil while she studied lists. Saying that she had to keep an engagement downtown and would leave them to tour the White House and talk things over, Mrs. Wilson warned them specifically not to go near her husband's quarters or disturb him in any way. It was seven in the evening when she returned, and she was surprised to hear Mrs. Harding's voice coming from the kitchen. When Mrs. Coolidge later heard of the criticism of Mrs. Wilson for not having stayed with Mrs. Harding she came to Edith's defense and said that she had handled things in a particularly courteous manner by letting Mrs. Harding have the run of the house without interference.

Their next meeting was on March 3, the day before inauguration,

329

when the President-elect and Mrs. Harding came to call. Wilson waited downstairs to receive them when they arrived and then accompanied them to the Red Room. "We tried to make things go, but they both seemed ill at ease and did not stay long," Mrs. Wilson reported. She was disapproving of Harding's casual manner when he threw one leg over the arm of his chair as he talked to her husband.

That night she gave thought to what lay ahead of Mrs. Harding. She had already heard that this clever businesswoman from Ohio "had made Warren Harding." She also knew what a factor Mrs. Taft had been in her husband's rise to the Presidency, although her voice was silenced soon after he took office and she had a crippling stroke. In a quiet way Theodore Roosevelt, too, had listened to his wife's clear voice and had been quelled at times by her commanding glance. Mrs. Wilson alone knew what her own influence had been, as she prepared to leave the White House forever.

For the most part Edith enjoyed the association with her successors, and was both awed and annoyed by Eleanor Roosevelt's omnipotence. Edith saved all her physical links with the White House—the invitations, announcements, place cards, menus, programs of historical events, Christmas cards, pressed flowers, ribbon bindings, small flags, and favors until she had a stunning collection. Old clippings showed her with other Presidents and their wives—such as the dedicatory exercises at the Folger Shakespeare Library with President Hoover and Mrs. Hoover, and the Princeton commencement of 1947 with Mrs. Truman and Mrs. Thomas J. Preston, Jr., widow of President Cleveland.

A major event in which Mrs. Wilson figured was the dedication of the League of Nations building in 1939 at New York's World Fair, with Henry A. Wallace making the address. Boy Scouts and the Red Cross, war bond drives and garden clubs, ship launchings and war memorials—she was always being caught by the camera. Mrs. Wilson at a political convention, Mrs. Wilson with the Franklin D. Roosevelts, Mrs. Wilson with the DAR—the story went on and on, although she continued to dislike her pictures, as she did the press. Mrs. Wilson was particularly honored at the official functions for King George VI and Queen Elizabeth when they visited America in 1939, and for Queen Elizabeth II and Prince Philip in 1957. And only once in forty years did she miss the White House garden party for war veterans that she had initiated.

Although she did not live to see Lyndon Johnson take office after the assassination of President Kennedy, she knew him well and recognized his power as a politician. Her husband's links with Texas had been strong. It was the native state of Colonel House and also of Jesse Jones. It pleased her to receive a letter from him in 1955 saying that few Congressional acts had given him more personal satisfaction than the passage of the bill assuring her a pension. It had been fixed at $5,000 a year, the amount that Mrs. Theodore Roosevelt was getting. This had been a long time coming, but Edith had decided not to ask for a pension after her husband's death, and she was now comfortably off.

Senator Johnson said in this letter that Woodrow Wilson had been one of his boyhood heroes and the passage of the years had left him with a memory "untarnished and undimmed." He predicted that the place he already held in history would become even more secure as "time gives us greater perspective."

# 31. *An Indulgent Matriarch*

EDITH WILSON'S zest for life diminished only slightly with the years. The constant flow of relatives from far and near kept her young at heart. Whether it was a Kentucky Derby, a flower mart at the cathedral, a good play, an embassy party, or a game of cards, she would show up as a striking figure, not to be ignored. The all-time champion bridge player among Presidents' wives was unquestionably Edith Bolling Wilson. In her ruby-red drawing room she challenged some of the world's most famous men, for none could escape her. In spite of all the work she did on her Woodrow Wilson projects her passion for bridge and other card games became almost obsessive as she aged.

She played with intensity and she played to win. She could not bear the dilettantish spirit or interruptions, and her regulars remembered this as they met for tea, luncheon, or dinner at one another's houses. Sometimes they played far into the night with everyone ready for sleep but Edith. When they broke up for refreshments she was keen for fun and laughter. Their bets were infinitesimal and winnings were immediately applied to charity.

If anything came up even remotely related to the old Wilson policies, Edith would dash away from the bridge table, the only exception she ever made in her well-established routine. Aside from the steady round of official engagements, Edith liked to give small dinners for ten or twelve. With the end of World War II life grew more abundant again in official circles and she reverted to the rich Southern cuisine that delighted many of her guests, particularly the great-nephews attending prep school and college. Her trunk room was constantly jammed with suitcases and bundles, skis, tennis rackets, and camping outfits.

But her interests were legion. On an April day in 1949 she detailed two days of her activities. She had the Visiting Sisters for lunch at S Street, then went to the British Embassy to serve as hostess for a tour to benefit the Home for Incurables, which she visited regularly. At night she attended a Washington and Lee Centennial celebration. The following day she worked on a peach taffeta dress and nearly finished it. Then she took her niece Barbara Fuller to the Thrift Shop where there was always useful work to be done. That night she dined at the home of Jesse Jones. Next day she had Mrs. Eleanor Tydings in for lunch, and visited Dr. Ruffin at the hospital.

Like Woodrow Wilson she greatly enjoyed her cars and the country drives. They came in a swift succession of new models as fashions in cars changed. In the late 1940's she was shepherding her friends around in a sleek black Buick lined with gray upholstery. In 1949 an RCA Victor television set was installed in Woodrow Wilson's old bedroom. Wilmer enjoyed it, but it took her some time to get used to it. Even while she watched it she knitted or sewed. She did not believe in idle hands, and it took her no time at all to knit an afghan 50 by 45 inches for the veterans at Walter Reed Hospital.

Edith changed her way of living after her first heart attack. She had always risen early when her husband was alive, but she now took the rest the doctors ordered by spending her mornings in bed. She worked constantly while resting. In pastel-tinted negligees, with her hair becomingly done up in lace, she welcomed relatives in her bedroom, surrounded by papers, documents, and letters, her breakfast tray by her side, flowers scenting the room, and her canaries singing on the porch. When she felt extra lazy she would get up after twenty birds flashed by the window. Cardinals and humming birds were her special delight.

Because of her heart condition Edith needed a paid companion, and the perfect choice was made in Mrs. Margaret Cherricks Brown, a lively, well-informed, and amusing woman of the world who became as close to her as a member of her own family. Known to everyone as Cherie, Mrs. Brown understood the social game and knew how to get things done. She seemed to sense intuitively what Edith wanted, and she helped to keep the wheels running smoothly at S Street.

Cherie was small, bright-eyed, and quick-witted. She took care not to ruffle Mrs. Wilson, and her clear handwriting was useful for social notes and for copying letters that were sometimes almost illegible. Up to the time of her death Edith maintained a steady flow of correspondence, from thank-you notes to long, chatty family letters almost invariably in her own handwriting, even when she was in a cast.

She gave and received gifts on a generous scale, and she took infinite care with the wrappings, from the little bags of candies for the children hung on the Christmas tree to a priceless piece of Chinese porcelain. She liked to give a rare vase with camellias or a single spicy red rose in a choice glass holder. She would find an old print or something rare in china or glass. Her own jellies and jams were enjoyed by many of her friends and she was expert at rounding up delicacies of all kinds.

She continued to make the most of her trips to New York. They were usually timed for meetings of the Woodrow Wilson Foundation, but she enjoyed her own worldly pleasures at the same time—window-shopping, attending the theater and opera, stopping in at art galleries, and dining with friends. She liked the life and excitement, the bright lights, the stir of an opening night on Broadway, just as she had in Woodrow's time. She attended the Horse Show with Lucy and Red Moeling to watch their daughter Lucy show her fine horsemanship in competition. If Altrude was not away on one of her trips, they would meet and discuss the new world in which they lived. The old strings were quickly pulled together again, for Edith was always intensely interested in her friends and liked to talk about them and their families rather than about herself.

As of old she sought to escape observation in New York. She did not want attention and it did not worry her when salesgirls gave no response to the name Mrs. Woodrow Wilson. But her presence was usually noticed in the hotels and theaters, for she was a striking figure in any gathering and when she and Fannie Hurst got together at a luncheon in the Plaza they made a distinctive pair. She had chance encounters with many writers of both sexes. From her earliest years it had been her custom to read the books of the day. The President had steered her into deeper channels in the historical field, but during his illness she had read so many mystery stories to him that she shied away from them in her later years. The novels, memoirs, and biographies that were being discussed were usually on her library table.

Friends remembered her constantly with the books of current interest, from *The Son of Talleyrand* to J. P. Marquand's novels. Like most young girls of her day in the South she had been well indoctrinated in the classics and knew the poets. Her literary interests grew strong in her years with Woodrow Wilson and she read omnivorously in the expansive years that followed. She never failed to read or have read to her the books that concerned her husband in any way. In general she favored biography, reminiscences, witty books, and social satire. She was a critical reader and liked a book to have wit or substance, but she followed the popular trend.

In November, 1961, shortly before her death, she was being brought up to date by Barbara Fuller's young son Richard, then at Rollins College, who wrote to her to be sure to read Harper Lee's *To Kill a Mockingbird.*

She was treated with great respect by all ages and even with a touch of awe by the younger generation. The teen-agers thought her a good sport and the little ones were easily beguiled by her entertaining stories, affectionate ways, and the sweets and toys she gave them. Sterling Bolling was a favorite from his earliest years. When she gave him a bath as a little boy he eluded the towel she held and went dashing through the house stark naked, an astonishing event in Edith's Wilson's dignified house.

She was proud when Sterling "got his wings" in the Air Force in the summer of 1943. After the war he and his wife were regular visitors at

S Street, and when little Sterling was born he was placed on Woodrow Wilson's historic bed and admired. Young Sterling grew up with much devotion for his Great-Aunt Edith, writing to her from his home in Bronxville that "from my earliest memory of you . . . you have always been associated with all that is gracious, sweet and entirely charming."

The boys all sat up straight and kept their hair neatly brushed on their visits to S Street. "Aunt Edith" demanded certain standards. She wanted to know what they were doing at school, what marks they were getting, and who their friends were.

There were Republicans among her relatives as well as among her friends, and in the heat of the 1960 campaign young Cary Fuller drove his mother to S Street for a visit. He was eighteen at the time and had a bright red car known as his Red Fury, which bore a "Nixon for President" sticker. He parked the car boldly across from Aunt Edith's. Cherie was amused and felt sure there would be a storm. There was. When the former First Lady looked out the window she was shocked and furious. "Cary, either move that car or go home," she told him severely. The car quickly disappeared from view.

All holidays and anniversaries were celebrated in the grand style until Mrs. Wilson's last days. Her Thanksgiving and Christmas parties were famous. The warm family spirit of hospitality continued as in the time of Woodrow Wilson, but death thinned the ranks in the 1950's. The younger members of the family were settled in homes of their own, but any within reach never failed to call on Aunt Edith on Christmas Day. She was still the family matriarch.

# *32.*    *Valiant to the End*

MRS. WILSON entered the 1950's with her usual optimism and gay spirits, but it was to be a decade of illness and family deaths as well as of impressive events. With the Wilson Centennial coming up in 1956 she was ready for anything that would enhance the memory of her husband.

But on March 4, 1951, she took the sort of backward look in which she did not often indulge, and wrote to Lucy Moeling, "It is 30 years today since we left the White House—and how many changes these years have brought." She was sitting up in bed, trying to write as she recovered from a severe bout of influenza. One of her doctors was intent on keeping her from attending a dinner at the Brazilian Embassy, and she hated to miss a party.

Without Dr. Grayson, she was facing a difficult period in her life, for her health was poor, she had a number of small accidents, and there were family deaths of shattering impact.

"Wilmer's death has left me numb," she wrote in November, 1951. Wilmer had been a strong and companionable brother who possessed both her sense of humor and her efficiency. They had traveled together and it had been his custom to spend Saturdays and Sundays at S Street and to be on hand for all the holiday gatherings. His card club had met regularly at her house.

Randolph's death in the summer of 1952, coming right after Wilmer's, was a severe blow. She had given him the most understanding care for the better part of a lifetime, encouraging him, helping him with his music, and responding to the constant demands of his precarious health. He had been a vital part of her household, too, acting as amanuensis, a buffer on business matters, and a spirited companion at cards, games, or magic. Everyone who knew Edith Wilson knew Randolph and how much he meant to her. His scrapbooks in the Library of Congress testify to the zeal with which he collected clippings and memorabilia of all kinds on the life of his sister Edith.

Gertrude was so stricken by the loss of her brothers that Edith closed up the apartment in which her sister had lived for nearly forty years and moved her to S Street. Gertrude had become an invalid and Edith found it necessary to have a nurse in the house again to care for her. For a time she was in a hospital, but in the end a hospital bed was installed and Edith gave her the most zealous care. Her mother had died in 1925, soon after Woodrow Wilson, and Bertha had died in 1935. She had survived them all, and now her brothers, too.

# Valiant to the End

Edith's life was full of so many things and her days were so busy that she gave no outward sign of her sorrows. She was a conspicuous figure at the dedication of the Woodrow Wilson Hall at Princeton in June, 1952. She had laid the cornerstone which was later displayed in the hall as a historic memento. President Harold W. Dodds paid her every honor, as he always did when she visited Princeton, and she was entertained at Prospect House, which had once been her husband's home.

All his troubles at Princeton had come before her time, but she was familiar with the story of his attempts to abolish the undergraduate eating clubs and to house the students in quadrangles, where they would live and eat together, with faculty advisers. As he worked out a plan for the reorganization of the campus social life he headed into trouble with a divided faculty and some of the alumni, who accused him of threatening to destroy the class and club spirit that engendered loyalty. The subsequent battling cost him the friendship of John Grier Hibben, who had succeeded him as President, and to some extent of Grover Cleveland. But when he became Governor of New Jersey and then President much of this was forgotten, and his image there grew stronger with the years. Edith nourished Woodrow's class spirit and encouraged his ties with the university. She welcomed all gatherings of Princetonians at the White House or S Street, and the university events were scrupulously observed.

Following the family deaths and illnesses in the early 1950's, she began to circulate freely again and when Claude Bowers met her at a luncheon of the Women's National Democratic Club in April, 1954, he noted in his diary, "Mrs. Woodrow Wilson, who very seldom goes out now, appeared today. I had not seen her since 1915, when we were luncheon guests at her house." He had a long talk with her after meeting her at the club and they discussed the Joseph McCarthy controversy raging at the time. Edith deplored McCarthyism. Bowers had been a favorite of her husband's, and he admired her for the role she had played in his life, and also for her charm as a woman. He had served as ambassador in Spain, and the embassies always took pride in Mrs. Wilson.

The year 1954 brought her special satisfaction when her house was taken over by the National Trust for Historical Preservation. It was agreed that she would continue to live in it, but that it would not be

337

open to the public. The plan had been considered for some time but the question of endowment held things up.

Signing the deed, she remarked on the coincidence that the thirteenth had always been Woodrow's lucky number. In October she was unanimously elected a member of the National Trust for Historical Preservation, and this became one of her keen interests.

She transferred to the trust some possessions not previously assigned, including the leather chair the President had used in presiding at Cabinet meetings. It had two plaques and two inscriptions—the first from the Cabinet members who had given him the chair, and the second, signed by himself: "Presented to my dear wife, whose inspiration meant so much while I occupied this chair."

The house was painted when the trust took it over, and Edith gave a party to show it off proudly in the spring of 1955. She thought that her garden was looking its best that May, with her white peonies and roses in full bloom. She made good use of the Cape jasmine that a friend had been sending her for twenty years, and she arranged on the terrace sixteen red geraniums that she had found at the Cathedral Flower Mart. She felt more responsible than ever for the house now that it was a landmark, but she and Cherie had a severe scare late that year over a boiler explosion. Edith smelled smoke one night and hurried downstairs to find the first floor filled with dense fumes. She called to Cherie and groped her way to the basement, unable to see her hands when she stretched them in front of her. She tried to reach the office to telephone for help but was stopped in her tracks when she heard one explosion, followed by a second one.

Cherie was already in the office telephoning for help. She thought after hearing the explosion that Mrs. Wilson must have been killed or injured downstairs. The firemen came quickly. The firebox of the furnace had blown out, bringing bricks and soot with it. The trunkroom and coat closet had been blown open by the blast, and things were scattered about. The firemen reassured Edith and Cherie, both blackened with smoke beyond recognition. They had not had time to wash up when their near neighbors came in to offer help. Viscountess Harcourt, wife of the British ambassador who lived nearby, brought her maid with her to help clean things up, and a bottle of brandy with glasses to revive the intrepid survivors of the blast.

The friendship continued. The viscountess invited them over for

## Valiant to the End

Christmas carols that year. There were sixty English guests who celebrated in the traditional way, with mulled claret and Dickensian echoes. Edith was preparing for a year of great occasions—the Woodrow Wilson Centennial of 1956. The campaign opened at Staunton in January with the sale of a new stamp struck in his memory. A luncheon was held, and the *Town Meeting of the Air* carried the message far afield. Old friends and government officials sang praises of Woodrow Wilson.

Edith Wilson was expected in Staunton the day before the ceremonies began, but no one dreamed that she could make it because of the sleet and glazed streets in Washington. She was warned not to go. Edwards, her chauffeur, had tonsilitis but she had his throat sprayed before he left. He was never at his best on slippery roads; he had smashed one of Mrs. Wilson's cars. But it was all for Woodrow, "so I felt I must go."

The weather improved as they neared their destination and found Staunton decked with flags. A large crowd gathered next day. The room in which the President was born had been turned into a post office and 2,500 of the memorial stamps were sold there that day.

The commemorative events came in such swift succession that on April 21, 1956, she wrote to Baruch, quoting the song, "Darling, I Am Growing Old," and regretting that she could not attend every event, to show her appreciation of what was being done in her husband's memory.

She listened to hundreds of speeches about him, one of which was delivered by Arthur Krock at Mary Baldwin College at Staunton. In general the famous correspondent's talk on this occasion was laudatory but he threw in some double-edged comments on the mistakes he thought Wilson had made, such as not taking Taft and Root to Paris with him.

He feared some reaction from Mrs. Wilson, who was seated at the luncheon table, but she looked amiable and untroubled. A few days later he met her at the Gridiron tea and plunged right in with a reference to the luncheon both had attended. "You must have been very much gratified at Staunton on the occasion of the centennial of President Wilson's birth," said Krock. "It was a very great occasion."

Mrs. Wilson smoothly replied, "Yes, it was. I'm so sorry you could not have been with us."

In May Woodrow Wilson was elected to the Hall of Fame, and Mrs.

339

Wilson was a proud participant in the ceremony. Dr. Ralph Sockman, the well-known New York clergyman who officiated, wrote to her, "Your husband's entry into the Hall of Fame would not have had adequate significance were it not for your presence, and I hope that the exercise compensated in small measure for your trip to New York and to the University."

With Francis Sayre and his family she was present for the unveiling of a plaque at the Presbyterian Church where he had worshiped in Washington. The Armistice Day service at the cathedral in 1956 to her was one of the great days of the Centennial Year, and she maintained the pace until the New Year dawned. "I have been to so many things in honor of Woodrow that I am glad the Centennial year is over," she said in the fifty-seventh handwritten letter she sent in January, 1957, concluding her obligatons. But she had enjoyed it all and had been much honored. There was work still for her to do. In the last few years of her life she made many public appearances and in 1958 she watched Sterling Bolling drive the first pile for the Woodrow Wilson Memorial Bridge. A platform had been built over the water and once again she was singing the "Star-Spangled Banner" and listening to speeches eulogizing her husband.

That same year she stood with Madame Alphand, wife of the French ambassador, for the tape-cutting at the Rochambeau Bridge in Washington, honoring the French general who fought with the American Colonies against England. She was still a fashion picture. The orchids were there, the ropes of pearls that she had always loved, and the flattering touch of fur. With age she had become much slimmer and stooped a little. Her features had softened, her hearing was failing, but her gray eyes still glowed with interest.

When in 1958 she visited the Institute of Physical Medicine and Rehabilitation directed by Dr. Howard Rusk at Bellevue Hospital, in New York, she greeted Roy Campanella among the patients. He had been one of Randolph's heroes. Room 623 at this famous health center was dedicated to Mrs. Woodrow Wilson on October 15 of that year. Rehabilitation was a field of medicine in which she was deeply interested, and she followed all the advances made with a rare degree of understanding but with little comment. Belle Baruch endowed a room in her name, also, at the Walter Reed Hospital in Bethesda, Maryland.

# Valiant to the End

After an emergency operation in 1957 Edith's health improved. Although she and Cherie had a series of falls and mishaps, she always brushed her own off as mere trifles. Beset by arthritis, various allergies, and a series of accidents, Cherie accepted her own afflictions with the same insouciant spirit. A motoring accident in which all her front teeth were knocked out, a fall from a stool, which injured her back, a bout of pneumonia or a violent rash were part of Cherie's history, but in 1974 she was still enjoying life at Chincoteague, Virginia. She helped to brighten Edith Wilson's last days and was always greatly missed when she made quick visits to her family.

"Old age fell like a benediction on Mrs. Woodrow Wilson. . . . In mind and spirit she was young to the end of her days," said Dr. Link at the memorial service held at Staunton after her death.

She was able to stay active until she died, attending to her flowers and talking to them lovingly, cleaning the bird cages, and getting off notes to relatives and friends. She was apt to hear from any part of the world. Her adventurous family had scattered everywhere. She heard from Alaska, Japan, Panama, and Central Europe, as well as from hamlets in the American West. Woodrow Wilson Sayre, who one day would successfully scale Mount Everest, was tackling Mount McKinley in 1954 by way of preparation. She had relatives in the diplomatic service, on college faculties, in banking, law, radio, publishing, real estate, the church, and the arts.

To the end she looked much younger than she was and was carefully and becomingly dressed for the functions she attended. But after World War II she ceased to care so much about what she wore. She became bored with the emphasis on her clothes and hats. Although she would still turn out for all the Woodrow Wilson functions, she cut down on social engagements as her deafness grew worse. For a time she tried the old-fashioned ear trumpet, and although she could jest about that she did not like it.

Few realized that Mrs. Wilson had a troublesome tic on her right side and sometimes had great difficulty steadying her pen. Some days she was worse than others, but no one could tell if it was due to arthritis. Although it accounted for her curious and irregular script, it rarely kept her from getting off a letter or going wherever she wished.

Edith Wilson lived her last year gallantly but under great stress. In

341

February, 1961, she had a bad fall that caused back and arm injuries. After a series of tests her arm was put in a cast. Her discomfort increased when a car door was slammed shut on her fingers, but she made light of this as she did of her broken arm, planning gaily to spend Easter in New York. The Sayres, the Bolling relatives, and Dr. Grayson's sons, Cary, Gordon, and William, kept dropping in to see her, and Lucy Moeling came from Chicago to visit her when she could. Edith worried because her hair was falling out in handfuls and she was pinning her faith, she jestingly told her friends, on a scalp preparation that would give her a growth of hair resembling the Seven Sutherland Sisters. She was also taking iron capsules because her blood count was so low.

Gertrude's death in May, 1961, came as a surprise to Edith although, in her own words, she "had tried to prepare herself but up to the last week Gertrude was so like herself that it came as a real shock." Edith's eldest sister's ten years of invalidism at S Street were over, and letters poured in from friends who understood the care Edith had given her. Mrs. Kennedy sent her a personal note on May 23, 1961: "The President and I were so sorry to hear of your sister's death. Please know that you have our deepest sympathy, and you are very much in our thoughts. Affectionately, Jacqueline Kennedy."

One day, while in New York, she had not been feeling well after lunch and she fell in a dead faint. "When I got myself together," as she put it, she was taken back to the Dorset Hotel. The doctor ordered her to bed, but she felt so unlike herself that she decided to return to Washington at once. Describing her collapse to Lucy, she wrote on June 16, 1961, "I think it was the result of Gertrude's illness and death and so much rich food . . . ."

But she soon recovered and in July received "three gentlemen working on the publication of the Woodrow Wilson papers." She charmed her guests but she still held firm about the way in which things should be done. She hoped that no loose ends had been left, for great changes were under way in 1961 at Princeton. A large bequest had made possible the establishment of an international center and the assemblage of Woodrow Wilson material. "A great tribute and a just one," she said. "What it would have meant to him if it had been done in his lifetime!" She had traveled to Princeton and had met Dr. Arthur S. Link, who would be in charge. She wrote to Baruch, who had decided to give his papers to Princeton, that she had liked him and believed that an outstanding job would be done on the papers.

While the Princeton negotiations were going on, another crushing personal blow fell. Altrude, her oldest and dearest friend, died in London. She had gone abroad in April with a group of friends, planning to travel around the world, but in Greece she suffered a knee injury. She was hospitalized and when she felt better she went on to London, where she arranged to have her sons meet her in August. But she became desperately ill on her arrival and had an emergency operation for stomach ulcers. Her sons were notified and Gordon caught a plane at once, arriving an hour after her death.

Edith could scarcely believe that the vital and fascinating Altrude had left her life. They had been friends for fifty years and her thoughts reverted to their early days together and the influence each had on the other.

That October, two months before her death, Edith had one last great fling at the White House when she was the star guest at a ceremony, sitting beside President Kennedy as he signed into law a commission to plan a suitable memorial to Woodrow Wilson. This memorial was something she had longed for but did not live to see. She looked around the White House on this last visit, and was pleased with its pervading spirit of youth and energy. The President had described Woodrow Wilson as the "first shaper of the plan for international cooperation among all the peoples of the world," and he viewed Mrs. Wilson with fond approval.

In a purple suit, with a black hat and white gloves she stood while the President moved her chair closer to his and said in a genial way, "You just sit right there and then we'll sign it."

He gave her the pen and she said meekly, "I didn't dare ask you for it."

This was greeted with laughter. No one had ever thought of Edith Wilson as meek. There had been so many important pens in her life, but this one mattered to her deeply—a memorial to Woodrow, by grace of Congress. She was conscious of the irony of this. And she felt sure that the vital young man before her was probably the last American President she would live to see. She was right. She lay at rest close to Woodrow Wilson in the crypt of the cathedral when John F. Kennedy was assassinated.

At Thanksgiving, she developed a cold that she could not throw off. Although suffering severely from respiratory congestion, she still tried to keep her engagements. By Christmas it was clear that she was failing. But she was determined to keep one final pledge to unveil a plaque at the dedication of the Woodrow Wilson Bridge over the Potomac on the one hundred and fifth anniversary of Woodrow Wilson's birth. The day before the ceremony, she wondered how on earth she would manage it. No one who knew her doubted that she would be there, in spite of the icy weather. But she died that night—on December 28, 1961, Woodrow's birthday.

She slipped away quietly in the late evening. Lucy Moeling and Mrs. Jane Powell, another of her relatives who had been staying at the house, were with her. Her heart condition had been severe for a year and there were respiratory complications at the end.

The news quickly flashed around the world that Mrs. Woodrow Wilson was dead at eighty-nine. The funeral services were simple, as she wished them to be. Dean Sayre officiated. She was buried in the crypt, at the west end of St. Joseph's Chapel, in the lower level of the cathedral. Her name was carved into the stone of the sepulcher where her husband's casket, encased in limestone, had been since its removal from Bethlehem Chapel. Few of her old friends were still alive to attend the services, but there was a strong gathering of the younger generation.

Messages flowed in from around the world. With the United Nations a working reality, her death evoked memories of Woodrow Wilson in distant places, and of the work she had done in the years after his death. She was described in some American and European papers as the First Woman President, a title that she had always disowned. Aside from the influence she had wielded in affairs of state she was remembered in diverse ways, since her interests had been far-reaching and had touched the lives of many. Her role was unique in White House history, and her work after her husband's death kept her in touch with world celebrities for forty years. She was remembered as an accomplished hostess, a diplomat of sorts, and a humanitarian who worked tirelessly for children and incurables at home and abroad. Time dimmed old animosities; she had outlived waves of criticism, and the buoyant spirit that had carried her through every crisis left her at the end with a strong sense of optimism and fulfillment. Above all, she was remembered as the sympathetic and loyal wife who had shared to an extraordinary degree in Woodrow Wilson's triumphs and his sufferings. Her own accomplishments were lost in the dramatic sweep of a revolutionary era in American history, but she never thought of honors for herself. It was enough for Edith Bolling to be remembered only as the wife of Woodrow Wilson. That, to her, was the greatest honor of all.

# Acknowledgments
## and Sources

Edith Bolling Wilson's life story is exceptionally well documented because of the wide range of her social and official activities as the wife and widow of Woodrow Wilson. She lived to be eighty-nine, and her long life span enabled her to follow the development of aeronautics and nuclear power, to welcome the establishment of the United Nations, to see seven Presidents' wives follow her in the White House, to become again a patriotic war worker when America in the 1940's engaged in the major war that Woodrow Wilson had predicted after he lost his fight for participation in the League of Nations.

Her name and presence had a certain magic up to the day she died in 1961, and although her power was never clearly defined, she remained an attractive, mysterious and enduring figure in White House history. Long before the official biographies of Presidents' wives became customary, Edith Wilson proved to be the best news gatherer of them all. With the help of Ray Stannard Baker, her husband's official biographer, and the cooperation of Cabinet members, friends and close associates, she assembled a stunning amount of evidence that she used to strengthen his image around the world and right the wrongs that she felt he had suffered.

Although Mrs. Wilson became internationally known when the President lay helpless with a crippling stroke and she stood between him and the outside world, she deplored the stories that overplayed her role. Essentially reserved in her instincts she shunned personal publicity and was concerned only for the recovery of her desperately ill husband.

Wilson's voluminous papers and memorabilia in the Library of Congress supply ample evidence of the unique part his wife played in American history and her links with world celebrities. Her life was so closely tied to the major events of the First World War era that her history is reflected also in Woodrow Wilson's official papers, since she was always at his side, his thoughtful adviser, his trusted confidante, his helpful wife in his days of triumph and of despair. When the limelight beat on him, it caught her in its nimbus.

347

## Acknowledgments and Sources

Some of the most important letters addressed to Mrs. Wilson are in her husband's official papers, and there are many allusions to her in his correspondence since he seemed always to be conscious of her presence. But in dedicating her papers to the public, Mrs. Wilson ordered his letters to her sealed until fifteen years after her death. Like her husband, she was a tireless correspondent, and hundreds of letters in her rounded and distinctive script help illumine her own and Woodrow Wilson's history.

Her correspondence with Ray Stannard Baker I found particularly revealing on the personal as well as political level. Much of the political material was assembled after the President's death as his friends and colleagues responded warmly to his widow's requests for letters. The papers were in Baker's custody at Amherst until she deposited them in the Library of Congress in 1939. They are now being studied and reappraised at Princeton University, a center for Woodrow Wilson material from all sources.

Dr. Arthur S. Link, a noted authority who has written and edited a succession of books on Wilson, is directing operations sponsored by the Woodrow Wilson Foundation and Princeton University, involving a multivolume compilation of the Wilson papers. Dr. Link remembers Mrs. Wilson well and recalled for me her wit, charm and acute perceptions as she discussed her husband's papers with him in the last days of her life. Some of my material came from Mrs. Wilson's papers at Princeton and from Bernard Baruch material deposited there, as well as from the Library of Congress.

Edith Wilson figured often in the books and papers of her husband's associates and, most significantly, in the diaries and papers of Colonel Edward M. House, which I studied at Yale University. His numerous references range from friendly and affectionate comment at first to an acerbic view of her influence with the President. She is viewed from various angles in the papers of Josephus Daniels, Newton D. Baker, Norman H. Davis, Bernard Baruch, Jesse Jones, Henry White, Robert Lansing, Cordell Hull, William Howard Taft, John Barrett, Bainbridge Colby, James W. Gerard, Gilbert M. Hitchcock, Carter Glass, Homer Cummings, Charles R. Crane, William C. McAdoo, Rear Admiral Cary T. Grayson, Joseph P. Tumulty and many others.

Mrs. Wilson's social life as First Lady is well documented in her pa-

348

## Acknowledgments and Sources

pers, in the correspondence of Mrs. Edith Benham Helm, and in the enormous scrapbooks in the Library of Congress, compiled by her brother, John Randolph Bolling, while he worked as her secretary at the house on S Street. She was punctilious about observing protocol, and her letters to other First Ladies at times showed warmth and spontaneity. She saved memorabilia of all the historic functions she gave and attended at home and abroad, and her papers include courtesy correspondence with the British, Italian, Belgian, Spanish and Rumanian sovereigns, with the Emperor of Japan, and the Prince of Wales, who later became the Duke of Windsor, as well as with his parents, King George V and Queen Mary.

After she attended the Peace Conference, the international strings lengthened as Lord Balfour, Earl Grey, Lord Cecil, David Lloyd George, Clemenceau, Poincaré, Foch, Smuts, Orlando, Paderewski, Herbert Asquith and his wife, Margot, all pass in review in Mrs. Wilson's papers. A witty, perceptive judge of men, she showed a tenacious and unforgiving spirit to her husband's enemies, but in her late years she softened and became more tolerant, except in the case of Henry Cabot Lodge.

Family reminiscences in Mrs. Wilson's papers and her autobiography, *My Memoir*, published fifteen years after the President's death, chronicle in detail her early days in Wytheville, Virginia, one of eleven children born into a Southern family impoverished during the Civil War. She worshiped her father, William Holcombe Bolling, a lawyer and circuit judge; her mother she viewed as a "saint," but it was her tiny crippled grandmother, Mrs. Archibald Bolling, who taught her to read, write and count, to absorb impressions as she traveled, to work hard, to stand by her convictions and express her likes and dislikes with freedom.

In her memoir Mrs. Wilson tells of her arrival in Washington as a girl of eighteen to visit one of her married sisters, of her twelve-year marriage to the well-known Washington jeweler and silversmith Norman Galt, of her business career when she was left a widow. For one who sought privacy all her life but never attained it, Mrs. Wilson described with astonishing candor her first meeting with Woodrow Wilson, his ardent courtship and what he said when he proposed to her. She alone could have been so explicit, but her story is firmly backed by Admiral

Grayson, who was of paramount importance in her history since he brought them together. Dr. Grayson encouraged their romance, was close to them all through the war, the Peace Conference and the dark days after Woodrow Wilson's collapse when he alone understood the role played by Mrs. Wilson during the interregnum.

I am particularly indebted to Admiral Grayson's three sons—Gordon Grayson, Cary T. Grayson, Jr., and William Grayson—for a wealth of family material, including some of their father's correspondence with Mrs. Wilson, their mother's diaries with many allusions to her when she was Mrs. Galt, and an exchange of letters between these lifelong friends. When Alice Gordon's father died, he asked Mrs. Galt to look out for his young daughter. They traveled together to Europe before President Wilson and Dr. Grayson came into their lives, and the Grayson material documents the start of this great White House romance and carries it to the final stages when Mrs. Galt became Mrs. Wilson and Alice Gordon (Altrude) became Mrs. Grayson. They died within a few months of each other and kept up their association to the last.

Mrs. Wilson was never able to shed her fame or retire into obscurity during the thirty-seven years she survived her husband. She traveled the world over as an ambassador at large. The camera caught her in Cairo and Peking. These years are richly documented through her letters to her family and her numerous friends. They illumine her many interests before and after her life with Woodrow Wilson. They mirror the times in which she lived and the changing mores. She discussed books, plays, films, music (her special interest), fashion, the races and the great sports events of the era. Her work for children and incurables, for church, charity and the Red Cross is reflected in her abundant family correspondence. She followed the history of the young Bollings and Sayres with scrupulous interest and was ready to lend a helping hand. Her correspondence with Norman Davis, Josephus Daniels, Bernard Baruch and some of the leading lawyers, bankers and scholars of the day was enlightening on the role she played in the early days of the Woodrow Wilson Foundation. She did everything she could for the restoration of the President's birthplace at Staunton, and she attended scores of Woodrow Wilson events and memorial ceremonies in his centennial year, all of which is reflected in her correspondence.

Her own impressions of many of the public and private events of her

350

life after the President's death are embedded in her letters to Mrs. John Moeling (Lucy Maury), the niece whom she regarded as her daughter. Lucy visited her aunt at the White House and S Street while the President was still alive, and although her home after her marriage was in Chicago, she was constantly in touch with Mrs. Wilson and visited her regularly. She accompanied her aunt on the historic trip to celebrate the independence of Poland in 1931 and drove with her through cheering crowds in Warsaw and Poznan. They exchanged hundreds of letters in which Mrs. Wilson gave almost a running commentary on her busy days, and the letters, which Mrs. Moeling was good enough to let me see, were a rich source of information on her distinguished aunt. Mrs. John A. Goodloe, Mrs. Moeling's sister Anne, was also most helpful with memories of Mrs. Wilson. Among others who assisted me were Mrs. Robert Evans of Fairfax, Virginia, and Mrs. Drake Campbell and Mrs. E. W. Robischon of Washington.

Various members of Mrs. Wilson's family gave me information and reminiscences of "Aunt Edith," as she was known to them all. Her nephew Sterling Bolling and his wife, Jane, were in touch with her constantly up to the time she died and have many warm memories of her kindness, wit and courage. Two of her nieces—Mrs. Robert Ruckman and Mrs. Barbara Fuller—were equally helpful, as were a number of friends who still remembered her. She was a Washington dowager for so many years that she never ceased to be a striking figure in the capital, in spite of her desire for privacy.

For official events in which Mrs. Wilson figured, during and after her years with Woodrow Wilson, I have drawn from the files of the New York *Herald Tribune,* the New York *World* and the New York *Times* and have personal recollections of her on various occasions, including the scene at Woodrow Wilson's funeral in 1924. Randolph Bolling's monster scrapbooks mirror her life at home and abroad, and she was much publicized in the magazines of the day.

Miss Katharine E. Brand, who worked with Ray Stannard Baker at Amherst for years on the Wilson papers and was custodian of the Woodrow Wilson Collection in the Library of Congress after they were deposited there, was particularly helpful in giving me her recollections of Mrs. Wilson and in suggesting various sources of information. Miss Kate M. Stewart assisted me at the Library of Congress, and Mrs.

# Acknowledgments and Sources

Wanda M. Randall, assistant curator of manuscripts, at Princeton University Library.

Various librarians, archivists and custodians of landmarks gave me assistance in my research for this book. The late Mrs. Ruth Dillon and her associates at the Woodrow Wilson House in Washington were skilled hostesses, evoking the memory of Edith Bolling Wilson and the years she spent there in much the same setting.

Raymond F. Pisney, director of the Woodrow Wilson Birthplace Foundation at Staunton, let me see Mrs. Wilson's papers there, involving her years of work with Mrs. Herbert McKelden Smith, its director, Mrs. Cordell Hull and various Virginia ladies engaged in the restoration and furnishing of the spacious manse, with its bowknot garden, Woodrow Wilson's cradle and the old Pierce Arrow he preferred to all his other automobiles. Mrs. Odile Cleveland and Mrs. Charles Blackley were the hostesses at the birthplace, where the documentary film of President Wilson's triumphs in Europe is shown to the thousands who visit the house on the hillside each year. His first home and his last bear the stamp of Edith Bolling Wilson, who demanded excellence in all things relating to her idolized husband.

After devoting years to the disposition of her husband's papers Mrs. Wilson gave her own to the Library of Congress in successive batches between 1957 and 1961, and more were acquired after her death. The collection of more than 20,000 items is studded with the names of world notables with whom she communicated. It includes the manuscript of *My Memoir*, showing the changes made in the text. The range of interest is wide, from the detailed record of her business dealings with Galt's to the brief but intensely personal entries in her diaries of 1907, 1909, and 1915. Mrs. Wilson was not a diarist at heart. Letters to her family and friends were her natural form of expression. It was not until she wrote *My Memoir* that she opened the floodgates of self-revelation. She left notes for a sequel she intended to write, but in her busy life she could never find the time.

# Bibliography

ALLEN, FREDERICK LEWIS. *Only Yesterday.* New York: Harper, 1931.

ALLEN, ROBERT S. *Washington Merry-Go-Round.* New York: Liveright, 1931.

ARCHER, WILLIAM. *The Peace-President.* New York: Holt, 1919.

BAGBY, WESLEY MORRIS. *The Road to Normalcy: the President's Campaign and Election of 1920.* Baltimore: Johns Hopkins Press, 1962.

BAILEY, THOMAS ANDREW. *The Art of Diplomacy: The American Experience:* New York, Appleton-Century-Crofts, 1968.

———. *Woodrow Wilson and the Great Betrayal.* New York: Macmillan, 1945.

———. *Woodrow Wilson and the Lost Peace.* New York: Macmillan, 1944.

BAKER, NEWTON D. *Why We Went to War.* New York: Harper, 1936.

BAKER, RAY STANNARD. *American Chronicle.* New York: Scribner, 1945.

———. *What Wilson Did at Paris.* Garden City, N.Y.: Doubleday, Page, 1919.

———. *Woodrow Wilson and World Settlement.* Garden City, N.Y.: Doubleday, Page, 1922. 3 vols.

———, ED, WITH DODD, WILLIAM E. *The Public Papers of Woodrow Wilson.* New York: Harper, 1925–27.

———, ED. *Woodrow Wilson: Life and Letters.* Garden City, N.Y.: Doubleday, Page, 1927–39, 8 vols.

BARUCH, BERNARD M. *Baruch: My Own Story.* New York: Holt, Rinehart and Winston, 1957.

———. *The Public Years.* New York: Holt, Rinehart and Winston, 1960.

BELL, HERBERT C. F. *Woodrow Wilson and the People.* Garden City, N.Y.: Doubleday, Doran, 1945.

BLUM, JOHN M. *Joe Tumulty and the Wilson Era.* Boston: Houghton Mifflin, 1951.

BOLITHO, HECTOR. *Twelve Agains* the Gods.* New York, Simon and Schuster, 1929.

BOLLING, JOHN RANDOLPH. *Chronology of Woodrow Wilson,* compiled for Mary Vanderpool Pennington by John Randolph Bolling and others. New York: Frederick A. Stokes, 1927.

BOWERS, CLAUDE. *My Life. The Memoirs of Claude Bowers.* New York: Simon and Schuster, 1962.

BRADFORD, GAMALIEL. *The Quick and the Dead.* Boston: Houghton Mifflin, 1929.

BULLITT, WILLIAM C. *Thomas Woodrow Wilson. A Psychological Study by Sigmund Freud and William C. Bullitt.* Boston: Houghton Mifflin, 1967. *See* Freud.

BURLINGAME, ROGER, AND STEVENS, ALDEN. *Victory Without Peace.* New York: Harcourt, Brace, 1944.

353

# Bibliography

CARY, CONSTANCE HARRISON. *Recollections Grave and Gay*. New York: Scribner, 1911.

CLAPPER, OLIVE EWING. *Washington Tapestry*. New York: Whittlesey House, McGraw-Hill, 1946.

COIT, MARGARET L. *Mr. Baruch*. Boston: Houghton Mifflin, 1957.

COLBY, BAINBRIDGE. *The Close of Woodrow Wilson's Administration and the Final Years*. New York: M. Kennerley, 1930.

COLSON, EDNA MAY. *White House Gossip from Andrew Johnson to Calvin Coolidge*. Garden City, N.Y.: Doubleday, Page, 1927.

CRAMER, CLARENCE H. *Newton D. Baker*. Cleveland: World, 1961.

CRANSTON, RUTH. *The Story of Woodrow Wilson*. New York: Simon and Schuster, 1945.

CREEL, GEORGE. *The War, the World and Wilson. Rebel at Large: Recollections of Fifty Crowded Years*. New York: Putnam, 1947.

CROUSE, RUSSELL. *It Seems Like Yesterday*. Garden City, N.Y.: Doubleday, Doran, 1931.

DANIELS, JONATHAN. *The End of Innocence*. Philadelphia: Lippincott, 1954.

_____. *Frontier on the Potomac*. New York: Macmillan, 1946.

_____. *The Time Between the Wars: Armistice to Pearl Harbor*. Garden City, N.Y.: Doubleday, 1966.

DANIELS, JOSEPHUS. *The Cabinet Diary of Josephus Daniels 1913–1921*, D. David Cronon, ed. Lincoln, Neb.: University of Nebraska Press, 1963.

_____. *The Life of Woodrow Wilson 1856–1924*. Philadelphia: Winston, 1924.

_____. *The Wilson Era: Years of Peace 1910–1917*. Chapel Hill: University of North Carolina Press, 1944 and 1946. 2 vols.

DAVIDSON, JOHN WELLS. *A Crossroads of Freedom: The 1912 Campaign Speeches of Woodrow Wilson*. New Haven, Yale University Press, 1956.

DAY, DONALD. *Woodrow Wilson's Own Story*, selected and edited by Donald Day. Boston: Little, Brown, 1952.

DODD, WILLIAM E. *Woodrow Wilson and His Work*. Garden City, N.Y.: Doubleday, Page, 1920.

DOS PASSOS, JOHN. *Mr. Wilson's War*. Garden City, N.Y.: Doubleday, 1962.

_____. *Social History in All Countries*. New York: Harcourt, Brace, 1934.

ELLIOTT, MARGARET RANDOLPH (AXSON). *My Aunt Louisa and Woodrow Wilson*. Chapel Hill: University of North Carolina Press, 1944.

FLEMING, DENNA FRANK. *The United States and the League of Nations*. New York: Putnam, 1932.

FREUD, SIGMUND, AND WILLIAM C. BULLITT. *Thomas Woodrow Wilson: A Psychological Study*. Boston: Houghton Mifflin, 1967. *See* Bullitt.

FURMAN, BESS. *Washington By-Line: The Personal History of a Newspaperwoman*. New York: Knopf, 1949.

# Bibliography

_____. *White House Profile: A Social History of the White House, Its Occupants and Its Festivities.* Indianapolis: Bobbs-Merrill, 1951.

GARRATY, JOHN A. *Woodrow Wilson: A Great Life in Brief.* New York: Knopf, 1956.

GEORGE, ALEXANDER L. AND JULIETTE L. *Woodrow Wilson and Colonel House: A Personality Study.* New York: John Day, 1956.

GIBBS, SIR PHILIP HAMILTON. *People of Destiny; Americans as I Saw Them at Home and Abroad.* New York: Harper, 1920.

GRAYSON, REAR ADMIRAL CARY T. *Woodrow Wilson: An Intimate Memoir.* New York: Holt, Rinehart and Winston, 1960.

GUNTHER, JOHN. *Roosevelt in Retrospect.* New York: Harper, 1950.

HARBAUGH, WILLIAM H. *Lawyers' Lawyer. The Life of John W. Davis.* New York: Oxford University Press, 1973.

HARRIMAN, MRS. J. BORDEN (DAISY). *Politics and Pinafores.* New York: Holt, 1923.

HATCH, ALDEN. *Edith Bolling Wilson: First Lady Extraordinary.* New York: Dodd, Mead, 1961.

_____. *The Lodges of Massachusetts.* New York: Hawthorn, 1973.

HELM, EDITH BENHAM. *The Captains and the Kings.* New York: Putnam, 1954.

HENDRICK, BURTON J., ED. *The Life and Letters of Walter Hines Page.* Garden City, N.Y.: Doubleday, Page 1922–25. 3 vols.

HOOVER, HERBERT. *Memoirs of Herbert Hoover.* Vol. 2. New York: Macmillan, 1952.

_____. *The Ordeal of Woodrow Wilson.* New York: McGraw-Hill, 1958.

HOOVER, IRWIN HOOD (IKE). *Forty-two Years in the White House.* Boston: Houghton Mifflin Company, 1934.

HOUSE, EDWARD MANDELL. *The Intimate Papers of Colonel House,* in narrative form by Charles Seymour. Boston: Houghton Mifflin, 1926–28. 4 vols.

_____, AND SEYMOUR, CHARLES, EDS. *What Really Happened at Paris: The Story of the Peace Conference.* New York: Scribner, 1921.

HOUSTON, DAVID FRANKLIN. *Eight Years with Wilson's Cabinet 1913–1920: With a Personal Estimate of the President,* Vol. 1. Garden City, N.Y.: Doubleday, Page, 1920.

HULBERT, MARY ALLEN. *The Story of Mrs. Peck: An Autobiography of Mary (Allen) Hulbert.* New York: Minton, Balch & Company, 1933.

HURD, CHARLES. *Washington Cavalcade.* New York: Dutton, 1948.

_____. *The White House: The Story of the House, Its Occupants, Its Place in American History.* New York: Harper, 1940.

HURLEY, EDWARD NASH. *The Bridge to France.* Philadelphia: Lippincott, 1927.

355

# Bibliography

_____. *The New Merchant Marine.* New York: Century, 1920.

IRWIN, INEZ HAYES. *Angels and Amazons.* Garden City, N.Y.: Doubleday, Doran, 1933.

_____. *The Story of the Woman's Party.* New York: Harcourt, Brace, 1921.

JAFFRAY, ELIZABETH. *Secrets of the White House.* New York: Cosmopolitan Book Company, 1926.

JENSEN, AMY. *The White House and Its Thirty-two Families.* New York: McGraw-Hill, 1958.

JENSEN, OLIVER O., KERR, JOAN PETERSON, AND BELSKY, MURRAY. *American Album.* New York: American Heritage, 1968.

JOHNSON, GERALD W. *Incredible Tale.* New York, Harper, 1950.

_____. *Woodrow Wilson: The Unforgettable Figure Who Has Returned to Haunt Us.* New York: Harper, 1944.

JONES, JESSE H., WITH EDWARD ANGLY. *Fifty Billion Dollars: My Thirteen Years with the RFC (1932–1945).* New York, Macmillan, 1951.

KENNAN, GEORGE F. *American Diplomacy 1900–1950.* Chicago: University of Chicago Press, 1951.

_____. *The Decision to Intervene.* Princeton: Princeton University Press, 1958.

_____. *Russia Leaves the War.* Princeton: Princeton University Press, 1956.

KIERNAN, R. H. *Lloyd George.* London: G. G. Harrap, 1940.

KOHLSTAAT, HERMAN H. *From McKinley to Harding.* New York: Scribner, 1923.

LANSING, ROBERT. *The Big Four and Others of the Peace Conference.* Boston: Houghton Mifflin, 1921.

_____. *The Peace Negotiations: A Personal Narrative.* Boston: Houghton Mifflin, 1921.

LASH, JOSEPH. *Eleanor and Franklin.* New York: Norton, 1971.

_____. *Eleanor Roosevelt: A Friend's Memoir.* New York: Doubleday, 1964.

_____. *Eleanor: The Years Alone.* New York: Norton, 1972.

LAWRENCE, DAVID. *The True Story of Woodrow Wilson.* New York: George H. Doran, 1924.

LINK, ARTHUR S. *The Road to the White House.* Princeton: Princeton University Press, 1947.

_____. *Wilson: The New Freedom.* Princeton: Princeton University Press, 1956.

_____. *Wilson: The Struggle for Neutrality.* Princeton: Princeton University Press, 1960.

_____. *Woodrow Wilson: A Brief Biography.* Cleveland: World, 1963.

_____. *Woodrow Wilson and the Progressive Era 1910–1917.* New York: Harper, 1954.

# Bibliography

LLOYD GEORGE, DAVID. *Memoirs of the Peace Conference.* New Haven: Yale University Press, 1939.

———. *War Memoirs of David Lloyd George,* Vol. 5. London: I. Nicholson & Watson, 1933–36.

LONGWORTH, ALICE ROOSEVELT. *Crowded Hours.* New York: Scribner, 1933. 1933

LOWRY, EDWARD GEORGE. *Washington Close-Ups: Intimate Views of Some Public Figures.* Boston: Houghton Mifflin, 1921.

MCADOO, ELEANOR RANDOLPH (WILSON). *The Priceless Gift: The Love Letters of Woodrow Wilson and Ellen Axson Wilson,* Eleanor Wilson McAdoo, ed. New York: McGraw-Hill, 1962.

———, AND GAFFEY, MARGARET Y. *The Woodrow Wilsons.* New York: Macmillan, 1937.

MCADOO, WILLIAM GIBBS. *Crowded Years. The Reminiscences of William G. McAdoo.* Boston: Houghton Mifflin, 1931.

MAMATEY, VICTOR S. *The United States and East Central Europe 1914–1918.* Princeton: Princeton University Press, 1957.

MARTIN, LAURENCE W. *Peace Without Victory: Woodrow Wilson and the British Liberals.* New Haven: Yale University Press, 1958.

MAY, ERNEST R. *The World War and American Isolation.* Cambridge, Mass.: Harvard University Press, 1959.

MAYER, ARNO J. *Political Origins of the New Diplomacy 1917–1918.* New Haven: Yale University Press, 1959.

MILLER, DAVID HUNTER. *The Peace Pact of Paris: A Study of the Briand-Kellogg Treaty.* New York: Putnam, 1928.

MILLER, HOPE RIDINGS. *Scandals in the Highest Office: Facts and Fictions in the Private Lives of Our Presidents.* New York: Random House, 1973.

MORRIS, LLOYD R. *Not So Long Ago.* New York: Random House, 1949.

NEVINS, ALLAN. *Henry White: Thirty Years of American Diplomacy.* New York: Harper, 1930.

———. *The United States in a Chaotic World: A Chronicle of International Affairs, 1918–1933.* New Haven: Yale University Press, 1950.

PALMER, FREDERICK. *Newton D. Baker: America at War, Based on the Personal Papers of the Secretary of War.* New York: Dodd, Mead, 1931.

PALMER, JOHN MCAULEY. *Washington, Lincoln, Wilson; 3 World Statesmen.* Introduction by General John J. Pershing. New York: Doubleday, Doran, 1930.

PARKS, LILLIAN ROGERS, AND LEIGHTON, FRANCES SPATZ. *My Thirty Years Backstairs at the White House.* New York: Fleet, 1961.

PAXTON, FREDERIC LOGAN. *American Democracy and the World War.* Boston: Houghton Mifflin, 1939.

# Bibliography

PERSHING, JOHN J. *My Experiences in the World War,* Vols. 1–3. New York: Stokes, 1937–1940.

REID, EDITH GITTINGS. *Woodrow Wilson. The Caricature, the Myth and the Man.* London: Oxford University Press, 1934.

ROOSEVELT, ELEANOR. *On My Own.* New York : Harper & Row, 1958.

————. *This I Remember.* New York, Harper, 1949.

————. *This Is My Story.* New York, Harper, 1937.

————. *You Learn by Living.* New York: Harper & Row, 1960.

ROSS, ISHBEL. *An American Family. The Tafts 1678–1964.* Cleveland: World, 1964.

————. *First Lady of the South: The Life of Mrs. Jefferson Davis.* New York: Harper, 1958.

————. *The General's Wife: The Life of Mrs. Ulysses S. Grant.* New York: Dodd, Mead, 1959.

————. *Grace Coolidge and Her Era.* New York: Dodd, Mead, 1962.

————. *Ladies of the Press.* New York: Harper, 1936.

————. *The President's Wife: Mary Todd Lincoln.* New York: Putnam, 1973.

————. *Sons of Adam, Daughters of Eve.* New York: Harper & Row, 1969.

SEYMOUR, CHARLES, ED. *American Diplomacy During the World War.* Hamden, Conn.: Archon Books, 1964.

————. *The Intimate Papers of Colonel House.* Boston: Houghton Mifflin, 1926–28. 4 Vols.

————. *Woodrow Wilson in Perspective.* Stamford, Conn.: Overbrook Press, 1956.

SIMS, REAR ADMIRAL WILLIAM S., and HENDRICK, BURTON J. *The Victory at Sea.* Garden City, N.Y.; Doubleday, Page, 1920.

SLAYDEN, ELLEN (MAURY). *Washington Wife; Journal of Ellen Maury Slayden from 1897–1919.* New York: Harper & Row, 1963.

SMITH, GENE. *When the Cheering Stopped: The Last Years of Woodrow Wilson.* New York: William Morrow, 1964.

SMITH, MARIE D. *Entertaining in the White House.* Washington, D.C.: Acropolis, 1967.

————, AND DURBIN, LOUISE. *White House Brides.* Washington, D.C.: Acropolis, 1966.

STARLING, EDMUND W., AND SUGRUE, THOMAS. *Starling of the White House.* New York: Simon and Schuster, 1946.

STEINBERG, ALFRED. *Woodrow Wilson.* New York: Putnam, 1961.

STEED, HENRY WICKHAM, *Through Thirty Years 1892–1922.* Garden City, N.Y.: Doubleday, Page, 1924.

STODDARD, HENRY L. *As I Knew Them: Presidents and Politics from Grant to Coolidge.* New York: Harper, 1927.

# Bibliography

TAYLOR, ALAN JOHN PERCIVALE. *Lloyd George: Rise and Fall.* Cambridge, Mass.: Harvard University Press, 1961.

TILLMAN, SETH F. *Anglo-American Relations at the Paris Peace Conference of 1919.* Princeton: Princeton University Press, 1961.

TUCHMAN, BARBARA W. *The Guns of August.* New York: Macmillan, 1962.

_____. *The Zimmermann Telegram.* New York: Macmillan, 1967.

TUMULTY, JOSEPH P. *Woodrow Wilson as I Know Him.* Garden City, N.Y.: Doubleday, Page, 1921.

VIERECK, GEORGE SYLVESTER. *The Strangest Friendship in History: Woodrow Wilson and Colonel House.* New York: Liveright, 1932.

WALWORTH, ARTHUR C. *Woodrow Wilson.* Boston: Houghton Mifflin, 1965. 2 vols.

WECTER, DIXON. *The Saga of American Society.* New York: Scribner, 1937.

WHITE, WILLIAM ALLEN. *The Autobiography of William Allen White.* New York: Macmillan, 1946.

_____. *Woodrow Wilson: The Man, His Times and His Task.* Boston: Houghton Mifflin, 1924.

WILSON, EDITH BOLLING. *My Memoir.* Indianapolis: Bobbs-Merrill, 1939.

WILSON, WOODROW, *Constitutional Government in the United States.* New York: Columbia University Press, 1961.

_____. *George Washington.* New York: Harper, 1902, 1910, 1918.

_____. *Mere Literature and Other Essays.* Boston: Houghton Mifflin, 1896, 1924.

_____. *The New Freedom.* Garden City, N.Y.: Doubleday, Page, 1913.

# *Index*

# Index

363

# Index

# Index

# Index

# Index

# Index

# Index

# Index

# Index

# Index

# Index